ROAD-BOOK AMERICA

ROAD-BOOK

- -

AMERICA

*Contemporary Culture
and the New Picaresque*

Rowland A. Sherrill

UNIVERSITY OF ILLINOIS PRESS

URBANA AND CHICAGO

Library of Congress Cataloging-in-Publication Data
Sherrill, Rowland A.
Road-book America : contemporary culture and the new picaresque /
Rowland A. Sherrill.
p.   cm.
Includes bibliographical references and index.
ISBN 0-252-02546-6 (alk. paper)
1. American fiction—20th century—History and criticism.
2. Picaresque literature, American—History and criticism.
3. American prose literature—20th century—History and criticism.
4. Travelers' writings, American—History and criticism.
5. Travelers—United States—History—20th century.
6. United States—Civilization—1945–   .
7. Travelers in literature.
8. Travel in literature.
I. Title.
PS374.P47S54   2000
810.9'355—dc21   99-006869

C 5 4 3 2 1

For the sheer JOY of it all

CONTENTS

Acknowledgments   ix

Introduction: The Road Work of the New American Picaresque   1

Part 1: The Literary Work of the New American Picaresque

1. The Picaresque Old and New: The Question of Continuity   11
2. The Picaresque Borrowed and Blue: The Matter of Change   34
3. The Picaro in Fiction, the Picaresque in Fact: Blurring Genres   57

Part 2: The Social Work of the New American Picaresque

4. The Picaro's Recovery of the Sovereign Self: Road Cures   83
5. The Picaro in Social Space: Stranger Still   108
6. The Picaro in the Nick of Time: Virtues of the Margin   140

Part 3: The Cultural Work of the New American Picaresque

7. *Homo Viator, Homo Spectans:* Slants on the Size of America   175
8. Road Work: Detours into the Renewal of American Meanings   208
9. Postmodern Religious Conditions and Picaresque Gifts   242

Notes   275
Index   341

ACKNOWLEDGMENTS

Since I first took up this topic in the middle of the 1980s, several "life-stages" have come and gone, administrative terms have run their courses, task forces have been chaired, and the like. Over the course of it all, intermittently at work on this study, I have amassed a huge number of debts, some of which I am glad to be able to acknowledge here.

Early on, I explored before exceptionally receptive audiences at scholarly meetings and at other venues some of the facets of the subject, and I must thank those groups at the Great Lakes meeting of the American Studies Association at Kent State University (1984), at the national meeting of the American Academy of Religion in Chicago (1984), at the Midwest meeting of the AAR in Rockford, Illinois (1985), and then, for invitations to address them, the faculty and students of McMurry College in Abilene, Texas (1985), the alumni at the Mini-University at Indiana University, Bloomington (1986), the faculty and students at Indiana State University, Terre Haute (1987), and the gathered colleagues at a conference of the Center for the Study of Religion and American Culture at Indiana University/Purdue University at Indianapolis, my home institution (1994). The enthusiasm for the topic on these occasions provoked my continuing work: indeed, for months after some of these presentations, I continued to receive leads, suggestions, and queries about it from persons who had attended.

I have also had the great, good fortune of splendid colleagues scattered around out there who have kept an abiding interest in this work, who have "fed" me bibliography and ideas, and who have encouraged me to continue when spirits were flagging. Although they are far too numerous to name them all, several very special people among these should be mentioned because of their direct contributions at several points: John Roth, Ed Linenthal, David Chidester, William Dean, Jay Moseley, Liz Dulany, Giles Gunn, and Tracy Fessenden.

Nearer by, at IUPUI, I have enjoyed some fine colleagues, friends, and students throughout the university and a sabbatical in 1995 that helped greatly to advance the work. I much appreciate the work of Philip Tompkins and his University Library staff who have provided me with a "faculty study," with generous services, and with good cheer. Here to thank Kari Jahr is, I hope, to thank them every one. From IUPUI's Department of Religious Studies, Center for American Studies, and School of Liberal Arts more generally, important support has been everywhere. Again, these are far too many to be identified individually, but special thanks go to Paul J. Nagy, John D. Barlow, Richard C. Turner, Carol Brooks Gardner, William P. Gronfein, Susan Sutton, and William M. Plater, these often fueling the work with their own insights. In my home department, Conrad Cherry, Thomas J. Davis, William J. Jackson, Jeffrey T. Kenney, E. Theodore Mullen Jr., Andrew D. Walsh, and, now retired, James F. Smurl and Jan Shipps, have sustained an environment for continuous intellectual challenge, and Conrad Cherry, most especially, has put a more or less constant Texas "spur" into my mental hindquarters with his acute sense of my arguments and expositions. Two exceptional secretaries in Religious Studies, Evelyn Oliver and Kimberly McVey Long, have encouraged me, have protected my time, have contributed their skills, and have attempted to ameliorate my technological stupidity. A certain clear debt runs deep to Rebecca Vasko, my secretary in American Studies, who has virtually adopted this book—taking on roles, quite beyond any reasonable expectation, as research assistant, critic, proofreader, indexer, and so on. She has been an extraordinary friend of and "gift" to this project.

Beyond the walls of the university, a wonderful collection of other friends in the city has both encouraged and patiently inquired about my work over the years, and I appreciate the continuing support of Ann and Dave Frick, Phyllis Gamage, Margie and John Hittle, Jean and Ned Hornback, Sue and Martial Knieser, Barb and Bill McLin, Diane and Charlie Robinson, and Carol and Bill Vincent.

Deepest standing gratitude, of course, goes to my family. My mother, Elise, has gone without some visits, as have my dear, late brother David and his Debbie, Josh, and Jason. My in-laws, Aurora and Troy Glidewell, have also permitted me many excused absences. Fairly launched into their own lives now, my children, John and Amy, and son-in-law, Mark, have likewise been very forgiving, encouraging, and inspiriting over the years, while remaining a source of pure pride and delight. And, now, there are the newest little picaresque adventurers in the Sherrill bloodline, grandson Sam, whose favorite songs include "Movin' Right Along" (from *The Muppet Movie*), and granddaughter Katie, soon to toddle along her own route. Beyond that to all others, my gratitude flows to the one to whom this book is dedicated, my dear wife Joy, for her continuous help and inspiration, her threshold for neglect, her independence of mind, her creative negotiations of family existence, her unending compassions and energetic enthusiasms, and her very nearly unaccountable love. On every day, in every way, she makes meaning, and, without her, I hope she knows, it would indeed be a "long and lonesome road."

ROAD-BOOK AMERICA

INTRODUCTION

The Road Work of the New American Picaresque

"The road," old Cervantes observed, "is better than the inn," and many Americans in recent decades, allured or captured by some such sentiment or necessity, have not only hit the road but have then, like the old master, written about it. This is a book about their "road books." Since the mid-1950s, an astonishing number of Americans have found themselves literally or imaginatively "on the road" in their country and have apparently felt compelled upon their returns to write about these various journeys through America. Some of these books, like William (Least Heat Moon) Trogdon's *Blue Highways* and John Steinbeck's *Travels with Charley*, propose themselves as works in the genres of autobiographical writing. Others, as different as Kurt Vonnegut Jr.'s *Breakfast of Champions* and Barbara Kingsolver's *The Bean Trees*, arrive to the reader as "pure" fiction. A number of these journey narratives—Peter Jenkins's *A Walk across America* and Charles Kuralt's *On the Road with Charles Kuralt*, for two—have the presentation of documentary-style "portraits" of the land and people as their stated purpose. With still others (and, arguably, *all* such books), the issues of genre seem utterly confused: Robert Pirsig's *Zen and the Art of Motorcycle Maintenance*, David Rounds's *Celebrisi's Journey*, Edward Abbey's *The Monkey Wrench Gang*, among a great many others, clearly employ the elements of fiction and a form of pseudo-documentary but equally and "visibly" entangle with authors' personal experiences, outlooks, and sentiments. Jim Lehrer's *Kick the Can*, Joe David Brown's *Paper Moon*, and Bill Terry's *The Watermelon Kid*, from different angles of vision and memory, converge in forms of narrative nostalgia as they evoke and explore ear-

1

lier, "simpler," and expressly poignant American landscapes. Larry Mc-Murtry's *Cadillac Jack* rides blithely, sometimes hilariously, through a maelstrom of contemporary confusions. And, of course, Russell Banks's *Continental Drift*, Norman Mailer's *An American Dream*, Nelson Algren's *A Walk on the Wild Side*, Earl Thompson's *Caldo Largo*, all variously explore the dark underside or seedy visage of the American scene, just as Thomas Pynchon's *The Crying of Lot 49* travels across the terrain of an America apparently caught in an apocalyptic moment. The sheer number of these and other such books that present some traveler / writer hitting the narrative road stands as a huge phenomenon in contemporary American cultural expression, and the task of this study is to explore its cumulative character, implications, and significance.

The phenomenon is not only huge but obviously "messy," in the sense that these various texts are so widely disparate in nature and style of presentation. Indeed, the dozens of American "road books" that have appeared over recent decades are so various in genre make-up, in point of view, in expressed purposefulness, in motive and message, in literary success, in cultural import and implication, that any presiding rubric or containing pattern or common denomination for them might seem at first blush quite improbable. Beyond the narrative presentation of some figure's movement in space, in fact, there would seem little relationship at all among Peter DeVries's *The Blood of the Lamb*, James Crumley's *The Last Good Kiss*, and Saul Bellow's *The Adventures of Augie March*, an odd "set" indeed even without conjecture about how any or all of these might then bear some relation to Robert Penn Warren's *A Place to Come To*, or Mona Simpson's *Anywhere but Here*, or Elizabeth Berg's *The Pull of the Moon*, much less indeed to Harrison Salisbury's *Travels around America*, Eddy L. Harris's *South of Haunted Dreams*, Andrei Codrescu's *Road Scholar*, or David Lamb's *Stolen Season*. Dozens upon dozens of such books have appeared over the past four decades that feature at the narrative core some figure "on the roads," short or long, traveling in full, continuous motion, whether within narrow confines or in far-flung ways, and the critical question is what this phenomenon might indicate about the cultural place, America, and its times.[1]

With an interpretive "gathering" of these texts, this study proposes that the road book phenomenon is freighted with cultural significance when approached by way of a particular critical perspective. To the extent that these books can be understood to stem from and to be responsive to a complex of situations and issues in the contemporary American culture of their origin, as narrative expression is conditioned by its place and time, then this specific mode of literary formation—the journey story—might be thought disclosive of that complex, indeed even thought elicited by the cultural situation. Even more pointedly, however, not just any form of journey literature would suffice. The general contention of this book is that these American "road books" not only appear as responsive to contemporary American culture but also represent a powerful reappearance and significant transformation of the old literary form of the picaresque narrative, a form apparently especially equipped for grappling with American life in the second half of the twentieth century and into the new millennium. This picaresque form appeared as an early variant of the Western novel, flourished into the eighteenth century and beyond, and includes among its early, classic examples *Lazarillo de Tormes* (1554), Thomas Nashe's *The Unfortunate Traveller* (1594), Mateo Aleman's *Guzman de Alfarache* (1599), Alain-Rene Le Sage's *Gil Blas* (1715), Daniel Defoe's *Moll Flanders* (1722), and Henry Fielding's *Tom Jones* (1749).[2]

At the center of the old picaresque narrative moves the picaro or picara, most often an innocent but (mildly) delinquent figure who, for one reason or another, is at least temporarily dislocated—removed from any particular place—in order narratively to enter an expanded space. Thrown back solely on his or her own wits, this character is loosed to travel the highways and by-ways of the land. The plot of the narrative, to outward appearance anyway, simply follows the traveler's wandering as the picaro or picara winds along randomly from one episode to the disconnected next one, buffeted about by the experiences of the road, as he or she successively engages elements of the topographical and social scene. Such designs work less in terms of unifying the narrative under one broadly enclosing experience than in proposing the focal character's fractured existence in which events from moment to moment occur quite apart from perceptions of a "progress" or, even, a "logic." In tone, concordantly, the picaresque narrative often belongs to comedy: naive blundering or roguish mischance often border on burlesque; the picaro possesses that remarkable, endearing resilience that must exist to counter the results of his/her utter credulity; and even apparently dangerous episodes occur in the larger framework of implied authorial assurances that life will sooner or later right itself.

Along with those attributes of protagonist, plot, unity, and tone, an element of the expressive structures of the classic picaresque narrative has to do with social stock-taking. By virtue of the socially marginal character of the picaro or picara, his or her ingenuous demeanor, and a fair degree of literary license, the figure easily (or impishly) trespasses social boundaries, thus serving as a catalyst or a "lens" for one of the major purposes of the old picaresque narratives—namely, running the social gamut of the culture in question. Though not a satirist—he or she is too insufficiently directed and too unsophisticated for that—the picaresque traveler can venture into the drawing rooms of lords as well as into the huts of bondsmen, can stumble alike across clergyman, farmer, philosopher, merchant, and soldier, and can, thus, encounter and propose those targets for an author's satirical thrusts. Indeed, for the work of imaginative authorship within those traditional, highly stratified, and deeply codified Anglo-European societies, the picaro or picara provided a literary device for virtually unlimited access to the social scene, and the picaresque narrative could ride this vehicle at full satirical tilt.

As this tradition of picaresque literature reappears in American culture in the second half of the twentieth century, there are clear likenesses and differences, continuities and changes. The essential or at least "generic" character of the new picaro or picara seems largely continuous with forebears in the classic formations: as naifs or rogues, Don Wanderhope, Joey Celebrisi, "Cadillac Jack," and Taylor Greer suffer spatial and social dislocations, operate on the margins, proceed by happenstance and wit, and embody the kinds of reciprocating guilelessness and resilience, that make them largely of a piece with Lazarillo, Jack Wilton, Moll Flanders, and Tom Jones.[3] The courses of their mobility in space are likewise random, episodic, disjointed, without apparent destination. No unifying pattern of plotting, tricked out by an over-riding author, subsumes the focal actions of the picaro's engagements with the disparate aspects of the road, and the road itself, even in those rare cases of the most conscious metaphor-making, always maintains its semantic ground, never completely surrendering to abstract reference. Moreover, the sustaining tone of the narrative, in most cases, often participates in the comic sense of life, again standing in continuity with the classic texts. Owing to the prevailingly open and essentially innocent temperament of the picaro and picara, even in the midst of his or her accidents and blunders, the new American picaresque narrative, in general, seems to accredit a hopeful outlook or at least to posit a way to survive the contingencies met and to move forward.

That there are women, picaras, on the new American road is only mildly surprising within a genre that, at first blush, would seem for obvious reasons to belong generally to a concentration on male protagonists. For every "new" Taylor Greer or "Dutch" Gillis, however, there is a precedent in "old" Moll Flanders or Justina. In some respects, of course, their narrative lives on course, in route, are clearly more hazardous and meet different obstacles, and how they move and see are quite importantly "engendered": as they render their takes on American existence, they significantly enrich the inventory by providing different angles of vision, indeed even restoring to view things that otherwise might have been neglected or ignored altogether. In some other respects, perhaps ironically, the difference gender makes becomes a matter of indifference: to the extent that these female narrative "characters" qualify as *picaresque* figures, then to virtually that same extent they become defined less by sex and gender and far more by the shapes and movements of the road life that define picaro and picara alike, just as with Justina and Moll Flanders.

If characteristics of central character, plot, and tone appear at least in these general ways as demonstrably continuous with the stuff of *Gil Blas*, *The Unfortunate Traveller*, or *La Picara Justina*, the most immediately visible elements of change between the "old" and these "new" picaresque narratives are those related to cultural context and structural intentionality. In contemporary America, such narrative formations cannot presume (or presume to re-present) broadly homogeneous social scenes and hierarchically stratified social groupings and cannot either count on readers to recognize social "types" codified by time and traditions. In short, that kind of social reality, whose internal boundaries are certain and clear and whose groups and types set up for the work of the satirist, simply does not correspond to an American social scene that is fluid, heterogeneous, regionalized, and fragmented. The predictable targets of the old form of satire refuse to stand still, and, in any event, the driving intentionality of the new American picaresque narrative seems bent on different purposes altogether. Originating in and entangled with a social scene not fixed but fluid, not full of commonalities stemming from longstanding traditions, marked less for sameness than difference, the new picaresque forges its particular form of cultural response not in satire but in exploration, discovery, and map-making in an America in so many ways become terra incognita.

After Part One here, devoted to the questions of literary continuity and change, critical attention turns to these "different purposes." In its responsiveness to its new American location, the new American picaresque opens with its literary evidence onto three main levels or facets of cultural significance. First, just in the ways that the various picaros and picaras can be regarded in their cumulative character, the "generic" figure that emerges can be interpreted emblematically. The picaro/picara can stand not only as embodying problems of the contemporary American "self" but also, by virtue of his or her "road work," as locating, even eventually inculcating, solutions to such problems. Even those picaros who fail on this count turn out to be quite revealing with respect to the problems. Second, as the picaro explores the terrain of American life in its hugeness, variety, and pluralism, the picaresque narrative becomes a means for taking inventory, recovering resources, making new maps of all that "otherness." In this respect, the significance of the accumulated "new American picaresque" lies in its being equipped, as nothing else seems quite to be, for the cultural work of wrestling with the meanings of the topographical and social whole. Third, the significance of this new picaresque formation in contemporary narrative suggests that the American imagination, at least in this instance, continues its attempt to posit an inhabitable America, even as the late modern national experiment seems, to many, largely in ruins. Indeed, a significant feature of the new American picaresque appears in the ways it posits, or at least proposes, an avenue into the postmodern situation. Traveling such a transitional epoch, the forms and actions of the central characters extend the cultural work by crossing through some of the spiritual conditions of the age, and, without any concertedly religious outlook at all, these characters cover the cultural territories in a manner that begins to clarify the terms in which religious sensibility might move in new motions or at least to clear the grounds on which postmodern religion might likely have to stand.

In the chapters that follow, then, these matters of continuity and change that align the old literary form with what here is denominated "the new American picaresque" provide a beginning avenue of exploration, but the more abiding concern fastens to questions of the parts, places, and implications of these numerous road narratives in the context of contemporary American culture. Such a concern forces critical scrutiny of this cultural phenomenon to go beyond strictly literary questions into other spheres of intellectual inquiry and, thus, in probing into the significance of the road-book phenomenon, to promote and follow out a certain model of interdisciplinarity that imports into the explorations the various interpretive tools that the task itself seems intermittently to require. In short, the interdisciplinary work here simply follows the invitations of the new American picaresque. As different facets of the narrative formation entice different disciplinary perspectives, the study yields to such eclectic necessities. While utilizing the resources of literary history and criticism, genre studies, and discourse theory in order to reckon with the narrative formation, the interpretive work here also entails appeals at various, necessary points to some of the conceptual vocabularies belonging to the disciplinary stores of anthropology and ethnography, communications theory, sociology and social-psychology, humanistic geography, popular culture studies, cultural criticism, religious studies, and the like. To contend that an "explosion" onto the scene of a number of contemporary American "road books" stands in continuity with the formations characteristic of the classic picaresque narratives—or to posit that such American travel stories have their common denomination in a construct called "the new American picaresque"—is, of course, to propose a study involved in the work of literary history. But, in attempting to calculate the *terms* of the reappearance of the picaro and the picaresque venture and the *work* it performs in American culture, the interpretation also enlists itself in the business of the broader shapes of cultural studies. Indeed, as constructed here, the "new American picaresque" is an interpretive invention, a notion devised out of "interdisciplinarity," designed to corral and control a disparate cultural phenomenon, to bring into patterns of coherence these accumulated "road books" waiting to be deciphered. Subsequent chapters drive along this interpretive road.

PART 1

The Literary Work of
the New American Picaresque

1

The Picaresque Old and New:
The Question of Continuity

In contemporary popular parlance, perhaps most often in the "blurbs" on dust jackets, the attribution "picaresque" seems to refer to any rollicking adventure presented in a story that delivers the travels and travails of a central character as he or she careens along the narrative way. In point of fact, the word has a history and, in the scholarship, a tradition of critical usages stemming from a particular culture-scape in the Anglo-European world, most notably Spain. Thus, to contend that a "new American picaresque" has emerged in the second half of the twentieth century is not only to call for an eclectic, yet responsible use of the designation "picaresque" but to propose an extended continuity in formal literary terms with narrative configurations that had their quite distinctive origins in other lands in the sixteenth and seventeenth centuries. "Continuity," of course, is not "identity." E. L. Doctorow's *Billy Bathgate* (1989)[1] is not *Lazarillo de Tormes* (1554), however much the pattern of the latter-day, underclass youngster's vagabondage, his originating innocence, his service to strange masters, or his trespassing social hierarchies might put the reader in mind of Lazarillo's own narrated career. Nor is Doctorow's book a simple echo of Mateo Aleman's *Guzman de Alfarache* (1599) with its own "autobiographical" rehearsal of ejection into a seamy and disarrayed situation, its confession of incidents of episodic criminality, and its retrospective moralism, inserted in narrative course in questionably reliable forms of self-justification. No matter how anti-heroic its narrator/protagonist, anti-romantic its presentation, or anti-social its message at one level, *Billy Bathgate* does not merely mime Quevedo's *El Buscon* (1626), even if some dark satirical ironies—the victim swindled, the swindlers victimized, the reader exposed—might have been on Doctorow's narrative agenda or if the ostensible inversions of the normal social world in the depiction of Dutch Schultz's "underworld" might have come pat to novelistic purposes. Whatever else the character Billy Bathgate is or presents himself to be, he appears as no formulaic revivification of the abandoned Lazarillo or the climbing Guzman or the vicious Don Pablos, any more than he is any mirror reflection of Jack Wilton in Thomas Nashe's *The Unfortunate Traveller* (1594) or the title characters of Jeronimo de Alcala's *Alonso* (1624) and Alain-Rene Le Sage's *Gil Blas* (1715).

Nevertheless, there are enough literary elements and traits discernibly in common among Doctorow's recent American novel and these early Anglo-European "prototypes" and later exemplars of picaresque fiction to warrant the ideas that these texts are in many respects of a narrative piece, regardless of correct and necessary distinctions, and that *Billy Bathgate* scarcely stands alone as a contemporary American permutation of the centuries-old tradition. Some contemporary American authors, with their variations on picaresque patterns, are clearly aware of elements and forerunners in the tradition. Oblique and direct allusions appear here and there to *Don Quixote*[2] and others, and Erica Jong's *Fanny, Being the True History of Fanny Hackabout-Jones* (1980), obviously relishes its replication of several eighteenth-century British versions. Quite clearly, however, there is no unbroken or at least traceable line of influence, imitation, or redaction that persists from the point of fictional origin to the present day and from the Old World to the New: literary history only seldom secures any such provenance. The continuity between old *Lazarillo* and the new American texts is a matter, rather, of compellingly comparable narrative forms as these invite interpretation to detect how the old tradition enables and reaches forward to include the new variations and how, in turn, the more recent innovations in picaresque narrative, in a different time and place, enrich the capacities, functions, and effects of the tradition.

Just such an invitation establishes an agenda for inquiry. In the ensuing discussion, then, after brief attention to the history and geography of picaresque "origins," the effort will be, first, to isolate a number of those formal characteristics that belong to the more or less prototypical or exemplary picaresque narratives in the earlier stages. Even without a dense literary-historical account, this exposition can suggest how the old tradition opens to include a number of new American texts that decisively share the characterizing form. From this necessarily broad rendition of the controlling aspects of the genre, the focus will turn to a more specific concentration on the central and defining figure in all such texts, the picaro or picara. By detailing something of the status, situation, character, and operative mode of this distinctive habitue of narrative, there arises, again, the prospect of a new American company of such figures, progeny of old Guzman or Jack Wilton or Gil Blas. Finally, these sketches of the contours of a picaresque genre and of the nature and life of a generic picaro/picara lead to another kind of consideration of the permissible expansion of the "reach" of the picaresque tradition, this in the context of cultural history. As the earliest picaresque represented a shape of narrative surely responsive to its cultural surround and as this shape was continuously altered in succeeding decades, even centuries, to have cogent entrance and affect in different environs, the genre itself seems genial in adapting to new times and places when social and cultural circumstances seem to require its reappearance.[3] Somewhat like its own Protean focal characters, the picaresque apparently changes masks, shifts, dodges, proves resilient, and survives, all the while maintaining its essential nature. In this context, however, the question of the continuity of picaresque refers to the capacity of the genre to sustain its core structures under what might be significantly different cultural conditions confronting narrative expression. This is easy enough for the mythic Proteus, more challenging perhaps for the picaresque in contemporary America. In this context, then, as always, "continuity" not only implies but includes "change."

Old Tradition, New Texts

The originating texts and authentic forms of the picaresque genre are currently and highly contested.[4] Still, for many literary historical accounts, the first formally "genuine" picaresque narratives were *Lazarillo de Tormes*, its first part published anonymously in Spain in 1554, which provided an original narrative design, and Aleman's *Guzman de Alfarache* (1599), also Spanish, which then significantly advanced the construction. The former, *La vida de Lazarillo de Tormes y de sus fortunas y adversidades*, became genuine perhaps because, unprecedented in its total fictional makeup, it appeared first and, later, could be seen to have "started something." In quick, abstracted version, it is a story, narrated autobiographically by one Lazaro, presumptuously of himself. It presents the life of a lowly and insignificant "orphan," the young Lazarillo, abandoned by the world and yet cast out into it to cope with its ambiguous and brutalizing forces, wherein, in necessary service to several different kinds of suspect masters, his innocence gives way to the "realism" such circumstances required, and his candor turns to guile. Lazarillo's wayfaring movement toward a new life turns on surviving by wit and cunning through episodes whose connection, at least to him, are not apparent. *Guzman* follows essentially the same course; Guzman, however, arrives from more sordid backgrounds with compounding consequences: his father was a sheer reprobate and usurer, his mother entirely promiscuous, and his "orphaned" state, therefore, appears more darkly painted in a more confusing and more dangerous situation. Somewhat like the "settled" Lazaro's recollections, Guzman's autobiography is self-justifying, if more morally reflective in the stance of retrospection permitted by his new life, but he nonetheless admits with occasional delight that, left to bad inheritance and sorry fortune in a venomous world, he followed an earlier criminal and "lewd life" far outstripping the milder roguish behaviors of the more likable Lazarillo.[5] This additional and intensified delinquency, enacted in a starker world, confirmed the anti-heroic "outsider" status of the focal figure of the emergent picaresque, solidified the roguish necessity, and reiterated the principle of narrative movement in a life lived by the wits, "on the road," in discontinuous episodes.

In broadest outline, then, *Lazarillo* and *Guzman* put in place the fundaments of the structure and contents of the picaresque form. These would continue to be developed, amended, and manipulated in later works, but, with Aleman having so to speak "confirmed" the unique work of his anonymous predecessor, a new kind of narrative entered the Western literary tradition. As one critic describes it, "the picaresque novel as a genre . . . emerges out of the confluence of the *Lazarillo* and of the autobiography of a criminal."[6] Moreover, the two entered the territory of cultural expression in several ways that would prove commanding for their narrative legatees. In focus and outlook, style and trajectory, both narratives pitted themselves against the standing order, again establishing aspects of the form that would come to be thought generic criteria for the picaresque mode.

By concentrating on *las vidas* of lowly, marginalized, even criminal characters, these progenitors of picaresque immediately confronted the powerful literary traditions of heroic figures, those mighty pageant creatures at the centers of the epic, the romance, and the chivalry book, that for centuries had defined fit, high, and proper narrative subjects for aristocratic readerships. Guzman might well follow a career of travel and travail, but he is clearly no stately Odysseus: indeed, his character might have had a place in that Homeric "world," at best if at all, as one of those attempting to swindle the household during Odysseus's absence. Lazarillo could only have been a bit player in *Sir Gawain and the Green Knight*, no doubt entrapped, in his insignificant life, to hover at the edges of the drama in service to one of the emblematic, heroic-sized actors enmeshed in a clash of clearly huge moment for sustaining the community. If the focal figure of picaresque has any epic dimension whatever, it is because his or her narrated career constitutes a representation of "the epic of hunger,"[7] recapitulating in complete obverse the socially mighty epic hero whose own intermittent deprivations are the "daily fare" of the outcast picaro. Nor does this new (anti-)hero on the scene enact out of heightened romantic character or idealized duty some noble errand on behalf of the larger moral community: he or she parries and thrusts, self-protects and aggresses, reflexively against a "moral" community that would as not do him or her in. If romance there be about such a figure, it is a "romance of roguery,"[8] bent on the survival of the self. Acknowledgment of epic or romantic heroes in the picaresque is nearly unfailingly tacit as the picaro's status and character simply and decisively affront and counter the "heroic" traditions. With *Lazarillo* and *Guzman*, the challenge went beyond literary competition; they were indictments as well of cultural conventions and social preferences deep-seated in a readership still not weaned from the succor of its "unreal" models.

As the earliest picaresque "fronted and centered" an anti-hero, it thus also depicted the world in styles and terms decidedly resistant to all species of the world view of the "romance," in whose fictive worlds the operations of emblem and symbol remained reasonably clear, heroic characters went unmitigated by any but minor flaws, distinctions between good and evil, commanding and trivial, high and low, were consistently enforced, social hierarchies stayed intact, communal responsibilities were unmistakable, acceptable didactic purposes were maintained, *and* closures arrived with certainty, *just as* lessons came clearly.[9] *Lazarillo* and *Guzman*, of course, portray a world not coerced by narrative romance into those ideal shapes to serve dramatic and moral purposes but a world gritty, "real," frequently dangerous, always opaque, rendered in a style more empirically attentive to the tractable stuff immediately at hand. The players on the scene, including the picaro, are not constant in character or consistent in action (unless marked for satirical purposes) but full of masks, changeability, hidden motive, mixed desire, driven as they are by the claims of sensate existence. Good and evil come disguised, shift places, "lower" elements of life are ascendant, as "higher" ones suffer diminution. What is important in this world of picaresque—food, clothing, shelter, just "getting by"—are the very things scarcely attended to by the bent of romance toward life "heightened" and sublime. In this unromantic, even grimy world, life seems in complete flux: one's status changes from one episode to the next; one's primary duty is to move oneself along. No full-scale dramatic climax occurs, and, thus, any clear denouement and certain closure are problematical: the lessons to be learned, at least until retrospective narration, and perhaps even then, remain obscure.[10] With this kind of mimetic activity, the representation of life in the earliest picaresque poses a real effrontery to the world view at the heart of epic and romance. When recalled at all, the dramas of ideal action in those clearer and steadier fictional worlds are notable in the picaresque only in their absence or in the reader's recognition of the imitation of demeaned "heroic" action in an altogether diminished world.

Beyond the subversions of the regnant narrative and high-cultural traditions posed by the focus on the anti-hero and by the "realistic" depiction of the world, the picaresque further confronted the standing order with an undisguised disposition to mock the stature and pretense of elements of the social hierarchy. Although the full narrative contours of *Lazarillo* and *Guzman* are not given over only to satire, the picaro's trespass of social boundaries, "hit and run" mobility in the socialscape, and wily engagements with a variety of recognizable social types all enable intermittent episodes of satirical presentation and exposure. A definitive element of the picaresque genre is the "social motley" it contains, as the picaro encounters beggars, thieves, prostitutes, landowners, chevaliers, churchmen, small aristocrats, and the like, all playing the bit characters temporarily "on stage" for the picaro's survey and response. Although these represent a vertical as well as horizontal social field of view, the cleric, the student, the school master, the innkeeper and other figures of "business," the faded *hidalgo* in *Lazarillo*—each quite predictably invested in maintaining the hierarchy, coinage, and commerce of the social order—are regularly personae in the old picaresque and occasional targets in satirical episodes, delivered in biting retrospection as the narrator recounts his or her earlier life on the road. The picaresque is not satire per se: its attention is fixedly on the picaro and not on the objects of mild or vitriolic scorn; the subjects and modes of satire appear through the picaro's eyes and are important only in terms of his or her *vida*. But, by virtue of its content and principles of narrative movement, the earliest picaresque clearly folds into its possibilities the frequent inclusion of satirical elements and episodes, utilized again to disrupt the repose of the standing order, to force a shock of recognition in a readership whose own various "types" can come in for ridicule.[11]

From such beginnings, the picaresque persisted across the decades and immigrated across national boundaries of the Western cultural worlds of narrative fiction in works like Nashe's *The Unfortunate Traveller*, Francisco Lopez de Ubeda's *La Picara Justina* (1605), which introduced the first female protagonist, Jeronimo de Alcala's *Alonso* (1624), Quevedo's *El Buscon*, H. J. C. von Grimmelshausen's *Simplicius Simplicissimus* (1668), Le Sage's *Gil Blas*, Daniel Defoe's *Moll Flanders* (1722), Tobias Smollett's *Roderick Random* (1748), among a large number of others, including, later, North American progeny like the 1816 Mexican picaresque novel *El Periquillo Sarniento* (*The Itching Parrot*) by Jose Joaquin Fernandez de Lizardi and the 1885 American *vida* in *The Adventures of Huckleberry Finn* by Mark Twain. In these and other works, while sustaining the basic frame of picaresque focus, pattern, style, and thrust, narrative interests were obviously predicated on and conditioned by the pertinent and pressing temporal concerns and the dynamics of specific cultural settings. Each new entry into the genre variously modified the emphases, amending or amplifying the narrative potentiality, and, withal, shaped and reshaped the genre. *La Picara Justina*, for instance, not only complicated the gender of the focal figure but displayed a propensity to allegorize the stuff of the genre, with the effect of domesticating its subversive potentiality. On the other hand, *El Buscon*, with its picaro Don Pablos, raised delinquency to a new "height," while *The Unfortunate Traveller* again mollified roguery, displaying good, solid Anglo-Saxon virtues in Jack Wilton even in the midst of his misadventures. *Gil Blas*, demonstrably more morally mannered in French eighteenth-century styles, cultivates remorse in the picaro to distinguish its title character from his morally debauched Spanish forebears.[12] In some variations, the picaro's character remains more constant while fortune appears more chaotic; in others, *caractura y fortuna* fit hand in glove. In some, detectable remnants of romance emerge, with satirical thrusts blunted, or, again like *Gil Blas*, nostalgia for the once-dominant but now waning social order is to the fore. At another extreme, as in *El Periquillo Sarniento*, revolutionary foment—the urge for a new order—is scarcely contained. In still others, like *Gil Blas* or Henry Fielding's *Tom Jones* (1749), the haphazard tale possesses the elements of comedy or seems animated by the comic sense of life,[13] an animus not a feature of John Bunyan's *The Life and Death of Mr. Badman* (1680) in its pursuit of high Puritan edification, or Louis-Ferdinand Celine's *Journey to the End of the Night* (1932), one of the darkest narratives in the picaresque tradition.[14] Given all of these shifts and adaptations, it seems reasonable to observe, no one text exemplifies the genre, even if *Lazarillo de Tormes* and *Guzman de Alfarache* stand at the point of its origins and inaugurate some of its definitive features. The picaresque narrative is obviously variable and the tradition of the genre malleable.[15]

Nevertheless, the works in the genre across its first several centuries evince a number of other traits that would become broadly characteristic if not universally present in all picaresque narratives, however much these might be transformed by cultural-historical modification or calibrated within particular picaresque texts. In short, in one rendition or another, some aspects of picaresque can be seen to have accumulated as generic markers. Beyond the concentration on a solitary figure, whose nature or circumstance renders him or her a socially marginal, sometimes shady character dislocated from any "home," the narrative voice of the picaresque is most frequently from the first-person viewpoint, retrospective and "autobiographical," but at all events invariably presented through the consciousness of the one whose *vida* the story is. This narration, realistic in tenor and tone, presents life "on the road," always moving across a *fairly* sizable panoramic vista of cultural topography and social reality, nearly always a vista that is constantly confusing, always challenging, sometimes predatory, or occasionally bordering on disintegration for the picaro or picara who has to enter it, learns to cope with it, and exercises a more or less unfettered moral freedom respecting it. The lonely and anxious *figure* is, thus, thrust into a life without ties and responsibility, free to traverse the landscape but confined by having to meet the conditions of survival. Under the control of the retrospective narrator, the plotting of the tale, the *principle* of movement, is episodic, frequently simply sequencing the chronology of incidents and encounters of the focal character, and each episode, though possessing a kind of unitary character within itself, seems discontinuous with other episodes, a fact that makes the world view of picaresque all the more one of random and haphazard existence, one of chance and fortuity. Emphases are on mobility and survival, the latter often predicated on the former, but the protagonist largely works *sine itinerarium:* moving on becomes a necessity; the next destination appears as a matter of chance, the final stop forever receding into the future. And, as the picaro is buffeted about from one experience to another, duped or duping, blundering along, the narrative movement can range to scenes working to comic effect or to increased anxiety. Such mobility on the part of the picaro, moreover, follows—indeed creates—the panoramic sweep and introduces to the reader, through the picaro's trespassing eye, a plethora of characters and character-types, varying echelons of social status, a veritable carnival of humanity, a *galeria* trait that can open to satirical thrusts, even if the narrative only "hits and runs," the picaro never content or able to remain long at the present venue, the picaresque committed to the venture of the road.

Throughout the narrative, then, the presiding sensation is one of intermittently but continuously "beginning again," starting all over, as each new episode initiates a new stage of chaotic existence or commences a different cycle of experiences without apparent conjunctions. Only when the active figure reaches some repose, ceases to be in constant motion, *stops* being a picaro, can the work of retrospective, autobiographical narration really begin to spy out the coherences that make this jumble of experiences into the stuff of *una vida*. Out of this welter, some broadly shared themes of the picaresque emerge—innocence and disillusionment, gullibility and savvy, liberty and captivity, literal and spiritual hunger, isolation and the craving for a "home"—and some consistent motifs often appear from text to text, like the picaro's odd birth or childhood, the ejection from family or community, the skill for and execution of tricks, the capacity for role-playing, the witnessing of a horrible incident that compresses the nature of the world into one dark scene, all working under the governing theme of motion, the style of episodic presentation.[16]

Just as the numerous works of the old picaresque tradition hang their particular fictional enfleshments on this generic skeleton, thus confirming the nature of the narrative frame and encoding some of its possible figurations, exemplars of the new American picaresque continue to substantiate and renew the defining form. Again, J. D. Salinger's *The Catcher in the Rye* and John Barth's *Giles Goat-Boy* are not identical to *La Picara Justina*, but, then, neither was *Roderick Random* or *Tom Jones* a literary clone of *The Unfortunate Traveller*. Given the structures, thrusts, themes, and motifs, however, each and all—including the contemporary American cases—stand in formal continuity with the earliest instances, the inaugural narratives of the picaresque tradition, and align with what have discernibly emerged as the "general laws about the existence and evolution of a picaresque mode."[17]

John Kennedy Toole's posthumously published *A Confederacy of Dunces*[18] provides a good introductory case in point because, under critical inspection, its broad course, contents, and contours apparently fill out the narrative frame and follow the "general laws" of the picaresque more or less effortlessly. The novel is the *vida* of one quaintly educated Ignatius J. Reilly, a singular, marginalized figure, unwonted and unwanted, solitary even as he makes his way through crowded streets and a kaleidoscope of odd characters. Although the point of view is the third-person omniscient, the narrational consciousness attaches to and largely remains with Ignatius from the fourth sentence forward, and, since some of his own various writings (railing critiques of the modern world written on Big Chief tablets) are interpolated into the story, the narrator always invites, and frequently forces, the reader to see and "feel" through this focal character. What is seen is the unromantic, though often comic, panorama of life in New Orleans, and, for the nearly helpless Ignatius, this world supplies little nurture: he experiences it as forever falling apart, threatening in its chaos and dangerous figures, full of small disasters and hinting of larger ones, its frights and ambiguities further intensified by the disjunctions among the self-contained episodes through which Reilly passes as he blunders haphazardly from one scene to another. Very much like several of his sixteenth-century progenitors, he at one point indeed exclaims, "'Oh, Fortuna, blind, heedless goddess, I am strapped to your wheel. . . . Do not crush me beneath your spokes. Raise me on high, divinity'" (p. 27). Forced to cope in such a world, however, he displays his own unique shapes of guile, plays tricks, dupes the victimizers, but, continuing to seek the terms of his survival, he also falls into the service of strange masters, like the proprietors of Levy Pants and, later, the supervisor of a hotdog street-vending operation. These belong to a large cast of human types randomly dancing in and out of the narrative action—the black petty-thieving, jive-talking Jones, bent on swindle; the hapless cop, Mancuso, trapped by his confused tender-heartedness; his own mother, Mrs. Reilly, arthritic and daft; her friend, Santa Battaglia, busy-bodying; the absent love-interest, Myrna Minkoff, off to revolution in New York—and a variety of other, smaller players who appear from incident to incident to suffer at least quasi-satirical blows as Ignatius's peripatetic course crosses over them.

Although the strange ride of Ignatius Reilly unfolds under the control of a retrospective narrator who knows full well how this history of misadventures will close, poor Ignatius Reilly in medias res has no such foreknowledge, and he, along with the reader, proceeds without benefit of causal "plot," animated only by episodic happenstance, moving on, without itinerary and entering each new, apparently unsuccessive experiential location with mingled foreboding and hope, starting every day as if brand new. Serving and enforcing this narrative rhythm of un-fettered mobility and constrained possibility are the thematic staples of naive innocence and morose disillusionment, of guilelessness and craft, of the literal and existential starvation for "something more" (Reilly has a huge, unsatiated hunger in several senses), and of alternating dislo-cations and desires for a "place to be," these themes nicely accompanied and confirmed by the motifs of the unusual childhood, the "ejection" (Mrs. Reilly hurls him into the world of work), the performance of tricks (mostly rhetorical), the role-playing of the "hero" (he often writes his vitriolic tracts and letters under pseudonyms like "Zorro" or "Gary, your militant working boy," or even one of his bosses, "Gus Levy"). In fact, were such reminiscences of the old picaresque not enough for Toole, this anti-hero, Ignatius Reilly, whom Walker Percy's foreword calls "a fat Don Quixote" (p. vi), even carries a sword about the streets of New Orleans as if to remind the reader of the distance of this man, with all of his flatulence and gaseous belches, from the old knights-errant and other heroes of romance, the heroes undercut by the likes of Don Pablos, *el buscon,* and other early picaros.

But *A Confederacy of Dunces* is far from the only contemporary Ameri-can book operating within and plying anew these "governing laws" of the texts in the picaresque tradition. In urban formations, Jay McInerney's *Bright Lights, Big City,* Ralph Ellison's *Invisible Man,* and James Leo Her-lihy's *Midnight Cowboy,* for instance, move the narrative panorama from Toole's New Orleans to New York City, but each also operates under executive structures of the picaresque form—the socially marginal figure, the episodic venturing through a chaotic, hostile, and ambiguous city-scape, the theme of hunger, the passing parade of human types, and so on. Broadening the territory of coverage to the western United States, James Crumley's *The Last Good Kiss,* Robert James Waller's *Border Mu-sic,* and Edward Abbey's *The Monkey Wrench Gang* travel vaster expanses, with the variety of the human gallery perhaps more attenuated, but each too deals in the singular, eccentric anti-hero whose character and circum-stances have dislodged him from any place simply to be and commit-ted him to life "on the road," the unplanned, episodic course of chance and happenstance that channels the narrative progress. Some shift the temporal scene. Bill Terry's *The Watermelon Kid* (1984) follows the criss-crossing movement of A. J. Poole through Arkansas during the 1950s as this good-natured "rogue," a kind of "knight-erring" in a pick-up truck, gathers and disperses his cronies (Will and Leroy, Pierpont, Rainbow,

Pepper, Doodle Sockett) as they all blast their episodic way along the road-house circuit. E. L. Doctorow's *Billy Bathgate*, mentioned earlier, pushes back further as it follows the vagabondage of Billy through his own narration of "orphanage," ejection into an ambiguous and tumultuous world, tricksterism and role-playing, living by his wits in gangster-land America as "bondsman" to the "lord" Dutch Schultz's underworld. And, although narrated in 1952, "as told to" a "historian" of the American West, Thomas Berger's *Little Big Man* drives back further still, into the nineteenth century and onto the western plains, as the 111-year-old Jack Crabb revels in and "ravels" his frontier misadventures, including his necessarily shifting outer "identities," his living by wits and cunning, his several shapes of delinquency, and his survivalist service to various masters, most notably General George Armstrong Custer. As such contemporary American texts and a great many others participate in the general structures of the old picaresque formations, later, closer scrutiny of some of them will reveal that such American "road books" belong to the narrative category in much more specific ways as well. For now, as their particular forms of creativity both recall and reconstitute the terms of the tradition, they invite a closer inspection of their continuity with Lazarillo, Jack Wilton, Guzman, Don Pablos, Gil Blas, Tom Jones, and other old picaros, in whose legacy the likes of Ignatius Reilly, Billy Bathgate, Jack Crabb, and A. J. Poole can be thought to stand.

The Picaro/Picara: Forebears and New American Avatars

Despite the wandering character at the center of attention in *Lazarillo de Tormes*, the term "picaro" in fiction was first used by Aleman to describe his Guzman, another indication perhaps of the latter's confirmation of the new kind of narrative, with a new kind of focal figure, brought into the literary world by his anonymous predecessor. The debate continues about the origins and meanings of the term—everything from "kitchen-boy," to "low life," to "rogue," to "army deserter" (*piquero*), to those knaves of Picardy, thought by the Spanish to be scurrilous types.[19] If the etymology and original associations remain shrouded, however, the inclusion of Jack Wilton, Gil Blas, Tom Jones, and others in the cadre amplifies the possibilities of "picaro" beyond the stuff of peasantry and of "delinquency," much less "criminality." In this accumulated tradition of the older picaresque narratives, the character of the picaro or picara has come to include any narratively focusing figure whose existence, by fortune or volition, has pushed him or her to the social margins, there to be free and mobile in a manner quite "unheroic": by wit and chance, he or she lives and moves episodically through an ambiguous world in relation to which he or she remains an outsider. Additional features of his or her character, style, and aspiration while "on the road" further define the literary form.

In the episodic engagement with experience, the picaro or picara twists and turns as a creature of almost pure immediacy and reflexivity. While on the road, still in transit, his or her existence crystallizes only in the scene, whatever scene, is currently to the narrative fore. The visuals, tactiles, olfactories command attention: the picaro's life by wit necessitates his commitment to the press of immediate sensation upon him. No simple materialist, he must nevertheless respect the material order of life for the sake of his survival.[20] *Yo soy solo*, Lazarillo reminds himself (and the reader) early on, and he must be alert in order to care for his life. Thus, although the retrospective narrator, himself no longer a picaro even in the autobiographical mode, is settled in to tell the tale, to detect pattern, to exercise the "literary convention of perfect memory," the picaro, living here and now (or actually "then and there"), works without any such extended recollection, responsive only to the present moment, the near at hand, as he or she is caught in its terms and dynamics. Part of this is a result of the picaro's constant "inconstancy," his playing different roles from scene to scene, each role predicated on situational demands. If a flicker of memory occurs in the picaro while still in mobile career, it is frequently as a streak of recognition he suspects playing him false in a world requiring him to have to start over, begin again, in successive moments. "Perfect memory" remembers the picaro's apparently caring not a farthing about the last episode. His understandable self-absorption makes the world matter only as it presents itself most simultaneously to him, as it elicits the knee-jerk responses by which sensate life rules him. Occasions for more than the quickest, necessary reflection in the midst of the bombardments of experience surrender to reflex, thus lending the figure what often seems a kind of "shallowness" and an "amoral" posture, both of which traits are apparent functions of the self-concentration and continuing movement such a homeless *vida* requires.[21]

These very attributes, indeed, contribute to the picaro's style of engagement and response. If he appears notably light in his hit-and-run mode, it is not only because his life permits no place to stay, to sink in, to gain depth, but also because he operates in a frame of kaleidoscopic ambiguity that requires as primary response the matter of dealing with a world of appearances, sheer surface, before supposing depth in it. Such wonted shallowness, moreover, makes the picaro a veritable "democrat of experience" in the sense that his lambent, even facile touches on life ordinarily refuse to distinguish the high from the low, the sacred from the profane, the noble from the common, the mannered from the vulgar, as these categories are exerted in the conventional and hierarchical evaluations of experience, especially those of epic and romance. He regards each and all with equal eye, and, because his picaresque life forces him to begin anew in each episode, he brings forward a form of equanimity that, however ambivalent, continuously challenges the reader to reevaluate as well.[22] For Lazarillo, Guzman, even Don Pablos, beggars and squires, soldiers and thieves, priests and prostitutes, are of a piece, to be sifted through in the immediacies of engagement, to take their places in the *galeria* according to the picaro's encounters with them, to fall into the (sometimes satirical) scheme later dictated by retrospective narration. In a world without governing principles, the ostensibly unprincipled life of the picaro, even in his role-playing, follows this one constant principle of equilibrium, adaptability without constant (and sometimes expected) conventional judgmental discretions. His "amoral" style functions for him as a structure of moral balance on his twisted course through a tilted world.

Thus, despite being forever an *isolato* or outcast, caught in the swirl of circumstances in a difficult world, the picaro or picara—in most mutations—displays a persistent kind of openness, an enduring innocence, with respect to the experience of the road, even as his or her background, ejection, and subsequent ill treatment might have instructed otherwise. Clearly capable of craft and cunning when required in a particular episode, Guzman, Jack Wilton, and especially Lazarillo, and many another picaresque wayfarer consistently move to the next experience with some wariness but also armed with candor and prepared to think life can now, perhaps, right itself. The settled, "settling" Lazaro (the adult Lazarillo) and the smug narrator of *Guzman* might well be jaded, but their retrospective depictions of their own earlier selves, of themselves as picaros, present figures unusually resilient and animated by hope. Although the picaro can in the midst of things despair sometimes about his condition and apparent fate, he ordinarily proceeds to the "next thing" with readiness, opened to its prospects. As Guzman remembers in retrospection on his younger self: "Well, when I saw how the world went, and that there was no helpe for it, I pluckt up my spirits, set a good face on the matter, and drew strength out of weakness."[23] Picaros are forever "plucking up" their spirits, renewing themselves in hope. This sustained and sustaining hopefulness might be born of the picaro's sense of fortuitous or crafty escapes from his earlier predicaments, his delight in his own capable guile, his surmise about the intercessions of providential good fortune, his idea of a good turn of the *rota Fortunae*, his detection of "the will of God," or in some alternating perceptions of these. Whatever the fundaments of his hope, he is able to continue along the solitary course of his hard-scrabble life and to remain open to what it will bring when less intrepid travelers would have forsaken the road altogether, to relent to apparent conditions and settle for the present place, just as Lazaro and Guzman have by the time their tales are finally told.

This quality of the picaro's hopefulness, overt or more muted, suggests an essentially romantic craving in him. Even if decidedly unheroic or anti-heroic in background and bearing, in social status and self-concentrated actions, the picaro's implicit yearning—signaled perhaps only by his aspirant movement toward an as-yet unknown better condition—is for some place to be and belong, some locus of order and coherence that will render his life meaningful, some point of repose that yields significantly and significantly more than the road affords.[24] There are frequent instances in which the remarkable thematic "hunger" of this character in exile and tumult is nothing other than starvation for a realm of meaning. Indeed, the old picaro's desire is often for facets of the lost "world" of the romance, with its clarity, order, and purposefulness, even as his customary realism in grappling with experience can evoke such a world only by its altogether conspicuous absence. His notable homelessness, his orphaned state in an unresponsive world, often has him alternating between some nostalgia for the home from which he has been ejected, however sordid it might have been, and some futuristic dreaming about that better place he might yet find in which to lay his head. As the earlier picaresque mode in the hands of an Aleman or a Le Sage or a Nashe assumes the romance in order to invert its meanings, the old picaro is nevertheless captive to the nature and quality of the past order his experience occasionally permits him, sometimes forces him, to imagine in his own versions.

Given these presiding traits, a number of contemporary American "characters" represent permutations of this old picaro. Salinger's Holden Caulfield, for example, certainly displays not only that ejected "outsidership" while he is cut loose in the city to make his way but also, saturated in the immediacies of his episodic adventures, that reflexive responsiveness, leveling style, perduring innocence, and hopeful openness, that belonged earlier to Lazarillo. Despite the empirical style of realism Holden practices and the biting invective sent in retrospection toward some peoples, he sustains his willingness to "begin again," to pluck up, and his closing dream of standing in the rye to save the children pointedly evokes the now-missing world of the romance. Or, again, Jay McInerney's *Bright Lights, Big City,*[25] though told in alternating past and present tenses and from the second-person viewpoint, exercises this unusual tactic to obliterate the distinction between narrator and focal character, thus also giving the reader a sensation of immediacy with the once-insider now outsider, yet narratively centralizing figure operating by sense and reflex in his exiled existence. In Manhattan, the panoramic scene is geographically confined, as with Holden Caulfield or Ralph Ellison's "invisible man" in their own parts of New York, but the chaotic, episodic scenarios tumbling randomly upon each other are equally plenteous, as is the carnival of humanity to be seen by way of the dark life of bar prowling, partying, and drugs, all induced by losses of home, of mother, of wife, of job, of any coherence. "You described the feeling you'd always had of being misplaced" (p. 166), he reports, and, as he tosses about from one discontinuous moment to the next, free but desperate for some "home," he recognizes that each experience requires that "you will have to learn everything all over again" (p. 182). Or, for another kind of example, Billy Bathgate, in the Doctorow novel, is fully the outsider, indeed for a time lives secretly in the basement of an orphanage, even takes his surname from the area he came from, "Bathgate Avenue." But, as an *isolato* of full-fledged picaresque capacities, he manages from episode to episode to start over, to self-preserve, to be attuned as a matter of conscious "style" to even the minute modulations in the immediate situations of his gangster life, to avoid overestimating the apparently important and underestimating the obviously trivial characters around him and the experiences he undergoes. The very attribute that first called him to Dutch Schultz's attention—the extraordinary skill as a juggler—signals an essential equilibrium in Billy that gives him resilience through the hard going and hopefulness for something more, a constant moral balance that belies his outwardly "amoral" stances. Deep into the narrative, remembering being tempted to steal from the gang, the retrospective Billy reveals that even then "I knew I would do nothing of the kind, I didn't know what I would do but I sensed that the nature of my own business opportunity was still to make itself known, life held no grandeur for a simple thief, I had not gotten this far and whoever had hung this charm over my life had not chosen me because I was a cowardly double-crosser" (p. 271).[26]

Toole's Ignatius J. Reilly again presents a sufficiently ample and conveniently synoptic case in point. From virtually the first paragraph of the novel, as his "supercilious blue and yellow eyes" scan the street scene in front of the Holmes department store in search of others' "offenses against taste and decency" in their manner of dress, it becomes quickly evident that it is Ignatius who is a social affront, a marginal figure, an outsider even in a New Orleans where "normalcy" runs to extremes. A medievalist by training, he is undauntedly jobless, preferring to live in the house of a mother whom he scorns. He is a fat man of eccentric dress, huge hunger, and outrageous decorum, who is full of enormous flatulence, both literal and verbal, the released rages of which erupt from his sense of the lack of coherence after "the waning of the Middle Ages." Stranded thus in historical as well as social terms, he is "driven into" virtually complete self-absorption, but he discovers that he is exiled even from his own body: were the continuous betrayals by his digestive system not enough, his once masturbatory delights ("flights of fancy and invention," worthy of high romance) now only become frantic, mechanical acts that fill him with depression (pp. 27–28). He is also soon "driven out," expelled into the bigger, complicated world of livelihood, wherein his unique embodiment, but characteristic style, as a picaro runs its course.

On the streets of New Orleans, Ignatius is full of anxiety, even paranoia, that leads to a highly empirical mode of presentation. He suffers the slings and arrows of his life like a raw nerve-ending, and the third-person retrospective narrator, so deeply entrenched in the picaro, delivers these compounding disasters likewise. As picaro, Reilly's extraordinary self-consciousness, beset by the swirl of immediate sensations in each episode he undergoes, becomes an ever-shifting, nearly instinctive matter of avoiding the bludgeoning he anticipates that the *rota Fortunae* will soon deliver. Even the stylized language of medieval culture that he uses to heap vitriol on the chaotic and threatening environment comes less out of any quiet and extended reflection than as a reflexive rhetoric of his picaresque role-playing, a self-defensive measure (like his sword) enacted in burlesque, whether in the shadowy and sorrowful barroom called "Night of Joy" or in chasing down the cat through the company's storeroom of hotdog buns. Through it all, Ignatius the picaro arrives before the reader's eyes, from one disconnected episode to the next, as a "democrat of experience," making no distinctions in his mobile misadventures between trivial and important incidents, authoritative or outcast figures, protectors or perceived enemies: he regards all with equal trepidation and / or scorn, treats each only and equally as a function of his own necessities, and, withal, proves resilient in these tactics of self-sustenance.

Nevertheless, for all of his nastiness and duplicity, for all of his apparent axiological bankruptcy, this hefty picaro balances off his "amoral" style with his constancy in openness and innocence. Regardless of what befalls him, indeed fells him, he gets up and dusts himself off, enters each new day prepared to begin anew, refreshed in the hope that things will work out, that life will right itself. Such romantic and often comic expectancy, even following closely upon this or that small or large episode of catastrophe, propels him along, each day preparing to seize all over again, as he must, the tactics or the luck that might gain him a better cycle of fortune. The world for which Ignatius Reilly hungers but cannot find, as he chases around near or on "Desire" Street, can only be emotionally reclaimed from an earlier, a much earlier time. "Once a person was asked to step into this brutal century," he fears, "anything could happen. Everywhere there lurked pitfalls like Abelman, the insipid crusaders for Moorish Dignity, the Mancuso cretin, Dorian Greene, newspaper reporters, stripteasers, birds, photography, juvenile delinquents, Nazi pornographers" (p. 325). That other, earlier world he continually aspires to enter is an imagined medieval order of clarity and stability: "'what I want,'" Ignatius tells his mother, "'is [to have] a good, strong monarchy with a tasteful and decent king who has some knowledge of theology and geometry and to cultivate a Rich Inner Life'" (pp. 183–84). Ironically, as the narrative closes, this picaro—at first afraid to leave his room, then to travel beyond the bounds of New Orleans—now moves toward his anticipated new "cycle of life" when fortuitously spurred forward by the reappearance from New York of his Myrna Minkoff. For his highly tuned hold on immediate sensations, her hair, scented by "soot and carbon," brings him as well a vision of "glamorous Gotham": moving yet, he decides, "'I must go flower in Manhattan'" (p. 331). The new American picaro is off again and running, though across a different geographical terrain than that traveled by his forebears in the tradition.

Continuity of Cultural Contexts: Old World and Contemporary America

By this point in the second half of the twentieth century, no reader of imaginative literature should any longer be surprised to discover a non- or anti-heroic figure, a Billy Bathgate or an Ignatius Reilly, as a character of narrative focus. Indeed, in picaresque version or otherwise, the contemporary anti-hero seems reasonable and appropriate enough in those newer fictional worlds that have long since kicked the mimetic traces of "romance" for the renditions given by rhetorical, social, and psychological "realism." These worlds more or less *predictably*, and quite acceptably, contain underworld thugs, insipid crusaders, alcoholic mothers, hapless cretins, corrupt politicians, newspaper reporters, crooked cops, jolly rapists, jive artists, busy-body neighbors, and Nazi pornographers.[27] In some views, the sixteenth-century rise of the picaresque fiction, which put to rout the books of chivalry and other shapes of medieval romance and allegory, was an originating point, or at least a catalytic moment, in the evolution of narrative forms toward the recognizably modern novel.[28]

Still, it should not be forgotten that the appearances of Lazarillo and the world portrayed in *Lazarillo de Tormes* were not quite so predictable at all in the last days of medieval Spain, in a culture experiencing not only the emergence of new social prospects amid the final throes of antique feudalisms but also the unprecedented wealth attending new forms of commerce, the incredible growth of glamorous urban centers in Sevilla and Madrid, the administrative unification of the regions, and the glories and triumphs of an ever-extending nationalist empire. To outward appearance, Spain had entered and was enjoying its Renaissance, a "Golden Age." In social and cultural reality, things were and were apparently "felt" as quite different. The new social order, not yet fully formed, was in disarray, status and privilege up for grabs just because of the transformed shapes of economic life. An increasing middle class suffered the discontents of the civilization as the rural peasants flooded the cities, there creating an under-culture of poverty, hunger, and crime. The subsumed regions contended with and resented each other. The "empire" drew enemies, fought competitors, experienced significant financial crises. As in the rest of Europe, new forms of science—in mathematics, astronomy, optics, and anatomy—collided with old myths and meanings and challenged old faiths. Counter-Reformation surges in Catholic Spain were accompanied by huge actions of intolerance against Jews, Moors, and the few Protestants, but, instead of creating any new religious consensus, they seemed to contribute to the general chaos. Culturally centralizing and controlling ideas and values were evaporating: the so-called medieval synthesis clearly could not hold. In the face of such a situation, the empowered—the royalty, the clergy, and the old aristocracy—nonetheless clung desperately to the "ideal" past that had empowered them and that they

hoped might stabilize the current chaos: it was the past of the clear, ordered, and ennobled world posited by heroic romance, the crystalline
values in the stable world prompted by Christian morality plays, the
gentrified social models proposed in the world of the chivalry books.[29] The
possibility of some royal decree to reify this world of medieval order probably disappeared when Charles I of Spain, the "chivalric king," the king
for Christian unity, abdicated in 1555 (the year after *Lazarillo* first appeared) and left a real vacuum of leadership. He retired to a monastery,
it should be noted, himself obviously yet seeking the certitudes of the old,
but now rapidly vanishing order of meaning. And comparable social,
economic, religious, and political upheavals, with similar efforts at literary-cultural and socio-political bulwarking undertaken by "elites," were,
of course, occurring quite broadly throughout the Anglo-European world.

Confronting such anxious attempts by aristocracy to codify in the new
culture this old, "ideal" version of its life, *Lazarillo de Tormes, Guzman de
Alfarache,* and *Don Pablos, El Buscon* clearly received little approbation
from these would-be arbiters of literary taste, religious meaning, and
cultural order, no matter how much an increasingly literate middle class
might have gobbled up this new kind of narrative. The picaresque narrative venture must have seemed to the entire reading audience to have
opened a new front in the more and more evident "culture wars" then
being waged during this era of transitions and turbulence. For the lower-
and middle-class reader or auditor, Lazarillo or Guzman no doubt displayed a more recognizable character in a more real situation than any
glorified knight-errant, and, through the various picaros' travels and
travails, the reader could spot out and delight in the exposure and vic-
timization of those pitiful creatures in the human gallery still preening
themselves on former status or "office" or chivalric pretense. For the old
religious and cultural aristocracy, Guzman and Don Pablos were surely
not only unworthy figures for narrative concern but subversive anti-
models for individual and social existence, and, with the picaresque,
these kinds of readers evidently considered Aleman and Quevedo, in
their "epics of hunger," to be fueling the fires of perverse disarray at the
very time Spain most needed centers of order and coherence. Little wonder, then, that the picaresque, especially as it bent toward parody of the
old literature, satires of elements of the authorities, and ridicule of waning values, struck many across the spectrum of cultural officialdom as a
subversive form. *La Vida de Lazarillo de Tormes* was quickly put on the
church Index or Catalogue of Prohibited Books in 1559 and was censored
by the Inquisition upon its reissue in 1573.[30]

Even such a stunted survey suggests the particular historical setting and timing for the origins of the picaresque form, the cultural-historical circumstances in which it found its place and to which it was responsive, and the literary and cultural "displacements" it attempted to generate.[31] With respect to the question of continuity, this survey begins to indicate as well why the picaresque narrative is the kind of expressive formation that might be required by some other broadly analogous cultural-historical circumstances and might flourish within a comparable cultural context even centuries later across a wide ocean. Like the new American picaro Ignatius Reilly, the transfigured picaresque narrative might "go flower in Manhattan" and other contemporary American parts.[32] This kind of continuity, of course, is not successive, in the sense that social and economic situations and forces in sixteenth-century Spain followed any direct and traceable trajectory directly into the United States in the second half of the twentieth century. "Continuity" here, rather, refers to general social and cultural conditions broadly shared by the two periods and places, conditions providing an interpretive link at one level between that moment in old *España* and the other in contemporary American culture.

If sixteenth-century Spain seemed on its face to be in a "Golden Age," life in the decades of post–World War II America appeared to confirm that this was indeed "the American Century." Outwardly, the movement from rural agriculture to urban commerce and suburban landscapes signaled both the ensconced character of middle-class solidity and affluence and the new prosperity of industry and business, and the increasing consolidations of economic, military, and political powers created huge vectors of global control and "imperial" influence. As an international "superpower," in short, America could be seen as a contemporary version of fifteenth- and sixteenth-century Spanish glory and triumph. In social and cultural reality, things were and have been "felt" as quite different. A new set of complex social matrices increasingly confused the scene, stemming from racial conflict, from generational battles during the Vietnam era, from new feminist waves, from heightened immigrations to American shores, and from the appearance of an evidently permanent underclass. Amplified social and cultural pluralisms and "new ethnicities" widened the interspaces of reserve and distrust among people and frequently led to hostilities and resentments. The distances between rich and poor were exacerbated, and the middle class suffered its modern shapes of discontent. The urban world turned more and more to blight, violence, and crime. From within, the regions of the "unified" country came into political conflict, and the state fought its "un-American" competitors. From without, the "empire" drew its predictable cold-war enemies and waged wars on "non-American" peoples. There was a series of economic crises. New forms of science and technology (like life-sustaining systems, organ replacements, and genetic engineering) continued to challenge old religious meanings and to complicate received values. Intra- and interreligious contentions, indeed, were increasingly intense, contributing to the scenarios of disarray, disgruntlement, and disillusionment. The chivalric "king," Kennedy, was assassinated in 1963: Camelot was dead. An elected successor in effect "abdicated" ten years later, and corruptions in officialdom were more or less continuously exposed. In the face of such a generally chaotic situation, desperate to maintain social order and stable meanings, the empowered—the royalty, the wealthy, the cultural elite—clung to a romanticized past, or promoted ideal visions of the future, or both, by calling for instruction in a stable American "canon" of necessary learning and citizenship, by vaunting ideas of "the Great Society," by pleading for "a new American covenant," by pumping for the old morality, especially from the "Religious Right." These and other attempts to codify an ideal version of America, comparable to such efforts among the remnants of the "authoritative" order in Spain, far from achieving consensus and stability, only pointed up the chaotic situation, compounded the tensions.

However foreshortened, even these abridged depictions indicate a continuity of social and cultural upheaval between old Spain and the recent United States—a comparability of conditions that made the setting ready and the timing right for the reappearance of the picaresque narrative in contemporary America, just as tumultuous conditions had originally called it forth in the Anglo-European world of the sixteenth century. As a narrative formation, the picaresque seems more or less uniquely suited for and responsive to these kinds of contexts of cultural transition, disorder, and ambiguity. With its capacities to render the experience of the non-heroic or anti-heroic figure, to gather and present the *galeria* of myriad human types, to expose and pique the recognizably perverse, silly, or vain shapes of social existence, even to carve out a kind of realistic narrative "place" for itself in the fields of cultural expression, the picaresque emerged again transformed in and by its new American modifiers, but, as other chapters argue further, it "arrived" or was re-created in America with fundaments intact, still endowed with its capacities to evoke immediate scenes, to engage experience "on the road," to withhold assessment, to maintain equilibrium, to render its "lower" epic of hunger and hope, and to move toward a next episode, a new cycle, in which might be found the locus of order and meaning allowing one finally to be still. After the gang has been wiped out, Billy Bathgate realizes that "now that he [Dutch Schultz] was dead, I was on my own" (p. 311) all over again, but, resilient though newly cast out, he soon realizes that "nothing was over, it was all still going on": "I thought it was indeed possible my days were numbered but my competitive spirit was reawakened" (pp. 317–18). With this expectancy, even in troubled times, the old picaresque venture continues and renews, though now its narratives, in America, have to travel new and different social, cultural, and geographical territories.

2

The Picaresque Borrowed and Blue: The Matter of Change

At the levels of the narrative shape, the life and style of the focalizing character, and the cultural context, *Billy Bathgate*, Billy Bathgate, and late twentieth-century America clearly present continuities with—structural parallels to—*Guzman de Alfarache*, the picaro Guzman, and late sixteenth-century Spain. But it is just as clear that the narrative of Billy's strange ride as a picaro and indeed his characterizing nature and style play out under quite altered circumstances and move toward some altogether different ends with the renewal of the picaresque by the hand of E. L. Doctorow. Toward the end of the narrative, the reader discovers that "Bathgate" will remain the picaro's pseudonym because, after having finally learned his lessons from Dutch Schultz, the now "settled" retrospective narrator has gained a "certain renown" in America and, thus, must keep his earlier life completely hidden. If for no other reason than the twisted Horatio Alger kind of closure, this puts a decidedly American cast on Billy's *vida*, a kind of romantic consummation that could not have been fully expected from the earliest picaresque novels. Even more, however, the reader finds in the matured Billy a typical shape of American insouciance. He has no regrets about his youthful delinquencies, does not despise his exile on the road like Lazarillo and Guzman, and never imagines he will be read "out of heaven." He is, rather, most grateful for the experiences: "I drop to my knees in reverence to think of it, I thank

God for the life He has given me and . . . I praise Him and give all reverent thanks for my life of crime and the terror of my existence" (pp. 321–22). Other new American picaros, of course, display other kinds of American transformations.

But it is not only the case that some general traits of American character create modifications in the central figure. If American literary expression of the past three or four decades taps the generic reservoir of the picaresque, the fact is as well that the special cultural case represented by recent American life puts its own special channels on the narrative currents, tapping them for its own needs, releasing what remain identifiably picaresque streams, to be sure, but forcing them and thus changing them to flow in a different age, in different cultural conduits.[1] As *Gil Blas* was apt for and responsive to its time and place, it shifted the terms of engagement from those of *Lazarillo de Tormes,* and there is good reason to think that the nature of these "shifted terms" discloses something about both the force of the picaresque current and its malleability in the work it performs to serve different cultural functions.

The central concern of this chapter relates to the matter of how this continuity of the picaresque involves change of the picaresque—change largely predicated on the altered cultural situation, from *España antigua* to contemporary America. The following discussion, then, seeks first to sketch in general terms some of those facets of cultural life in contemporary America that not only distinguish it from sixteenth- and seventeenth-century England and Europe but that also put distinctive and altering pressures on the reemergent picaresque form in its understanding and depiction of the world. The continuities abide, but the changes are apparent, all the more when the expository focus turns to a consideration of the ways that the new American picaro lives and moves and has his or her narrative "being" in this American "world" of picaresque. As he or she participates in some typical American forms of ideation and exhibits what are arguably some defining traits of American "hunger," this road figure arrives not as Gil Blas or Don Pablos or Moll Flanders but in ways apt for and responsive to his or her time and place—the picaro and picara still but in new American embodiments. These inquiries into the shifted terms conditioning the picaresque form and into the cultural "precedents" at home for the new American picaro finally lead to critical reflection on the cultural "space" in America occupied by these recently emergent and newly shaped narratives. *Lazarillo* and *Guzman* wedged open roles for themselves in the arena of creative cultural expression in their age, but the task of reckoning with the texts inheriting the picaresque tradition in twentieth-century America forces criticism to calculate their functions and measure their possible effects in new and different ways.

The New American Setting and Permutations of the Picaresque

Old Spain and recent America might well seem in a continuity of social condition, in the sense that both glitter from without while suffering turbulence, disorder, and ambiguity from within, but the change from one to the other, of course, has a radical and even self-evident character. Not only is there a continental shift, attended by huge geographical and topological transformations pressing on human sensibility; there is also the significantly different historical course of social, political, and cultural evolution. Not only is there an enormous temporal divide, differentiating late medieval, early Renaissance outlooks from modern and postmodern views; there is also a chasm between ideas of human nature and destiny, the senses of the scene and situation, the calculi of "realism," and the character of hope. That a genre can persist through such changes is remarkable; that it must change in order to do so is inevitable. The sheer size of the culturescape, the increased rapidity of life, the unmitigated motley of the social scene—place, pace, and pluralism—all begin to suggest the "difference" of the new setting for the picaresque venture. Still, for the paradigmatic structures of such a narrative tactic, this "new" America appears daunting, proves transforming, and yet seems approachable.[2]

Wanderer though he was, the old picaro's path was for the most part circumscribed and the picaresque narrative's range of survey truncated, at least in comparison with the nearly unimaginable length and number of the roads and the size of the cultural territory unfolding for engagement on the contemporary American continent. Compounding the incredible geographical field, of course, are the nearly infinite topographical variegations, the mixed and mingled natures of the regions, the size and number of the cities, the crowds and varieties of and within the crowds of people. While the old picaresque entered and presented the panorama of its social and cultural scene with some confidence about prying open and exposing its nature for readers prepared to recognize it, the new picaresque faces no such prospect of exposition, of returning to the reader the character of America in any way comparable to the identifiable France in *Gil Blas* or the recognizable England in *The Unfortunate Traveller* or the familiar Spain of *Lazarillo*. The place is too big, the culturescape too kaleidoscopic, the dynamics too pulsed with energy, the urban territories too complex, for any "unfortunate travel narrative" to see steadily, essentially, and whole. This is an America always immense, once partly hidden beyond its frontiers, now become again in the second half of the twentieth century a kind of *terra incognita*, a land so huge in several senses as to create an amplification of the ambiguous world of the old picaresque beyond hitherto understood proportions.[3]

The staple of picaresque represented by the old picaro's mobility, his or her capacity to roam unfettered in spatial terms, created both the occasion and the means for the narrative gathering of the panoramic scene and the exposure of the familiar culture itself to itself. The contemporary American picaro retains and even extends this capacity and need for movement and, thus, also extends the capacities of the picaresque to cover even broader fields of purview. Robert James Waller's *Border Music*, for instance, can follow its Texas Jack Carmine, one of "the last real unbonded men on earth,"[4] from northern Minnesota to Otter Falls, Iowa, to Alpine, Texas, to Charlotte, North Carolina, and around again, and his "unbondedness" inspires his uncle, Vaughn Rhomer, finally to become a "roamer" himself, to cut out for a new experiential territory. Or, Larry McMurtry's title character in *Cadillac Jack* can zoom about large stretches of the country at the spur of the moment, or on the impetus of the last episode, or upon the attraction of something simply having caught his attention, thus affording the narrative a panorama from the West coast to the District of Columbia. James Crumley's C. W. Suhgruc extends the range of *The Last Good Kiss* with his cycles of disjointed experience as an innocently roguish private detective, following his "clues" or his nose through Montana, the Southwest, and California. Like Kerouac's *On the Road*, these and other contemporary American examples of picaresque follow a course far too huge for Mateo Aleman or Alain-Rene Le Sage in their times to have imagined, much less traveled.

However, while such mobility, with its American increases, remains part and parcel of the new picaro's life, thus enabling an even greater range and reach of narrative sweep, the narrative purpose now is often less one of exposing a familiar cultural surround than of entering and experiencing elements of a *terra incognita*, this huge, almost imponderable new America, somehow become, even for Americans, newly "alien" in its sheer size and variety. Texas Jack Carmine, the seasoned traveler, entices his temporary road companion to west Texas by telling her "'You'll see what I mean before long. Different place altogether, and if you feel it, you'll live it and start believin' you're from a foreign country compared to everythin' else of an American nature" (p. 139). After crossing the border into this unknown landscape, Linda Lobo "thought about . . . this being another land entirely." An American from Iowa, "she was used to green fields and towns . . . and the arid distances and high buttes out here made her feel small and vulnerable. It was no place to be running on empty" (p. 142). On the part of Vaughn Rhomer, having played Walter Mitty for years resourced by travel books and the *National Geographic,* the decision to take to what he calls the "Big Road" sends him not to Borneo or even to Bermuda but to the alien exotica of New Orleans, as different from his Otter Falls as Arizona plateaus are from the Lower East Side of New York City.[5]

As the size and alien character of twentieth-century America presses on the genre, as a vaster and more opaque "place" stretches the panoramic possibilities of narrative view, the accelerated "pace" of contemporary life presents additional challenges to the adaptability of the picaresque genre. On the narrative "go" as they were, *Lazarillo de Tormes* and *Tom Jones* seem slow motion indeed in comparison to post-Kerouac America. Quite beyond the high performance automobiles and the interstate highways on which they run, quite beyond the systems of air and ground rapid-transit and the routes on which they zoom, and quite beyond the technics of simultaneity (telephone, television, facsimile machines, electronic mail), all of which obliterate the time required to get "from here to there," there are many more indicators not only of increased mobility but of the speed with which contemporary American life moves and its effects on cultural sensibility. Fast-food restaurants, drive-through banking, fast-forwarding on the VCR, and the like, point toward a population bent not only on racing through experience but consuming it at ever more rapid rates, regarding it as quick and expendable. The motels are chained: even room for sleep is plotted with quick movement in mind. The leisures of baseball, once the national pastime, seem to belong to an earlier, slower era, some antique, past time, as they give way to the games of continuous and quick movement. The hectic style of individual life—more, faster—shapes and is shaped by general cultural preference, itself shifting with alarming speed not only in politics but in the vernacular worlds of fashion and music.[6] While this new speed of life creates a sensation of rushing, of course, it also complicates further any steady view of the surrounding scene. The number of images multiplies, but any one of them grows indistinct during the race through them, and their proximity one to another presents swirling new combinations, strange new enjambments. From the 1950s forward, the pace of the cultural style simply intensifies in ways both absorbed and signaled by the popular culture of the country. When Chuck Berry sang "Maybellene" in 1955, it became clear that to seize one's heart's desire (a woman in this case) one would have to run faster: the poor man in his Ford cannot chase down the rich man's Cadillac.[7] The old picaro, on foot or in ox-cart, would never have a chance.

Thus, not only the size of the new setting but its rapid pace and quickly changing character pose terrific challenges to the new American picaresque narrative. The basic characteristics of the old form remain—like the commitment to "realistic" presentation, the style of empirical attention, and the episodic plotting—but by now the disorderly and ambiguous "world" of the likes of *Lazarillo* has been exaggerated many times over. The unaccustomed rapidity of the cultural pace, with its jumbling and interflow of images, poses serious obstacles to mimetic realism, to the constitution of accurate perception and rendition, to the narrative convention of full, much less perfect memory, and to any authorial confidence in "connecting" with readers by way of a recognizable world. Similarly, the old style of delivering the sensory character of scenes can be thought deeply compromised by the sheer number and opaque character of the stuff of the contemporary American scene, not to mention the dubious or expendable nature of the material order encountered. Sensate authenticity of style might well only disguise inauthentic *realia*.[8] The suddenly felt recessions of the past under the arriving onslaught of the future might well be suited at one level to the concentration of the old picaresque on the episodic "now," but at another level unabated confusions about what is "here and now" or "then and there" occur in the compacted simultaneity of contemporary experience.[9]

If any standing literary formation can begin to accommodate such a frenetically experienced world, the picaresque, again, would seem the most likely. Always moving, and always apparently moving by coincidence, rebound, fortune, and fortuity, the old Anglo-European picaresque bequeaths its evidently "plotless" but "realistic" course through ambiguous realms of experience generously to the narrative structure of the new American picaresque. James Leo Herlihy's *Midnight Cowboy*, for instance, follows its Joe Buck through a labyrinthine set of incidents of confused sexuality, macabre situations, incomprehensible masquerading, camouflaged characters, and unanticipated relationships, and so moves in a way that does not violate the canons of realism for a contemporary American audience, even with instantaneous and nearly inexplicable narrative shifts. Thomas Pynchon's *The Crying of Lot 49*, far less committed to the empirical validities of its rendition, nonetheless enters the opaque experience suffered by its picara, Oedipa Maas, in ways that resonate "realistically" with those American sensibilities forged in the cultural style of speed, blurred images, interpenetrations of a fantastic past with an enigmatic future. Or, again, Waller's *Border Music* posits Jack Carmine's centrality in its picaresque form, plotting its narrative movement often on Jack's "episodes," but its structural necessities in giving readers the picaresque rendition of experience require shifts in point of view, flashbacks to earlier life, senses of simultaneity in order to account, on the new American scene, for the course and affect of this particular *vida*. Jack himself senses that the accelerated nature of experience involves "'a kind of space-time curtain rifflin' in the wind'" (p. 139). With the sheer speed of life, the perceptions of rushing change, the blurring rapidity of images confronted, the episodic character of the picaresque genre can stand by the new narrative in continuity as its most congenial literary antecedent, but the shape and character of picaresque styles of representation, these and other texts suggest, must come in for change: they must be bent less now on the old forms of "realism" devoted to depiction of a certain objective world and more on grappling with the terms of coherence that can be achieved in an American experiential and perceptual world whose objective status is problematical.

If geographical size and cultural experience represent "road-blocks," as it were, to the renewal of the picaresque in American literary expression, the character of the "human gallery" at century's turn in the United States complicates the possible life of the form further still. *Gil Blas* and *Moll Flanders* could issue up characters in the social array predictable enough—that is, types recognized more or less quickly by the readership—in terms of social, economic, and cultural status and, thus, could confidently fulfill this criterion of the picaresque genre. In the times and places of these works, moreover, social hierarchies remained sufficiently intact, codified in the traditions, such that relatively patent presentations of social figures, charactered nearly by way of caricature, could often "stand still" in mode, means, and motive for the narrative use of them in quick satire or parody. Even when *Lazarillo* offers up the impoverished squire who yet refuses to admit hunger or the decadent priest who, the picaro suspects, dines on corpses at funerary feasts, the *galeria* is still in large part made up of cultural "familiars" in status and expectable behavior. Although doubtlessly plural, however, the social world of the old picaresque pales in comparison with the new pluralistic American setting to be encountered. Quite beyond what a couple of centuries of democratic "individualism" and ethnic, racial, and religious immigrations had done to prevent any facile understanding of hierarchy and status or any easy identification of social types, the motley of the social "voices" in America by the middle and late decades of the twentieth century had become ever increasingly polyphonic. Combining with the old pluralisms and calibrating them and each other, new and particularized life-style assertions, forms of gender consciousness, regional differences, intra-racial and -ethnic divides, single-issue politics, more recent waves of immigration, religious fractures, and so on, have also meant no real comfort to be had in finding social familiars in the midst of the intricate variables operating in social existence. Attributions of "type," much less stereotype, erode immediately upon scrutiny of the mode, the means, and the motives of individuals: no "type," in any event, would stand still long enough to become a target of satire.

The picaresque commitment to provide a broad survey of the human types in the social gallery is thus confounded from the outset in the new American setting, even if the structure of picaresque plotting—the designs of continuous, if erratic mobility—persists in pulling the narrative across the paths of numerous, different human characters. When even the various thugs in the Dutch Schultz gang in *Billy Bathgate* have to come in for sharp individualization at the level of narrative depiction, the rendition suggests that a formulaic painting of "underworld types" cannot connect with the social reality of contemporary America. Nor can a quick identification of an "urban cop type" be found in the picaresque recounting in Toole's *A Confederacy of Dunces:* Mancuso's mode and motive defy the type; he combines too much in his countenance for an easily pragmatic account to serve. No simple "man-eating woman type" in Waller's *Border Music,* Linda Lobo ("pretty wolf") comes unique, soon in narrative possession of her own forms of fear and hope. Even the "freak band" in *The Crying of Lot 49* manages to exceed stereotypical grasp. The disposition for "typing" might well remain present in the new American picaresque, as perhaps an unfailing form of social perception, but, time and again in a world of almost infinite varieties of individualisms, the characters encountered on the road supersede the categorical impulse initially used on them. At points when broadly characterizing attributes might be brought momentarily into narrative play to help give the picaro or the reader a "hold" on this or that figure, the attributes are quickly dissolved in some distinguishing act or statement. The portraits might well be thin indeed in the instances of the intersection of the picaresque with minor characters, and from time to time such "bit" sketches verge on parody, but the presentation of the *galeria* in the new American picaresque attests generally to a recognition not of type but of difference, variegation, modulation, or abolition of what might have seemed the assignable character.

The pressures of unmitigated social and cultural pluralism on the picaresque venture in American prose, then, lead to or result in some other decisive changes for the work of the genre in the new setting. First, the social landscape, now much more complex and ambiguous, forces the narrative entrance to arrive in a "world" not mapped by the certitudes of long-standing codifications and hierarchies. In response to this new social reality, so marked for the pluralism of backgrounds, choices, styles, and outlooks of its constituent members, the main work of the picaresque at this level is not—and cannot be—a matter of pushing forward the socially and culturally familiar for the picaro's tactics or tricks and the reader's inspection; it is, rather, an effort of encyclopedic inventory, a catalog appropriate to the variety, a new map of the social wilderness.[10] If the old picaresque appeared as a counter-fiction, designed to make strange the old familiar motley, the new picaresque, in many respects, arrives to assay the prospects and possibilities for coherence in a social world newly filled with "strangers." As a second matter of change, then, with the new American picaresque frequently purposing exploration and discovery of a kind of uncharted social territory, the narrative capacity and instinct even for intermittent satire recedes. Exposing elements in the social world of pretense or sham becomes far less certain business indeed when the whole of the social realm has become alien, too thickly complicated with strangers, too kaleidoscopic as the crowd swirls by, too variable and opaque even in small, individual instances. Narrative ridicule and scorn fall away, and the task becomes coherence, connection, and relation in an American social reality itself having become *terra incognita*. At the end of *The Crying of Lot 49*, the narrator is poised still, waiting along with the picara Oedipa Maas for the enormously complex American reality to open to clarity, to fall into coherence, for a way to be in it and of it. The problems of picaresque denouement and closure persist.

If the size, speed, and social complexity of the new American setting have the effect of changing some thrusts and functions of the picaresque genre, however, another set of notable changes surely occurs with respect to the picaro or picara, that character at the narrative center of focus whose life on the road defines the form, whether in its Anglo-European origins or its new American variations. The new American picaro, just *as* "American," pulls some traits of the "old" character forward much more emphatically, while other attributes—more important for Gil Blas or Moll Flanders—appear in this "new" figure somewhat more sporadically or recede virtually from view.

American Prospects and Precedents for the New Picaro

When Lazarillo and Tom Jones appeared on the literary horizon, they entered their worlds as solitary, low kinds of figures who presumed to obtrude themselves upon the attention of readers unaccustomed to democratic assumptions about the narrative "worth" of the individual human being and most especially about any non-heroic specimen of the race. Each arrived, moreover, not as emblematic of the human condition—indeed as a counter-character to the medieval "Everyman"—and each preened himself on his singular circumstance, as a kind of "Only-Man," stranded by and from the regular social order of existence.[11] On the other hand, when Joe Buck comes before the reader in *Midnight Cowboy* or Sal Paradise roars into view in *On the Road* or Oedipa Maas is awakened to move in *The Crying of Lot 49*, they appear in what are distinctively American embodiments, and they draw on democratic assumptions about the high valuations placed on the common person and on individual existence. More or less ordinary folk, they are to be regarded as significant until narratively proved otherwise, presumed worthy of attention if they can "typify" something of and for the broader society. Each is an American "Anyman" or "Anywoman," now become a picaro or picara, whose *vida* might play out importantly. Playing out as an American life in the contemporary American setting, however, each moves and weaves and dodges hazard on an altered field in the picaresque game, and the picaro / picara's defining situation, mode, outlook, and aspiration necessarily operate therefore under a different set of genre tactics.

In terms of originating situation, the new American picaro can be but does not have to be a waif, either in age or circumstance. In fulfilling the requirements of the form, the centralizing character must be or become or feel an outsider and must enter upon the tumultuous road as an innocent in some manner, like the classic picaro, but this "outsidership" in relation to the normal runs of social organization might well stem from a psychic dislocation, or an unmooring incident, or a self-conscious choice (or all three, as with Sal Paradise's impulse to go "on the road" in the Kerouac novel), as much as it might result from any literal abandonment by or ejection from the familial or social world. Indeed, it is frequently the case that the overwhelming size, the bewildering spectacle, and / or the strangeness of the social motley are the alienating causes. The picaro's exile onto the ambiguous and haphazard twistings of the road, into the life of continuous mobility and encounter, results from his or her sense of marginality, of being or being made "eccentric," however temporarily, of being pushed to the peripheries and away from the center of American social "normalcy," however perceived. Thus marginalized by background, lacking any normal human relationships in small-town Texas, Herlihy's Joe Buck leaves of his own accord, determined to get his slice of America in New York by being a male prostitute. Closer to Guzman in terms of family background than many others, Joe turns out to be driven less by simple acquisitiveness than by a "hunger" to connect, even in the midst of the ambiguous social "otherness" he enters: he chooses a picaresque route, it soon becomes clear, that holds out to him the promise of a sense of relation, of belonging, of a place to be in America. Oedipa Maas is unexpectedly made eccentric, pushed to the outer edges of American society, rendered marginal, because her earlier affair with wealth gives her a legal duty that sends her in and through wasted, outer-boundary human territories so starkly "other" as to play havoc with her (and the reader's) idea of America, to raise for her the closing question of how or even why to belong to the country in which, before her journey, she had been so comfortable.

While maintaining the characterizing mobility of the old picaro, then, this new American picaro travels not to meet the literal needs of survival in hand-to-mouth existence but, rather, to carry out a kind of "errand into the wilderness," to engage the newly alien character of American experience, to restore or locate the terms of relation when senses of community have been fractured, to render the whole sensical somehow by deciphering the chaos on his or her particular pathway. All or part of such a tacit charter is precisely what propels the overt picaresque trajectories followed by Toole's Ignatius Reilly, Doctorow's Billy Bathgate, Salinger's Holden Caulfield, Terry's A. J. Poole, Kerouac's Sal Paradise, Pynchon's Oedipa Maas, Waller's Jack Carmine, and, arguably, many more. The fabled mobility of the old picaro remains, charged with this new freedom to discover, and the episodic course stays intact as well. Of course, the needs to push into the wilderness, to exceed even the frontier settlement, to refuse the boundaries, are well-known elements of American life, legend, and lore—from Cooper's Natty Bumppo, to Melville's Ishmael, to Henry Thoreau's version of himself at Walden pond, to Mark Twain's Huck Finn—as pursued by *isolatos,* orphans, and outcasts who have discovered or willed their marginal status. This urge to trespass, to keep moving, invites the rogue, even the renegade, in other kinds of examples, but, clearly, the needs exemplified can arise from romantic vision as well as, or instead of, wilderness delinquency and can issue up innocent idealism as well as, or instead of, pragmatic cruelty.[12] Certainly with the new American picaro, the episodic life—forever starting different cycles of experience, always finding fresh beginnings, starting almost each day all over again—not only remains but conjoins with the tradition of the Adamic impulse in American letters: it is no mere matter of necessary survival as with old Guzman but, now, a matter of essential innocence and abiding hope in a new territory to be entered, a new "wilderness" to be charted.[13] The picaro's mobility, founded on such American precedent, is not at all *necessary* but, for narrative purposes, it is compelled, in the ironic way this frees the picaro to move along, to locate where and how to be in America.

On the new picaro's or picara's episodic course, the terms of movement echo the erratic mobility of the old picaresque figures, but now these dynamics of his or her narrative existence bend to different purposes. As always, the picara, despite any larger projections, finds herself buffeted through chaotic, sometimes rude, largely self-contained, always disjointed incidents, without any exact itinerary. Whether seen in Elizabeth Berg's *The Pull of the Moon* or Mona Simpson's *Anywhere but Here*, the movement seems apt for the bewilderingly complex American landscape. For the new American picara, however, the movement through these experiences—and from one episode to the next—tends to follow not a course of escape from the last place or a manipulation of events toward the next place or the promise of material gain in some other place but a career of pure fortuity, coincidental discovery, new curiosity, odd lead, or simply a restlessness animated by hope to move on. In happenstance, for picara and picaro alike, Joe Buck's cowboy costume makes him sufficiently odd to get an invitation to a party of "strangers," or Oedipa Maas is pulled forward because she spots the image of the mysterious horn, another tug at her anxious curiosity, or Texas Jack Carmine enters a new episode, meets his hunger, simply because "a sign screeched BEST CINNAMON ROLLS IN THE WORLD" (p. 71). In the midst of this careening, highly random mobility, although the episodes lack integral conduction with each other and no real "progress" is obvious, the accumulation of experiences seems what is most at stake, as one or another of them might well provide the figure the clues to find authenticity, to locate connections, to begin to solve the apparently undecipherable character of American experience. Promising a new avenue into American existence, then, each new episode, no matter how unconjoined with past experiences, has the potential for the picara or picaro upon entering it to contain the stuff to be taken up in reflection for the sake of the larger map of cultural life he or she needs.

Entering each arriving cycle of experiences in this way, the new American wayfarer continues to utilize the style of open engagement and empirical attentiveness ineluctably the practice of the picaresque forebears, and the presentation of experience through the retrospective narration steadfastly maintains the style of realistic rendition within the episodes. But now such close attunement to the palpable specificities of scene in the experiential life of the picaro is not so often a survival tactic, a prompt of frightened reflex needed for a life lived by one's wits, as it is a means of seeking connection to the place, a form of taking stock in the midst of multitudinous images and sensations, a manner of discovering what might be hidden out there. Because Joe Buck wants to locate a place to belong, he must develop as quickly and as completely as possible a rapport with each place he enters, as confusing as it might appear; he must be fully participatory at all levels with the intricacies of the life of the party. As Oedipa Maas negotiates the ways into the furtive thing America has become for her, she must be completely open to all hints and clues, like a raw nerve, even to the point of a paranoid attention to detail. If Texas Jack Carmine wants to decipher the enigmatic legacy of drift America has given him, he cannot simply taste the cinnamon rolls but must feast on every exquisite detail of an episode, even when he and Linda accidentally stray into the middle of the Thorvalds' wonderfully ordinary fortieth anniversary party in a northern Minnesota inn to relish the moment with this "short and stout" (p. 36) couple not met before or encountered again. As a function of the new map-making or encyclopedic aim of the new American picaresque, the picaro thus becomes a kind of megaphone through which various aspects of muted America shout themselves into objective existence, as the picaresque becomes a form of cataloging the infinite, confused variety of America.

To achieve this rapport with the world external to him or her, the picaro or picara, even in the contemporary American socialscape, must continue to possess and to renew that persistent equilibrium and equanimity of the classic figures in the tradition, the very trait in him or her that must accompany the new American shape of his or her innocence and hope. In the new setting, however, this remarkable attribute serves not only the purposes of moral balance in a world of confused and competing values but also the difficult, requisite work of approaching the "stranger," all of those strangers out there, without the predisposition to type and without the penchant to judge in advance. As bizarre or perverse as the various temporary partners are in the picaresque dance, Herlihy's Joe Buck has little choice—given the social *galeria* of his American "world"—but to dance, with the resilience necessary to sustain him when betrayed by this partner or that, with the hope that out of the masquerade the authentic relation might emerge. Oedipa Maas, in Pynchon's picaresque novel, likewise must maintain her balance in the encounter with an American social reality now marked for its sheer "otherness": her expectations are continuously beguiled as she attempts to discern the shape of a human community to which she might belong, one possibly composed of all of those strangers. Each of them, thus, must be approached in his or her own terms, for each is—potentially—the key piece of the puzzle. Although Texas Jack Carmine would seem on the face of the matter to fit in anywhere, to be the very paragon of equanimity in approaching an alien social scene, his hard-won equilibrium results from a sustained balancing act based on a self-recognition of his own alienation. Such a perception, of course, contributes to his failure to connect fully in the realm of social life, but at the same time this sense of himself in his own marginality creates for him a democratic equality of condition with all those others out there encountered or to be encountered, and always to be respected in their human integrity, on the picaresque way.

In terms of the persisting traits of the picaro, then, the mobility, the defining innocence and hope, the empiricist or sensory commitments, and the style of equanimity all remain, but they reappear in the new American picaresque altered to become consonant with standing American values and traditions and to be folded into the service of contemporary American cultural situations and needs. The mobility, the episodic life of ricochet, aligns with a trait of freedom from restraint in the context of American space, a chance to begin again.[14] Eluding masters, remaining unbonded, this life is an action of self-service as much as any imposed exile; it operates not for purposes of escape for a life of minimal survival but as a function of discovery or rediscovery of a way and a place to be. The catalyzing innocence, no longer merely some young naivete to be lost at the hands of rude experience, becomes something to be achieved and sustained in order to gain a new kind of access to chaotic experience. Charged with hopefulness, this purposing openness becomes a means of seeing anew, locating the resources that will cure one's affliction of marginality, participating in the Adamic impulse in an alien new world or a world newly become alien. The finely calibrated attunement to the visuals and tactiles of experience is no longer simply a necessity of a life lived by the wits but, rather, a means for taking inventory, of locating the keys to unlock the whole, of grounding a craving for a cultural metaphysics in the empirics of the immediate surround. And the celebrated equilibrium of the picaro now functions less to define the stabilities of that character in a world of familiarly ill creatures, motives, and acts than to pose a tactic of approach and relation, a means to take stock in a strange world full of those socially "other" ways of being. As the narrative life of the contemporary American picaro moves with these new outlooks, needs, purposes, and aspirations, the picaresque narratives themselves are comparably converted to new designs and ends, driving as they do through their fictional worlds with that new American "Anyperson" who is loose in the exotic cultural territories. While yet drawing on the old genre repertoire, the new American picaresque occupies different space in the realm of cultural expression.

The Cultural Place of the New American Picaresque

While the new American picaresque formations arrive on the contemporary cultural scene and adjust themselves to the new context in ways that the originating structures of the old genre demonstrably enable, they also have had—like *Lazarillo* and *Guzman* and *El Buscon*—to find or to pry open space for themselves in the spheres of creative cultural expression. At one level, to be sure, simply the range, style, and focal figure of picaresque serve the purposes of moving through and attempting to decode an incredibly large and complex world of American experience, of taking inventory, and of attaching to the impulse of hope. Such narrative formations clearly fill an expressive niche by renewing and extending a literary genre appropriate for the cultural-historical circumstances. At another level, however, this is far more than merely a matter of a culture era finding its literary vehicle: it is also crucial testimony to the fact that other forms of cultural expression have become inadequately responsive to those same circumstances. Just as Mateo Aleman and Alain-Rene Le Sage vaunted early examples of the picaresque because other literary forms of the day seemed incommensurate with the realities of existence, the appearance and aptness of these new American narratives suggest that some shapes of creative authorship have sought to fill gaps in the mimetic record left by other forms of fictional response. The high romance of the *Chanson de Roland* defaulted on the depiction of experience that came to the fore in *Gil Blas*, the "heroics" of *Sir Gawain and the*

Green Knight failed to correspond to the "realities" faced by *The Unfortunate Traveller,* the chivalry books in general missed the fundaments lived out by an audience of more ordinary folk who quickly recognized Lazarillo as decidedly nearer by, and the allegorical clarities and didacticism of *Everyman* and other morality plays simply did not obtain in the later and much more confusing world inhabited by Moll Flanders.

Thus, the old literature had in part to yield mimetic ground under competition from the picaresque formations, not only because the new narratives had found a readership but because of genre displacements,[15] and a comparable kind of battle for literary space seems to have occurred respecting the burgeoning presence of the new American picaresque. In one of the fine ironies of Western literary history, the early venture in realism by picaresque fiction, which many critics believe the prototypical narrative form that would evolve into the "realistic" modern novel of the nineteenth and twentieth centuries,[16] finds a point of revival just when the "modern" novel has apparently hit a certain limit. As the novel of descriptive verisimilitude shaded into the narrational stuff of so-called psychological realism and then, further, into the hyper-realisms of postmodern expression, the "high" literary artist increasingly refused to pretend to represent any objective external reality and submitted fully to what Erich Heller has called "the artist's journey into the interior."[17] Alienated by the vulgarities, onslaughts, and disintegrations of modern existence, authors have sent their narrators further and further into the inner worlds of subjectivity, which become both refuge and subject, and thus more and more into contrived worlds of personal and imaginary artifice, which preen the fictions on private visions and disdain connection with any "world" shared by readers. Such novelistic forms, of course, testify vividly and profoundly to the huge perceptual interspaces separating human beings and, thus, concord narratively with those senses of social and spiritual alienation diagnosed as the nature and upshot of the modern condition in Western life. Indeed, the authors of such fictions—from James Joyce, William Faulkner, and William Burroughs to Jorge Luis Borges, Umberto Eco, and Gabriel García Márquez—have constructed in brilliant labors of *tour de main* worlds redeemed in moment and import by inner life. Concomitantly, however, they have also testified in a radical way to what Andrei Codrescu, in a different context, has referred to as "the disappearance of the outside."[18] For all of the stunning virtuosity involved in devising elegant order out of inner sensibility, these fictions have largely relinquished efforts of imaginative grasp on the common life or, better, life more fully held in common. With their own good reasons, such narrative attempts have rejected the course of engagement and rendition with respect to that outer world, external to them, where subjectivity must play alongside of and stand in the service of broader, shared experience, a "world" beyond the exclusively personal. Their answer to the problems of artistic exile, to the general condition of modern alienation, has generally been to drive deeper into perceptual privacy, into a kind of security of subjectivity, and there to execute those personal explorations, to create those imaginative constructs, to achieve those private syntheses that will substitute for the brutalizing world and sustain the prospects of inward existence.[19] The lacuna left by this evolved style of fiction is precisely the one the new American picaresque apparently seeks to fill.

In answer to Marcus Klein's 1964 question about what the American literary artist will do "after alienation,"[20] the renewed and transformed picaresque both adumbrates and seeks to answer to the need for another, different kind of narrative, one that struggles back out again, out of interiority, to find, engage, and render "the outside." As intractable or missing, as impenetrable or disappointing, as inauthentic or suspicious, as some sophisticated literary and cultural outlooks might find that world external to the interpreting self, the reappearance and modification of the picaresque in recent American narratives bespeak authorial choices about coming "out" again, after alienation, to test the exterior stuff, to take inventory and to take stock, to measure remaining resources in any America still usable for the debilitated modern self. The choice is broadly one to locate a "literature of replenishment" after the truncations of the "literature of exhaustion," but the shapes of replenishment are not now to be sought in the stillness and repose of private artifice but in the mobile, experiential life through the external world.[21]

This is the very *vida*, of course, at the center of new American picaresque attention. Following the picaro's compelled career of exile *into* the surrounding world forces the reader to accompany him, and, as the new picaro ventures forward on the wayward course, the posture of openness, the practiced naivete, the style of attunement, the search for a sense of the whole, and the hope for some relation or "connection," commit the narrative itself, through the picaro's eyes, to reenter and attempt to represent a world "out there" quite independent of any private subjectivity's imaginal propositions about it. If the picaro or picara fails to elude the captivities of his or her own inwardness or succumbs to an utterly private world of his or her own pure construction—and this sometimes occurs—then the picaresque game, by definition, is lost. On the other hand, if the external world merely disappoints or even if it fails completely to yield to the picaro's craving, the narrative game simply remains unfinished: the world "out there" continues to be out there; the territories still beckon discovery or rediscovery; the map still needs making. And even if the world forces or enables one finally to settle, the essential picaro's heart can continue to beat. As Saul Bellow's Augie March concludes even as his vast career on the road has come to a close, "Why, I am a sort of Columbus of those near-at-hand and believe you can come to them in this immediate terra incognita that spreads out in every gaze. I may well be a flop at this line of endeavor. Columbus too thought he was a flop, probably, when they sent him back in chains. Which didn't prove that there was no America."[22]

Thus, while the sixteenth- and seventeenth-century picaresque proposed to detect the "real" life literarily and culturally screened by romance and allegory and to exercise interpretive suspicion about the world of chivalric pretense, the motive charge and desired effect of the new American picaresque come in for change. To meet the external world of contemporary America—a world outsized in geographical vastness and variety, in pluralistic character, in confused and confusing experience, in contested symbols and meanings, in multitudinous and accelerated images and energies—the picaresque charter alters from the old "hermeneutics of suspicion" in its interpretive designs on the world to a "hermeneutics of restoration." To that world external to the self's subjective constructions— a world alien and alienating—the new American picaresque utilizes the old formative structures of narrative mobility, episodic engagement, the social gallery, and the like, now not for the sake of a wariness that will supersede innocence but rather for the sake of developing a kind of "second naivete" that can replace the self's alienated wariness.[23] This converted objective entails viewing experience anew for the unspent possibilities it might yet contain, gauging how the picaresque inventory of American life might serve replenishing effect for those hungry for meaning and connection, and so, like the American picaro at its center, the new picaresque goes to meet the world more than halfway as its defining figure rejects any retreat into interiority and seeks to restore himself to the world and restore the world for himself. Hitting the road is more, therefore, than the opportunity to flourish in the spatial freedoms of exile; it can also be the occasion, after alienation, to find a form of new implacement, to find a way, as Oedipa Maas hopes, "to be in America."[24]

The exercise of this sought and practiced new naivete on the part of the picaro or picara consistently belongs, at least in one sense, to his or her narrative stock in trade, that sustained equanimity that allows him or her to approach each new episode in experience new and alert to what it might

contain. But in the new American picaresque such a narrational commitment has the consequence of transforming the mimetic thrusts of the narration away from the satirical exposures of the old familiar world into efforts designed to give rendition to a world perhaps latent with renewed
or new disclosures. Given the style of encounter of its American picaro and
picara, the new picaresque more or less naturally has the capacity, when
the shared world of experience permits such retrospective narrative tack,
to execute its representations of life as a project of defamiliarization with
respect to both picaro and reader. Under the control of retrospection, the
continuously innocent picaro, always approaching new cycles of experience with fresh eyes, can be or be remembered as astonished by the potency of something utterly habitual in one moment while, in another, as
bent on rendering something exotically new to him into a shape his consciousness can recognize. The part of the project of making that which is
strange into something more familiar, then to be plumbed, is a crucial drive
for the new picaresque in an America felt to have become alien territory,
but, for the sake of taking full and usable inventory, the converse operation of seeking out new disclosures in the old familiar places and people
is also a significant operation. From a reader's standpoint, as the episode
arrives in *Border Music*, nothing could seem more ordinary and predictable or, indeed, rife with parodistic possibilities, than the fortieth-anniver-
sary party of the Thorvalds, the stout upper-midwestern couple, but coming upon the scene with Texas Jack Carmine allows a depiction of the
experience that, if not profound, is not parody or satire either and that, yet,
yields more and better than the original, banal promise. Approaching the
strange and familiar through the picaro's eyes and actions, the reader is
thus invited to make fresh entrance and to defamiliarize customary views.
While all good imaginative literature arguably works at the business of
defamiliarizing its implied audience, the terms of engagement that the new
American picaresque establishes with that world "out there" recognized
and shared by readers affords it additional charge, if for no other reason
than the multiplication of episodes through which the studiously naive
picaro must necessarily move in order to pass genre muster. With this and
other prospects like the size and diversity of its social *galeria*, the new and
reformed picaresque would seem to be one of the forms of narrative expression best equipped in some senses to enter and engage that mimetic
space open "out there" on the literary-cultural horizon.[25]

    With all of these changes in the social and cultural context that modify
the narrative performance, in the American ideas and assumptions that
convert the nature and craving of the picaro, in the literary-cultural space

that alters the picaresque aim and function, the critical question reasonably arises about the extent to which the genre can remain discernible as the new narratives stand in continuity with old picaresque structures but permute them to accommodate the contemporary American circumstance. Although it is obvious, in the case of the continuity and change of the picaresque, that some of the old structures and forms have fallen away or, as Alastair Fowler states it, "have long been smoked over by time's tenebrosity,"[26] it also seems clear that the accumulated "redundancy" of the genre—the surplusage of narrative possibilities that no one picaresque text could ever exhaust—enables vast variations, especially as the genre evolves through what Fowler calls the "secondary and tertiary phases," wherein individual texts consciously or unconsciously manipulate elements found in the primary phase toward far different uses and ends and, in doing so, contribute to the evolution of the type. As history moves toward the new American context and circumstance, the *staples* in the nature of the picaresque narrative make the genre "available" to American writers because its constituting structures propose it as commensurate with the literary-cultural situation while many other narrative types (Homeric epic, heroic ballad, allegorical romance) would prove counter-intuitive except for parodistic or antithetical purposes. By the same token, it seems, the *mutabilities* in the nature of the picaresque genre make its narratives "cogent" for approaching contemporary American experience because its redundant repertoire can afford formations that shift and move and adapt to the specificities of the American case while at once endowing the genre itself with possibilities for its further evolution.[27]

As the new American picaresque venture in fiction works to propose a utile "space" for itself in the realm of contemporary literary expression and, thus, to carve out its own transformative niche in the picaresque tradition, however, the complex cultural dynamic of the picaresque's new territory has itself created or required a new sense of the situation and new forms of response in the sphere of interpretive affairs. The shifting, and sometimes perplexing, conditions and dilemmas confronting those seeking to "read" and "represent" the terrain have had yet another consequence, indeed a profoundly shaping effect, on the formations and prospects of new picaresque narratives and on the malleability of the genre. In the face of the enormous intricacies of social and cultural existence and the onrush of the reorganization of knowledge in the second half of the twentieth century, a phenomenon has appeared in the various fields of interpretation that anthropologist Clifford Geertz has noted and explored

as a situation of "blurred genres"—a situation in which numerous interpretive texts commingle, enjamb, and confuse modes of description and
forms of exposition usually considered discrete and remote from each
other.[28] One finds, he writes, "scientific discussions looking like belle lettres
morceaux (Lewis Thomas, Loren Eisley), baroque fantasies presented as
deadpan empirical observations (Borges, Barthelme), . . . documentaries
that read like true confessions (Mailer), parables posing as ethnographies
(Castenada), theoretical treatises set out as travelogues (Lévi-Strauss)," and
so on (p. 20). Such interpretive sallies, which Geertz sees as signals of a
"genre dispersion" (p. 21), are not simply arcane acts of intellect or arch
attempts to vaunt eccentric views: rather, their nimble, if complex renditions seem required somehow by social and cultural realities so daunting
that interpretation would be stymied without such genre-blurring or something comparable to reconceive the boundaries. In Geertz's view, the situation leading to this "jumbling of the varieties of discourse" reveals and
requires not "just another redrawing of the cultural map" but "an alter-
ation of the principles of mapping" (p. 20) as a necessary element in the
effort of reconfiguring social thought.

Appearing in the midst of all manner of interpretive forays into the
geographical, social, and cultural spaces of American existence and in the
midst of the enjambed discourses required by the complexities of those
spaces, the new American picaresque has been as prone to the blurring
of genres as the next literary type. The picaro or picara and his or her
narrative vehicle, in short, are not the only figures and the only means of
interpretive transport into the complicated datum contemporary American experience poses. When it occurs to once secure cartographers that
their maps might well have missed the continent, the search begins again
and intensifies. As Geertz observes, "the woods are full of eager interpreters" (p. 21). And when the interpretations more and more entail confusions and interpenetrations among the varieties of discrete discourses, as
genre boundaries often become sieves, then it should come as no surprise
that the new narratives of American picaresque, for all of their tradition-
ally identifying structures, likewise extend their mimetic reach, share the
genre redundancy, trade with and borrow from other shapes of exposition, color with the dye of other narrative types, in order to construct new
principles of mapping and to carry out the map-making required by the
new American terra incognita.

Given the standing character of the genre, its mutable possibilities,
and its pressing charge to explore a difficult contemporary America, the
new picaresque cartography has clear affinities with the interpretive tac-

tics of other forms and types. If the structural anthropologist Claude Lévi-Strauss can present his theoretical treatises in the shape of travelogue, it is quite easy, indeed, to see how the picaresque movement of Waller's *Border Music* or Larry McMurty's *Cadillac Jack* or Russell Banks's *Continental Drift* can borrow on the shapes of travelogue or tourism narratives, or to measure how the picaresque rendition of a *vida* in Bellow's *The Adventures of Augie March* or Jim Lehrer's *Kick the Can* trades in elements of narrational memory that smack of "purer" (nonfictional) examples of the *ars autobiographia*, or to determine how the picaresque encounter with the *galeria* in Herlihy's *Midnight Cowboy* or Toole's *A Confederacy of Dunces* shade off occasionally into the kinds of narrative case-study expositions and diagnoses characteristic of some new shapes of sociological analysis. Indeed, as subsequent chapters will suggest, it is not much more difficult to discern in various narratives of the new American picaresque some fundamental traits of the literature of confession and conversion, of works in the categories of spiritual journey or pilgrimage narrative, of expository forms belonging chiefly to new ethnography, humanistic geography, and cultural history, among others. Again, the American shapes and purposes of the new picaresque can draw such alliances into the service of their own altered and particularized narrative ends.

By far the most exceptional change created in the new picaresque as it enters, engages, and reaches modification in the contemporary American context, however, follows just from this situation of interpretive dilemma and blurred genres—to wit, the blurring of the boundaries between fictional and nonfictional cases to the degree that, at a number of levels, no completely certain distinctions can finally be maintained between them. It would seem natural enough and even appropriate, given Geertz's "genre dispersals," for some picaresque narratives to employ creative stripes of new ethnography, even to become a kind of inadvertent anthropology, as the picaresque searches out and engages habits of the American cultural heart. Or, to the extent that this or that picaresque formation inclines to see America as a hugely difficult "text" to be deciphered, narrative recourse to the strategies of literary criticism follows logically and consistently. Indeed, the unconjoined, zig-zagging episodes through the world the genre sponsors lend themselves fully and quickly to the tactics of the "encyclopedia," just as the episodic attunements can have the photographic effects of "documentary," especially as the new American picaresque designs to take inventory, to catalog the multiplicities of the country, even if in a more haphazard and experiential, non-alphabetic fashion. These and other prospects accompany predispositions structured into the seat and center of the narrative type. The genre "rub" occurs when John Steinbeck publishes *Travels with Charley*, or when William Trogdon (Least Heat Moon) produces *Blue Highways*, or when Eddy L. Harris zooms narratively across the interpretive landscape on his big blue motorcycle in his *South of Haunted Dreams*, and when all three, along with a great many others, beg admissions into the genre shape evolved into the new American picaresque.

Just as the new American picaresque fiction appears as such because of the distinctive and defining structures borrowed from the likes of *Lazarillo de Tormes, Gil Blas,* and *Roderick Random,* the works by Steinbeck, Least Heat Moon, and Harris, among many others, arrive on the scene in ways that are clearly participatory in the situations, structures, and aims of the new American picaresque, even to the extent that they play in those complex "genre dispersals" that send the picaresque toward cultural history, toward ethnography, toward documentary, and so on. On their narrative roads, intent at once on working their ways out of the narrator's marginality and on attempting to see America steadily and see it whole, these works operate in and through episodic narration committed to the empirics of scene, exercise the convention of perfect memory, seek to see experience fresh and new, ricochet about in disjointed progresses, attempt to sustain that American insouciant equanimity and hope, and struggle to locate a way to be and belong in the baffling new America through which they ride. That they want to rediscover America is no surprise; certainly and clearly "the woods are full of eager interpreters." That they elect a picaresque "exile" to carry out their explorations in the form of the dislocated, mobile *vida* is consistent with the new American frame. That they approach the exceedingly complex *galeria* of American pluralism is part and parcel of the venture. That they frequently configure themselves in the forms and styles of fiction, even while posing as "purer" autobiography, suggests that the "redundancy" of the picaresque genre not only includes but enables them on their blue motorcycles and on their blue highways.

3

The Picaro in Fiction, the Picaresque in Fact: Blurring Genres

When William Trogdon, later to become William Least Heat Moon, found himself expelled into the broader territories of contemporary American experience because he simply could not remain "in place," he set about on a solitary trip to reckon with an America that had become alien to him or he to it, and, later, in 1982, the re-presentation of this trek reached publication in *Blue Highways: A Journey into America.*[1] Having lost his marriage and—some academics would probably say "worse"—his teaching job at a small Missouri college, Trogdon went seeking to resolve the conundra of his own life and, as an element of that effort, to engage the larger conundrum of America in an attempt to restore to himself the land so entangled with his own self-identity. The "blue highways," of course, refer to the back-roads, the secondary roadways, designated with blue on the maps to distinguish them from the interstate freeways and other main routes criss-crossing the United States, and Trogdon chose these roads because he was convinced that the "real" America was there to be found. Naming his van "Ghost Dancing" after a Plains Indian "resurrection" ritual, he went looking for, he reports, an America wherein the continent and the culture might still support authentic life: "with a nearly desperate sense of isolation and a growing suspicion that I lived in an alien land, I took to the open road in search of places where change did not mean ruin and where time and men and deeds connected" (p. 5). The well-wrought narrative he returns to the reader of *Blue Highways*—Trogdon was an English professor, after all—is a thick autobiographical record of this "journey into America."

But *Blue Highways* works its narrative way not simply and not only as a signature formation of *ars autobiographia*. Groping for a form of literary expression commensurate with its untidy personal subject, its subject's animating alienation, its motive of recovery, its sprawling terrain to cover, and the like, the book operates in mixed and mingled discursive modes, alternating its forms even from paragraph to paragraph to rescue the topic immediately to the narrative fore. At one moment it smacks of self-analytical confessional literature, while at another it appears as documentary "realism," and at yet another as cultural criticism or new interpretive ethnography. Content for a time to move as stolid travelogue, it interrupts that progress here and there with landscape *poesis* or philosophical meditation. Occasionally becoming a form of exegesis of the mythic "text" of America, it again turns into an intermittent and jocose restaurant guidebook. Confronting the pluriform human realities of the culture, Trogdon works alternately as steady interviewer, intent new-journalism featurist, and severe caricaturist, singing *encomium* here and blasting off parody there. This autobiographical text clearly belongs in the category of "blurred genres," decidedly participating in what Clifford Geertz identifies as "genre dispersion."[2] Moreover, all the while mixing its discursive tactics and posing as nonfiction, *Blue Highways* reads like a novel and, given the central figure and the structures of its narrative presentation, like a novel belonging to the new American picaresque form of contemporary expression.

Blue Highways is certainly not the first or last American book to arrive on the scene since mid-century that mixes modes or confuses boundaries among types of narratives or blurs fiction/nonfiction distinctions, or even does all three in ways that suggest other examples of the contemporary American picaresque. Along with a great many others, John Steinbeck's famous *Travels with Charley*, published precisely two decades before Least Heat Moon's "road book," stands also as the "autobiographical" travel record of mingled discursive forms delivered by an alienated American loosed in the culture, as the subtitle says, *In Search of America*.[3] And, nearly conversely, the description of *Blue Highways* above, with only a few minor adjustments, could serve broadly in characterizing any one of numerous American picaresque fictions of the past several decades, from, say,

Bellow's *The Adventures of Augie March* in 1953 to Robert James Waller's *Border Music* in 1995, even if some of the fictions are somewhat less overtly "in search of America." This is especially the case with respect to those new American picaresque novels grounded deeply in the specific biographies of their authors, fictions with highly autobiographical casts about them, like Jack Kerouac's *On the Road* (1957), Robert Pirsig's *Zen and the Art of Motorcycle Maintenance* (1974), David Rounds's *Celebrisi's Journey* (1982), and Robert Penn Warren's *A Place to Come To* (1977).

Even on its face, the situation of such apparent literary "exchange" between fictional and nonfictional road books, between fiction and non-fiction *within* individual texts, suggests that the new American picaresque might well contain narrative formations other than the standard novel and, indeed, that the inclusion of those "nonfictions" that belong to the genre type has the effect of complicating and extending the significance of this phenomenon in contemporary American cultural expression. Closer scrutiny of such an inclusive possibility is the business of the discussion here. Attention will be given, first, to the ways that a number of road narratives proposed as strictly autobiographical journeys through America in fact correspond to the structures of the new American picaresque. To the extent that *Blue Highways, Travels with Charley,* and others present parallels, even duplications, of the structures, effects, and functions of picaresque found in E. L. Doctorow's *Billy Bathgate,* John Kennedy Toole's *A Confederacy of Dunces,* James Leo Herlihy's *Midnight Cowboy,* and others, then the genre blurs indeed. There follows from this a consideration of how the purportedly nonfictional self-presentations of Moon, of Steinbeck, and of others push their narrative "selves" forward as close kin of the new American picaro as that centrally defining character of the literary form appears in Billy Bathgate, in Ignatius Reilly, in Joe Buck, Oedipa Maas, Texas Jack Carmine, Jed Tewksberry, A. J. Poole, and others. Although lacking the same *degree* of fictional license in positing protagonists, Least Heat Moon, Steinbeck, and many another construct themselves imaginatively for narrative purposes in *kind* with the fictional picaros and picaras. Finally, the exposition will turn to an account of the complex reciprocities of fiction and nonfiction in the new American picaresque mode, as these narrative strategies converge with each other and as both converge on their broader work of self-recovery and American discovery. In this convergence, inquiry can begin to detect how the blurring of narrative types creates both the picaro in fiction and the picaresque in fact, and, thus, the prospects of such American road work to be extended well beyond the literary sphere.

The Picaresque and American Travel Writing

In an essay devoted mainly to John McPhee, David Espy makes an off-hand observation about famous and prolific American travel writer Paul Theroux that begins to account for the character of his travel, the quality of his writing, and the central status he has among contemporary travel writers: "Theroux plots a general journey . . . and proceeds in leisurely fashion, looking for the chance encounter, the noteworthy, the seedy. He reads widely on the region through which he will travel, but he has only a loose idea about what he is after. The form of his writing—chronological, episodic, and picaresque, reflects the casual style of his actual travel. He travels alone, and he is the major character in his writing."[4] Theroux, of course, is best known for his writing about his travels abroad, but the particular form of his travel narratives, as synopsized here, has attributes (loose itinerary, "episodic, picaresque" movement, solitariness) with clear affinities not only to *Augie March, On the Road*, and Theroux's own *Picture Palace*, a picaresque novel that "travels" America, but also to the structures of *Blue Highways, Travels with Charley*, and other travel books by recent Americans who have stayed nearer by, have sought to surpass their various senses of "exile," and have gone in search of America. Their more purposeful searching might seem to clash with the attribution of a "casual style" to Theroux's travels, but that statement seems somehow amiss, especially because Theroux, like Least Heat Moon and like Steinbeck, is also clearly seeking out the terms of rapport with the places he travels and doing so by openness to the "chance encounter, the noteworthy, the seedy," and so on. In any case, either Least Heat Moon's or Steinbeck's "loose idea about what he is after"—something called "America"—creates a narrative procedure of the "leisurely fashion," in the sense that both follow a more or less random and meandering course and not a frantic pursuit causing them to fail in attuning to the episodic scenes or making them fly by what might be the main chance.

Beyond these well-known works by John Steinbeck and William Least Heat Moon, a large number of other such contemporary American autobiographical journey narratives, usually consigned to the category of the "travelogue," present comparable picaresque patterns for inspection: for example, Bill Moyers's *Listening to America* (1971); Richard Reeves's *American Journey* (1982); Harrison Salisbury's *Travels around America* (1976); Eddy L. Harris's *South of Haunted Dreams* (1993); Walt Harrington's *Crossings* (1992); Laurel Lee's *Godspeed* (1988); K. T. Berger's *Where the Earth and the Sky Collide* (1993); Bill Bryson's *The Lost Continent* (1989); Andrei Codrescu's

Road Scholar (1993); Hans Habe's *The Wounded Land* (1964); Lars Eighner's *Travels with Lizbeth* (1993); David Lamb's *A Sense of Place* (1993); Natalie Goldberg's *Long Quiet Highway* (1993); W. Hampton Sides's *Stomping Grounds* (1992); and additions to this baker's dozen—"road books" by Americans autobiographically in search of America, travelers intent on discovering or recovering the land and culture—could obviously continue.[5] Their structural participation in the new American permutations of the picaresque form puts them in full company with the fictional texts— Bellow's *Augie March*, Doctorow's *Billy Bathgate*, McMurtry's *Cadillac Jack*, Terry's *The Watermelon Kid*, and so on—that decidedly belong to the form.

With respect to the broadest, defining structures of the contemporary American picaresque, each of these nonfictional travel narratives—like the autobiographical *Blue Highways*, on the one hand, and the fictional *Midnight Cowboy*, on the other—fulfills the genre criteria after its fashion. In narrational mode, figure of concentration, "world-picture," narrative movement, field of survey, obligatory social motley, style of presentation, and studiously patterned intentionality or objective, they both conform to and exploit the expressive capacities of the new American picaresque, itself continuous with the likes of *Lazarillo de Tormes*, *The Unfortunate Traveller*, and *Gil Blas*.

In the presiding terms of narration, just because they operate in autobiographical mode, all of the nonfictions present first-person retrospective narrations that concentrate the focus through a segment of *la vida* in question, a period of that life, moreover, voluntarily or involuntarily compelled to occur on the road, into territories grown alien, disarrayed, confusing, or somehow exotic, but in all events "unfamiliar." After ten years "isolated" on the East Coast, Bill Moyers informs, "I learned that it is possible to write bills and publish newspapers without knowing what the country is about or who the people are. Much changed in America in those ten years. There were thirty-five million more of us, we seemed more raucous than ever, and no one could any longer be sure who spoke for whom. . . . [And so in 1970], I boarded a bus in New York to begin a journey of thirteen thousand miles through America."[6] For Hans Habe, a naturalized citizen, after the two-month American tour in 1963 upon his return from years in Europe, the "old" America he had earlier known has "suddenly" become filled with hitherto unacknowledged and alienating tensions—class conflicts, racial divisiveness, regional battles, and competing political ideologies—submerged for him until, late in the trip, the great dislodging episode of the assassination of John F. Kennedy makes them come pointedly forward for him and

makes him reconstruct his retrospective travel narrative around this signal event.[7] Richard Reeves, for his part, follows Toqueville's course one
hundred and fifty years later because "streets in Detroit were a modern
wilderness. There was gunfire and there were riots in Philadelphia
. . . [and] an ex-President [was living] in a sort of exile"—facts that meant
"the question was still American democracy: What had it become? Did
it work? Could it peacefully translate the will of the people into life, liberty, and the pursuit of happiness for each of those people?"[8] America
having become problematical as a place and as an idea, Moyers, Habe,
Reeves, and others—feeling themselves estranged in one way or another—put themselves into the solitary journey narrative, the exile of the
road book, the picaresque venture.

In this exile, the focal figure of the narrative, as recollected, bumps
about "with only a loose idea about what he is after"—that is to say that
he or she possesses no exact itinerary—and moves in erratic or random
fashion, a mobility reflected in the episodic, disjointed movement of the
narrative from each self-contained scene to the ostensibly unconjoined
next one. Searching the country's "Empty Quarter" to answer "What is
America? or Who are the Americans?"[9] David Lamb receives a chance
invitation to dinner from a stranger, Jack Dawson, a "former professional
rodeo rider" (p. 41) and now a rancher on the family place in Montana,
an invitation that leads both to Dawson's children's asking "if they can
bring . . . [this city fellow] to school the next day for show-and-tell" (p.
47) and to Lamb's hearing and encouraging Dawson's father, George,
into "reminiscing about his eight decades on the land his father had
homesteaded" (p. 48). The narrative episode closes with a pithy rhetorical question old George poses, and the next episode opens, without the
slightest causal transition or logical conjunction, in Bethel, Alaska.[10] For
another kind of example of vague itinerary and episodic movement,
there is Moyers again. He wants, he says, to "listen" to his countrypersons, to measure their senses of the American experiment, and this
takes him across the wide land, with stops in thirteen states and dozens
of towns. Throughout, he works for the "chance encounter," follows his
nose. After talking with folks in Idaho about environmental concerns, for
one instance, he prepares to head for Seattle, but the trip moves into an
unplanned new cycle—he is pulled instead into Colfax, Whitman County, Washington—when his eye catches an announcement about a meeting of residents and students about "campus unrest" at Washington State
University. "Seattle," he quickly concludes, "will still be there Monday"
(p. 162). Rather like Waller's Texas Jack Carmine enticed into a new epi-

sode by a sign declaring the "best cinnamon rolls in the world," Moyers's path ricochets about according to what experience presents. Along with Steinbeck, Reeves, Least Heat Moon, and others, the most general itinerary might well be there for Lamb and Moyers, but following a more exacting, guiding map or schedule would preclude the episodic, experiential cycles of the road and would prevent engagement with the America they think is "out there." Deflections off course, self-contained episodes, erratic or random "progress" are the narrative means for their kind of entrance into the world.

As these travel narratives converge with the formations of the new American picaresque, the panoramic sweep the road books enter, however expansive or constricted, is highly variegated and sometimes deeply confusing, and the narrative works to promote the idea that the fortuitous itinerary that results, the microcosm of America in the specific travel, reflects and could be a "key" to unlock the principles of mapping the broader country.[11] Hampton Sides stomps through eight American "subcultures" in order to gain his sense of American "sense." Lars Eighner necessarily travels the trails of poverty and drift and writes to expose the conditions of being homeless, a situation to the American forefront. For the operations of narrative construction, Eddy Harris's *South of Haunted Dreams*, for instance, tracks about—actually motorcycles about—the regions of the southeastern United States, with Harris's following the loose intention, from Owensboro, Kentucky, down, around, and back again, of taking "A Ride," as his subtitle suggests, "through Slavery's Old Back Yard."[12] "I have no idea where the road will go," he observes at the beginning of the journey (p. 25), but as an African American he knows that this haunting, confused topography has everything to do with who he is in America: "I did not go to Africa to find my roots. My roots are here" (p. 30). Comparably seeking the America of rooted personal identity, an America apparently utterly altered from the experience of forebears, Harrison Salisbury conducts a journey that crosses the terrain of the familial ancestors who made the country once great. Feeling exiled from that past, he begins his *Travels around America* with only a vague itinerary: "I have no blueprint, just some jottings on old envelopes, some penciled lines of highway maps . . . some old letters, some new talk, fresh as paint."[13] His episodic course begins and ends with the assertion "that America is bigger than any plan, too vast for a map" (p. 3), but his effort of discovery, to go "looking at *my* continent, *my* America" has him "traveling forgotten trails, sticking my head into nooks and crannies, old attics and new condominiums, talking to the old and the young, looking for my country," and, he adds, "trying to find something of myself as well" (p. 2). Harris, Eighner, Salisbury, Reeves, Lamb, Steinbeck, and others, all travel their particular, specific territories with the hope that those "roads" will yield for them, for each in his own way, an answer to Salisbury's question, "Where is the real America?" (p. 9) and Oedipa Maas's question in the closing pages of *The Crying of Lot 49* about the reality of an American legacy. Each and all have to cope with the complicated panorama of the land that, as Salisbury notes, is too vast, too full of mutability, too elusive: "the images twist and turn, dissolve and resolve again in changing form. There are a thousand thousand strands in the American tapestry. The warp and woof is beyond the art of a weaver like myself" (p. 3).

As a crucial element of the engagement, aligned with the work of the new picaresque encounter with America, there is the narrative business of traversing across and into the pluriform social reality that those by the side of the road present. In the part of the world wandered, each of the narrative journeys must approach, engage, and render the diversified human world, the realities of American pluralism, the virtually infinite myriad of "types," and this requires that they tune carefully to the human element in their attempts to take stock in, of, America. From Habe and Eighner, to Moyers, Reeves, Harris and others, the produced works literally fill the narrative "worlds" with the ordinary, the odd, the generous, the nasty, the reflective, and the stupid, bankers, ranchers, baseball managers, laborers, ecological warriors, political hacks, waitresses, waitresses, waitresses, writers, policemen, service-station attendants, barkeeps, among "the thousand thousand strands" of the racial, religious, ethnic, gendered, generational, classed, partisaned, human beings "in the American tapestry." Of a size and complication that makes Toole's "confederacy" or Herlihy's urban hordes look like limited fare, the American human world is there for the engaging by these "travel narratives." And indeed, hundreds of figures come into represented view, as Least Heat Moon attempts to offer up the record not only of *homo viator* but also of *homo spectans*, as Eighner depicts them, as Reeves and Salisbury encounter them. Numerous others speak themselves into the reader's attention, as Moyers and Lamb "listen" to Americans and as Andrei Codrescu interviews them, recreates them, and provides time for them on stage. Some pass quickly by, fade into the crowd or in the rear-view mirror, in the quickest survey of a scene. Others remain "on page" for a time in order to be able to claim their distinctiveness. For these, Salisbury, Eighner, and others must attempt to calibrate the encounter, engage with care, notice the nuance, in order to carry out that exploration of America, and themselves, that concentrates a thrust of the narratives on the enormous *galeria*. For one instance only, as David Lamb "delivers" Mike Wisdom of tiny Wray, Colorado, momentarily out of anonymity, the reader sees and hears the son of a lumberyard owner, a former wrestler, a volunteer fireman, who lives on his savings and quietly returns his salary to that community recreation center he and others have built to help Wray in its decline. Lamb writes, "I told him I thought that [his] attitude had probably helped snatch Wray from the death rolls of the Great Plains but doubted it was applicable to the problems of urban America." The episode closes abruptly, with the fuller sense of the man disclosed in Wisdom's reply: "Why not?" The collection of such examples from Lamb's book and the other "travelogues" would constitute—in its inventory of the good, the bad, and the ugly Americans of all shapes and sizes—a full-scale social encyclopedia.[14]

The finely tuned ear, the roving and receptive eye, and the narrative presentation alert to the human nuance, all suggest the orientation of the renditions to the world external to the narrating self. Subjective they are, to be sure, but, as with the concerted work generally of the new American picaresque, theirs is a subjectivity that finds itself engaged with "the outside" instead of one that regards external life only as a function of interiority. And this attention to the telling, the distinctive, human trait or gesture or motion, the accuracy respecting detail required by such efforts at new social map-making, has its corollary in a honed narrative style of broad mimetic attentiveness in these picaresque structures of American travel literature. Each forces subjectivity into the fronting of the immediate surround in each episode through which the protagonist passes, and this narrative commitment to empirical "realism," poised to seize the "chance encounter" and prepared to take full inventory, means approaching the "noteworthy" and the "seedy"—but, at all events, what is "out there"—with equal and ready eye, regarding the world as potentially full of disclosures, to be restored to the self and the self to it, the experiential realm as the place of connection, after alienation. This increases the burden for more or less exacting representation in the sense that, with a few words or many, the narrative seeks to convey both a recognizable scene and the perceptual sense of the scene, never sacrificing the former for the latter.[15] Two quick examples stand for this style of mimetic attention. As Richard Reeves enters the village of Haverford, Pennsylvania, he remembers that "less than a mile from the railroad station, I turned into the stone gateway of the college and walked down a long road through a perfect landscape of small hills. There was a duck pond just on the other side of the split-rail fence along the roadway, and a child's bicycle leaned against the fence near the pond. . . . As I got closer, I saw that the bike was chained and locked to the fence" (p. 253). As Bill Bryson makes a stopover in a small town he tags "Dullard," Illinois—renamed, he says, to protect the innocent—he recollects:

> I went into a dark place called Vern's Tap and took a seat at the bar. I was the only customer, apart from an old man in the corner with only one leg. The barmaid was friendly. She wore butterfly glasses and a bee-hive hairdo. You could see in an instant that she had been the local good-time girl since about 1931. She had "Ready for Sex" written all over her face. . . . Somehow she had managed to pour her capacious backside into some tight red toreador pants [and] . . . looked as if she had dressed in her granddaughter's clothes by mistake. . . . I could see why the guy with one leg had chosen to sit in the farthest corner.[16]

Although neither scene looms large in its respective narrative, they both fold their selective alertness to small details into the formal and intentional commitments of "authentic" depiction: not just a pond but a "duck pond," a "split-rail" fence; not simply tight pants but "tight red toreador pants." In the course of the various inventories of America undertaken by Bryson, Reeves, Harris, Salisbury, and others, the picaresque "convention of perfect memory" must use its retrospection to take note of even the smallest, present potentialities, and the style of rendition—representation conditioned by empirical detail—is a means to recover, to restore, the American world outside the self to overcome the self's exile.[17]

The objective of the new American picaresque is, after all, the new Columbian expedition, the rediscovery of America, and these and numerous other American narratives of travel, fictional and nonfictional, participate in that search and research. Subtitles of some of these road books indicate this general picaresque initiative: Reeves, *Traveling with Tocqueville in Search of Democracy in America;* Moyers, *A Traveler Rediscovers His Country;* Bryson, *Travels in Small-Town America;* Lamb, *Listening to Americans;* Sides, *A Pilgrim's Progress through Eight American Subcultures;* Habe, *Journey through a Divided America;* Goldberg, *Waking Up in America;* Berger, *America through the Eyes of Its Drivers;* Codrescu, *Coast to Coast Late in the Century.* To these "nonfictional" entries into the new American picaresque, numerous others can be added whose titles or subtitles begin to suggest their membership in the genre form. For example, Phillip L. Berman's *The Search for Meaning: Americans Talk about What They Believe and Why* (1990); Pete Davies's *Storm Country: A Journey through the Heart of America* (1992); Frances FitzGerald, *Cities on a Hill: A Journey through Contemporary American Cultures* (1986); B. C. Hall's and C. T. Wood's *Big Muddy: Down the Mississippi through America's Heartland* (1992); Walt Harrington's *Crossings: A White Man's Journey into Black America* (1992); Jim Lilliefors's *Highway 50: Ain't that America* (1993); David Lamb's *Stolen Season: A Journey through America and Baseball's Minor Leagues* (1991); Joseph J. Thorndike's *The Coast: A Journey down the Atlantic Shore* (1993); Jonathan Yardley's *States of Mind: A Personal Journey through the Mid-Atlantic* (1993); Mark Winegardner's *Elvis Presley Boulevard: From Sea to Shining Sea, Almost* (1987); Bo Whaley's *Rednecks and Other Bonafide Americans* (1986); Mort Rosenblum's *Back Home: A Foreign Correspondent Rediscovers America* (1989); Stephen K. Roberts's *Computing across America* (1988); Peter Jenkins's *A Walk across America* (1979); Thomas Rawls's *Small Places: In Search of a Vanishing America* (1990); and Geoffrey O'Gara's *A Long Road Home: Journeys through America's Present in Search of America's Past* (1989). If the picaresque poses itself as an "epic of hunger," the yearning adumbrated in such titles suggests at least the nature of the kind of appetite that belongs to the new formations of the form in contemporary America.

Although no single one of these "nonfictional" travel narratives could be claimed perfectly to duplicate all of the "key" or defining structures of the picaresque genre,[18] their autobiographical modes, solitary and exiled figures of concentration, chaotic or confusing "worlds," episodic movements, panoramic surveys, social motley, realistic styles, and objectives of discovery and inventory all propose them as narratives of picaresque character.[19] To the extent that each such road book follows the genre's narrative pattern, moreover, then that travel autobiography, like one of Theroux's works, has its own narrator as the "major character" and thus invites further examination to determine how completely or convincingly its focal figure corresponds to the nature and actions of the picaro.

The New Autobiographical American Picaro

Habe, Moyers, Salisbury, Reeves, Least Heat Moon, and Steinbeck, among others, acknowledge in their works that the temporary versions of themselves that they find out on the road were ejected into those wandering careers because, from whatever particular causes, they had sensed themselves, in effect, exiled or alienated, as described above, in an America that had become a question for them. As remembered, the narrative "selves" that appear on the pages are literally and literarily propelled forward to engage some broad segment of American society and culture "out there," to encounter its variety, to surrender to the episodic experiences of the place, in order to take stock of it and of themselves in it—in short, to enter America in picaresque terms, to encounter it in its immediacies, and, at last, in retrospection, to render it realistically. With this agenda, whose overall objective is American interpretive inventory (Salisbury's effort to take hold of "*my* continent, *my* America"), a certain kind of autobiographically composed "self" on the road is required for these travel narratives to meet the criteria that make them entries into the new American picaresque. And, again, upon investigation, Moyers, Lamb, Reeves, Bryson, and others deliver their "major characters," themselves represented on the road, in ways that surely associate them not only with some smaller traits of the picaro (as trickster, role-player, upstart) but with that Adamic hope and innocence, that resilience and continuous self-renewal, that equilibrium and equanimity, necessary for them to walk the walk with fresh eyes and open hearts.

That many of these American travel writers in felt exile nonetheless take to the thoroughfares is itself one kind of signal, of course, that, despite senses of alienation, they both retain hope and exude a distinctively American kind of hopefulness about the possibilities of the world to be located in spatial movement. The road—or at least what it might lead to—looms up for the American Adamic cast of mind as an opportunity to start over, to begin again, innocently to refuse the captivity of the deeper or more recent past, and to explore the world anew. Admittedly embittered by the racial history of the country and the way it has pressed, alienated, in personal terms, Eddy Harris still climbs aboard his blue motorcycle to "try" the American South empirically, to seek out the terms of some rapprochement, however tenuous, that can connect his life to his country. Salisbury fears the loss of an old America of sturdy pioneer virtues, Reeves worries about truncations in American democracy, Moyers is anxious about the loss of any centering chorus to the disparate cacophony of voices, Lamb has read that the American way of life is in chaos and decline, and so on, and all feel, at least at journey's beginning, somehow "alien" in their own strange and bewildering land. But each, like Harris, goes on his meandering course for purposes of that discovery, survey, stock-taking that might locate the redemptive possibility of connecting or reconnecting with America: "I seek a confrontation with the South and with the past"; he remembers himself on the road, "face to face—a baptism of the spirit, a reconciliation, and, in the end, a salvation. I seek a new way of seeing" (p. 91). Over and over in the books of travel that belong to the new American picaresque, that "major character," the autobiographically composed self, arrives both sensing exile and feeling hope.

An element of this hopefulness from one such character to the next reveals itself in the willingness to adopt and enact an operative innocence in approaching the experiences at the side of the road—not a form of callow naivete but an Adamic regard that commits the traveler at least to attempt to see things as he or she had not been wont to see them before, to practice a kind of unselfguarded responsiveness, to be open to the strange in the familiar and the familiar in the strange. For instance, as prepared as Eddy Harris is by racial conditioning and experience to despise the South he enters on his journey, he nevertheless seeks his "new way of seeing," and, with this, only one state deep into his southern course, in the woods around Lake Cumberland, Kentucky, he begins to "feel the place in my bones," the place that had created African-American warmth and passion and soul, "where my people lived and died": "the color red flashes, streaks across the corner of my vision, vanishes, and flashes again. A cardinal dashes from branch to branch. . . . And suddenly that which yesterday was unthinkable takes shape in the trees I conceive the inconceivable and this time give voice to it. Could I like this place?" (p. 94).

For another kind of example of these "opened eyes," this "innocent" responsiveness, Lars Eighner, perhaps the most down and out of the contemporary autobiographical wanderers, comes upon a scene that his own homeless condition might well have made him resent. Thrown in for a time with a fellow named Dallas, a cigarette thief who robs quick-markets along the road, Eighner begins to realize his own unwitting work as accomplice. Despite his own poverty and his temporary criminal partner, within three brief paragraphs, Eighner, at the peak of a southern California rise, peers out on a valley of vast wealth and records: "in every direction were the shimmering lights of the thickly populated valley below us: rose sodium lights, blue mercury vapor, neon and yellow incandescent; all before us glittering in the darkness. Tears rolled down my cheeks. It was beautiful and, so I hoped, somewhere down there Lizbeth [his dog] and I might get off the road."[20] Then, for a final example of this attempt to see anew, to approach with innocent eye, to dig the potent out of the mundane and the coherent out of the bewildering, Richard Reeves remembers attempting the stance quite self-consciously:

> I didn't know exactly what it was I wanted to hear, or to see, but I had come to Newport to begin traveling the United States, to try to see, perhaps to understand, America and Americans in my time. I think I was trying to be a stranger, a foreigner, someone in a strange place. But it was hardly foreign to me. It seemed quite ordinary, a quiet American street. . . . [But, simply by tuning in local radio,] I was instantaneously, miraculously, swept into, engulfed in storms of facts, of ideas, of information, of opinions, of urgings, of preachments. I was on the unpeopled streets of a corner of America, in this torrent, amazed and confused. (p. 20)

Harris, Eighner, Reeves, and the other autobiographically represented "selves," are prepared like their fictional counterparts—Joe Buck, Billy Bathgate, Ignatius Reilly, among others—to venture forth with such fresh forms of vision, to receive the episodic scenes with unaccustomed eyesight. Like their fellow American picaros and picaras in the novels, some will succeed better than others at this real or practiced naivete, and most will be disappointed, even abused, in one cycle of experience or another, but then this is the nature of the opaque and difficult world through which the "exiled" figure passes, making his or her "innocent" way.

Of course, to the degree that these traveling "selves" fulfill the requirements of the picaresque life, then they likewise possess that measure of quick resilience, that capacity to begin again and anew, from one episode to the next, all the while sustaining their animating hopefulness even after some particular experience bullies them about. Harris will several times encounter in the white South those persons who, without knowing him, despise him, but he will also find Andrew, the belly-laughing, white, gas-station attendant in Raleigh, North Carolina, who cares to hear the story, who permits Harris to rant about racism, and who instructs him that he is "'missing so much more'" (p. 121). And, picking himself up, Harris moves on. Or, for a different instance, after being chased from a park by the police, Eighner, though briefly nonplussed, simply moves to another spot, locates another "residence," begins again. Or, again, this capacity to start over, *volver nuevo*, appears when the young, hirsute Peter Jenkins, in his *Walk across America,* is chased from the roadside by "rednecks" and, fearing for his life, sleeps hidden uncomfortably in the brush, without even campsite in the woods. This fills him with trepidation, but it does not preclude his beginning again and—familiar to strange—later receiving an unlikely apology for the incident. Such examples of the picaro's resilience, adaptability, and renewal multiply in the presentations of Bryson, Lamb, Moyers, and others, and, again, they signal the kinship between these autobiographical travelers and their fictional cohorts.

Throughout, then, as a necessary element of the picaro's narrative existence, one finds in the self-remembering narrations of Salisbury, Least Heat Moon, and others, that quality of equilibrium and that defining trait of equanimity lived out on the pages. These "major characters," protagonists of their own stories, possess or seek to enact that balancing stability or consistency of response, an accoutrement of their open approaches to things, which prevents or defers judgments about what is high and what is low, what ennobling and what tacky, in a kind of calm reserve. In the experiential inventories they seek to take as each auditions for the part of a main player on the picaresque stage, the usual and the bizarre, the sublime and the vulgar, must at least en route receive a brand of equal attention and weight, or an unexpected reversal of trivial and significant, in a sustained perceptual democratization of experience. And so the reader discovers the "exposition" concerning the salesman who picks up Eighner and Lizbeth as they are hitchhiking to Austin, Texas: "The driver asked if I could drive. I replied that I could, but was not licensed. After a pause he said for me to get in. He was fiftyish, deathly pale, grown fat with age, and he was wearing only boxer shorts. I wondered at this at first, especially as the opened fly of the shorts exposed his sex whenever he shifted in his seat, but eventually I concluded that the driver's attire reflected only his practical nature. It was a very hot day" (p. 94). Without the slightest query about the man's behavior, without any judgment beyond the brief "wondering," and indeed without the least further evaluative commentary on the salesman, Eighner draws the episode to a close three short paragraphs later.

Different forms of this disposition to withhold judgment appear in Harris's account of his "self" on the road, until he is rebuffed or insulted, and in Bryson's narrative recollections of himself, as he scoffs at, scorns, or ridicules virtually everything (but everything equally), in Moyers's text, as he usually prefers simply to "listen," and in others. One further illustration, at this point, should suffice. Although the picaresque protagonists only rarely have any patience with most "tourists"—those ersatz travelers who follow guidebooks, seek prepackaged experiences, follow schedules, bring home along with them, hate the unanticipated event, and withal, thus, often present themselves for parody—David Lamb can exercise reserve even so. As he gazes at the landscape around

Three Forks, Montana, and contemplates the fact that Lewis and Clark had taken four months to cross the Montana territory, during which time "the Corps of Discovery would encounter not a single human, red or white," his own fine solitude is abruptly interrupted:

> "Angela, where's my camera?" The voice startled me. It came from a shirtless man with Wisconsin tags on his car. He had three children in tow, and he barked orders like a drill sergeant. "Get over there with Grandma so I can take a picture. Hurry up, Angela. It's bitchin' hot, ain't it? *Bitchin'* hot!" The child obeyed, squinting in the August sunlight. In the background, where Lewis and Clark had spread their soaked cargo on a grassy bank to dry, complained about the mosquitoes and hunted elk, three rivers—the Jefferson, Madison, and Gallatin—quietly joined to form the Missouri and begin a 2,466-mile journey to St. Louis. (p. 21)

Like the trouserless salesman Eighner encounters, "Shirtless" from Wisconsin, so ripe for satirical or parodistic picking, is never mentioned again after this paragraph. Of course, not all of the various picaros—nonfiction or fiction—encounter people in various states of undress. Respecting them and other people engaged or sights seen, however, Moyers, Salisbury, Reeves, and others meet them and narrationally treat them with a form of "indifference"—not in the sense that the picaros are inattentive or that they fail in regard, only rather in the sense that they most frequently refuse to make partisan discriminations or to cast judgments.[21] With the picaro's task of taking full stock, the business at hand is not evaluation but the business "at hand," seeing, listening, gathering the experiential inventory.

In these and other ways, then, the figures on the road in many contemporary "nonfictional" travel narratives live and move and have their narrative being as picaros or picaras just as much as the fictional Joe Buck or Oedipa Maas, Ignatius J. Reilly or Billy Bathgate, Jack Crabb or Jed Tewksberry belong in the new American picaresque. Lamb, Least Heat Moon, Eighner, and Reeves all convert their "exile" to the work of the road, and there they channel the hunger for connection to the panoramic movement, the episodic encounter, the need to keep starting over, the innocent approach, the work of new map-making, the job of restoration, fully as much as the major characters of picaresque fiction.[22] And, just as the contemporary American fictions borrow from nonfictional narrative forms—autobiography, journalism, social analysis, documentary, ethnography, and so on—there are good reasons to think that the nonfictional entries in the new American picaresque enter into significant exchanges with the forms and techniques of fiction. William Least Heat

Moon, after all, began as English professor William Trogdon, no more unaware of the strategies of fiction in his careful composition of *Blue Highways* than Jim Lehrer is unconscious of television journalism's scene-setting, sequencing, and "sound-biting" in constructing the "episodes" of his picaresque novel *Kick the Can.*

The Work of Fiction in the Autobiographical Literature of Fact

Travel literature is often thought of as a form of "the literature of fact" for the very reason that it proposes to deliver to readers objective, real-istic, and thus, "authentic" renditions of real places and people, natural landscapes and human culturescapes, customs and behaviors. But the "nonfictional" travel narratives that belong in the category of the new American picaresque not only align with the basic structures of a genre that had its origins in fiction and not only present those "major charac-ters" parallel in situation, attitude, mode, and style to the fictional *vidas* of Lazarillo, Guzman, Gil Blas, Joe Buck, Texas Jack Carmine, and Oedipa Maas; they also trade in the shapes of fiction, of narrative art, in other significant ways. In some cases this is not surprising in the least. Paul Theroux is both travel writer *and* novelist, and, as both, his work inter-mittently pushes or "blurs" into anthropology, history, sociology, and so on, as well as calling on the arts of fiction in his travel narratives and the arts of travel literature in his novels. Examination of Bryson's *The Lost Continent,* Harris's *South of Haunted Dreams,* Habe's *The Wounded Land,* and other comparable examples of the "authentic" travel book makes pointedly clear that in cases of the new American picaresque heavy lines between the "real" and the "created," the "genuine" and the imagined, the autobiography and the novel, fact and fiction, cannot be confidently drawn. Quite beyond the constructions of dialogue, dramatizations of episodes, characterizations of people, penchants for metaphor-making, rhetorics of effect, editings for unity and coherence, all of which natu-rally are conscripted into the service of numerous kinds of narratives, fiction and nonfiction alike, the American picaresque nonfictional "lit-erature of fact" is, in fact, slicked up with the work of subjective imagi-nation and licensed, almost ineluctable creativity.

The complications occur, the boundaries blur, because both the fictional and nonfictional examples arrive through the shapes of the first-person point of view, the "autobiographical" narration—Least Heat Moon as his own picaresque player, Bill Moyers in his own travels, Jack Crabb and Sal Paradise as their own picaros, all of their lives "on the road" told retrospectively by themselves[23]—and it is in that tricky work of representing one's self in the midst of one's experiences, the very essence of autobiographical expression, that fact and fancy often become deeply entangled, the objective world and the interpretive response become "con-fused," and the "real" and the "imagined" become, willy-nilly, simply functions of one another. Brief considerations of a few facets of these autobiographical accounts—the retrospective composition of the self as picaro, the artful principles of narrational memory, subjectivity, and selection, and the imaginative narrative bent, and bending, toward broader American literary purposes, as these converge and intersect—reveal a more or less full collusion of fiction and nonfiction, fiction *in* the nonfictions, in the new American picaresque. This coalition obliterates most distinctions between the "actual" and the "imagined" at the level of the literary character of the form. And the work of fiction in the autobiographical travel "literature of 'fact'" begins, in turn, to suggest how all of the narratives in the new American picaresque might have more than exclusively literary significance in the road work they propose to readers.

First, simply, there is the matter of the fictional quality of the "traveler" appearing on the pages. Resulting from the retrospective, autobiographical reconstruction of the picaresque self, the picaro or picara, this figure who, because living only in narrative, is as much a concoction of authorship in Bryson's *The Lost Continent* or Moyers's *Listening to America* as Vaughn Rhomer is in Waller's *Border Music* or Don Wanderhope is in Peter DeVries's *The Blood of the Lamb*. Even if Bryson and Moyers, as they move along the road, must remain Bryson and Moyers—and so cannot match the wonderful picaros' names like "Rhomer" and "Wanderhope" and "March" and "Cadillac Jack"—the "Bryson," the "Moyers," the "Salisbury," the "Reeves," posited by their respective authors as the "major characters," are not Bryson, Moyers, and so on, but *versions* of themselves, limited to those periods of *las vidas picarescas* spent tramping America, constructed by retrospective narrations and created studiously for narrative purposes. As "remembered," these exiled literary personae do not have to be the "real" Bryson or Moyers but only have to be compelling in their claims on the reader's attention; their alienations must appear genuine and serious, their missions must strike the reader as sufficiently notable and promising, and this means that early strategies of autobiographical "self-invention" need to be employed. The narrator Bryson, for instance, begins to establish the character of the picaro "Bryson" in his very first paragraph: "I come from Des Moines. Somebody had to. When you come from Des Moines you either accept the fact without question and settle down with a local girl named Bobbi and get a job at the Firestone factory and live there forever and ever, or you spend your adolescence moaning at length about what a dump it is and how you can't wait to get out, and then you settle down with a local girl named Bobbi and get a job at the Firestone factory and live there forever and ever" (p. 3). The life weariness in that opening from the so-called litera-ture of fact scarcely seems different from a comparable kind of despair in the first paragraph of Walker Percy's novel *The Moviegoer,* as the nar-rator, Binx Bolling, presents in the present tense the picaro he is or is about to become: "This morning I got a note from my aunt asking me to come for lunch. I know what this means. Since I go there every Sunday for din-ner and today is Wednesday, it can mean only one thing: she wants to have one of her serious talks. It will be extremely grave, either a piece of bad news about her stepdaughter Kate or else a serious talk about me, about the future and what I ought to do."[24] The question is whether it makes any significant difference that the *actual* Bryson is world weary when the literary picaro, then narrator "Bryson," clearly is. While only the most unsophisticated reader would equate Binx Bolling—narrator, picaro, or both—with Walker Percy, many apparently would assume a complete identification of "Bryson" the picaro, Bryson the narrator, and Bryson the author. But, as true of autobiography as of fiction, Bryson the "major character" is in most respects as "made up" by the author Bryson as Binx Bolling the major character is made up by the author Percy. And the point is that, however "autobiographically" committed *The Lost Con-tinent* is, however much its author might want to deal in the "facts" of the traveling self and his experience, the picaro that emerges is only a product of a narrator, and that narrator, no matter how closely allied with the author, is nothing other than a result of authorial decisions about the best temporary and "created" *version* of himself or herself to assume for the sake of promoting the narrative construction at hand.[25]

Moreover, in order to execute the necessary narrative expeditions into America, the picaro clearly must be represented in a certain way—as open, resilient, innocent in approach, attentive to the world, full of equanimity, and so on—and even the authors of the "nonfictions" must create themselves "on the road" accordingly if readers are to follow the characters' traces through the experiences of contemporary America. In short, the autobiographical "presumption" of picaresque—some figure's obtruding himself or herself into a reader's presence and at-tention—must be warranted by the reader's interest in the possible gains to be had by continuing to witness the picaro's career. Just as

Lazarillo de Tormes promised its audience glimpses of the actualities of life hidden from view in the literature of the age and Lazarillo, the picaro, therefore had to arrive on the pages in a way to enable those views, *Travels with Charley* swears "to try to rediscover this monster land" and, thus, the Steinbeck "on page," the figure as a contemporary American picaro, has to be construed so as to make good on the determination. To prove equal to and appropriate for the set task, the reconstructed "self," the picaro, stops being John Steinbeck, famous author, and self-consciously becomes a fiction. As the retrospective narrator tells the reader in the opening pages, he arranged himself to become, as picaro, a kind of "Anyperson," the anonymous, ordinary man, with whom the people encountered might more freely and easily converse, all the more with his tactic of appearing "lost" in whatever local spot and, the coup de grace, with the dog in tow as ice-breaker (p. 9). He vows to be open, ready, and attentive along the way, he says, to be poised for the main chance, and, in good picaresque fashion, to act on the wisdom that "we do not take a trip; a trip takes us" (p. 4). For another example of the creative work involved in constructing a character adequate to the picaresque course, Peter Jenkins, likewise stranded in his remembered perception that "there seemed to be no hope for the United States of America, once the greatest country in the world and my homeland,"[26] concludes that he must see for himself: "I made a decision about what we would do. Cooper [his dog] and I were going to walk across the U.S.A. That's right! We were going to give this country one last chance" (p. 24). And, with this choice for the solitary walk, he remembers, he prepared as well to fulfill crucial traits of the picaro. As he prepares for open encounter, endurance, and resilience, on the walk, he recalls as narrator, "I promised myself we would follow two laws. One is a Sioux law: 'With all beings and all things we shall be as relatives.' The second law was one I made up during training . . . [that said] 'Every morning we will leave our campsite as a deer would, with only a few hundred bent blades of grass to show we have been there'" (pp. 33–34). Others like Reeves, Lamb, and so on, remember taking to the road with a comparable resolve—to let the trip "take them," to engage and relate, to see firsthand and anew, to become, in short, the picaro, to act out in America the life of that literary nomad. As Jenkins, in recollection, puts it, "my main purpose was to be where[ever] I was. Most important, I wanted to find the real people out there, what they were made of, experience who they were, how they lived, and how they worked for a living" (p. 34), and this form of resolve requires Jenkins and all to "compose" themselves narratively as picaros, to work themselves up for that narrative living.

Such exacting narrators' recollections of their road-selves created to travel the narrative highways point toward another element of fiction in the autobiographical travel "literature of fact"—namely, the exercise of the convention of "perfect memory." As a convention, of course, it is pure artifice—simply a working agreement between author and reader that, for the course of the "telling," the narrator remembers fully, accurately, and precisely—and, as artifice, it can obviously be as artfully handled in an autobiographical work as in any fictional one. If the adage holds that the biggest liars in the world are solitary fisherpersons and solitary travelers, at least as they recount their own splendid "adventures," it is not necessarily that they seek to deceive or to create tales whole-cloth, so much as it is that, in narrating, memory omits, selects, and shapes, pours through the stuff of subjectivity, works to achieve effect, mistakes the past, supplies that "additional" detail to smooth the ragged edge for purposes of narrative credence.[27] In the case of autobiographical travel literature, the narrational memory, self-evidently, is not exhaustively but selectively employed and shaped. Lars Eighner straightforwardly admits that his is a designed reconstruction of his "road" experiences and not a complete record of them:

> I do not think I could write a narrative that would quite capture the unrelenting ennui of homelessness, but if I were to write it, no one could bear to read it. I spare myself as much as the reader in not attempting to recall so many empty hours. Every life has trivial occurrences, pointless episodes, and unresolved mysteries, but a homeless life has these and virtually nothing else. I have found it best in some parts to abandon a strictly chronological account and to treat in essay form experiences that relate to a single subject although they occurred in disparate times and places. (p. xi)

For his part, David Lamb discloses that his "travels" occurred at different points over a number of years, even as the narrative representation of the travel has the kind of seamlessness that, without the author's admission otherwise, certainly suggests that the account remembers one continuous picaresque journey. Eighner and Lamb are decidedly in the business of shaping and reshaping their travels as picaros, of reorganizing and of representing those experiences, not as they *exactly* happened

but as fully *indicative* of what happened, not as "lies" but under the aegis of autobiographical purposefulness, as "fiction" and "nonfiction"
converge in the narrational memory.

Other autobiographical travel narrators of the new American picaresque are less candid: they draw on and deploy the writing convention
of perfect memory without caveat. But it is nevertheless the case that even
their narrative presentations, "from memory," work fully on principles
of selectivity, and the selections have everything to do with the authorial
imagination. How does Lamb—months and perhaps years later—remember from Three Forks, Montana, the name of the child with "Shirtless,"
whose car has "Wisconsin" tags, much less how the child "squinted" in
the sunlight? As improbably remembered as the description is in that case,
the scene would seem to belong to fictionalization by an imagination intent on seeing the discrepancy between the enduring patience of Lewis
and Clark and the irritable haste of "Shirtless" against the backdrop of the
same natural vista. How does Bryson, as retrospective narrator, remember, out of all of the images that flew before his picaro's eyes, that the
barmaid in "Dullard" had butterfly glasses and a beehive hairdo? As it
turns out, *numerous* middle-aged women he encounters in his journey
through small-town America appear on the pages with their butterfly
glasses and beehive hairdos, and the terms of these recollections, that
smugly push all such women into the category of generic tackiness (the
one-legged man *must* be an "added" effect), are an element of the narrative point of *The Lost Continent*. Or, for another instance, out of the huge
welter of images during his travels that Reeves recalls having plunged
down upon him, leaving him "in a torrent, amazed and confused," he yet
insists on his "perfect memory" even months afterward of the bicycle
chained to the "split-rail" fence in the quiet little village of Haverford. This
very small detail—not from exhaustive description but from selective and
creative memory—comes into narrative play when, to be sure, other, more
powerful images have been discarded in this particular piece of retrospection. But the chains on this bicycle to prevent theft surely work toward
narrative effect when the reader recalls that Reeves has troubled about
crime and violence in the midst of American democracy, that his journey
into America follows Tocqueville's nineteenth-century course, and that
Tocqueville was in America on the "official" business of inspecting the
prison system. Whether the chained bike was really there or not is in virtually every respect quite irrelevant: the "added" detail reverberates with
the concern about the polluting effects of crime, even in a small Quaker

village. Such examples of creativity multiply, appearing on practically every page of the autobiographical travel "literature of fact."[28]

To contend that these and other autobiographically composed travel narratives—just because they *are* autobiographical—also contain elements of the art of fiction, operations of (only perhaps) fettered creativity, is not at all to suggest that they are pure fictions, much less to invalidate their legitimacy. The fact that they fictionalize through the lenses of authorial subjectivity no more diminishes their possible effects as travel literature than the realistic style of empirical or "factual" observation in picaresque fiction renders it merely travelogue.[29] In the operations of the new American picaresque, the fiction extends its capacities by trafficking in the realistic ("factual" or not), and the nonfiction meets it with the creative work of generating new images ("fictional" or not), so long as these are realistic. The differences perhaps are only in degree. As bizarre as the character might seem, Tombaby Barefoot, the odd, misshapen and malignant, half-breed son of a madame, who crosses Joe Buck's episodic path in *Midnight Cowboy*, is plausible enough in the sexually perverse fictional world in which Joe travels,[30] and the "created" Tombaby is no more improbable in this context than is the "observed" character John Williams, in his context as the "justice of the peace" of Jarbidge, Nevada, the "Judge," as depicted by Hampton Sides, who wagers to all takers that he can bite his own eyes.[31] Indeed, the certified existence of the "Judge," "certification" through Sides's autobiographical account of this American "character," only makes the possible existence of some Tombaby Barefoot out there in America all the more plausible, just as the imagined character, Tombaby, serves to enforce the likelihood of there being a "Judge" Williams. In the work of the new American picaresque, both are stock in the whirling American social cavalcade as both come to life "on page," neither any more nor less significant or memorable, as each is represented to the reader through subjective narrational memory. If Sides had not discovered Williams and recreated him for readers' inspection, it would have fallen to Herlihy or some other novelist to have created the "Judge" from scratch. The participation of the autobiographical American travel narrative in the formations of contemporary picaresque simply suggests the blurring of the genre, fictional and nonfictional, required—as Jenkins would have it—"to give this country one last chance" at the level of the interpretive venture. Such "blurring," Clifford Geertz would remind one, is probably inevitable, given the sheer size of the predicament that interpretations of America must confront.

In effect and function, then, as "fiction" and "nonfiction" converge in this particular framework, the intriguing shapes of subjectivity in narrative presentation are precisely the advantage: without them, the texts would degenerate into mere guidebooks, tourist information brochures, or the work of the gazetteers; without the shaping work of the creative imagination, the texts would be not only dull compendia but completely inadequate to the task at hand, the job of grappling with Steinbeck's "monster land" of America, the labor of swimming in Reeves's amazing and confusing torrent of American experience, the work of exploring something so big, various, and confounding that nothing less than the creative imagination can begin even to approach it, much less to reckon with it. Thus, as the autobiographical travel accounts posit themselves in structural terms that belong to the picaresque narrative, as the focal figure in such a text lives out the American picaro's road life, as the controlling work of imagination in these books shades them ineluctably toward fiction, it is not simply because Least Heat Moon or Lars Eighner or Eddy Harris somehow chimerically concluded that it would be great, good fun to represent his journey in the form of a picaresque fiction.[32] The interpretive situation, the American cultural-historical vista and problematic, dictated or at least conditioned the narrative possibilities, and the bent and potential of picaresque, when newly shaped to meet the contemporary "territory ahead," made it emerge as an efficacious formation, a literary form, available in the reservoir of genres, that might be adequate for the encounter and responsive to the character of contemporary American experience. The nonfictions join the fictions in undertaking this interpretive errand.

But the genre blurs further still. As fiction, nonfiction, or both, the new American picaresque also intermittently pulls into itself—just because it is picaresque and just because it newly faces the complex American territory—the operations of geographical documentary, social-psychological analysis, historical retrieval, mythological decoding, cultural criticism, and so on, which become necessary en route or in retrospection to meet the interpretive challenges. Although these interpretive modes remain subsidiary to the overall structures of picaresque, their presence in *Blue Highways, A Confederacy of Dunces, Stomping Grounds,* and *The Crying of Lot 49* suggests that the appearance of the new American picaresque is more than merely a small and curious section of a chapter in literary history, that the road work it proposes also moves into broader social and cultural spheres in America.

PART 2

The Social Work of the
New American Picaresque

4

The Picaro's Recovery of the Sovereign Self:
Road Cures

In the narrative lives created or constructed for Bill Trogdon, Billy Bathgate, Bill Bryson, Billy Pilgrim, and Bill Moyers, the longevity of the literary character of the picaro extends across the Atlantic and across the ages into America in the second half of the twentieth century. With the appearance of travel texts like *Blue Highways, Billy Bathgate, The Lost Continent, Slaughterhouse-Five,* and *Listening to America,* and others, this new American picaresque—with its broad and mobile mission of rediscovering the "monster land" America—occupies a certain literary space that opens for it, indeed calls for it, when other narrative forms have refused the tricky interpretive challenge of the world "out there," external to the refuges of alienated interiority. That challenge, as one of David Lamb's titles reminds readers, is to develop and to render "a sense of [the American] place," and the narrative structures of the picaresque form (its autobiographical narration, panoramic sweep, episodic mode, realistic style, and focal character) clearly have availed it to Lamb, Moyers, Doctorow, and Vonnegut as an apt one for their literary purposes, as commensurate with the narrative requirements they face in grappling with the rapid-fire, confusing, pluriform nature of contemporary American experience. With changes and additions, the continuity of the picaresque in terms of literary work would seem secure: Salisbury's *Travels around America,* Yardley's *States of Mind,* and

Steinbeck's *Travels with Charley* join with Waller's *Border Music* and Toole's *A Confederacy of Dunces* as they, in turn, appear on a literary-historical line reaching back to *Gil Blas* and *Lazarillo de Tormes*.

Given the charge of American exploration and stock-taking in the midst of complex new circumstances, however, the work of the new American picaresque is scarcely completed with the literary alignments. While the representational work of the picaresque is effectual for broadly panoramic inventories and the picaro can surely be an appropriate narrative vehicle for engagement and receptivity, that picaro—any picaro—must, as it were, "prove out" for the effectual life of the narrative form. The "self" he or she musters for the necessities of life on the road must be equal to the interpretive charge of the picaresque form. Certain obstacles confronting selfhood in recent America, however, conspire severely against the ability of any "self" in the arenas of experience and interpretation, and, as it frequently happens, the new American picaro or picara begins his or her road career as a "carrier" of the ills that beset contemporary selfhood. In fact, the figure's alienation, his or her sense of exile, psychic dislocation, and marginality, all of which can erode the integrity of the self, often prompt or require the mobile life, send the figure out to accomplish the road work that could also prove to be a form of self-recovery or -discovery.

Just as the work of the new American picaresque involves efforts at the renewal of the world for the self and the restoration of the self to the world, one designed objective, in this light, is not only American inventory but the recuperative work of self-recovery. As Salisbury remarks it, he ventures forward "looking for my country," but, he soon adds, "perhaps I'm trying to find something of myself as well."[1] For Peter Jenkins "to give this country one last chance"[2] is also, it becomes quite clear, to give himself another chance. The inquiry of this chapter, then, is first given over to those dilemmas of contemporary selfhood that impinge on the life of the picaro, the conditions and factors of recent cultural existence that conspire against the self in its experience, the dilemmas of which the picaros and picaras themselves are often bearers. If the authorized "eye" and "I" of the picaro, as used by the creative memory of the narrator, warrant the potency of the picaresque, then much militates against the capacity of the central figures to gain such authority. In developing the distinctive mode of experiencing they are challenged to learn during the requisite work of the road, the emphases fall on openness, immediacy, and freshness, but this innocent approach is less a birthright in contemporary America than a hard-won achievement as the picaro or picara labors to "come to his/her senses." Further exposition will thus be directed toward the ways the focal self in the new American picaresque narrative both suffers and surpasses these conditions. In this, the picaro or picara stands both as "case-study" of the dilemmas and, if successful in the road work, as a model of "remedy." As the picaro or picara struggles for his or her own required self-authorization, the picaresque narrative operates as a social-psychological diagnostic tool of the "ills" that afflict selfhood, and the picaresque curriculum, the experiential course of life, might be instructive of a special kind of cure. In turn, the job of engaging all of that "otherness" of American life depends, is completely predicated on, the achievement of this recuperative work of the self.

The Loss of the Creature and the Picaro's Dilemma

For the new American picaro, the mission is experiential, the job of the immediate, sensate reception of what the episodic course presents. David Lamb understands this as the traveler's developing "a sense of place"; Peter Jenkins, in preparation for his road trip, commits himself "to be where[ever] I was" (p. 34); and Vaughn Rhomer in Waller's *Border Music* wants to push further into experience than his Yellowstone vacation permitted, to engage the far places he thinks of as the "Big Road" encountered and "won" by his nephew Texas Jack Carmine.[3] But the active and mobile and experiential *vida picaresca* requires not just a road stretching ahead; it needs as well an experiencing "self" fully authorized to meet it, a self both responsive and integral that can engage, search, and sift American life, that can receive experience and revive it under the aegis of potent imagination and interpretation. According to some of the most telling contemporary cultural analyses, however, the existence of such a contemporary selfhood is perhaps deeply imperiled by current social-psychological conditions, a situation that, in turn, can undermine the possible life of the new American picaro.

Kenneth Gergen's explorations of the so-called technologies of social saturation[4] indicate one kind of debilitation that he believes puts "the self under siege" in this era. In pointing out the effects of "low" and "high" technological delivery systems—everything from the railroad, radio, postal service, and television, to electronic mail, facsimile machines, satellite dishes, and televideo media—Gergen contends that these have so amplified the range and numbers of a person's social relationships that, by now, an individual self finds itself "overpopulated" and, in fact, over-

whelmed by its often obligatory and frequently unavoidable connected-
ness to far too many other selves. Although a possible salutary effect of
this technological, social "closeness" might be a stronger realization of
human interdependence, Gergen believes that such new social propinquity can also—perhaps far more likely—eventuate in a person's becoming saturated and over-saturated with human relationships to the extent
that he or she suffers a paralyzing "multiphrenic condition," a dizzying
sensation of a "vertigo of unlimited multiplicity" that can cost a person
any constant, stable, persisting sense of self.[5] Out of balance, the self becomes nothing other than an accumulation of myriad other selves and a
function of their claims. When a person's selfhood becomes only a residence inhabited by the numerous, ghostly, commanding "voices" of those
others who have entered it, this overpopulated self cannot distinguish its
own separate identity, agency, or authorizing form of outlook and response for meeting experience, any more than it can either choose among
or find a way to coordinate the competitive and often contradictory perspectives and perceptions of the multitudes within it.[6]

But there are other, compounding factors in the contemporary conspiracy against the authority of the individual self as it goes to engage
the world. Walker Percy's diagnosis of the situation in *The Message in the
Bottle* points to the pathology he calls "The Loss of the Creature," the
dismantling of the prospects a person might have for direct, immediate,
and sensate encounter with the elements of experience. For anyone who
would seek "the sovereign discovery of the thing before him,"[7] the problem, according to Percy, is that contemporary life has created a condition
in which any "direct" experience—of the Grand Canyon, of a dogfish, of
a Shakespearean sonnet, of virtually anything—has become so utterly
mediated, or packaged for certain consumption, or overridden by theory,
or surrendered to the cult of the expert, that a person who fails to "work
at it" stands little chance of eluding the intermediate barriers between him
or her and the thing encountered. A person's approach to the Grand
Canyon, Percy argues, is by now thoroughly preceded by a prefigurement
of it delivered by postal cards, home movies, snapshots, television, and
the like, conditioning the encounter to the degree that the highest "term
of the sightseer's satisfaction . . . is the measuring up of the thing to the
criterion of the preformed symbolic complex."[8] Moreover, if one forges
ahead to seize on what might be the actual character of the place, the tour
is prepackaged by the National Parks Service, which manipulates or dictates just how the "experience" is to be accomplished and, indeed, even
understood. Comparably, the encounter of a student with a dogfish in the

biology laboratory not only extracts the thing out of the *ecos* wherein any "direct" or integral encounter must take place, and not only packages the thing for a certain kind of inspection, but also overrides the quite particular fish on the table by regarding it as a specimen to be understood under and only under the authority of "piscinological" theory and convention. Even more, the students' responses to the specimen must fall under the guiding and corrective sway of the presiding pedagogue, the biology "expert," whose lab it really is, authority on the matter confirmed.

Even were the student, without all of this preparation and intermediation, to blunder directly upon a dogfish in its natural element, a dogfish somehow unaccompanied by any "preformed symbolic complex," the inclination of the modern self, having in effect "waived" the capacity for the self-authoritative encounter, would be to doubt the authenticity of the experience until or unless it could be warranted by some expert. Percy depicts the amusing, but also somewhat touching plight of the young couple, off the beaten path, who inadvertently come upon a native ritual. Although delighted to think they might just have seen "the real thing," they then drag an anthropologist friend back to the scene in order to certify the authenticity of the experience. Relinquishing the right of sovereign response, Percy recognizes, is not necessarily a voluntary or even conscious surrender: it is an almost predictable inevitability in a time and in a culture that "manages" and "mediates" experience to the extent that the self's capacities and even desires erode, leaving the self to expect nothing other or causing the self to fail to recognize even the "real thing."

Such dilemmas of the modern American self presented by Gergen and Percy are compounded when the very structures of contemporary technology, quite apart from "overpopulating" the self and "mediating" its responses, alter the nature of experience itself. As Joshua Meyrowitz argues, the sheer omnipresence of electronic media especially makes it not only possible but actual that one need not ever leave a room to gain access to experience of a certain kind of the world "out there," experience once closed off by one's being situated in a particular place. "More and more," he observes, "people are living in a national (or international) information-system rather than a local town or city."[9] Although his study concentrates mainly on "the impact of electronic media on social behavior," Meyrowitz recognizes that one of the significant changes wrought on experience by the media of simultaneity—especially television—has been the felt obliteration of the self's distinction between "here," the place one is in, and "there," that place physically and formerly somewhere else. He realizes as well, along with Daniel Boorstin, among others, that the technical capacity for "simultaneity" can also lead to the creation of "pseudo-events"—that is, *apparently* important "happenings" arranged, framed, edited, even titled, and presented by the media as "significant experience," at which and to which the place-bound viewer can be electronically "present" and indeed is told he or she cannot afford to miss.[10] Thus, not only do technological delivery systems have the potential effect of confusing experiences by enjambing distant places and discrete occurrences in rapidly successive images, but, purposely or not, they can so manipulate "events" that the responding self has difficulty determining even the actuality of the occurrence, much less its character and significance.

Such self-determinations can become more difficult still when the self has lost any sense of placement that might help one at least gain some bearings. When "here" and "there" are virtually, electronically, the same place, "home" can no longer provide any locus of self-orientation. As indistinguishable from any other place, "home" is robbed of the resources it could afford for self-identity in an earlier era, and all the more so, Gergen would add, when a huge "population" can now enter and inhabit one's home so freely. Further, the engagement with the "other" so crucial for the self's own definition is lost when the other place, the other thing, and the other person, have all become so electronically present and familiar, and all the more so, Percy would add, when the altogether familiar "other" has been completely "demystified" because delivered through electronic packaging, mediating, and managing. Thus, while the electronic media would seem to promise "a new sense of access and openness to all places,"[11] Meyrowitz proposes, the effect is the creation of a kind of "placelessness," with the self stranded from any consistent and authorizing center of perception and response, the self dubious about the legitimacy of its own reflexes, the self distrustful of the integrity of its own witness.[12]

Directly or indirectly, these dilemmas of and challenges to contemporary selfhood in America radically hamper the work of that receptive and engaged person involved, like Lamb, in attempting to experience "a sense of place," a sense of the other person, a sense of the episode. It is not a matter of the end of the interpretive self: with Lamb, Ignatius Reilly, Steinbeck, Oedipa Maas, and others the task remains, and there are obvious reasons to think that, as Clifford Geertz avows, "the woods are full of eager interpreters," even in the midst of such tight social-psychological binds. But it also seems certain that these developments in recent social and cultural history put special constrictions on experience and interpre-

tation by compromising the sovereign discovery and encounter, by threatening the legitimacy of a person's perceptions, by draining the integrity
of the self's unique or distinctive responses. One's achieving a sense of
the place or the other person or the thing becomes no minor feat when
any such "sense" might only be a function of the saturating "voices" resident in one, or when it might result only from the "sight-seer's satisfaction" in confirming the preformulated image or in corresponding to the
proper packaging, or when the thing or event might well be a "pseudo"
thing in any "event." It becomes a triumph, in some respects, for a self
to find or make realistic "sense," most importantly, when that self is beset by doubts about either the authenticity of an experience or the effectual nature of the self's own responses to it.

Selves so straitened by this conspiracy of social, psychological, and
experiential conditions naturally, if perhaps largely unconsciously, take
several forms of recourse, some of which interrelate in social-psychological pathology. First, such a self can simply sign what Percy thinks the
"waiver" of sovereignty by surrendering completely to the "preconditioned" world, all without ever daring or caring to attempt the direct
engagement with experience, or can succumb totally to the cadre of the
populating "voices" within oneself or to the cultus of expertise all about
one, without ever seeking to locate one's own distinctive voice or viewpoint. Second, feeling its affectlessness, the self's inability to touch or be
touched or to possess any "affect" with respect to even the close sur-
roundings, the self can likewise sink into apathy, numbing itself to the
sensations from the external environs and retreating into the refuge of
utter privacy, deep interiority, exclusive subjectivity, even paranoia. But,
third, if those external sensations continue to assault too brutally, as Rollo
May has noted, the apathy can turn to radical assertion in a rage that
seeks "affect" through violence against the world.[13] Fourth, as Christopher Lasch discusses the matter, even if the sensations from outside are
more benign, a self so atrophied, so made "minimal" by any conspiracy
of factors, can locate a different form of assertion in the totalizing affect
secured by a self "absorbed," a self "concentrated," a self imperiously
narcissistic in its insistence on its own centering and self-centered image
as both the organizing principle and the essential meaning of the world.[14]
Any one of these courses of reaction can combine with or follow from
the others, but all such avenues of self-defense in the face of the afflicting
conditions only drive the attenuated self deeper into its malady, shrinking further still the possibilities of any effectual engagement with and
interpretation of the experiential order. Finally, of course, such a "self

under seige," as Gergen puts it, can attempt to find those healthier alternatives that lead out of these ailments of psychic life, those remedies
that secure the self in its integrity, those prescriptions for existence that
are self-restorative for dealing with the world. Before a self can work at
recovery or can learn to respect the authority and integrity of its own
distinctive experience, however, that self must first recognize itself as
"under siege," suffering affliction.

The Picaro as Symptom and Carrier

In a narrative form like the new American picaresque that devotes itself
to follow realistically the course of the solitary self's episodic career of
experience on the road, it comes as no surprise that these dilemmas and
ailments show up abundantly. Indeed, well before the new American
picaros and picaras even enter the recuperative process and sometimes
even in the midst of it, scarcely a one of them does not suffer some one
or more of these straitening predicaments or diseases of the self. The situation or illness might be expressed or revealed, directly or indirectly,
mildly or egregiously, through the picaro's own attitudes and recourses,
through faulty approaches to experience, through his or her truncated
actions of engagement, through disclosive hints dropped by narrational
memory, and in other ways, but, in all cases, the picaros arrive as "symptomatic," as etiological indicators of the conditions and afflictions of
contemporary selfhood. Part of this, obviously, is signaled in general by
their beginning senses of disaffection, of alienation, confusion, and loss.
Their very recourse to the "exile" of the road suggests that, for the time
being anyway, where they are is insufficient, that the self's relation to that
place does not adequately obtain, that the experiences there or the self's
responses fail to render that sense of self required for integral identity.
And such "dis-ease" in the current place, "home," is exacerbated in any
event by the "placeless" character of home that Meyrowitz describes.
With the new American picaro, however, the signals are also present
much more particularly of those conditions and ailments of selfhood
identified by Gergen, Percy, Lasch, and others. While some picaros suffer these problems only briefly in an instance here and there, others are
much more continuously afflicted, and all are, in some respect, at least
for a time "carriers."

On the matter of the multiphrenic condition that saturates the self to
the point of its overpopulation by the urging voices of others and thus
debilitates any distinctive self-identity, the symptomology from one picaro

to the next is present and telling. Oedipa Maas in *The Crying of Lot 49* represents an especially vivid case because of its severity. Throughout this picaresque novel, she "moves" not so much as herself but as the executrix of the legacy of the wealthy and powerful Pierce Iverarity, whose commanding "voice" continues posthumously to compel her. Now surrendered to him, she has involuntarily "earned" this position because of her adulterous affair with him, and, as other voices come increasingly to populate her "self," she grows even everless herself and evermore the object of seen and unseen others' wills for her seduction into their designs. Her shrinking self-definition is dramatized in a scene in which, having forgotten that the mirror in the motel bathroom had been shattered earlier, she attempts to glimpse herself there and discovers no reflection.[15] In *Travels around America*, the self-inhabiting others are the ancestors and the childhood friends, and Harrison Salisbury, saturated with them, their lives, their outlooks, occasionally moves into scenes that disappoint and frustrate him because his experience in the present fails to correspond to that of these ghosts from the past in him who have in some respect commandeered his own integral responses. In seeking out the old "Home Place" near Lake Canandaigua, for instance, he declares "Finally, I found Number 9. I wish I hadn't" (p. 30). The house, he learns, has become a party-house for the family of a real-estate developer. Or, again, as he approaches a class reunion, his habitation by other people from the past and the shrinkage of his own self are revealed quietly in his notation that "in their persons as in mine something of those distant days must survive. Perhaps in them I would find some reflection of myself" (p. 55). For David Lamb in *A Sense of Place*, the voices that saturate the self are those of the articulate people and the authors of books about America, and these voices have become sufficiently powerful in him that he has begun to worry some about the authenticity of his own outlook: "I may well be out of sync with common sentiment, but the pessimism I hear expressed when learned people gather to discuss our country mystifies me."[16] And, a paragraph later, he adds that, "coming home from a trip, I often felt the America I read about and the one I had seen were two different places—the former teetering on the brink, the latter muddling along" (p. 5).

For a final example of this picaresque self decidedly more whelmed than Lamb by the others who have taken up residence in it, there is Joe Buck in *Midnight Cowboy*. Virtually an empty cipher in self-identity and desperate for human connection, Joe travels the experiential realm as almost purely other-directed, without any defining inner compass to help him make his way. Constantly looking in mirrors to assure himself that he exists—a bit like Oedipa Maas's and Harrison Salisbury's attempts to catch reflections of themselves—Joe's eyes beg onlookers "Help me, but he had no idea any message at all was being transmitted."[17] His selfhood, shriveled by a lifetime of being nothing other than a function of other people, invites all takers to come in, to authorize him somehow with their authority, and he becomes prey, then, to the likes, among many others, of the haughty homosexual Perry, whom he misperceives and admires: "Joe felt he was living through some miracle: This stranger, a fine and handsome and knowledgeable and authoritative person, was turning his powers, his focus, his friendship, upon such an unworthy object as himself" (p. 66). Later, drugged, lachrymose, and physically held down to the floor by Perry, Joe thinks "Pinned. He was pinned down, pinned down by somebody friendly, wise, calm. Good. At last!" (p. 69). The saturated self in this case is so innocent that it is relieved, even joyful, to be overtaken and commanded: without the others living within him, filling up the empty cipher, Joe would disappear.

In some cases, then, Gergen's "ghosts" within that populate the self coincide with the waiver of integrity to the "experts" that Walker Percy identifies. Lamb, for an admitted time at least, pays attention to the "learned people," even though this obfuscates his own understanding, and Joe Buck gladly surrenders himself for a time to the "knowledgeable and authoritative" Perry, even though his waiver to this "expert" leads to mayhem. To relent to the expertise of any one or more of the "voices" is, in one form, also to put a mediating filter between the self and experience. Such defaults on self-sovereignty can only interfere with the picaresque mode, the direct and immediate engagement with experience that sees it, feels it, responds to it through the picaro's and picara's fresh eyes and untutored engagements.

The problems are compounded when the picaresque figure's responses meet places, sights, and people in ways that suggest those other kinds of interventions described by Percy as they preempt or constrict the integral response. Even without the self's default, the immediacy of the grasp on experience becomes problematical when the sites, events, things have been thoroughly overtaken by the "pre-formed symbolic complex" or have been obscured somehow by packaging or presentation that the picaro's "creaturely" reflex is tuned to the preformulation or the theory or the package as much as to the site or thing itself. This occurs to the extent in some cases that the site or thing is completely lost, supplanted by the mediation, and again, the symptoms of such a dilemma appear frequently, if indirectly. By the time Bill Bryson approaches Cleve-

land, after his rendition of the small town he calls "Dullard," the reader
pretty much expects that this picaro, almost unfailingly predisposed or
preconditioned in outlook, will only "find" or "discover" the dreary rust-
belt city he already and completely "knew" was there.[18] This, after all, is
the man who has already disregarded a fair number of middle-aged
women—"beehive hairdos and butterfly glasses"—because, failing to
approach each with some expectancy of her distinctiveness, he treats all
only as specimens within the genus "tacky," much as Percy's student in
the lab has learned to see the dogfish on the table out of context and has
been conditioned to deal with it only as a packaged example within some
more general, overriding theory. Salisbury, in effect, "misses" Canandaigua even while in it (found it "but wish I hadn't") because he cannot
see past the preformed idea of the place handed down in family lore and
conditioned by nostalgic memory. Binx Bolling, in Percy's *The Moviegoer*,
suffers a kind of disaffection because the "packaged" figures and actions
on the silver screen intercede between him and the, therefore, disappointing experiences of his life. After the Kennedy assassination, Hans Habe's
responses to America in *The Wounded Land* belong almost totally to the
preformed symbolic complex of racism and violence that henceforth controls his interpretive encounter and that leads to a preachy scold on the
country in closing. Vaughn Rhomer's venture onto the road in *Border
Music* is almost stifled altogether because his "over-preparation" for his
own Yellowstone vacation made that trip a debacle for him, and his reading of exotic "travel literature" and *National Geographic* convinces him
that he cannot locate the "Big Road." Eddy Harris, in *South of Haunted
Dreams*, begins and continues his journey pre-prepared and angry in his
preparation for the racist South he expects to find, and Bill Moyers, in
visiting a small, exclusive, liberal arts college in Ohio, immediately poses
to two of the obviously few African-American students on campus the
question of "how many blacks are enrolled at Antioch."[19] In these and
comparable instances, a kind of "pre-flex" has displaced the reflexive life
of the creature, and the picaro must continuously battle against these
predisposals in him or her that, in the mediated, conditioned world of
American experience, are almost ineluctable and unavoidable.

Other intercessions between the self and its experience similarly suggest the odds against the picaro's and picara's direct encounter when some
form of the population within, the packaging without, or the waiver to
some other authority exerts pressures along the way. Reeves's picaresque
efforts in his *American Journey* to follow Tocqueville's itinerary put that old,
admired voice inside of him, precondition what he will see by preceding

it with what Tocqueville saw, and lead him to consult en route with a large cadre of other "experts," consultations that saturate him with other voices still.[20] Sal Paradise in *On the Road* journeys toward expectations preformed by his admiration of Dean Moriarity. The "One-Eyed Mack" in Jim Lehrer's *Kick the Can* is so young and so "green" in self-definition that he concocts a romantic model out of adventure literature to mediate his course through the experiential, unromantic world into which he is loosed. Nan, in Elizabeth Berg's *The Pull of the Moon*, often recalls on course the ways husband Martin had formerly interceded in, directed, evaluated, and even defined *her* experience for her. Rojack in Norman Mailer's *An American Dream*, after his initial "horrible incident," somewhat like Hans Habe in this regard, approaches and enters the picaresque course now predisposed to suspect the violence and danger everywhere that he has identified in himself. In *A Walk across America*, Peter Jenkins confesses to diving for the underbrush along the southern highway because of that "preformed symbolic complex," besetting him in his "hip" youth, regarding the automatic danger posed by those approaching rednecks. Such conditions and dilemmas afflicting the picaro's self, consciously recognized or not, put real roadblocks in the way of the sovereign engagement with the experiences to which the journey might lead.

In some cases, of course, such examples of default or surrender to preconditioning, of appeal to other authority, of failure to possess an autonomous response, are altogether predictable and rather simple human failures stemming from the inevitability of "typing," laziness of independent perspective, and so on, although even these, even so, are truncations unacceptable in the picaro's particular kind of life. In other cases, however, these constrictions binding the authority and ability of the self appear symptomatically in the picaro or picara as evidence of his or her deeper psychic ailments. Atrophied under such conditions, the self can fall into the kind of relieved apathy that Joe Buck goes through in the throes of his affectlessness, as he willingly gives up to Perry, or the kind of cynical apathy that Bill Bryson exhibits in his refusal to touch or be touched, as he retreats into the safety of sneering at everything, or the kind of smug apathy that Hans Habe inculcates in his rejection of anything that would ameliorate his darkly superior inner lights, or the kind of "worldly" apathy that Binx Bolling permits himself in his recourse to the alternative world of the movie theaters. A recognition of another form of apathy occurs in Berg's Nan, who frequently berates herself as a shrunken self that paralyzed her desires to help an abused woman and who awaits, and ultimately gets, a "second chance" after taking to the road. As a result of the failure of "affect," this apathy in the face of the onslaughts of experience and of the truncations of the self can eventuate finally, as the self reasserts itself, in those forms of pure self-concentration expressed in rage or paranoia or, in milder cases, fortressed subjectivity. Herlihy's "cowboy," Joe Buck, senses after one episode of abuse at the hands of experience that he must evict those two soothing voices populating his inner life (Sally Buck and Woodsy Niles), the only generous ghosts from Joe's past, because they were "much too rare to find a place for in any useful view of the world": they needed to be "placed out of the range of his thinking . . . [because] they were dangerous to him, they caused the anger to run out of him. And somehow he had come to know that if he was going to manage in the world, he'd need all the anger he could keep hold of" (p. 95). Pynchon's Oedipa Maas is driven to self-absorption in a different way, not in any calculated anger but in the paranoid convictions that, personal identity very nearly shredded, the heaped-up hostility of the world is being heaped up on *her*, paranoia as the only certainty, in this case, into which an unsecured self can flee. These radical kinds of responses by the "self under seige" occur less often than other less extreme mechanisms of defense, to be sure, but they serve to dramatize how the new American picaro, like other American selves, also suffers the situations and dis-eases impairing the creature in his or her experience.

This is decidedly the case, if in milder form, even for that contemporary American picaro perhaps most renowned of them all. For John Steinbeck in *Travels with Charley*, the blockades on experience and the predicaments of selfhood that lead to "untoward" self-concentration are revealed when he temporarily abandons the road, retreats into the security and privacy of the Ambassador East Hotel in Chicago, and rejects out of hand the outside world in favor of his own comforting subjectivity. Desisting in the role of "Anyperson" constructed for the highway at the outset, he wants briefly to resume his famous persona—he remarks his being quite "well and favorably known"[21] in this hotel—and simply rejects the hard lot of the picaro's difficult empirics, the engagement with "the outside," displacing that factual world by making it *merely* a subject, a slave to his own imaginative fancy. As he waits for his wife to fly in to join him, to have a little "home" interrupting the "exile," he temporarily accepts a room not yet cleaned after its last guest, and there he admits to "conjuring" up a figure he calls "Lonesome Harry," that last hotel guest who is completely absent now but takes "shape and dimension" (p. 117) for the semi-retired picaro. Picking about in the very few things Harry has left behind, Steinbeck quite self-consciously "creates" this character, his job, his hometown and wife, his affair with another woman who had not stayed the night, and, at last, his empty, lonely existence, all of this to conclude that "I felt sad about Harry" (p. 119). Moreover, after having committed himself to engage the country, having traveled halfway across the continent at this point, having by now talked to dozens of people who *were* present to him, and now having briefly left the road, he asserts that, while Charley's dog nose might have detected even more about the lonesome man, "even so, Harry is as real to me as anyone I ever met, and more real than many" (p. 117). This is more than a writer's subjective shaping and directing of the facts, those narrational acts of uncovering or recovering the world by forcing subjectivity to be responsive to it: this is the stuff of repudiating the world, covering it with one's own imperious will for it, converting it to one's own solipsistic terms. Steinbeck needs "Harry" because, the experience of the road not yet yielding the kinds of generalizations hoped for, Harry helps Steinbeck cope: Harry "is not unique," he writes, "in fact is a member of a fairly large group" (ibid.). Beyond the stuff of "typing" and "lethargy" or apathy, both largely unacceptable for the picaro's mission, this instance in *Travels with Charley* suggests in a pointed way the form of self-absorption that prefers the clarities achieved in loose, unmoored interiority to the chaotic external world anchoring a more committedly engaged subjectivity. No real harm is done in such an incident—Steinbeck simply idling in his curiosity—except to the picaro's way of being in the world. But it reveals in its way another of those self-debilitations that the contemporary picaro is heir to as much as any other, and it certainly contradicts the picaro's defining mode of experience, flunks him out of the picaresque curriculum.[22]

Perhaps the most endemic ailments of the self that the picaro suffers, however, are the maladies associated with narcissism, the unhappy consequences of such self-concentration, even self-adoration, to the degree that the surrounding world is lost or missed or rebuffed altogether. These clearly attenuate the requisite picaresque forms of engagement with experience, and they reveal themselves in ways that suggest only slight and temporary lapses of the picaro or picara, on the one hand, and severe and continuous affliction, on the other. At some points, in momentary affliction, this or that picaro simply becomes a kind of imperious character, bolstered with enough self-esteem to run right roughshod through the episode at hand without decent regard for the full attentiveness he should be practicing, or inflated with enough self-regard to float himself as an expert in the cycle of experience to the fore.

In some instances, however, the basking in the reflected self-image becomes so enthralling and continuous that that image threatens to become the principle around which all of life is to be understood. In either case, such contemporary narcissism appears more or less inevitably
in a figure like the picaro whose solitariness ("*yo soy solo*," Lazarillo
exclaims) can lead to extremities of self-concentration, whose sense of
alienation or "exile" can turn to a sense of self-superiority, whose own
fine insights and responses can twirl into heightened self-satisfaction,
and whose movement through a difficult course can result in self-con-
gratulation, all of which forms of high self-centeredness can surely stem
as defenses from conscious or unconscious recognitions of one's self
made "minimal," marginalized, extraneous, lonely, and shriveled in its
distinctiveness and affect.[23]

In all cases, when these examples of intermittent or more enduring
narcissism appear in the picaro or picara, they have the effect of blockading the integral picaresque response to experience and, wittingly or not,
explicitly or more tacitly, the picaresque narrative performs the diagnostic chore on the self in its impairment. Sometimes the symptoms are clearly
charted or unmistakable—old Narcissus lost in the enamoring reflection
of himself in the water. Having personal identity so compromised that she
cannot find her own voice, cannot locate herself in the mirror, Oedipa
Maas, in executing the legacy of Inverarity, has to move about only as a
function of Inverarity's powerful self-regard in a town named San Narciso.
Or, again, Joe Buck in *Midnight Cowboy* spends so much time in front of
mirrors the reader is assured that, given Joe's shrunken sense of self, his
own beautiful image is pretty much all that is left to him. Even after a
particularly brutalizing experience, he finds this reflected friend there to
be consoled: "'Cowboy,' he said to his image, addressing it with a kind of
excited enthusiasm that looked a great deal like love, 'I'm gonna take care
of you, I'm gonna work my butt off for you, I'm gonna coddle you to
death'" (p. 91). In other cases, the disease is present even if the pathology
is more difficult to chart. When Salisbury attends his class reunion to see
if he can catch a glimpse of *himself* in the others there, one suspects that
the journey has—at least temporarily—become devoted less to the world
"out there" and more to the gaze at or search for one's own image. Or,
despite his declared efforts to go quite anonymously, to move as the American "Anyperson," on the picaresque course, Steinbeck, for another kind
of instance, quite frequently adopts an "imperial" attitude that preens itself on who he in fact *is*, the writer Steinbeck, who possesses refined abili-

ties and, thus, clear "rights" as he moves through life. Even in a moment of self-doubt about sifting through Lonesome Harry's privacy, he suggests that "although my conclusions may be wrong, I seem to be sensitive to the spoor of the human. Also, I am not shy about admitting that I am an incorrigible Peeping Tom. I have never passed an unshaded window without looking in, have never closed my ears to a conversation that was none of my business. I can justify or even dignify this by protesting that in my trade I must know about people, but I suspect that I am simply curious" (pp. 116–17). Hans Habe in *The Wounded Land* also tends to file American life into his own encasing sense of himself as writer, but his particular kinds of self-inflations seem even more to be a result of his alienated, romantic conception of himself in exile as "the superior European" whose delicately civilized sensibility and illuminating insights give him a kind of expertise with which to instruct the benighted Americans. Or there is the disaffected Bryson in *The Lost Continent*, who, in his marginalized state, regards himself as so "above" virtually all he encounters that his sheer carelessness respecting the world—his clever dismissals of people and things—signals the kind of troublesome self-regard that defensively manages experience only as a product of his own unfettered will for it, the world narratively colonized purely as a principle of his own smug agency.[24] All such self-concentrations veer away from the picaresque career, even as, just because they are culturally endemic, they suggest the odds against the picaro in contemporary America.

One of the most subtle revelations of the ways that the minimal self can become the narcissistic self and that the picaro's experience can thus be hampered occurs in *Blue Highways*—a somewhat ironic disclosure of the afflictions of Narcissus in view of Least Heat Moon's earnest Native American efforts throughout the narrative to avert the Caucasian illness of self-attention. In the third chapter of the first part, as he chooses his Native American name, Trogdon suggests just how minimal his selfhood has become in his own sense of things by seeing himself in a family declension. After his father, Heat Moon, and his older brother, Little Heat Moon, and after the spotted history of those giving him his Christian name and making him a mixed-blood, he can only become *Least* Heat Moon—"a long lesson," he reports, "of a name to learn."[25] And, even prior to that piece of self-shrinkage, he makes a pledge to the reader about this chapter of less than two pages: "I give this chapter to myself. When done with it, I will shut up about *that* topic" (p. 4).

Of course, such a conspicuous forecast of self-effacement—like Steinbeck's proud announcement that he will construct himself on the road as the ordinary "Anyperson"—ought to alert the reader that the narrative to unfold will not only give large heed to the afflicted self but will have that self as one of its major topics. The situation of the minimal self in place, the prospects of impending narcissism cannot be far off for Least Heat Moon. Slightly over two hundred pages later, now in Nevada, the sorrowful self-absorption remains intact, disclosed this time in his reply to a man who invites him to join "games of chance": not having played, he refuses by saying, in reference to his whole life, "'Haven't finished losing the first one'" (p. 210). And then, driving the next morning back into the rain-darkened desert, along a highway that "was a long, silver streak of wet," and wishing the desert could dry off to present itself, his sad self-concentration overrides his possible present experience:

> I looked out the side-window. For an instant, I thought the desert looked back. Against the glass a reflection of an opaque face. I couldn't take my attention from that presence that was mostly an absence. Whitman:
>
> *This the far-off depth and height reflecting my own face*
> *This the thoughtful merge of myself, and the outlet again*
>
> Other than to amuse himself, why should a man pretend to know where he's going or to understand what he sees? Hoping to catch onto things, at least for a moment, I was only following down the highways a succession of [self-]images that flashed like blue sparks. Nothing more. (p. 212)

With the world "out there" on the "blue highways" only witnessed as so many "blue sparks" of self image in instances like these, Least Heat Moon, like other contemporary American picaros, suffers those conditions and ailments of selfhood that interfere with the picaresque charge of immediate encounter, empirical response, integral experience. He discovers—as *some* others do—that, even if he can struggle through the cultural conditions that beset the efforts of experience, he might nevertheless succumb to his own self-absorption. While the picaro or picara might surmount the situations that saturate his or her views with those of others, that preformulate and frustrate "innocent" approaches, or that package scenes and events and thus prevent creaturely response, while he or she might well overcome such conditions, each picaro or picara might yet fall prey even so to the self's own defenses—the disaffections of apathy, the imperious approach, the unfettered arrogance of subjectivity, the narcissistic tendency to see the world in one's self instead of one's self in the world. Sent out to discover the world, the picaro or picara might also discover himself or herself as the largest obstacle on the course as the new American picaresque presents such a diagnosis as an element of its road work.

The Regimen of Road-Therapy in Self-Recovery

If the culture presents certain constricting conditions on experience and if contemporary selfhood must struggle against the likelihood of its own self-atrophying reactions, this is not to say, however, that the case is completely closed. Walker Percy, for one, recognizes that even in such peril of "the loss of the creature," even as the work is difficult, the self can yet prove nimble and quick in eluding the barriers between the sovereign response and the experience at hand. The cultural machineries creating self-saturations, preconditionings, packaging and manipulation, and mediating experts might well be thought to dominate the scene, and the afflictions of selfhood might well be epidemic in proportion, but, especially in democratic and pluralistic settings, individual life is rarely held so captive by one set of views that no other possibilities can be conceived: culture supplies the terms of thought, but this does not mean either that the singular self must accept those terms as dictated or that there is only a univocal set of terms. Even the most dominant forces in a rapid-paced and variegated culture are not eternal or absolute or even completely consistent, and, with these proximate cultural shifts, options, even contradictions, other pathways appear, avenues open, and roads fork, all permitting new movements into experience that hold out remedial prospects for "the self under siege." Just as the new American picaresque appears as a diagnostic tool, it also presents the prescription of the road for the picaro and picara in need of recovery, and they, by virtue of narrative definition and learned road alacrity, prove most often to be the "nimblest and quickest" of all.

Thus, while many of the picaros or picaras suffer the condition of Gergen's "saturated self," the situation of that person so filled up with others' views and voices that his or her own distinctive outlook and articulation are quite lost, the picaresque venture outlines a therapeutic road to the recovery of self-sovereignty. "Home" having led to this "multiphrenic sensation"—too much propinquity, too many within, too many contesting for command—"exile" onto the solitary course can become a means of leaving the resident "others" behind, putting one's self out of reach, and the multitude of others presented to the picaro and picara on the road, because of their continuous movements, can be, must be, left behind episode by episode. To the extent that the old "ghosts," the ancestors, accompany Harrison Salisbury along the way and "predict" his forms of responsiveness, his own integral experiencing is compromised in unameliorated disappointments. In the measure that the road teaches him perspectives allowing him to see some permuted form of sustaining American values in surprising "new" people and some attractive new valuations unanticipated in "old" familiars, he can free himself from the "crowd" within him, see the country in new ways, indeed even catch glimpses of new self-possibilities. For another case, although occasionally mystified by the voices of the learned people he carries within, David Lamb suffers them less, respects the integrity of his own experience more, and takes to the road again to confirm the authenticity of those of his responses gleaned from earlier trips. Nevertheless, he, like Salisbury, wittingly or not, must elude the "saturations" by others and their views in order to secure those senses of self-integrity without which fuller experience cannot be achieved.

Others suffer "over-population" more, must run even faster. While Oedipa Maas only increasingly finds herself filled with the voices of the others, as these reverberate for her against the commanding tones of the dead Inverarity, her picaresque career nevertheless introduces her to sets of voices quite different than any heard before her journey began. By herself, in her vagabondage, pushed to the edges of American existence, forced to cross boundaries, her "trespass" opens onto what are for her entirely new, entirely unsettling, vistas on experience, even if these are "authorized" only, as she fears, by her own paranoia. Herlihy's Joe Buck, himself shrunken practically to the point of extinction by the encroachments within of all those to whom he has relinquished any claim of self, finally finds on his hard road that Ratso Rizzo, one even more self-needy, without even any physical beauty to support him. At last having "connected," even in the strange shapes of relation the two accomplish, Joe's continued innocence, hope, and openness—as the picaresque prescription of encounter enables—leads him to a sense of self never before possessed. However, even as he declares to Ratso that "'I ain't going nowhere. I don't walk out on a buddy just 'cause I find out he's got some little bitty teensy something wrong,'" he has to rid "his mind once more [of] a brief picture of Juanita Barefoot" (p. 128), that vile hag within him whose "ghostly" presence attempts to preside over him.[26] Reeves, for his part, finds a road that follows but also frees him from Tocqueville's inhabiting voice, and, along the way, he learns to enjamb the various other expert voices he hears in order to create, on his own authority, new perspectives for himself on

American life. After his "consultations" in New York at the private university in Ithaca and at the state penitentiary at Auburn, two distinctive kinds of American democratic institutions, both of which had suffered recent riots, Reeves interweaves the discrete conversations to conclude that "Auburn was not all that different from Cornell."[27] First, however, he has had, and the road has given him the occasion, to free himself in his immediate engagement with the sites from the authority of old Alexis's opinion that, "'however annoying a law may be, the American will submit to it'": "If those words were ever strictly true, they are not today," and, with this, Reeves decides that "the Frenchman must have been exaggerating" (p. 55). In cases like these, then, as the picara or picaro plunges along alone and faces experiences that aid, indeed require, her or his repossession of the empirical life, the picaresque course provides a means not only to evict the all-too-numerous inhabiting voices that prevent necessary self-authorizations but also to discharge any one or more of those voices whose asserting "expertise," compelling inordinately, precludes the self's sovereign engagement.

But Percy's problem of mediated and manipulated experience remains even so. Even if the populating voices within can be expunged, as Berg's Nan slowly frees herself from Martin's rule, thus permitting the distinctive self to respond, the stuff of preformulated notions, of presiding theories, of preconditioned approaches, nevertheless beset the self intent on immediate engagement. Just as the picaresque form of life contains in its very terms the solitary drives into immediate experience that can help the self rid itself of "other-directedness," however, the very nature of the picaro's narrative existence withholds the possibilities at least of circumventing the prevailing conventions, to avert the preformulations, to locate the character of the sovereign response. The flow of culture might well seem channeled in one direction, but that does not mean that the picaro cannot swim against the current. Neither does it mean that some of the tributaries cannot provide alternative vistas or that, indeed, sometimes, the levees cannot break, creating new courses altogether.

One way to skirt the predisposed response, the intercessions between self and experience, is to get off the beaten path and into those areas not overlaid with prior images and ideas that precondition the terms of the engagement. While the picaresque road might not always take one completely out of the realm of mediating conventions, Least Heat Moon has the instinct that the secondary roads, the "blue highways," might provide a better chance of averting the "managed" experience of America. By staying off the interstate freeways that reduce the course to a kind of sameness

("Burger King here is Burger King there"), that emphasize speed as op-posed to "seeing," that promise predictability in travel, he can penetrate more completely into the local, the different, even the unanticipated. On the blue highways he can as well make those temporary pauses that might yield at least a quick sense of the distinctiveness of a place, the unique "feel" of a scene, a momentary, sovereign hold on things, that will help him go beyond the packaging, the conventions, the preformed complex. The very episodic, accidental career of picaresque to be followed can lead him to the Chiricahuas, an area in the Arizona canyons, which turns out to be "a new land of the eye, a new region of the mind" for him, one to be grasped in its immediacy: it was "one of the strangest pieces of topogra-phy I'd ever seen, a place, until now, completely beyond my imaginings" (p. 179)—in part "beyond" just because not pre-imaged for him in vast information dispersals. This experience is possible because the twisting picaresque trail, movement by chance and by rebound, has gifted him with a scene to which he can come fresh, with innocent eye, with Adamic im-mediacy. "And that was the delight," he says, "I'd never heard of the Chiricahuas. I expected nothing" (p. 178). A comparable "erring" move-ment beyond the inerrant, habituated path occurs in Peter Jenkins's en-counter, atop a Virginia mountain, off even the paved roads, as he, hav-ing arrived in the place, goes to see if Homer Davenport, a hermit, is "for real" (p. 70). What Jenkins finds far exceeds the preconceptions of the dangerous mountain man brought to the episode, including a log cabin with a front outside wall shingled with "old metal saltine boxes that had been beaten flat" (p. 72) and a sense of the wilderness, tutored by old Homer, that makes Jenkins feel suddenly reverent in his sense that "I was entering a wild paradise" (p. 71) with an uncommonly civilized man. Such examples abound, as the new American picaresque course itself frequently makes the picaro's travels "eccentric," off-center, away from the tracked, controlled, preformulated arenas of experience. In these areas, the picaro and picara might become amazed or dumbfounded in the face of things unprecedented for them, but for the most successful of them their re-sponses are at least and at last their own, direct and not totally conditioned by the forces of intermediation. The road itself, in this framework, can be "the road to recovery" as the self labors to achieve its distinctive and in-tegral ground.

In areas of experience more "tried out," considered more familiar, and therefore more likely to be encountered under the pressures of preformulation, the nature of the picaresque journey—the roving eye on its bumpy course—affords opportunities for the picaro to develop those new forms of vision in part enabled by the solitary course of the "unbonded" person. Since one part of the picaro's charge is to regard life without ranking or distinguishing "high" and "low," to familiarize the alien and defamiliarize the common, the picaresque tour entails trying out the innocent eye, and, however much any "mediating" structures seem to prevent the fresh view, the most successful of the picaros and picaras are nimble enough to manage this and are aided in it by their own vagabond situation. At least temporarily in exile, bound by no necessity to accept most received conventions of response and interpretation, the picaro or picara is thus also loosed not only to be introduced to eccentric spheres of America but, from his or her narrative status on the peripheries of social existence, to view more usual matters from an uncommon perspective, to trespass conventional understandings, to see ordinary things "anew" by seeing them "on the slant." Thus, a David Lamb isolates himself to go out in challenge of the viewpoints the "learned people" would foist upon him, and an Oedipa Maas, made peripheral, will learn to see from a new, unwonted angle of vision areas on the American periphery before impossible for her to see. For some on the road, the development of odd, new angles of outlook and insight arrives unconsciously, a result simply of seeing things from the picaresque vantage point. For others in their wandering state, it is a completely studied effort. Eddy Harris, for all the mediating history of white racism he lugs along, pushes the boundaries, puts himself on tense social edges, tries out the others' standpoints.

For a different kind of conscious evasion of the standard or conventional view that would settle an experience prior to one's having it, Least Heat Moon works strenuously to locate a new bias and to practice the lessons of simple receptivity. Driving through west Texas, he moves across "the Texas some people see as barren waste when they cross it," the area "they later describe at the motel bar as 'nothing.' They say, 'There's nothing out there.'" This picaro, however, "decided to test the hypothesis," the operative understanding, about these "miles of nothing" and stops, stations himself atop a broad mesa in western Crockett County, looks, listens, smells, touches, and even tastes, as he composes a list of thirty things—from wind to black ants, to orange ants, to an opossum skull— the barrenness gradually yields to him. After a while of thus coming to his senses, rediscovering himself as creature, he concludes, "that was all the nothing I could identify then, but had I waited until dark when the desert really comes to life, I could have done better" (pp. 164–65). Least Heat Moon's patient empirics, his tactics of reception, his feeling along

the boundaries of convention, are all learned or repossessed by the practice of the solitary journey, the roadside as an occasion for that self-recovery enabling the "innocent," immediate response to experience. As with
a number of these other narrative figures, seeking deliberately or not, the
location of the unaccustomed angle of vision, the strategy of different
perspective, can abet the picara's and the picaro's recuperative work of
self-recovery. When faced with intermediating structures between the
picaro and the scene or thing or when the scene or thing fails to render,
Least Heat Moon has learned, another slant is required: "a tactic returned
to me from night maneuver training in the Navy: to see in deep darkness
you don't look directly at an object—you look to the left; you look at something else to see what you really want to see. Skewed vision" (p. 129).
Having recognized a way to avert preformed complexes of sight and response in the possibilities of such skewed and peripheral vision, he is on
his way to becoming, as he had all along hoped, not only *homo viator* but
homo spectans (p. 418), as both picaresque movement and newly seized
forms of seeing emerge as elements of his road cure.

Other picaros learn such lessons much more slowly or not at all, but
from case to case it becomes clear that the road holds out comparable
possibilities for them all, and, of course, the invitation to move into that
"out there," beckoning one to experience integrally, is also a summons
to avoid the contemporary self's ailments of retreat into interiority, or of
the defenses of overweening self-regard or utile anger, or of any habit
of reducing the world to a function of one's superior will for it. The road,
or at least the picaresque response to it, is perhaps not the only therapy
for the self under seige, but it assuredly presents one prospective route
toward the recovery of Percy's "creature." Exiled into experience, dependent on the reflexive capacity, the picaro's tour into odd enjambments,
through the quick succession of things and images, the eccentric course
that allows or even requires "off-centered," peripheral or "skewed" perspectives, the renewing possibilities of accidental movement, the fresh
vista and the innocent view, and so on, all give the picaro and picara the
chance to see things "on the slant," in new bias, thus affording the situations of understanding the strange as familiar, the familiar as exotic, and
both as moments of unspent potency.

Managing to elude that which would intervene between the experience and the picaresque response is part of the therapeutic regimen, and
the very alienation that is the picaresque figure's initiating condition is,
thus, also one of his or her possible assets: solitariness can refresh autonomy; unbondedness can also mean "unconventional"; exile can be-

come the occasion for different perspectives. Some picaros and picaras prosper on the course, like Least Heat Moon, by devising new strategies of encounter, new tactics of vision. Others move toward self-correction or self-cure by observing the "failures" of other people on the road—as Lamb, for instance, notices the flawed responses of "Shirtless from Wisconsin," the paradigmatic tourist impatient with his daughter, or as Percy's Binx Bolling engages the college student on the bus, one whose intensity and posture expose his acting out romantic conventions to mask his shyness, conventions themselves preventing the very encounters he seeks.[28] Least Heat Moon, again, points to another kind of example of the faulty respondent from whom to learn the correct course in the encounter with the man he calls "the Boss of the Plains" (pp. 179–86), "a man concealed in his own life, scared to move, holding himself too close, petting himself too much" (p. 183), "an empty man full of himself," suffering the self's afflictions to the point that "things outside himself he found banal and not worth his attention" (p. 186).[29] Still other picaros and picaras stumble onto the prescription for cure quite fortuitously, like Eddy Harris in his encounter with the "accidental" cardinal, a momentary, flashing image that begins to bring him to his senses,[30] or like Nan in *The Pull of the Moon*, who gets just those "second chances" the life of temporary exile on the road tosses up for her, or like Vaughn Rhomer in *Border Music*, in his "main chance," as he dances with the mysterious, beautiful woman in New Orleans (pp. 166–68, 186–88). For them, picaresque fortune provides opportunity for self-recovery through the unanticipated character of an episode, very much like, again, Binx Bolling's quiet, shared moments with his crippled half-brother, fourteen-year-old Lonnie, at the drive-in theater, as they watch *Fort Dobbs*. In this more or less ordinary scene, Binx knows, there arrived—for one prepared to grasp it—that chance cycle of "the experiencing of the new beyond the expectation of the experiencing of the new" (p. 144), an apparently commonplace but actually extraordinarily powerful incident that provides him a stay against the grip of "everydayness" that usually drags at his life (p. 145).

While these picaros and picaras move toward the recovery of the integral self, while the picaresque venture enables the possibilities of cure, it is not the case that all succeed thoroughly, for there are frequent lapses and relapses. The written memories document these setbacks, sometimes unwittingly, as when Least Heat Moon tries out his arts and strategies of attuned reception to the outside world by locating the "somethings" in the desert "nothing," at one point, only to fall back into the trap of the "blue sparks" of his own self-image at another point. And, indeed, some

of the figures at the narrative center of the texts fail pretty much throughout, abjectly and utterly, in escaping the self-maladies even in the midst
of their best prospects otherwise, those obvious chances the picaresque
tenure affords them for remedy. At worst, however, even when the picaro
or picara suffers relapse or defaults altogether or fails even to begin to
realize his or her defining nature, the works belonging to the new American picaresque nevertheless serve at least an indirectly diagnostic purpose in isolating and exposing those instances in which the "dis-eases"
of the self can be discerned. At best, the new American picaro, in fulfilling
the picaresque charter, moves beyond the narrative diagnosis into the
regimen of cure "on the road." Learning to depopulate the self in order
to regain singular authority, learning the tactics to recover sovereign response by skirting preformulations and mediations, they might yet succumb from time to time to the temptations of self-absorption or the defenses of narcissism, the expected comforts of self-reflection that disdain
the fecundity of the unexpected in the world of experience. Nevertheless,
as the new American picaros and picaras answer to the charge of entering and engaging the complex, pluralistic social reality of the country—
of meeting and responding to the human "other"—the best of them will
come to realize that they cannot remain within the fortresses of adula-
tory self-regard if they are to take the inventory of America they themselves seek and that the picaresque work requires.

5

The Picaro in Social Space:
Stranger Still

As the picaresque tour provides Richard Reeves, David Lamb, William Least Heat Moon, Herlihy's Joe Buck, Toole's Ignatius Reilly, Doctorow's Billy Bathgate, and others with at least the opportunities and occasions to restore the sovereignty of the self, some seize on the complicated work of attuning to and responding to their episodic existences with growing integrity and respect for the authority of their own "empirics." These "cures," made possible by life on the road, go to suggest how the picaro's very charge as a literary figure can also help create reparations of the threats to full experience stemming from individual social-psychological dilemmas. But when the location or recovery of the picaro's self-sovereignty runs to the other extreme—that is, to the defensive mechanisms of radical and insulating forms of self-absorption—the problems appear most fully and disclosively in the various "social spaces" through which the picaro or picara necessarily passes in fulfilling the narrative charter of the picaresque form.

Commissioned by the picaresque genre to traverse, encounter, and inventory the human *galeria*, the "motley" of social types, the picaro or picara in contemporary America must enter the complex spheres of a pluralism so vast and variegated that it frequently befuddles in any case, confounding the sojourner with the strange and alien character of all of those shapes of human "otherness" that confront him or her along the way. If the picaro or picara suffers any of those untoward self-concentrations that beset recent life, however, if he or she practices those faulty responses that automatically segregate or insulate him or her from the people out there to be engaged, the problems compound, precluding that reflexive openness and equanimity that are among his or her defining traits. It is in this context that the picaresque narrative forms extend their diagnostic function, not now in tracing out the various constrictions of the self's authority but in displaying the predicaments of human engagement when the self *over*-authorizes itself. The picaresque figures encounter numerous cases of such social affliction in those met by the highway, but, again, they themselves also often present the symptoms, showing themselves infected by the diseases of human relation that belong to the social pathologies of self-concentration and that seem endemic in contemporary America. Again as well, however, the picaresque journey holds out the prospects of remedy: the life of the road, just because it crosses through so many human territories and bumps into so many strangers, can have the effects of depleting inflations of self-regard, of conquering the fear of the other, of pricking the propensity to stereotype, of breaking down protective senses of excessive superiority. For those picaros and picaras who already know such a "cure" at the level of natural reflex or who can quickly or gradually grasp it along the human way, the continuing, episodic cycles through the social experience with the country can take them, beyond alienation, into deeper senses of connection with their fellows or can at least allow them, like Moyers and Lamb, and Barbara Kingsolver's Taylor Greer, to "listen" attentively in their stock-taking, with the picaresque narrative all the while acknowledging and compiling that intractable diversity, the virtually whelming pluralism, in the human inventory of American life.

An account of this complex work of entering socially pluriform America and of meeting the strangers, as the picaresque existence demands its characters pursue the social realm, requires a particular order of exposition. In the following discussion, then, the first matter of attention is to portray briefly the totally ineluctable social and cultural pluralism of America, one of the central realities with which the new American picaresque must grapple. Even a quick vignette, clearly pointed, can convey something of the confusing and contentious character of a social reality that often results in forms of individual and group behaviors further widening the chasms between human beings, further paralyzing the possibilities of social interaction, and thus, further intensifying what are felt as "the pains of pluralism." This supplies backdrop, a mise-en-scène for the second matter of concern, the picaro's and picara's entrance into and witnessing of these social distresses of America.[1] Experiencing what seem the incoherence and assaults of a kind of social chaos, some people, the new American picaresque characters learn, recoil from intercourse with the American "others" and resort to those attitudes of protective self-segregation—personal superiority, ethnocentrism, xenophobia— that, as variants or offshoots of narcissism, defend the self with exacerbated and sometimes incorrigible self-regard and thus make the affronting other, the stranger, more alien still. Finally, however, some picaros and picaras in fact discover their own contagion, their own implication in the very social-relational ailments they have recorded in others. As their own social disabilities constrict the prospects for effectual encounter with the strangers out there, the American social inventory the picaresque has as a primary mission is jeopardized unless the picaros can find cure in their complex road encounters. Only with their narrative "selves" stripped of overweening personal regard can they even begin to deal with a world of American strangers.

The Pains of American Pluralism

In the middle 1980s, two wide-circulation magazines hired writers to take up the question of the possibility of any American "community" in the midst of the obviously and even wildly heterogeneous character of American social existence. *Harper's* magazine of March 1984 entitled its Forum section "Does America Still Exist?" and introduced the section with a nervous tone and a clear "worry" about the social diffusions created by rampant individualism and the cultural consequences of contending pluriform interest groups:

> The multiplication of so many [disparate] purposes has led to a good deal of confusion as to what, if anything, the dreamers of so many American dreams hold in common. Americans are forever asking the questions in variant forms—"Where is the lost consensus?" "What is the national interest?" Even a federation of sardonic democrats requires a store of common value and a lexicon of public myth, but among a people dedicated to the ruthless pursuit of individual liberty, how is it possible to sustain belief in a political [or social] entity greater than the sum of its collective desire? (p. 43)

To meet this perplexing question, the editors of the magazine charged writers like Michael Harrington, Richard Rodriguez, Eric Hoffer, and

Philip Berrigan to probe for evidence of any broad social agreements that might make for coherence. In celebration or lament about the great and real diversities of American society, the writers were able to answer "yes" to the question of whether America still exists, but, for the most part, they were forced to conclude that it exists only as the "collection" of sometimes highly competitive and contradictory desires, often in active conflict, among all of those discrete Americans. They had to confront the prospects that any "shared" society was probably a chimera and that a rampage of self-denominations and new tribalisms militated against the possibility of any perduring common life for the American peoples. Regarded as important by some of the writers and as less necessary by others, a standing social consensus among all of those individual, contending "dreamers" was not to be discerned by any of the *Harper's* writers.

For the editors of *Esquire*, in its Golden Collector's Issue of June 1985, the compelling question was about the location and terms of any presiding common "spirit" in pluralistic America that might comprise a current of unity, or at least some containing or centering pattern of values and convictions that could be identified as "The Soul of America." Instead of sending the assigned writers into the solitary tasks of thought-pieces as *Harper's* had done, the magazine pushed the likes of Sally Quinn, Ken Kesey, David Halberstam, George Plimpton, and Bob Greene, among others, out onto multiple and diverse American grounds—from Westwood, California, to New York City, from Portland, Oregon, to Lafayette, Louisiana—to have them attempt to spy out the unifying or connecting spirit that might reside among the diverse human shapes to be found in rodeo cohorts, workers in oyster bars, and laborers in oil fields; the life-forms of Vietnamese fishing villages, Pennsylvania mill towns, a Salt Lake City hotel staff, and Indiana basketball mania; the enclave cultures of the Philadelphia debutante circle, Houston opulence, a South Carolina military school, unemployed steel workers in Pittsburgh, the "Blues" crowd in Chicago, Jewish humorists in the Catskills, and sanctuary activists in Tucson. True to the commission, the writers dove into the more or less singular features of their assigned scenes, looked for the disclosive qualities of specific details, sought the sense of the unique action, the feeling of the immediate locale, and these they found and delivered. What they did not find was the social, spiritual tie that binds. The editors, apparently craving rubrics or labels that would organize all of the discrete scenarios in the issue, created headings like "Tenacity and Lasting Tradition" to contain alike the Wall Street process, the debutante balls, and the Albany oyster-shucker, and "Individuality and Reckless Imagination" to cover urban blues, the so-called borscht-belt, and the Arizona sanctuary movement, but the very headings themselves, in the sheer and obvious artificiality of the common denominators selected to reduce the diversities, signal the disparities and contradictions of the American social reality more than they manage to locate any really credible common grounds.[2]

The odds against the projects undertaken by *Harper's* and *Esquire*, according to many contemporary analysts, were perhaps too considerable even to challenge. Especially since the middle 1950s, Americans have become increasingly conscious of the multiplicities of backgrounds and outlooks, beliefs and aspirations, the contradictions of values, the competitive styles and shapes of being in the world, all resident in the variegated human quarters that comprise the social reality. The clashes and conflicts are everywhere evident, with different enclaves contesting, quietly or vociferously, directly or indirectly, about the nature, meaning, and modes of American life. More public militancy appeared in African-American claims on social existence, and a large and disaffected youth culture emerged visibly during the Vietnam era and continued to permute from one generation to the next. New shapes of feminist gender understanding and assertion began to take hold along with other kinds of movements designed for "liberation" from the regnant social hegemonies.[3] But the newly contending or newly visible cohorts were not confined only to broad racial, generational, and gender movements. New waves of immigration deposited in the land people of different color or culture—especially from the black Caribbean, Hispanic, Middle Eastern, and Asian worlds—in huge, unprecedented numbers, these too attempting to make places for themselves in America. Others, already present, retrieved or discovered and broadcasted the distinctiveness of their own "ethnicity," as more and more dedication to one's individual "difference" became not only a means of locating one's proper form of human association but also, once with the group, of securing or at least seeking social empowerment.[4] With new forms of possible "belonging" multiplying everywhere in "tribes" devoted to and grounded in visibly or palpably racial or gender or ethnic distinctiveness, the more abstract spheres of belief, values, and politics also began to emphasize the stuff of "difference." The splintering of long traditions of American religious life increased unabated, numerous religious or cultic formations arrived or erupted out of spiritual discontents or cravings in colorful new shapes, and new spiritualist orientations configured in individually customized terms.[5] Alongside these, the contemporary "culture wars," following on old ones long since present, began to occur in more public arenas and more vigorous terms as various, combative groups vied for the moral and intellectual life of the nation.[6] Standing political alliances grew more contentious one with another, and new single-issue politics among the citizenry, becoming more and more the order and mode of democratic partisanship, led to growing numbers of action committees, interest groups, and enclave communities, constituted out of sometimes unexpected caucuses and coalitions.[7] Withal, the possibilities of the broadest, most containing national community withered or dissipated in the face of, or just because of, Americans' having segregated themselves off into smaller and more immediate communities of identity, likeness, and self-interest. Publicly expressed cares for commonality seemed to many to be exclusive and self-advantaging, enclaves of "difference" seemed to promise more authentic community, and the very idea of any common culture seemed an insidious tool of the empowered and privileged.[8]

In such a chaotic situation, responses among the American people have varied. Celebrating the undeniable pluralism of the country as a valuable feature of American plenitude has remained possible for some, especially those enjoying or at least feeling a new kind of status and prospect predicated on some powerful American legal and institutional acknowledgments of richness in diversity. For others, however, the clear diversity has pointed to the clearly divergent lives of Americans and has led to concerns for the fates of any checks on rampant and greedy individualism, any politics of consensus, any care for the traditional values of the "common life," any shared discourse containing elements giving common cause, any broadly permeating and transmissible "soul" or "spirit" of America. For many thoughtful Americans, however, social pluralism has not been the problem: diversity does not necessarily mean divisiveness, much less fracture. The major difficulties, rather, seem to be in the ways many Americans have responded to this pluralism to style it as a kind of war of all against all. As the pluriform, contending parties have increasingly acted and reacted to one another in embittered, confrontational, and fractious tones and terms, those "different" from one become stranger still, not genuine countrypersons anymore but affronting and threatening aliens, even enemies. Among those seeking what they regard as the once-possessed but now "lost consensus," senses of alienation in the midst of discordant pluralisms apparently run deep. But even those who have prized and sponsored diversity the most, in recognizing and sometimes participating in the often vitriolic behaviors, have had reason to worry that the disparate threads of the social fabric cannot be raveled. For most, the question "Does America still exist?"

except as the cumulative dream of its myriad, diverse "dreamers" poses an unavoidable and perhaps ultimately unresolvable social problematic.

The dilemma reverberates dramatically in the numerous, cacophonous, contending, and highly combative voices that call for public attention, each claiming to be the vox populi or the only right and exclusive counsel for American society and each, thus, raising the dread, the suspicions, or the ire of some "other" set of Americans. So emphatically different is one group from the next that their very languages fail to communicate, creating the kinds of frustrations that lead only to louder voices, further misunderstandings, deeper distrust. At one metaphorical level, a certain kind of imagery for such a social situation parallels the biblical story of "Babel" and its difficult aftermath. As the story goes, the achievement of the tower to heaven seemed possible, at least to begin with, only because those human beings laboring at it shared a universal tongue, a language and a discourse, that enabled their mutual understanding and common pursuit. An unfaithful, untoward, and arrogant effort in the biblical depiction, the work on the tower is finally stymied by the divine action of introducing into the human world the multiplicity of tongues, the numerous languages that would separate the people, distance them in understanding, segregate them into spheres of discrete discourse, all further reinforcing the "fallen" character of human history by alienating people from each other. The subsequent linguistic and semantic pluralism and the attending divisions among the people, in brief, can thus be understood as a curse or punishment, interfering with the fullest possibilities of human community by disabling any common forms of discourse.[9] The socially "other," in such a world, is automatically a stranger at the gate, potentially an ally or friend but also, potentially, a danger and an enemy, and the human world is now full of such strangers, destined, without any common tongue, to remain strangers.

In the contemporary American case, such a "Babel of tongues," with accompanying dire social effects, has often been perceived or experienced as "the pains of pluralism." Whatever profits there are in human multiplicity, the fractures and divisions among people in the society also suggest the expenses, especially when the interspaces between one and very different kinds of "others" are filled with condescensions, fears, distrusts, or hostilities and when anyone's survey of the whole of the social gamut— with its segmented, kaleidoscopic, and apparently incommensurable character—can lead to sensations of its altogether alien and alienating aspect. When such a social situation persists, it generates or fuels certain psychological mechanisms: it makes the unfamiliar person arriving to one not only a "stranger" but an "other," evoking suspicion or trepidation just because of his or her otherness, and the more or less inevitable result is the anticipation of the stranger as a kind of threat, in one or more of several broad degrees. At one level of expectation, the stranger approaches simply as a figure quite reasonably and innocuously unaware of one's own ways, values, and commitments, and thus—in his or her trespassing ignorance—as an intruder on them until necessarily and properly disabused, somehow mildly instructed or invited into an amiable or at least tolerable familiarity. In another degree, of course, the defensive prescience one possesses in regarding the oncoming stranger, especially when the visible signs trigger negative stereotypes, elicits a tendency to reduce the other's humanity, to see him or her, even in sympathy, as everything one is not nor can abide, to locate in the stranger an intolerably alien character that smacks of inferiority. At an even more intense degree, the preconditioned stranger looms up in one's imagination in ways that make that alien an ominous and dangerous figure, almost if not entirely emblematic of whatever human shape fills one with fear or loathing or both, the sheer enemy, the social bête noire. Such preformulations of the stranger have always been with the human world, there is little reason to doubt, but they perhaps intensify or at least have more pervasive and immediate consequence in a contemporary social-psychological context wherein the projected strangers are not only foreign and distant but also American and nearby, not just occasional interlopers in one's territory but inhabitants of American ground itself, not few to be encountered but legion in their numbers, given the make-up of pluralistic, contending formations of the human reality of the country.

When these psychological complexes have taken hold, when such preformulations are no longer only tacit attitudes but become explicit behavioral indices, the pathologies of interpersonal existence appear in that self, those selves, whose responses to the others approaching or encountered reveal the pains and reflect the underlying dis-eases of a tumultuous American social pluralism. Each of these social debilitations, in its way, is a permutation or enlargement of a kind of narcissism that appears—quietly or egregiously—when a self, for its own self-protection, recoils from the different, the other, and retreats either into the stronghold of its perceived superiority or into the fortress of its perceived likeness with "familiars" in some segregated enclave, or both.[10] When on display in the American social realm, such self-focus, in the mildest cases, results generally in a kind of supercilious attitude and response to the innocently ignorant stranger, that benighted other whom the self quickly dismisses or over against whom the self simply asserts and exercises a surpassing and imperious will in order to bring the "different" one into the territory of personal familiarity. This a social form of the malady of narcissism, a kind of self-centrism bulwarking one in the face of plural-ism. In other cases, when the approaching stranger's altogether alien form of the human species makes the self doubt any humanity, or so fills one with repugnance that that human shape is intolerable, the response is disgust and avoidance or, if the other becomes unavoidable, disdain-ful treatment and prompt retreat back into one's own kind. This response represents a kind of intra-cultural ethnocentrism, a social ailment again associated with the pains of pluralism, an enlarging self-regard to make the self coextensive with the human ways of one's own enclave or vice versa and a refusal to acknowledge the ways of the other. In those inten-sive cases wherein the stranger presents to the self the terribly and fear-fully threatening other, the dangerously "foreign" form, the stranger who would or could somehow destroy one's self or way, the repulsive char-acter is again present, now more insidiously or ominously, and the reac-tions can range from suspicion, terror, and paranoia to anger, hatred, and violence. Again perhaps predictable in one suffering pluralism as a curse, this kind of response, fear of all but the comforting familiar, extends narcissism into the social neurosis of xenophobia.

When any of these social-psychological malaises reside at the level of attitude or disposition, predicated on stereotypes, they represent psy-chological afflictions of the self in isolation, compounding problems of psychic alienation and blockading the capacities for mutual understand-ing, much less empathy, or even cordial responsiveness. When they eventuate in the active sphere of social relations, when they translate into the world of behaviors, such ailments create huge impasses in so-cial existence. For those afflicted, the pains of pluralism—the daily pre-sentation of all of that human otherness—are suffered on the pulses. Pre-cluding even the effort to locate a common tongue, the social "dis-eases" drive deeper still the wedges of distrust or hostility already there be-tween people in a framework of what seems uncontrollable and acutely felt social and cultural pluralism, the overwhelming world of Ameri-can human heterogeneity. Surrounded by strangers, Narcissus is not tempted even to gaze upon the other. The power of sympathy is not strained by overwork, and the impossibility of any common life is a foregone conclusion.[11]

If the diseases are not suffered equally or epidemically, the pains would seem broadly endemic among those Americans who, in their various ways, care about the society. For some of these persons, especially those for whom the pathological retreats have become the only ostensible recourse, the human pluralities and diversities "out there" in the socialscape will probably remain always painfully "other," disgusting or threatening or, at best, odd. But even for others apparently less afflicted, those decidedly more prepared to embrace or at least to make do with the pluriform character of the social motley, the pains of pluralism are nonetheless felt, if only because they see and despair of the widespread narcissism, ethnocentrism, and xenophobia quartered in that accumulation of "sardonic democrats" who are their countrypersons and whose attitudes and actions threaten to rend the social fabric altogether.

The Social Witness of the New American Picaresque

Even on the face of the matter, the new American picaresque figure's situation, style, and charge in living out a narrative life suggest that, even with the initiating senses of exile and alienation, he or she must nevertheless confront the panoramic social world, must meet and engage the American "others" as a matter of literary self-definition. And at first blush, the frequently insouciant and even feckless style of the figures might suggest that approaching the wildly pluralistic spheres of human reality in contemporary America, entering the variegated social spaces undeniably full of all kinds and degrees of strangers, is a prospect that for them fails to daunt. Then, too, the reflexive alacrity that allows the picara and picaro to avoid harm's way—to "juggle" danger like Doctorow's Billy Bathgate—is matched equally with their standing or required temperament of equanimity, that trait that makes them slow to cut distinctions between high and low, tasteful and seedy, noteworthy and mundane. Such attributes would seem to equip the picaresque protagonists perfectly to cover even the most contested grounds and the most contentious strangers encountered along the way. Moreover, even if unawares, they operate within a narrative mission of broad social inventory, and this picaresque contract itself not only requires the focal figures to be open to all comers, however strange, and to follow their noses for the next episode into new social territories, however alien, but to trespass all manner of social boundaries among those in the pluralistic *galeria*.

Nevertheless, the new picaro or picara is frequently also a sufferer of the "pains of pluralism" because he or she, usually aware from the outset of the social situation of divisiveness, fracture, and fear, often enters this pluralistic American social space with some trepidation, feeling somehow estranged in the face of its alien and alienating or at least whelming character. But bent by the narrative form to be a vehicle for American discovery and stock-taking, the picaro or picara cannot blink or avoid the "foreign" and combative social parties and must engage them on course. Indeed, often just such concern about the confusions and contentions stemming from pluralistic life becomes a catalyzing factor for the picaro's socially encyclopedic journey.

Many of the new American picaros enter American "social space" acutely conscious of the painful pluralism that, in their perceptions, besets the life of the country and makes it seem alien, confusing, and often troubling to them. Bill Moyers, in an opening reflection on the American social reality, reports that "I wanted to hear people speak for themselves" because he could not "any longer be sure who spoke for whom," given the fact that, even as he writes in 1971, "there were [now] thirty-five million . . . of us, [and] we seemed more raucous than ever."[12] Walt Harrington, a white man with an African-American wife, who has convinced himself for years that his was "a life lived across the color line,"[13] informs the reader that his trip—his effort to "go out and travel America's parallel black world" (p. 3)—was more or less suddenly compelled because of a racist joke told by a white dentist while Harrington, in the chair, has his mouth crammed with dental dough. This joke meets with silence because Harrington's own white dentist and the attending white nurse both know Harrington's wife, but, of the "five thousand, maybe ten thousand" such jokes heard and shrugged off in his life, Harrington observes, this one stabs him "with a deep, sharp pain" (p. 1). Well before arriving in New York City, Joe Buck in James Leo Herlihy's *Midnight Cowboy* both acknowledges the pluralistic social order and, in his exile, suffers it, as revealed in his recurring dream:

> [It is] a dream of an endless chain of people marching across the side of the world. From his vantage point in some chill and dark and silent corner he could see them coming. . . . There were people of all kinds, bus drivers and nuns, musicians and soldiers and ten-cent store girls; there were Chinamen and pilots, hillbillies and fat men and red-headed women; you could find miners and bank clerks there, millionaires, store detectives, swamis, babies, grandmothers, thieves; look for any kind of person . . . and there would be one, a whore, a dwarf, a saint, a crazy man, cop, teacher, reporter, pretty girl, bookkeeper, shortstop, ragpicker. There seemed to be every kind of person but his own. He made many attempts to join them

[but] . . . the dreamer was forced to remain always on his chill and dark and silent edge.[14]

For his own part, John Steinbeck understands full well in setting out on his picaresque course that one aspect of America making it the "monster land" he regards it is its individualistic, variable, and frequently confusing and contradictory human array. One region of the country seems beforehand especially foreboding to him because of its opaque and alien character: having "moved through a galaxy of states, each with its own character, and through clouds and myriads of people, . . . ahead of me [there] lay an area, the South, that I dreaded to see. . . . Here, I knew, were pain and confusion and all the manic results of bewilderment and fear. And the South being a limb of the nation, its pain spreads out to all America."[15] Such examples of the picaro's concern for the distresses of pluralism multiply throughout the narratives of the new American picaresque, but, even realizing in advance the frights, pains, and bewilderments of a divisively pluralistic American social motley, the picaro qua picaro has little choice but to push ahead into that complex territory. Steinbeck knows, as do others, that the dreaded or not "social space," however much a theater of the pains of pluralism as felt by Americans, must be assayed.

On the road, in the narrative engagements with those people hitherto complete strangers to the picaro and picara, the speculative diagnosis—Americans suffering the throes of their own pluralistic society in worry, fear, suspicion, repugnance, and conflict—bears out in fact and in case after case. For example, in a foreshadowing created out of retrospection, presented *after* the picaresque tour has been accomplished, Moyers notes that "whenever I traveled, and no matter how innocent or casual my purpose, the people I met wanted to talk about the tribulations of America: war, campus unrest, crime, inflation, pollution, racism, and drugs" and, in view of the deep contentions among Americans on these and other matters, battles rendering Americans strangers to each other, he adds that "hardly a day passed that would be free of some demonstration of our woes" (p. ix). In Richmond, Indiana, he finds neighbors suspicious of neighboring Earlham College, a place where, he is told, many townspeople, especially American Legion members, "'believed some Communist influences were at work'" (p. 25). In this same venue, among the legionnaires, Moyers hears antagonisms toward college protestors, draft dodgers, money-spoiled children, parents who fail to provide religious upbringing, and, of course, attorneys.[16] In Little Rock he converses with a woman who informs him "'I used to be a helluva lot more of a Christian than I am now. My child is not going to [be bused to an integrated] school with the criminals they have over there. . . . They want to destroy us. They want to destroy our whole damn world'" (p. 293). In San Francisco Moyers locates "in the back streets and basements of Chinatown . . . a new rancor, nourished by resentments of a generation that determines it will not be 'the white man's yellow man'" (p. 206), a painful bitterness emanating from the kinds of childhood experiences reported to him by Loni Ding Welsh of having "'felt singled out for my Chineseness . . . and [of getting] that Ching-Chong-Chinese thing, you know, like burning with anger, when white schoolgirls would catch me if I came home and form a little ring around me while they sang this insulting ditty to me and knowing that my parents had forbidden me to get mad at them [or] . . . to say anything to them.'" Immediately beforehand, however, Ms. Welsh had revealed her own kind of childish ethnocentricity, at least at the level of attitude, smoldering in her perhaps because her parents insisted she not fight back: she remembers, out of her own sense of superiority, having asked herself "why are we doing these things [having to endure affronts 'with grace']? We were better than the whites. We were more refined, we were more self-restrained, we could take insults with dignity'" (p. 207). Among this random collection of what *Harper's* called "sardonic democrats," the idea of, much less the desire for, any common grounds with other, quite different sardonic democrats evaporates into an atmosphere of general antagonisms.

Mort Rosenblum's *Back Home* recapitulates such "pains of pluralism" and extends the picaresque survey. After years as a foreign correspondent, now tracking through the American social kaleidoscope in search of the country, he finds his curiosity struck in Boise, Idaho, for one instance, by "an American flag the size of a schooner sail"[17] and pays a visit to its owner, one J. R. Simplot. This billionaire potato tycoon's fortune had grown from a drying process he invented that allowed him to seize on military contracts and, later, to connect with a new "slick outfit named McDonald's" (p. 236). Although America has been good to him, Simplot allows, he despises some recent changes: he sees too many foreign imports of goods and products and too many jobs lost to foreign competitors; he is "especially worried about communists" and is "equally concerned about immigrants" and how to "keep 'em out" (p. 237). The "flip-side" of Simplot arrives, briefly, one page later, in Carl Yanick, who, despite an earlier, hardscrabble hobo's existence, "loves America just as much" as Simplot but who nonetheless worries about the president, Ronald Reagan, that "'actor,'" "'war-

monger,'" who says of Central America "'they can go kosher for all I care,'"
and who responds about African Americans "'I don't think it will be fifty
years before they take over the country, but by then maybe they'll be pretty
good people'" (p. 238). These Idaho encounters follow, among numerous
other instances for Rosenblum, from his inventory of the Atlanta of the
"New South." There he finds a "black mayor" also "statesman and diplo-
mat," black police leaders, black urban leaders, and the first African-American archbishop, but he also finds a recorded phone message gleefully contending that "'AIDS is the new white hope'" (p. 128) because the affliction
is "'killing niggers by the thousands'" and "'niggers are helping it along
with their sharing of needles and free love'" (p. 127). Somewhat later Rosenblum encounters Wesley Walraven, "a former Eagle Scout and biology
teacher," now the sheriff of "all-white Forsyth County" in Georgia (p. 128),
who despairs of "'a definite area of hatred'" to be seen in Nazi flags, new
paramilitary and survivalist groups, and the skinhead attitude (p. 129).
And, after a number of other, comparable episodes of suspicion and contention spotted in Americans caught in the pluralistic agon, Rosenblum
records an account of his exit "interview" in the United States as he heads
through the District of Columbia for Dulles International Airport with an
Iranian cabdriver. The cabby brings up the situation of American hostages
in Lebanon and argues that Terry Anderson and others were "'Spy, all
spies'" and that "'you Americans don't know anything'" (p. 445). To Rosenblum's retorts about Anderson's not being a spy, about having spent a
lot of time in Lebanon, and about the cabby's being a moron, the Iranian
screams "'Racist! . . . Typical American racist! . . . Why do you Americans
go to Lebanon? Why do you go anywhere? . . . [and, then, with no discernible sense of irony] You should stay in your own country'" (p. 446).

    As with *Listening to America* and *Back Home*, such examples placidly
or strenuously abound in many other texts of the new American picaresque, and they not only point to the socially endemic conflicts occurring
in the pluralistic realm, obvious enough in most cases, but also display the
associated anxieties, pains, and resentments. They reveal, through the
enormous inventory taken of American voices and behaviors, something
of the ways that American social pluralism, diversity, heterogeneity, have
whelmed many in the population and have in turn created in some those
self-superior certitudes, those intra-cultural ethnocentrisms, and those
xenophobic frights with which Americans regard the alien "other" Americans in their midst, all of which go to make those strangers "stranger still."
In *Travels with Charley*, for instance, three quickly successive episodes drive
the painful predicaments home. First, Steinbeck watches in New Orleans

the performance of a group dubbed "the Cheerladies," a cadre of middle-aged white women, inflaming a raucous crowd by practicing "the demented cruelty of egocentric children" as they scream obscenities at a little black girl, accompanied by marshals, making her way into a schoolhouse. This incident, which filled him with "a shocked and sickened sorrow" (p. 256), leads almost immediately, at least in narrative time, to an encounter with one Monsieur Ci Git, who despairs about the Cheerladies, who refers to himself as "'an enlightened Southerner'" and who, though acknowledging that as Steinbeck says "'the Negroes want to be people'" (p. 260), responds by observing he would be "'content enough'" for it *to happen* but, then, too, steeped as he is in the life of the region, he "'wouldn't understand it'" (p. 261) if it came to pass. Within a short span, beating a retreat out of the city, Steinbeck the next day, while stopped at a hamburger stand, gets begged for a ride by a lanky, young white man attempting to make his way toward Jackson and Montgomery. With this new passenger, the conversation turns again to the Cheerladies, a topic still very much on Steinbeck's mind, but this young man delights in the group, their willingness to sacrifice themselves to the cause: "'God bless them, somebody got to keep the goddamn niggers out of our schools'" (p. 268) and, willing himself to sacrifice similarly, he adds "'I'll sell my life . . . but I aim to kill me a whole goddamn flock of niggers before I do'" (p. 269).

Although the racial distrusts and animosities found by Moyers, Rosenblum, Steinbeck, and others are scattered broadly about among some of the various people encountered by the new American picaros and picaras in general, these American "quarrels" are not confined only or even mainly to the American South or to the white people met along the way or to black-white forms of embitteredness. Ethnic, national, and tribal enclaves—Hispanics, Middle Easterners, Asians, Native Americans, Koreans, and newly asserted ethnic groups—enter the general fray. Religious contentions abound. Broad sweeps of virulent anti-Semitism appear, Protestants pit themselves against Catholics and against each other. American Muslims are regarded with the deepest suspicion by many. Nor, of course, are the disputes and the angers always voiced on racial, ethnic, religious, or national-origin grounds. In Harrington's "bull-sessions" with students at his own old high school in Crete, Illinois, for example, he locates a world of insult and indignation, anger and hostility, toward whites among the black students when he interviews them by themselves and a different but parallel such world of slights and resentments among the white students when interviewed by themselves, and these worlds collide in an accusatory shouting match when all come together for conversations with Harrington, even with white turning on white and black on black (pp. 438–42) along class and wealth lines. A rather different kind of conflict among Americans appears to Hampton Sides in the Rainbow Family, a kind of loosely connected New Age, hippie, organicist, naturalist, communalist group contending with McDonald's (and thus Rosenblum's J. R. Simplot) and Burger King, on the one hand, and with local law-enforcement bodies and the National Forest Service on the other.[18] For another stripe of instance, duplicated from time to time in other picaresque inventories, Bill Bryson's temporary talking partner in Iowa City expresses a middle-aged distrust and contempt for the current college generation: "'I may have been that stupid once, but I was never that shallow. . . . they don't know *anything*. . . . they don't even know who's running for President. They've never heard of Nicaragua. It's scary.'"[19] Moyers, Steinbeck, Rosenblum, and others spy out these cases of generational hostility, and others as well in cases of labor and industry pitted, class antinomies, gender battles, single-issue socio-political and -cultural wars, farms versus cities, regional attitudes in embodied combativeness, straight/ gay clashes, ecological disputes, religious and intra-religious hostilities, and so on.

Indeed, for some Americans, this or that picaro or picara discovers, the world of strangers assaults to the point of requiring a radical retreat into personal or group solidarities and segregations, even xenophobia. It is a social world, the picaresque figures learn, in which *many* Americans distrust and fear *some* other Americans, in which *some* Americans are disaffected at best with *most* other Americans. And it is a world in which a *few* Americans are hostile to *all* others, as B. C. Hall and C. T. Wood discover. While attempting to get a good look at the Mississippi River on the outskirts of a town named Tomato perched along the Arkansas/Tennessee patch of the river, they blunder onto the property of a shotgun-wielding river rat. Without waiting to permit them to explain, this man, with a "feral look in his eye," cocks his weapon, yells at them, and chases them away: "'Whur the hale you thank yore going? . . . Yore own my place, sonsabitches, I could kill ye. . . . You git off my property, git away from this river.'"[20]

While few picaresque episodes of social conflict are as dramatic as this, the segmentations and hostilities of the social realm are also reflected in the world of social and cultural politics in numerous quarters. Sociopolitical conclaves or coalitions emerge (creating odd, even paradoxical partnerships), new communal cadres tribe into separate spaces, social or topographical, militia and identity groups move into areas of perceived mutuality and, in some vivid cases, geographical enclaves, all bent on survival in the face of enemies. Quite different "others" threaten "survival" from one of these bands to the next, but, in contending with their own perceived and designated American "strangers," each of these American groups seems to grow ever more hostile *to* the other and more and more frequently either to run *from* the other or to aggress *on* the other. They find refuge in interest and loyalty "armies" or "tribes" wherein they might also have safety in numbers and the power of numbers for contesting the "polar" others—feminist/anti-feminist, Pro-Choice/Pro-Life, Aryan Nation/Nation of Islam—or all "others" different from them in general. Senses of dislocation, betrayal, and fracture at the level of the national life reach embodied concern, fear, and distrust in the individual members of the local citizenry, with many believing some *other* Americans are foisting upon the country some intolerable versions of America. As Harrison Salisbury noted about the Americans encountered during his travels:

> At the bottom of all this lay that sense of alienation which I had found in my crisscrossing of the country, that inarticulate feeling that things had gone wrong; that the country was not what we had grown up supposing it was; that belief that it was not living up to the ideals of the forefathers; that, as Bly says, "the ministers lie, the professors lie, the television lies, the priests lie." The President had lied and Congress had lied and the newspapers had lied. Frustration had boiled up into one movement after another: the movement in the South; the movement in the colleges; the movement against the war; the movement for environment (against government and corporations); the movement for consumerism and Nader (against big business and government); the movement against Washington; against the media; against the White House; against New York City; for change in the church; against the CIA; against the young and against the old.
>
> Always *against* something, something *big* and if the drive was stated in positive terms—*for* civil rights, *for* women's rights, black rights, Indian rights, homosexual rights—it was against the status quo.[21]

These observations, published in 1976, sketch the broadest terms of some of the social divides creating conflict among Americans, while Salisbury's narrative also recognizes the ways such fractures play out in the smaller hostilities with one another felt by Americans estranged from each other. Two decades later, as many subsequent American picaros would discover, the social splintering and the accompanying alienation, suspicion, and anger had not abated. The "strangers" in the social midst were on the increase and were, if anything, even more dreaded, threatening, or enraging than ever.

Now, of course, in its canvas of the social reality, the new American picaresque discovers more than the outrage and embitterment of Americans, more than their estrangements from one another, and more than their frequent and presumptive personal superiorities, reflexive ethnocentrisms, or imbedded xenophobias that compound the pains of pluralism. There are too those kinder, gentler Americans with refined or heightened senses of the diversity of human kinds as a positive element of democratic possibility, with higher degrees of tolerance for the "others" in America, with more irenic regard for great varieties of human types, and with even a kind of ingrained instinct and ability to draw the stranger, no matter how very different, in as a familiar. But even they, the picaros often learn in the course of the social stock-taking the new American picaresque involves, fear for the fate of the social "whole" in view of the obvious and painful rifts among their countrypersons. For his or her own part, the picaro or picara must regard the socially diseased and the socially healthy with equal eye. Like Steinbeck's responses to the Cheerladies in New Orleans, the picaro's witness of the social scene might at times fill him with sickness and sorrow or, as with David Lamb's location of Mike Wisdom's tender mercies toward Wray, Colorado, the engagement may lead to respect and admiration,[22] but the former as well as the latter belongs to and must be included in the picaresque social inventory. Thus, in the midst of alien, alienated, and alienating social territories, the picaro or picara must attempt to maintain that defining equilibrium and equanimity, that openness and innocence with respect to all manner of encounters, that practiced diffidence that is slow to judge.

But this requisite temperament and the capacity for such social engagement are not simply present as automatic traits; in this picaro or that, indeed, such traits must be learned or relearned on the road, often against considerable odds stacked up by the picaro's own social-psychological biases, fears, and retreats. Ironically, then, some of the new American picaresque narratives, even those most intent on grappling with the strange, multiplicitous forms of humankind in America, put on display picaros and picaras not only in pain because of their concerns for the fate of common life under the onslaught of pluralism but also, consciously or not, ill with those same deeper ailments they have spotted in the general social motley. These picaros and picaras suffer the afflictions of narcissism, ethnocentrism, and xenophobia just as much as those they witness, and, without remedy, these maladies preclude the proper picaresque life of direct engagement with the socially "other" scattered about the national tour.

The Social Maladies of the New American Picaro

If a primary job of social work pursued by the new American picaro and picara is to engage the human *galeria,* the varied and disparate types in the "social motley," and to collect them as the multiplicitous human reality of the American panorama, that is one way of observing generally what Peter Jenkins, among other picaros, expresses specifically about his motives for trekking the country—namely, "to find the real people out there, what they were made of, who they were, how they lived."[23] On this score, the effort for the picaro is rather like attempting to apprehend the scene "from the natives' point of view,"[24] as anthropologist Clifford Geertz puts it. Although the picaro's course is one much more of ricochet, blunder, fortuity, and randomness than the designed purposes of the trained and dedicated ethnographer, the picaro or picara too must practice the strategic arts of gaining access to alien grounds, penetrating into the worlds of the strangers, operating there with a capacity for attentiveness, and rendering the others' ways in ways true to them. This labor and the picaresque inventory surely represent a more rapid and inadvertent anthropology—no formal education in participant/observer methods, no research design, no months or years of "field work" at one site—but those American picaros and picaras most intent on getting past the veils of strangeness shrouding the human other, given the American Babel, face comparable obstacles to inquiry and hazards to insight at home as the far-flung anthropologists encounter abroad, in the Ozarks as much as in Geertz's Bali, in Trenton as much as in his Morocco. That work of engaging the stranger, as Moyers, Jenkins, Laurel Lee, Steinbeck, Rosenblum, and others learn, is no small task, entailing as it does the overcoming of one's own superior disregard of the other's view, one's own habits of cultural "centrism," one's own trepidation about the threats the other poses. These ills of social relation, without finding cure, would certainly prevent the picaro's ability and credibility in taking the broadly neutral social inventory indispensable to the narrative form, and yet the new American picaresque presents just such diseases in its picaros and picaras, themselves legatees of Babel quite as much as those strange and contentious Americans the picaro or picara meets along the road.

In some cases, the responsive or relational failures showing up in the picaro are mild enough, simple breaches of local etiquette in highly pluralistic America, and can be quickly realized by the picaro or picara or gently corrected by the stranger who is willing to school the traveler on the near-at-hand forms of identity, sense-making, and behavior. These problems admit of easy enough repair. For instance, riding along, shortly into the first chat with the hospitable rancher Jack Dawson, David Lamb poses what seems to him an innocuous enough question by asking "how many head of cattle he had" (p. 47): "[Dawson] pretended to be occupied dodging ruts in the track and didn't answer. When I asked again, he said he didn't have an exact count. 'Well, *about* how many do you have?' I pressed, so lamebrained I was missing the message. Finally, he said, 'That's a question you don't ask in Montana. Just like I wouldn't come into your home in the city and ask you how much money you had in your bank account, you don't ask a man in Montana how many head he runs'" (p. 47). The particular conversation ends there, with Lamb disabused for a time of his ethnographic default and, now chastened, able to resume the engagement with Dawson and his family. This kind of intra-cultural ethnocentrism—the city slicker's unwittingly rude violation of rural manners—is comparably repeated and finds rebuff time and again by the picaros, but if left uncorrected such affronts by the picaro would preclude access to "native ground" and prevent his fuller engagement with the stranger.

Another variant of the remediable ethnocentric slip comes to the fore when William Least Heat Moon receives his own Montana comeuppance while seeking to help a "severely handicapped" boy having trouble filling his thermos from a mountain stream:

> He burbled again, then lost his footing, and fell hard on the wet rocks. The gush hit the flask and kicked it away. I went to help him.
> "Leave him alone!" someone shouted over the crash of water. A man who looked as if he had swallowed a nail keg came toward us. "Let *him* do it. You'll make him weak if you do it for him. He's my son. He understands. . . . He'll never survive if he gets turned into a pussy."[25]

To Least Heat Moon's insistent "'he'll never survive if he dies filling a thermos jug,'" as he and the father watch the boy continue to struggle, the man replies "'Malarkey! . . . this little gimp's got more white-water time than most of those canoe daredevils, and he can't even swim. Just never learned fear'" (pp. 291–92). Least Heat Moon relents, the boy delightedly succeeds, the interloper's socially intrusive right-mindedness, having met vigorous rejoinder, recedes into a more wonted picaresque diffidence, and the talk switches to the quality of the water, only now with the picaro's broader access to the locals' lives "from the natives' point of view." Such episodes of innocent and accidental effrontery, mild redress, and *then* fuller engagement are repeated again and again by the new American picaro or picara as he or she "blunders" along, however affably, trespassing into unknown social territories while yet, all the while, quite ignorant of the local ways and means out in the American provinces.[26]

Any full access to the strangers and their inlooks and outlooks, in some other kinds of cases met en route, meets blockade just because the other so frontally offends or assaults the picaro or picara that his or her defining equanimity cannot be fully mustered, much less sustained. When faced off by the shotgun toting river-rat, Hall and Wood do not stick around for fuller picaresque encounter with the alien other any longer than Lars Eighner practices any studied and congenial tactic of achieving relationship with the various police officers who roust him from his makeshift habitats in the parks. Filled with repugnance by the ugly scene created by the New Orleans "Cheerladies," Steinbeck can put them in the social inventory not by getting their senses of the matter directly from these "natives" but only through his own speculations about their motives and lives. His complete disdain for them makes them subhuman for him, and he simply cannot, will not, engage them. Or, in response to the hitchhiking youngster who admires the Cheerladies and who vows "'to kill me a whole goddamn flock of niggers'" (p. 269), Steinbeck dismisses him from the camper, puts him abruptly back out on the road, with a threat of menace. Like the river-rat, this young man appears in the composite social census of the new American picaresque as irredeemably alien, not to be known. Even though Steinbeck had earlier claimed in retrospection, regarding his time on the road, that "from start to finish I found no strangers" (p. 207), the Cheerladies and this hitchhiker, among some others, apparently do not qualify as sufficiently human to earn his anthropological efforts.

For yet one more example of the irredeemably "other," there is the experience of Mort Rosenblum, who for most of the narrative in *Back Home* proves out as a splendid exemplar of the picaro's deliberative balance and studied diffidence. In the closing episode, however, when challenged by the Iranian cabdriver's vitriol against Americans, Rosenblum cannot at last contain himself and, on departing the taxi, tells the man that "'one thing I really love about this country is that it still makes room for fuckheads like you'" (p. 446). As with other picaros in some cases of the lapsed neutrality that prevents careful attunement to the other, Steinbeck and Rosenblum realize retrospectively in these instances that they have foreclosed on the picaro's proper mode of engaging the other's ways of being in the world. With respect to the hitchhiker, Steinbeck candidly admits "it's true I goaded him" (p. 270) and recognizes that "if I could have kept my mouth shut I might have learned something of value" (p. 268). Rosenblum, immediately before quarreling with the cabdriver, thinks him "articulate, intelligent," stands to learn from him, and begins this last interview "scribbling like crazy" (p. 445). Immediately after the screaming match and the angry and sarcastic parting shot at the Iranian, Rosenblum *perhaps* senses his default on the journalist's calm reserve that has stood by him so well in his picaresque career when he adds "'Have a nice day'" (p. 446). These and other comparable, occasional breakdowns of the picaro's characteristic "style"— the loss of the habits of self-control and of the open manner of even-tempered and amiable engagement—do not invalidate the figure as picaro or picara in general, however, so much as they lend additional credence to the narrative survey: *some* strangers in the pluralistic panorama just naturally insult the picaros or aggravate them or anger them; the road runs long; patience sometimes runs quite short.

While the picaros' innocent blunders against the others' modes and manners can be quickly corrected and the failure of *constant* picaresque equanimity is more or less predictable and easily reparable, other shapes of self-centering, however much unconscious or innocent, do not come in for such ready solution, especially when these appear as full-blown "dis-eases" of social relation visibly deep and chronic in this picara or that picaro. Two more or less obvious cases of this stripe of extreme debilitation are indicative. For the one instance, the picara Oedipa Maas in Thomas Pynchon's *The Crying of Lot 49*, as her confusing movement in complex and opaque American social space pulls her further into paranoia, increasingly exhibits a totalizing form of self-absorption that "inventories" the others met on course only through her clouded, anxious, and wary eyes. For the other instance, there is the picaro Bryson in *The Lost Continent*, whose largely unearned cynicism about virtually everything outside of himself both stems from and adds to such concentrated self-regard in him that the strangers he encounters on the road are approached, cataloged, and repudiated as nothing other than occasions for his snappy wit or objects only of his careless scorn. In both cases, the picaresque social survey is present, the picaro is operative, and the *galeria* gradually comes into view, but these kinds of exemplars of the new picaresque must be read in terms of specific authorial tactics, as their narrational tilts instruct the reader, that present the strangers at roadside only as refracted through picaros who, for whatever reasons, cannot or will not prove capable of meeting the strangers in their own terms, of seeking, much less gaining access to their native points of view. And, although in less debilitating terms and less radical ways, many other picaros and picaras—even some of those most strenuously bent on relating to the American others—nonetheless also suffer, at least temporarily, from some form of these ailments of self-absorption to the extent that their "social work" within the new American picaresque is stymied for them in this or that intermittent episode.

One kind of case in point arrives on the pages when the picaro, quite beyond accidents of etiquette or occasional gaps of patience, not innocently but willfully pushes himself into the scene of an episode as more "knowing," as more masterful in experience or scruple, as personally and self-evidently better, or as belonging to some higher "caste" than the strangers at hand in the episode. For example, with another of his hitchhikers, this one reluctant to become a passenger, Steinbeck completely discomfits the stranger by presuming the superseding right to invade the other's privacy. He presses a ride on an "old Negro who trudged with heavy heels in the grass-grown verge beside the concrete road" and presses a question on him as well: "'how do you feel about what's going on . . . [about the schools and the sit-ins]?'" The old man's squirming response is only that "'I don't know nothing about that, captain, sir'" (p. 264), and Steinbeck, out of the corner of his eye, "could see that he had drawn away and squeezed himself against the far side of the cab." Remembering even in the midst of this situation a former African-American employee who had advised him that taciturnity and refusal to be implicated were standard black defenses against encroaching whites ("'I've been practicing to be a Negro a long time'"), Steinbeck, after a long silence, generously tells his present passenger "'I won't ask you any more questions'" (p. 265). Unnerved nevertheless, the man says he lives close by and asks to be dropped off, and Steinbeck, watching in the rearview mirror as the old man trudges along again, realizes that "he didn't live nearby at all, but walking was safer than riding with me" (p. 266). But to realize a failure of encounter is not necessarily to learn a lesson for Steinbeck. In an earlier episode, stopped for a night in a motel cabin in the mountains of Washington state, he had also inserted himself quite obtrusively, exercising himself on his superior knowledge, into the lives of the proprietors. Though he has been practicing to be a picaro for a long time, he forfeits again on the requisite diffidence by taking sides with twenty-year-old Robbie in a quarrel with his father about the son's going to New York City to become a hairdresser. Caring less to permit the two to speak themselves than to display himself, Steinbeck, full of superior urbanity, preens himself on his knowledge of the city, instructs the father on the potentials of hairdressing, and, withal, simply forecloses on the picaro's studied and sustained neutrality and equanimity (pp. 172–75).

But Steinbeck is scarcely alone among the new American picaros and picaras in those occasional self-vaunting behaviors that cut against the grain of their own stated purposes of social stock-taking in pluralistic America. On learning that Mike Wisdom had returned his salary to help bail out his hometown of Wray, Colorado, David Lamb admires the altruism but, I. A.-"centric" as he cannot apparently avoid being, he cannot resist contributing his own superseding expertise on the matter by telling Wisdom, "I thought that attitude had probably helped snatch Wray from the death rolls of the Great Plains but doubted it was applicable to the problems of urban America" (p. 75). In a studied phrase, instead of gaining additional access to this American Wisdom by asking *him* about the broader applicability of the small-town concern for community, Lamb, ordinarily so open to the ordinary stranger, simply pronounces himself. And, even one like Bill Moyers, intent as he declares himself to be on "listening" to the American others, sometimes runs similarly into the obstacles to proper hearing created by his own presumptive, self-righteous, and intrusive postures and posturing. While Least Heat Moon might innocently, if mistakenly, invade on others with his own values while trying to help the handicapped lad, Moyers at times quite purposely surrenders his equilibrium in order to lead with a jab out of his own intra-cultural ethnocentrism. In one instance, briefly off the road in East Texas, somewhere around Teneha, while sitting in a rural cafe, he notices the only black men in the place, four of them, in a back room off the kitchen. He immediately asks the waitress if "'they ever come up here'" into the main part of the place. When she replies "'naw. That's their place back there,'" he asks, "quite casually, 'Did you know that's against the law?'" and then instructs her and subsequently the owner on the Federal Public Accommodations Act of 1964, to the effect that "'You have to open the same facilities to everyone if you run a business that caters to the public'" (p. 278). A "vast square block of a man," the owner makes a first response with a laconic "No shit," his second is "Never heard of it [the law]," his third is to bring the black men out front to ask them if they think the segregated facilities are against the law ("'Naw sir. Naw sir.'"), and his fourth aims directly at Moyers: "'They don't think it's against the law. And I don't think it's against the law. And nobody's told me it's against the law but you. Now what are you going to do?'" (p. 279). Moyers reports "'I said, 'I'm going to hit the road.' And I put down a quarter, which included a fifteen-cent tip for my recent friend, the waitress, walked out of the diner, got into my car, locked the doors, and sped away" (p. 280). Such momentary self-promotions prevent getting the natives' views from the natives' *point of view* because they promote the picaro more than they attune to the others and because they frequently affront the strangers to the point of their angry reactions or their shielding themselves by clamming up. Such a self-obtrusive approach to "the other" on the part of the picaro simply precludes the work of polling the character, ways, and means of the stranger and leaves another small acre of the social territory largely uncharted.

Of all of those social-psychological ills besetting the picaro or picara, however, the one perhaps most damaging to the necessary openness, insouciance, and equanimity required by the picaresque mission of social inventory appears as an afflicting xenophobia—a stark terror of the stranger—that can prevent regarding the other in any way but in his or her sheer and threatening otherness. Although any picaro completely diseased in this way would probably forfeit the tour altogether, would surely leave the road for some form of seclusion no alien could enter,[27] a number of narratives in the new American picaresque nevertheless record at least temporary instances of such a disabling state of mind.

A dramatic, if somewhat "staged," example of a picaro's intermittent xenophobia appears in *Travels with Charley*. While Steinbeck's announced dread and loathing of the human other might well be largely reserved for his episodes with the racists of the American South, that is not the only place or set of situations in which his fear of the stranger comes into narrative display. In Maine, fairly early in the trip, Steinbeck camps overnight at the edge of a gravel road in the forest, and, as the rain falls on the cabin roof of his truck, he pitches himself into a "desolate . . . [and] frightening loneliness." Far away from any human presence, in this "country gone back to forest," he craves company and writes letters to simulate connection as the lonely solitude deepens. Over the noise of the drumming rain, somewhere outside, he reports, "I seemed to hear voices, as though a crowd of people mumbled and muttered offstage," and, as the rain stops, his fear is palpable:

> . . . I helped to spawn a school of secret dangers. Oh, we can populate the dark with horrors, even we who think ourselves informed and sure, believing nothing we cannot measure or weigh. I knew beyond all doubt that the dark things crowding in on me either did not exist or were not dangerous to me, and still I was afraid. I thought how terrible the nights must have been in a time when men knew the things were there and were deadly. But no, that's wrong. If I knew they were there, I would have weapons against them, charms, prayers, some kind of alliance with forces equally strong but on my side. (pp. 60–61)

In the midst of these dark-night horrors that make him all the more thirsty for human company, he is startled out of drowsiness by "the sound of footsteps . . . moving stealthily on gravel." Although he has longed for human alliance, the sound only signals "stealth," danger, the fearsome stranger, and he arms himself immediately, not with "charms" and "prayers" and not with the picaro's guileless and bluff countenance but with a two-foot-long flashlight and a 30/30 carbine. Instead of calling out a civil greeting, he demands to know "'What do you want?'" Despite the fact that his social encounters to this point have been nothing but hospitable, even generous, Steinbeck here candidly confesses to a momentary xenophobia born out of the isolation, the darkness, the rain, the forest, and his own histrionic self-haunting, and he soon realizes the "ridiculous pattern that had piled up layer on layer." What he had feared most immediately as "stealth" is nothing other than "a man in boots and a yellow oilskin," whose tread in the gravel was simply taking him home, "'up the road'" (p. 62).

When suffered, of course, the xenophobic attitude, the fear of strangers or of some category of strangers, is founded on or grounded in a species of negative stereotyping and always precedes the actual encounter with any particular stranger or strangers. The encounter itself, then, can either ameliorate the fear, as with Steinbeck and the late-night walker, or can reinforce the attitude, as Peter Jenkins discovers in his walk across America. As the semi-hip, long-hair from the Connecticut suburbs heads south toward the Tennessee–Alabama line in his walk across America, he reports in retrospection:

I walked and walked fast, dreading every step because I had nothing to look forward to. . . . Worse than that was knowing I had to walk through the entire state north to south. It was either here or Mississippi, and I didn't know which was worse. All my growing-up days, I was told horror stories about these uneducated, barefoot, racist states. As far as I knew, most people in Alabama never made it past the sixth grade.

. . . I imagined in living color how the ol' boys would see my backpack, red beard and blue jeans and for no reason blow my frightened brains out with at least one shotgun, probably two. If I was lucky, some friendly types might spare me and just run me over. I figured I had about a million to one chance of making it through this deadly state.

When I reached the border, it was the worse possible time, Friday night. As in many places in the U.S.A., Friday night was road-cruising, pickup-truck, hot-rod-cars and beer-slurping time. Their trigger fingers were certainly loosened by now, I thought. (p. 213)

The contingent life of the picaresque course veers him for a time in this case away from any contrived and self-fulfilling prophesy. Fearful of his lot, Jenkins puts himself in quick phone contact with the father of a young man met earlier on the trip, and the drawling, kindly Qualls, a doctor, not only takes him in without hesitation but insists he "stay put" until Jenkins's walking pneumonia has been treated. Then and only then, back on the road and now somewhat disabused of his standing terror of southern malignancy, Jenkins's *rota Fortunae* takes him into Shelby County and face-to-face with the reification of his xenophobic nightmare on "the black night I met the 'Shelby County Drunk Four'" (p. 219). Without benefit of introduction or opening amenity, the inebriated leader of this bunch—an "ugly-faced man" with "tobacco juice gobbed down the sides of his mouth" and breath "strong enough to patent and use as insecticide"—slurs into Jenkins's face, "Where you from, you ugly whiskered hippie?'" Upon hearing Jenkin's reply, the man "slyly and full of evil" says to his pals "'Looky here, this is a damn Yankee . . . Should I kill 'em now er later?'" (p. 221). The episode unfolds, the menace increases, and Jenkins's fear intensifies as he realizes he has somehow become accountable (since viewed as a long-haired, Yankee, draft-resisting, drug-peddler) for the man's Vietnam-veteran, drug-hooked son. At last, rather unpredictably, Jenkins briefly mollifies the man, gains some respect for standing up to him, and placates the lot by drinking a quick beer with them. Finally gaining his release, he heads, still frightened, for a hidden campsite in the nearby woods. From there, now with his generalized phobia having found specific embodiment and the reasonableness of his fear clearly legitimated, he watches from the bushes while "over ten times they came driving slowly by where I was hiding, the truck weaving from side to side." As with Steinbeck, however, Jenkins's xenophobic mania is soon put to rout, at least in this instance. In the light of the next day, out of hiding, as he hikes fearfully along the roadside, the man pulls up beside him again, this time to say "'Listen, boy, I took ma lunch break so I could cum and find ya. I'm plum sorry I raised sa much racket last night. I was jus' slam drunk out a' my head and crazy. I ain't never apologized for nothin' bafore, but I shore am sorry'" (p. 224).

A comparably disclosive example of the many cases of preflexive fear of the other or some class of the other that crop up in the narratives of the new American picaresque occurs in the midst of Walt Harrington's "white" journey through "black America." Well into his travels, on the far outskirts of Houston, he discovers black cowboys on a ranch owned and run by African Americans, and there he locates as well a wonderful hospitality. Upon leaving the ranch, he offers a ride to Michael, one of the just met cowboys, whose home is in Sunnyside, a poor black neighborhood back in the city. This passenger proves a quite congenial, informed, articulate, and remarkably forthcoming temporary companion, to the extent in fact that Harrington offers "to spring for lunch," during which "Michael talks about his life" (p. 344) in one of those encounters that suddenly can open for the picaro to pierce the veil hiding the stranger. Resuming the narrative ride, however, Harrington hits a rough, xenophobic patch:

> Back in the car, Michael directs me to his house through another of what I've come to see as America's classically poor neighborhoods—about two out of three houses are dilapidated, but about every third one is in nice, tidy shape, the grass cut and the siding painted. But Sunnyside . . . [turns out to be] a hard place, where ten, fifteen, twenty young black guys with no shirts are milling on strategic corners, sitting on car hoods, leaning against fences. And after about a dozen lefts and rights on Sunnyside's narrow streets, I realize I've got no idea where I am. Just then, it strikes me that I don't know this guy Michael Solomon from Adam. I'm relieved when we get to his mother's house, a nice little green home with clean white shutters and clean clothes drying on the line.
>
> "Thanks for the lift," Michael says, as he heads for the house. Once again my fears are unfounded. (pp. 345–46)

Although married to a black woman and accustomed to many black relatives and friends, Harrington here suffers and records yet another of his quick bouts with a confessedly unaccountable or at least "unfounded" fear of the black "other," even with one now who has become a familiar. To be cured of the social-psychological impairment of "other-terror" in one episode is not, apparently, to have a complete remission. With Harrington, as with other picaros and picaras, the road engagements might well have remedial value—as they clearly can, if only to show the fear of the stranger as groundless—but, for this imbedded dis-ease of pluralism, the series of treatments often seems as long as the road itself.

As with Steinbeck, Jenkins, Oedipa Maas, and others in these kinds of instances, Harrington's predisposed idea of the threatening strangers, these phobic anticipations of the others, might well prove quickly or gradually to be unfounded, but, in the midst and tumult of the American social Babel and the sheer "world of others," even these episodes in which the frightening alien anticipated and dreaded plays out as a more cordial stranger in the meeting do not always prevent the contagion of the picaro or picara by the kinds of xenophobia he or she has spotted on course in the social motley. In this sense, Steinbeck's late-night horror at the sound of footsteps in the gravel and his hostile, weapon-wielding response are not altogether different in kind from the threatened and combative reflex discernible in the river-rat near Tomato trespassed by Hall and Wood. Jenkins's preflexive fear of violent southern rednecks stands in clear and ready equation with the frightening menace to children and family posed from afar to the people of Shelby County, Alabama, by those hairy, destructive, hip, drug-dealers. Harrington's rising anxiety in Sunnyside is the functional equivalent of the fearful reaction Steinbeck receives from the old black man pressed to ride with him. The picaro or picara, in short, is no more immune than any of those found at roadside to fears predicated on demonizing images of "the others" lurking about or approaching one in a socialscape, a virtual haunt of xenophobias, marked for its divisive and conflictual character.

As the picaros and picaras labor on course to fulfill the mission of social stock-taking, then, picaresque retrospection often works to take stock of them as well. In this, the narratives frequently, sometimes unwittingly, display the ways that supercilious, ethnocentric, and xenophobic attitudes not only duplicate maladies endemic in the general social parade but also paralyze the picaresque figures' proper charge, even their raison d'être. If smug egotisms, suspicious provincialisms or stereotyping hatreds, and indeed unaccountable xenophobic frights reside in Americans scattered about the country, as the picaros and picaras and the picaresque diagnose those social ills, the picaresque venture into human relational space simply and broadly confirms and dramatizes such "pains of pluralism" as both causes and effects of diverse kinds of Americans in conflict with their own countrypersons. When the picaro exhibits such impairments in himself, however, the prospects for a significant inventory by the picaresque—getting the natives from their own point of view, penetrating into those forms of American knowledge that are always, as Geertz notes, "local knowledge"—are severely diminished: the itinerant ethnography enabled by the picaresque course cannot make a good job of work, without which toil the narratives can record the world of social conflict but cannot meet the picaresque objective of detecting the strangers' forms of sense, their shapes of sensibility. Steinbeck, for one, occasionally realizes or at least suspects such missed opportunities, lost because of his own contagion by social disabilities in him that create defaults on the picaro's equanimity, and suspects as well how these forfeits compromise his own declared, inaugural intentions to grapple with the American social reality. Remembering later the events in New Orleans and the road out afterwards, Steinbeck muses in perplexity about images "that walked across my eyes": there was "the grey man . . . and the faces of the Cheerladies, but mostly I saw the old man squeezed as far away from me as he could get, *as though I carried the infection, and perhaps I did.* I came out to learn. What was I learning?" (p. 266; emphasis added).

Fortunately, the life of the road supplies or can supply not only the theater in which the picaro's or picara's own social ailments might come dramatically into diagnostic relief but also the cathartic regimen, the course of "treatments" in manifold encounters with American "others," that can by-pass or wither arrogant self-regard, can prescribe remedy for ethnocentric constrictions, and can provide antibiotic for xenophobic infections. For the recluse, one in retreat from the world of social otherness, such medicinal regimen does not exist. For the picaro and picara, by definition, continuous exposure to the strangers is de rigueur, and the required empirics of the highway represent, in vastly pluriform America, a severe test of the essential nature of the figure's health. If the picaro cannot in his own character ultimately surpass or transcend those relational maladies of self-insulation or self-inflation so rampant in the socialscape, he simply fails as a picaro, and the narrative record of his picaresque tour remains purely self-diagnostic: it might perhaps provide a significantly revealing account of the problems associated with the pains of pluralism but only with the picaro himself as the major patient and with its survey of the "others" gained only through his diseased eyes.[28] It might indeed disclose a unique perspective born out of the picaresque self's several afflictions, but it cannot present a model of the picaro's best social-relational possibilities in and through a world of strangers. On the other hand, if the picaro or picara altogether eludes the ailments of self-centrism and xenophobia, or if he or she manages on the road to find the experiential cure, the picaresque narrative can present not only the endemic, pluralistic "dis-eases" of America witnessed on tour but also some brighter prospects, figured in the picaro or picara, for meeting and engaging the socially different, for demystifying or penetrating beyond the sheerly alien aspect of the stranger, for finding more cordial company with those out there among one's countrypersons who are finally, irreducibly other.

At the very best, however, even the most "socially" successful picaro or picara has to acknowledge in narrational recollection that no matter how comforting were the engagements, no matter how much the aliens became more familiar, no matter how completely achieved the civilities or deeply felt the connections, the strangers met along the way remain, at the last, "strangers still."[29] The wildly pluralistic character of the social reality, the huge interspaces between the discrete centers of social existence, the sheer differences among people in their forms of experience and sense-making, the always local nature of the natives' points of view, cannot be blinked. Nor can they be completely overcome, except in useless generalizations like those of the *Esquire* section headings and that of Herlihy's Joe Buck, who, searching for connections in the eyes of strangers, denominates them all out of his desperate loneliness as *"earthling! earthling!"* (p. 153) in order to belong in the same category with them.

In fact, the very nature of the picaresque course militates against increased intimacy even in those cases in which the socially successful picaro or picara has passed through the most rewarding encounter with the stranger. If the objective of the anthropologist on the ethnographic field is to move the "others" from their removes as "strangers" into the cohort of "friends," as Hortense Powdermaker avows,[30] the picaresque venture affords no such possibility or any such pretense. The picaro or picara cannot stay for the months or years necessary to penetrate the veils of otherness fully enough unless he or she ceases in picaresque life. His own form of ethnographical presentation will thus also reflect the twisting, unintentional, rapid, and even accidental movements of encounter that occur in episodic moments. If any cordial "connection," much less brief intimacy, is achieved with this or that stranger, the person is soon left behind, just as much an image in the rearview mirror as the old African American with whom Steinbeck *failed* to connect. The social encounters, in short, are brief "hit or miss" occasions, each of which, even the "hits," the *best* temporary relations, must be superseded by and for the sake of the journey and its mission of a broader social cartography.[31]

If the picaro or picara thus can do no other than to keep on moving, the lost opportunities for fuller relationships while on course are simply and ineluctably a rule of the picaresque game, and the rule means that the picaro or picara is always on social edge, continuously tracking into unknown territories of local knowledge and forever being brought by the happenstance of the highway into the presence of still more American strangers. But the toll on the picaro and picara taken by this lonely exile of the road, the solitary course of this kind of social navigation, is repaid by extending the "social work" of the new American picaresque yet again. Additional benefits can be derived for the narrative form just by virtue of its forcing the picaro or picara, or at least the more "knowing" narrator, to reckon with the fact that for every temporary "social" stop, in practically every episode of human encounter, the central figure of the narrative is central only in *narrative* space and is clearly marginal or peripheral in the various successions of social spaces he or she enters. The picaro or picara, in short, is always himself or herself the arriving stranger. Those odd Americans "out there" to be encountered as the "others," are already there, in place, and it is into *their* space that the picaro or picara ventures, trespassing *their* social borders and appearing at their gates. And as the picaresque narratives remember and represent those "border" behaviors, the social complications and implications of the form increase in the measure that the journey teaches the picaresque figure, the narrator, or the reader something about life on the edge, something of the virtues of the margin.

6

The Picaro in the Nick of Time:
Virtues of the Margin

Finding how the road can lend "cures" for those conditions and distresses of selfhood piled on by contemporary experience, the new American picaro or picara might very well learn or recover the kind of respect for his or her own sovereignty that gives the experiential trials of the episodic way some restorative character and permits integral approach to the strangers out there. Indeed, as the picaro toils in the midst of whelming social pluralism at engaging and ciphering the existence of those diverse American "others," narrative retrospection serves not only to point up the deeply raucous and conflictual terms of the social reality and the various psychic ailments that distance countrypersons from one another but also to display the picaro's own intermittent interludes of social-psychological atrophy. He often finds the regimen of the highways therapeutic in ways that return his picaresque abilities to him, in ways that thus promote his continuous encounters with the innumerable strangers in the human plenum, but the social work of the new American picaresque everywhere suggests that, even at journey's end, the others met en route, even in the best of moments, remain relative strangers still. The time passed with them having been too brief for much else, even if the picaro or picara in his or her loneliness might have craved more, he or she must soon leave behind that site, that cycle of strangers, that particular center of social life: the road ahead, the course de rigueur, is the picaresque way by definition. And, traveling again into a new succession of social stops, the picaresque protagonists will, must, as always, appear on those scenes as the approaching aliens. No more or less strange to those there, already in place, than they are to the picaro and picara, they arrive from the road on the borders of this, that, and the next social territory as the continual "odd persons out," forever the outsiders with respect to the irreducible and countless social centers comprising the American populace, and never to be very much more than fleeting, peripheral figures in relation to them.[1] If the literary nature of his and her existence dictates generic exile, the social terms of this life have them always "on edge."

This very condition militating against extended, much less intimate relationships, however, also increases the range and potency of the social instruction embedded in the works of the new American picaresque, and, in this context of concern, the contention here is that the career of exile, the tour on the boundaries, lived out in the terms peculiar to the picaro or picara, is a life represented at a crucial and propitious moment for American society, given the pluralistic perplexities and conflicts that inflame in its contemporary make-up. Into such a volatile babble of tongues, commitments, and ways, an American world in social fracture and combativeness, the picaro or picara succeeds best whose narrative walk approaches a horizon of yet unexhausted possibilities for a life lived in relation to strange others. At their best, their "embodied" traits and ways stand as a narrative resource for those worried about the failures of social rapport among the American aliens. Required by the genre to trespass a huge variety of social centers but recognizing himself or herself all the while as the eternal alien in these various socialscapes, the picaro or picara is poised by the narrative form to learn the virtues of the margin in a world of strangers—a world within which everyone is marginalized in some way, to some degree, and many suffer the social pains of pluralism, but in which few apparently can experience life even temporarily on edge as a boon.

In the following sections, then, the task is to take up the matter of the social benefits that can be derived, ironically, just by way of the picaresque character's condition of mobile social estrangement, the exile on the road, the "characteristic" ways of grappling with the complexities of human encounter, and the distinctive modes of human stock-taking. First, simply, despite the figure's alienation, there is the necessary effort, a genre requirement, of human inventory, and this forces inquiry into the way that the loneliness of picaresque life on the social edges itself shapes in the picaro or picara traits latent in him or her virtually by definition that are replete with social possibility. This beginning set of attributes often narratively realized in him or her is potentially heuristic for the effort to connect with the stranger, to come into human company. A second and related concern, then, is to examine how these picaresque attributes—experiential openness, bluff and innocent countenance, presiding temerity, alacrity to dynamic and nuance in a situation, hard-won resilience, crafted equipoise, and studious diffidence—all correspond to the social requisites of a life lived in rapid horizontal movements and, moreover, answer with such "adroit cosmopolitanism" to the threshold necessities for Americans living in the company of strangers. This in turn converges with the consideration of another visible asset of picaresque exile—namely, how the picaresque expenditure of labor in carrying out continuous trespasses onto others' grounds begins to propose a kind of model of approaches and responses to the strangers that has social utility significant in the American Babel. As the figures locate the means and terms for proper engagement, they put on display for readers the strategies and substance of a conduct of engagement perhaps sufficient for living in an ambiguous and even antagonistic world. In all of this, finally, the picaresque probes from the social edges made possible by following the picaro or picara in exile provide yet another instructive advantage, the terms of a "new civility" in American society enacted at least narratively by these figures arriving from the outer borders. Not belonging to or confined by any particular social center or hold, the picaro or picara exists on the fringes, and the cumulative new American picaresque narratives, with testimony refracted through those marginalized eyes, can thus afford readers some additional vistas, fuller human inventory, views accomplished from the margins of society without readers having themselves to go to those edges to begin to see and understand American "others." Understood in this manner, the picaro or picara presents no heroic figure or action, certainly not for those whose territories he or she only fleetingly passes through. Each appears "in the nick of time" not because each comes as a traditional stalwart here to save the day but, rather, because each is, like other Americans, struggling to get along as a continual interloper in a world of relational contingency, and the "peripheral vision," the vantage of the margin that road exile forces upon him or her, proposes to readers one form of what might suffice for social coping in an American time of need.[2]

Curricula of Exile and Loneliness, Strategies of Approach

Only shortly on the narrative road of exile, stopped for a time on his tour in Albuquerque, Joe Buck in *Midnight Cowboy* finds himself struck again with a long-term sensation "always just below the surface" but never before articulated, "the feeling of being a person with no real place in the world, an alien even under the red-white-and-blue of his birth, one who did not belong even in his own neighborhood."[3] Cast out now into a broader world wherein all he meets have been "strangers who had dealt with him brusquely or condescendingly or who had ignored him altogether" (p. 91), he comes to the recognition that he is himself "the stranger": "now, thinking it all over, carefully but inexpertly, there seemed to him to have been from the very beginning a campaign afoot to make him aware always and always and always of his own alien status" (p. 92). In the place of the contemporary "red-white-and-blue," a pluralistic welter within which anonymous others are everywhere, Joe's sinking feeling, according to the testimony gathered by the new American picaresque, is endemic.

Most often without the callow paranoia, such a realization occurs to nearly every picaro or picara at some point on course, the startling and somewhat paralyzing idea that no matter where he or she is or has arrived—Waco, Albuquerque, Des Moines, Kokomo, Dime Box or Dixon, New York City, Raleigh, Waycross, or Miami, all the same—he or she stands as the outsider, the alien, if not necessarily alienated quite like Joe Buck. As the title indicates, young Vic Messenger in Richard Hill's picaresque novel understands, sometimes dimly, sometimes acutely, that in his complex tour he is *Riding Solo with the Golden Horde*.[4] The longer, troubled course traveled by Texas Jack Carmine admits of no sustained or sustaining relationship for this "unbonded" man but for the accompaniment of favorite "road music."[5] Walt Harrington's journey through black America visibly marginalizes him in relation to those through whose territories he passes.[6] William Least Heat Moon begins and moves "distanced" from any viable connections, often longs for a "roadfellow" as he does in passing through the immensity and emptiness of the Great Plains, and, withal, struggles to find a "tribe" to which to belong.[7] John Steinbeck suffers his lonely, forest-secluded, miserable night of craving human connection and attempts to ameliorate it by writing letters home.[8] Every new "social" stopping point introduces a new conclave of anonymous others; with every turn of the human road there appears a new social center, each of which presents the picaro or picara with another set of native boundaries to cross. Strangers literally fill the worlds of the picaresque figures, and yet, in entering that world as they must, they sooner or later learn that they come to the others as "strangers" and that they must make their way into the others' places.[9] However much disgust or dread or terror of entry this might create for the picaro or picara, this self-recognition of "the self as a stranger to the others," this instructional exercise in loneliness, can be a crucial beginning for the picaro and picara to develop those virtues of social being that their marginal place demands, that the pluralistic world requires, and that the essential literary condition promotes. To the extent that any picaro can vitalize those assets in him that belong centrally to the definition of "the picaro" at large, then to that same extent can he convert exile into opportunity, estrangement into occasions for encounter, and the singular condition on the road into new social resources. The dilemmas, in short, also become the distinctive possibilities. Prospects of full relationship, enduring intimacy, are surely foreclosed upon by the picaresque life, but such a life might also open anew to a different form of human relation, one commensurate with persisting existence in the midst of a swirl of strangers.

In these terms, then, the introductory or, perhaps, remedial instruction in the social-work curriculum of picaresque exile is a study in the picaro's own outsider status and his long *mobile* solitudes, but even this sad and isolated condition can be converted into a virtue of the marginal life. Imposed or willed, the need to take to the road—to traverse spaces of social otherness, to become anonymous by entering an unknown and unknowing world—is necessarily to embark at least temporarily into a form of concerted loneliness, all the more when the itinerary can project no certain "welcome" at any day's end or even indeed any sure destination from day to day. The human inventory to be taken is huge and various to be sure, but its sheer size, far different from assuring abundant human connections, insures the more or less continuous impact of the picaro's reminders to himself and to him by others of himself as stranger to the others. Exile might well mean personal liberty, even a special margin of freedom, experienced from time to time in flights of exhilaration, but it also involves the strong recognition, as the picaro or picara from Gil Blas, Moll Flanders, Justina, and Jack Wilton to Joe Buck, Vic Messenger, "Dutch" Gillis, and John Steinbeck, has each learned, that, like their progenitor Lazarillo, *"yo soy solo."*[10] Autonomy on the trail also means, at best, episodic anonymity, being unknown, and, even should the picaro or picara manage to achieve familiarity or even brief rapport with someone one day in El Paso, the task must needs be undertaken all over again the next day in Corpus Christi or San Antonio or "even in his own neighborhood." Least Heat Moon discovers throughout that he is the outsider: "A Missourian gets used to Southerners thinking him a Yankee, a Northerner considering him a cracker, a Westerner sneering at his effete Easternness, and the Easterner taking him for a cowhand" (p. 30). The picaro's sense of himself as *isolato* only seldom abates, but because the autonomy of the trail makes the picaro ultimately autodidactical in the road curriculum, even when he or she fails at being "the ultimate autodidact," the perfect student, many of the picaros and picaras—or at least the retrospective narrators—also learn to recognize just how their alien singularity, their exile onto the edges, has put their desires for encounter and engagement on the increase and has created tactics, possible grounds, for accomplishing even temporary human connection.[11]

The experience of the conditions of loneliness might not be an absolute requirement for seeking social relation, but, for the picaro and picara, it clearly figures as a propaedeutic, especially after any extended, private sojourns on the road, for the virtues of openness and affability toward an other, any other, however strange, that might bring the two out of their estrangement. For those picaros who can transform the condition of isolation away from further self-enclosing misery and desolation into eagerness for company, life on the margin thus inspires an even fuller, more anticipatory conviviality. Among others, William Least Heat Moon, consciously or instinctively, hones in on this insight, accepting and even cultivating the loneliness, which comes his way in any event, just to enhance his social outreach. When asked why he does not have a dog along on his trip, he reveals one of his tactics for coming out of isolation into company: "'It isn't traveling to cross the country and talk to your pug instead of people along the way. Besides, being alone on the road makes you ready to meet someone when you stop. You get sociable traveling alone'" (p. 31). In other cases of picaresque solitariness, of course, Peter Jenkins, Lars Eighner, C. W. Sughrue in James Crumley's *The Last Good Kiss*, and Steinbeck, want the company of the pet but, utilizing the opposite strategy of encountering other people, also realize that in traveling with their respective dogs—Cooper, Lizbeth, the beer-guzzling Fireball Roberts, and Charley—the animal can serve to break the ices of anonymity and reserve between people unknown to each other: "A dog, particularly an exotic like Charley," according to Steinbeck, "is a bond between strangers. Many conversations en route began with 'What degree of dog is that?'" (p. 9).

Experiencing and understanding extremes of social isolation in his unbondedness, the picaro's lot even with strangers, these and other examples suggest, conduces to and even leads to plans for his own openness and amiability. Exiled as he is, a loner as he might well be, the picaro
nonetheless often possesses a kind of ingrained gregariousness, an appetite for moments of congeniality, that gives him a natural hunger for
social stock-taking and that his lonely trek only whets.

Other means and forms of coming to encounter similarly elicit out of
the picaresque situation of banishment some of the picaresque person's
own strongest suits for social life, traits that help them penetrate through
anonymities into others' companies. In this regard, along the lonely way,
the sheerly mobile course of the career can either evoke an inherent literary trait of alacrity or can train them in keeping poised for any sign of temporary "welcome," any human opening, and, indeed, the picaros and
picaras whose social means are most effectual are often the ones best able,
like Doctorow's Billy Bathgate, to juggle the situation, to wedge further
into the scene with the "other" or "others." For these exiles, even the accidental encounters, the advantages of the random and often blundering
passages into episodes, can pay social dividend by returning here and there
the socially informative interlude, even the congenial engagement, with
the American stranger, if, that is, the picaro or picara in question can muster
the tools of the trade bequeathed by the genre. Harrington's inveterately
picaresque curiosity leads him to the Texas ranch staffed by African-American cowboys, and here he trips across young Michael, with whom a cordial and instructive afternoon passes (pp. 344–46). Least Heat Moon's
encounter with an extraordinarily thoughtful woman in southwestern
Louisiana, he remembers, occurred in a completely fortuitous way:

> Because of a broken sealed-beam headlight and Zatarain's Creole
> Mustard, an excellent native mustard, I met Barbara Pierre. I had just
> come out of Dugas' grocery with four jars of Zatarain's, and we almost
> collided on the sidewalk. She said, "You're not from St. Martinsville,
> are you? You can't be."
> "I'm from Missouri."
> "What in the world are you doing here? Got a little Huck Finn in you?"
> "Just following the bayou. Now I'm looking for the Ford agency."
> "Coincidence. I work there. I'll show you the way." (p. 133)

Through their lunch at her place and conversing through the afternoon,
Barbara Pierre proves a brave, concerned, funny woman, full of ambi-

tion and native wisdom, and, attuned to possibilities, the picaro William
seizes on the main chance, however much it results from a brief collision
of fortunes.

Not all such social "accidents" are happy ones, of course. Loyal Blood
in E. Annie Proulx's *Postcards*, himself also alert to the social chance,
crosses the local border into an invited familiarity, a quite sudden and
unanticipated welcome, with a woman gas station attendant, but he
quickly learns more from her and about her than he wishes to and very
soon has to flee into the parking lot with his pants down around his
ankles.[12] Another stranger on the road, Bill Moyers, in a diner in east
Texas, arrives alert to the visible scene but not to the native "society,"
inadvertently confronts the owner, in fact manages to retrieve social "information," and finally possesses the alacrity to know when to leave.[13]
Uncongenial though these moments of social mischance might be, they
too must be taken up by the picaro for the sake of the inventory of the
motley, for what they can yield of the ways and means of the other, and
for what they might teach of social relation. If the picaro's feckless trespasses turn to conflict, innocent conflict is a course in the curriculum. If
the picaro's bluff countenance meets with stolid or hostile return, the
rebuffs, instructive in themselves, only call out another defining trait in
him, his resilience, his capacity to brush himself off and begin anew. Indeed, such resistance often only in fact increases his craving. Over and
again, the road presents the strangers in place to the picaresque stranger
arriving, with the latter simply stumbling across, recognizing, and accepting or prying open a brief cycle of social moment. Withal, human
encounters are lessons to be learned in exile, and to this course-work the
picaros and picaras, at their best, bring their own natural abilities of innocent openness, sustaining insouciance, eager alertness to moment,
intricate attentiveness to situation, and even occasional traces of mildly
roguish charm, traits that might allow the strangers to open to them when
there are any signs of welcome.[14]

At times, however, some of the strangers out there want to remain
no more than that, halting to respond even in conflictual ways, but this
form of challenging recalcitrance only presents occasions for the picaro
or picara to come even more completely into his or her own. Beyond the
appetite created by loneliness, the openness stoked by anticipation, the
advantage of the numerous accidental encounters, and the quickness to
ply welcome, the road also, sometimes, simply requires of the picaro or
picara ways of getting started with often reluctant or insular others that

might bring them into the light of the picaresque inventory. In this, beyond the strategy of inviting or "exotic" dogs, the ways of the dexterous picaro are many. No trickster he, the picaro nevertheless knows a few
tricks, tactics designed to trick the other stranger out of his or her shell
and into some fuller presence to the picaro. Taking a chance, Steinbeck
asks a weary and obviously unhappy waitress "'How soon you going
to Florida?'" (p. 46), and this opening gambit brings the untalkative
woman briefly to respond, even if only to place herself in the social inventory not as "a person who can saturate a room with vitality" but,
rather, as one "who can drain off energy and joy, can suck pleasure dry
and get no sustenance from it. . . . [and can] spread a grayness in the air
about them" (p. 46). In attempting to penetrate into the "glamours" of a
closed-off underworld, Doctorow's Billy Bathgate initially poses as a
numbers runner to mask himself, and in this role, delivers pastries to
achieve entrance to the Dutch Schultz enclave. His camouflaging ingenuity, meeting with the strangers' delight, wedges open a hitherto hidden social reality. Least Heat Moon faces in the frigid social territories
of the central North people "wondering who the outsider was" but observes also that "as soon as I nodded . . . [they] looked down, up, left,
right or turned around as if summoned by an invisible caller." This forces
him to resort to an old tactic: on the theory that "nothing breaks down
suspicion about a stranger better than curiosity," he recalls, "I even tried
my old stratagem of taking a picture of a blank wall just to give a pass-
erby an excuse to stop and ask me what I could possibly be photograph-
ing" (p. 322). Waller's Texas Jack Carmine crashes the parties of strangers, like the Thorvalds' anniversary occasion, and, once in, counts on his
unleashed roguish spirits to charm the others into responsiveness. Steinbeck reports that, in inducing engagement with indifferent strangers,
"the techniques of opening conversation are universal. . . . [his having]
rediscovered that the best way to attract attention, help, and conversation is to be lost. A man who seeing his mother starving to death on a
path kicks her in the stomach to clear the way, will cheerfully devote
several hours of his time giving wrong directions to a total stranger who
claims to be lost" (p. 9). Some innocent craft, backed up by temerity and
bulwarked by affability, goes a long way on the road toward the work
of creating those means of social trespass that the picaro's outsider status requires him to deploy among strangers.

Playing in guises of "lostness" or "helplessness" or "innocence," of
course, is not only a possible tactic but is a manipulation of the picaro's
actual condition on the road. *Being* "lost" or "helpless" is in fact part and

parcel of the picaro's essential condition in social exile, at least on intermittent bases. Again, however, these straits both require him and help
him to demonstrate other key facets of his stock-in-trade that answer to
his life on the margins in a world of strangers—namely, his persistence
and his resilience. Vic Messenger, a nimble, young, white, jazz/blues
saxophonist—who begins as a total stranger in the black musical world
he seeks to enter—practices no more guile in his intrepid but hapless efforts than Least Heat Moon employs in his seeking directions to Nameless, Tennessee. But Vic's adolescent innocence and need finally gain him
a relation to Tonto (Perkins), the black alto player, to a degree not possible without his own daring and dauntless persistence at boundary trespasses, just as Least Heat Moon's intrepidness accompanies his un-
feigned "lostness" on the road and at the door in seeking "Nameless," a
persistence that finally grants him a temporary but more highly cordial
and informative access to Thurmond, Hilda, and Virginia Watts. At last,
Virginia admits him to her sphere and warms to him only after having
"looked me and my truck over . . . clearly [sending the message that] she
didn't approve" (p. 34). Forced on the road forever to obtrude into the
presence of strangers just by dint of continuous movement, if not hunger for encounter and inveterate curiosity, the picaro continuously runs
the risk of social transgression, but, again, his narrative necessity of "trespass" is answered by those capacities for persistence and resilience that
accompany his insouciance, temerity, and bluff countenance. When having difficulty crossing the border, connecting with the stranger, Richard
Hill's picaro reports, he has learned two things: "'One: Grab his neck in
a headlock and hang on. Two: Think of something weird to do'" (p. 13).
These autodidactical lessons serve Vic Messenger well. They serve him
figuratively in his musical attempts to trespass his saxophone into the
"other" world of black jazz artists and to translate jazz and blues back
into the white high-school band, and they serve him quite literally in
street skirmishes with teenage toughs and in his mortal combat with the
vicious Ice, a black drug-pushing pimp, who enters the picaresque social inventory as a highly uncongenial stranger. And other picaros and
picaras, in dealing with the strangers, find their own versions of such
"neck-grabbing" ways of engagement, "holding on" persistence, and
"weird" or wily terms for connecting with the recalcitrant "other."

In these instances and literally hundreds of others in the accumulated
new American picaresque, the picaro or picara thus ricochets along the
highly contingent course of human encounter and, throughout, follows
the exercises dictated by the curriculum of exile. The cumulative testi-

mony suggests that, although the way is difficult and the challenges to even momentary social engagement are everywhere, the dilemmas of life on the margins, given the picaresque hunger, can also turn to advantage. In the career of isolation, the transactions along seemingly endless successions of social borders create the need for continuous movement on the road, itself in turn affording ample, indeed nearly overwhelming, opportunities for human inventory, from the likes of the despicable Ice to the generous Barbara Pierre, from Steinbeck's dour waitress to the forthcoming Tonto. If the marginalized life forces the picaro into necessary trespass into the territories of others, he can be forgiven his trespasses, like all characters in books, to the extent that these "border jumps" illumine some of the terms, means, and possibilities of meeting the "others" in that deeply pluriform and largely anonymous world in which society itself seems teetering on dangerously anti-social edges. Moreover, the picaro's or picara's standing assets point up some of the traits and strategies required to negotiate the pluralistic, estranging, and often rancorous social agon, those attributes he or she possesses or learns to help cross the tricky interspaces of reserve or suspicion or hostility between people alien to each other, and, in this work, the new American picaresque narratives suggest how the picaro's or picara's life on social edge, a life on the brink, might be more in social terms than approaching the "brink of disaster." This *vida*, posed in narrative, might indeed call for and give rise to those socially salubrious arts of "brinkspersonship" boded by the picaro's or picara's ability to juggle and maneuver situations out of harm's way, onto safer ground.[15]

In a time of social need, then, what the picaro or picara initially brings to human encounters are attempts to enact from scene to scene those forms of social meeting and threshold rapport that can be achieved in a strange world for those who wish to be and wish the other to be more than aliens to each other. In various ways, the pluriform gallery of strangers, in which all relationships are contingent, suits this character perfectly: it not only presents the perfect realm for his or her movement but elicits the realization of his or her operative abilities. Picaresque exile becomes possibility, marginality becomes glorious opportunity to trespass, the condition of estrangement becomes the advantage in exercising those very traits—by definition—the picaro or picara should possess. Few people generally perhaps would willingly choose picaresque banishment and loneliness as training grounds for coming to human encounter or as conditions for development of the picaresque social arts, especially those devoted to standing familiarities and intimacies. As Loyal Blood muses, the toll of road life is heavy: "The price for getting away. No wife, no family, no children, no human comfort in the quotidian unfolding of his life; for him, restless shifting from one town to another, the narrow fences of solitary thought, the pitiful easement of masturbation, lopsided ideas and soliloquies so easily transmuted to crazy mouthings" (p. 53). But one need not duplicate the exiled life of the picaro or picara in order to study in the picaresque curriculum. Many who are more confined in movement but who must nevertheless venture outside of their particular forms of housekeeping into the general, pluralistic human gallery might recognize in themselves something of the picaro's hunger for the cordial company of other Americans in that wider orbit, might discern in the picaro's ways and means some stratagems and assets for coming to first meeting, might indeed understand how the picaro's trespasses onto strangers' grounds can be practiced even in the narrower ambits of their own non-picaresque entrances into the outside world.

These persons might above all else take instruction on some beginning virtues of the margin. As the picaro or picara on the pages works through the road courses of social instruction and thus becomes or can become more fully what he or she most assuredly already is at the level of literary latency, the study habits themselves begin to propose answers to some of the perplexing questions of social life in a divisive world of strangers, wherein the human centers are hugely multiple, the boundaries between them are fixedly drawn, and the margins, thus, are everywhere. The picaro's continuous marginality, his more or less incessant solitariness, and his mobile existence in sailing toward still other strangers are only magnifications, after all, of the less extreme conditions and more localized social situations of contemporary Americans at large who do not live on the road. And, beyond exemplifying some tactics and terms for *approach* to the "other," the character of the picaro and picara also proposes fuller senses of what might be required and, indeed, what might be possible from the margins once the other stranger begins to open the gate.

Cosmopolitanism, the New Picaro, and Tactics of Fuller Trespass

According to the testimony of the new American picaresque, the title of Lyn Lofland's study of "urban public space," *A World of Strangers,*[16] aptly describes the kaleidoscopic swirl of people, discrete from and largely unknown to each other, that comprises the social reality of contemporary America, urban or not. The picaro's or picara's continuous and usually fairly rapid movement has the effect, in narrative space and time, of pressing him or her largely without respite into the presence of new strangers in all of their American heterogeneity and thus, in the effect on the reader, of demographically compressing even the quick successions of suburban and rural "strangers" into something like a throng. As in the cities, their unceasing numbers, forever appearing before the picaro, always seem legion, if only because, as in the city, he crosses the paths of new, unknown "others" virtually all the narrative time. Lofland's broad, opening description of urban existence, indeed, seems perfectly consistent with the sensations of the picaresque life on the road:

> The city [road] may be harsh, but it is [also] exciting. It may be cruel, but it is [also] tolerant. It may be indifferent, but it is [also] a blessed in-difference. . . .
>
> . . . To live in a city [to live on the road] is, among many other things, to live surrounded by large numbers of persons whom one does not know. To experience the city [or the road] is, among many other things, to experience anonymity. To cope with the city [road] is, among many other things, to cope with strangers . . . [continuously in that] very pecu-liar social situation [in which] . . . "pure" anonymity would be intolerable. (pp. vii–viii)

Such a life is possible for humans, Lofland contends, "because they, in fact, know [or learn] a great deal about the strangers who surround them" (p. viii). Beyond simply recognizing the spatial orderings of social life that give clues about the "others" (what types live and work where), the ones who would successfully negotiate this alien world, the ones she calls "the Phi Beta Kappas" of such an education, are those who develop and use "their knowledge and skills to confront the world of strangers head-on and to play, in the midst of this world, at some conventional and not-so-conven-tional fun and games," to the extent indeed that each becomes "the cos-mopolitan human confronting, with ease and ability, the constant stranger" (p. ix). In social-psychological terms, the objective is also the necessity, Lofland contends, and that is to make "the world of strangers . . . become routine" (p. 180). By narrative necessity, of course, the new American picaro or picara studies sufficiently in this curriculum of social difference in that he or she stands poised and ready, eager in loneliness, enabled by mobil-ity, even armed with tactics for "fun and games," prepared, potentially at least, to become Lofland's "cosmopolitan" stranger who moves with ease and dexterity in engaging the other strangers out there. Again, the very character of the marginal life—the road-exile, the condition of anonymity, the recognition of the self as "stranger"—works to the advantage of the vagabond who would be or become the required cosmopolitan, either in the cities or on the rustic trails or, with the new American picara and picaro, in both venues. Moreover, in order to meet just this necessity of cosmopolitanism, the picaresque virtues for conducting social life, for ameliorating the pains of pluralism, fully require the picaresque figure's work on "social edge," as "marginal person," itself in turn again potent in implication, if not indispensable for, some other, even deeper arts of engagement and inventory.

Lofland's general understanding of the requisite learning for coping or even flourishing among strangers is straightforward enough, and it corresponds broadly to the picaro's or picara's ways and means on the road of strangers when he or she is most socially adroit. There are, first, those "meanings" inscribed in the socialscape that must be mastered or lessons that have to be learned about decoding appearances, locations, and behaviors (pp. 98–107), and, like the adept urbanite, the interloping picaro possesses or develops his empirical know-how, his finely tuned senses, his eye for nuance and detail, his feel for the scene, and these usually serve him well in discerning that "look" about the strangers informative of whom to avoid or approach, in giving him an instinct for sizing up this or that "social space" as either dangerous or welcoming, in noticing the tell-tale behaviors of the others alerting one to sharper attentiveness, even when he runs counter to these "meanings" about what is out there. E. Annie Proulx's Loyal Blood, for instance, is full of such hard-earned and heightened alacrity to strangers' "meanings." Taking full note of appearance, situation, and deportment, he cheerfully picks up the hitchhiker-sailor-stranger Weener but those same coded messages fill him with some alarm when, so soon following, Weener encourages him to pick up a second "hitcher," an Indian:

> The thought occurred to Loyal for the first time that the pair might be in cahoots, close as a pair of nickels in a pocket, tight as two corks in a bottle, as single-purposed as a pencil sharpened at both ends. He didn't like the Indian sitting behind him in the backseat, didn't like the way sailor Weener had one arm over the back of the seat, and was half-turned toward him as if he was getting ready to grab the steering wheel. He pulled out onto the highway, steering north, but all the sweetness had gone out of the day from the minute the Indian got in. (p. 56)

As things work out, he deciphers correctly: he is badly used, injured, robbed of a year's savings, his vehicle, even shoes and socks, "'partially scalped'" (p. 61), according to a doctor completely unaware of the Indian. But, withal, Loyal nevertheless displays his acquisition of those social codes necessary in a world of strangers, even as circumstances prevented his acting upon them. Such scenarios, most with far less disastrous consequences, appear throughout the new American picaresque as the picaro or picara demonstrates knowledge of the encoded messages of the others' appearances, circumstances, gestures, postures, and behaviors.

Second, however, beyond such learned or instinctive understanding of how to "read" the approaching other, the cosmopolitan must have or acquire certain "skills" of his or her own, for, as Lofland notes, "to understand, without the skill to do" (p. 108) will not suffice for coping with the strangers. He or she must know or learn in medias res the way to appear, where to go, how to act, commensurately with the knowledge of appearances, locations, and behaviors descried in the surrounding strangers (pp. 108–17). Nor are these skills foreign to the acrobatic picaro, whose lot in exile frequently makes him a master improviser in response to the requirements of different masks to wear, the rise of odd boundary situations to venture, the need for new manners to employ. Indeed, the long lessons of loneliness for the picaro and picara teach them to generate certain stratagems and "skills" for momentarily inserting themselves into the presence of strangers. These are matters not only of reception of what the others' codes signal but of seeking, as the picaresque figures send their own messages as obviously as possible, for the others to decode, for others to understand just how the picaro or picara might "mean," and, in the new American picaresque, picaros and picaras have constructed themselves adaptively, variously and situationally, as everything from bewildered naifs, lost lambs, and inept blunderers to charming rustics, witty urbanites, and sophisticated experts, depending on the sense of what plays when with whom.

But the generalized "cosmopolitan" of Lofland's interpretive sociology and the cumulative "picaro" of new American narrative formations converge further yet in these terms. The knowledge of categorical social "codes" and the processive acquisition of introductory "skills," of course, are requisites simply for coming to initial approach to the unknown others, and, beyond these, as Lofland understands, the genuine cosmopolitan, he or she who would *flourish* in continuous, multiple, and diverse settings with myriad strangers, must at least borrow of certain key traits or crucial characteristics that belong to the prototypical cosmopolitan, the ideal figure for thriving in the midst of strangers, the type Lofland calls "the urbane hero."[17] Again, the picaro or picara brings to special narrative embodiment the features Lofland identifies in the (usually male) "idealized image." The figure's "dominating trait," she suggests, "is his coolness": always "at ease" and "never flustered," "never thrown by diversity," "he goes everywhere . . . and he encounters everyone," solidly and continuously in possession of an unflappable temperament. Nonplussed almost invariably, Lofland points out, the figure's "second trait is tolerance." The urbane hero or heroine might well be angered, disappointed, or repulsed by egregious acts of cruelty or violence seen in others, but, for the most part, the figure relishes human diversity in all of its shapes and sizes, quite compelled, as he or she is, toward the "wide array of life-styles [as] a source of genuine personal pleasure." In fact, this skilled urbanite engenders a kind of "toughness" to steel his or her tolerance, understands that life is often a struggle, even regards others' "minor vices," and his or her own, "with amusement and a certain fondness" (p. 159).

Like Lofland's "prototype of the adventurer," the picaro often finds allure in the passing social parade, the *galeria*, intriguing him or her with its successive, open possibilities, and the attitudes of cool demeanor, high forbearance, and remarkable imperviousness, of course, find something of full correspondence, even outlets, in numerous new American picaros loosed in the midst of strangers. The reader finds a kind of normative "cool" in Larry McMurtry's unassailably nonchalant "Cadillac Jack," Richard Hill's jazz-riffing Vic Messenger, Richard Farina's "exempt" and "immune" Gnossos Pappadopoulis, Bill Bryson with his insulating witticisms, and Bill Moyers, W. Hampton Sides, and Mort Rosenblum with their calm reserves. There is a kind of paradigmatic, if not unlimited, tolerance of diversity in them and, among other picaresque figures, in E. L. Doctorow's Billy Bathgate, Robert James Waller's Texas Jack Carmine, Elizabeth Berg's Nan, Thomas Berger's Jack Crabb, Barbara Kingsolver's Taylor Greer, Peter DeVries's Don Wanderhope, and the narrative personae of David Lamb, Richard Reeves, and Walt Harrington. In these and other picaresque figures, the reader locates a kind of tough insouciance or notable resilience, accompanying such diffidence and equanimity, in Bill Terry's A. J. Poole, E. Annie Proulx's Loyal Blood, Jim Lehrer's "One-Eyed Mack," James Crumley's C. W. Sughrue, and in the narratively presented "selves" of Peter Jenkins, Eddy L. Harris, Lars Eighner, and William Least Heat Moon. Withal, in the cases of these picaros and picaras, as with the prototypical "urbane hero," not only do they "sometimes find it enjoyable" but also somehow know themselves committed by the narrative vocation of trespassing on strangers "to seek out a little danger, to court a little fear, to engender a little anxiety . . . [that is,] to go adventuring" (Lofland, p. 159). Such sensations, indeed, need less to be sought out than simply to be noted for the picaro or picara who, in social exile, knows danger, fear, and anxiety as functions of a life lived marginally, a career always "on edge."

What makes these sensations tolerable for the genuine cosmopolitan, even enjoyable if they are "little" dangers and anxieties, and what securely funds his or her ostensible attitudes of easy coolness, calibrated social permissiveness, and moderate "hard shell," are that knowledge and that skill, instinctive or gained, that come in encountering strangers, in negotiating complex territories of mutual anonymity. He or she, Lofland notes, "is the star scholar of city know-how" (p. 159), and this knowledge, in turn, permits him or her "to operate amidst strangers with minimal risk" or, in more adventurous moods, "to take those minimal risks should he [or she] wish to" (p. 160). For the picaro or picara, of course, that requisite knowledge and skills have to do with road "know-how," and, just as with the development of the skilled urbanite's "attitudes," the world of strangers to be met is a highly parallel, if not identical experiential school. All told, in this context of concern, it amounts to the same or at least a deeply comparable experiential effect for the social lessons to be learned. The compressed world of strangers that results from more or less continuous and rapid picaresque mobility is identical, in the sensations felt by the picaro (and by the reader), to the congestions of anonymity met and felt by the confirmed city-dweller. And, as the most adept or intent picaros or picaras quickly or gradually con well the novel lessons of the "new cosmopolitanism," they move toward their road adventures with knowledge, skills, and attitudes fully intact, prepared for their own "fun and games." What these achieved "urbane" capacities afford are not only or simply the personality criteria for those who would take wide social inventory but, indeed, also fundaments for possible and even potent forms of social intercourse, enacted in narrative, for living in a world of strangers.[18]

With categorical social knowledge, basic interrelational skills, and learned dexterous demeanor in place, the social "games" of the new cosmopolitan follow naturally, and they bend decidedly toward the natural suits of the picaro and picara. Among the "conventional" forms of play in a world of anonymities, Lofland points out, the genuine urbanite employs "mechanisms by which total strangers are transformed into personally-known others" (p. 168), and there are three interrelated issues that comprise a "decision calculus" (p. 169) to be used in the conventions for establishing contact with any unknown other. The adept wayfarer among strangers must quickly use his or her most astute senses to decide about the *desirability* of meeting the stranger (the right place? the right time? the right appearance and behavior? the cosmopolitan's right mood?), about the *legitimacy* of engaging the other (interaction as expected, permissible, or disrupting?), and about the *appropriateness* of interacting with the other (how the stranger belongs to the locale? what signals he or she sends?) (pp. 168–72). Because the picaro or picara is able continuously to hone his or her abilities in such spontaneous decision-making, he or she is not only usually highly alert to these several factors but also has had the kind of experiential lessons that help tune to the exceptions, that give him or her a knack for knowing how the variables might play, when to expunge some factor from the calculation, or indeed why the formulaic might backfire and when to suspend it altogether. For the picaro, quite apart from moments in which there are "built in" interludes for permissible exchange with waitresses, service station attendants, or public servants, virtually all of the accidental encounters, as with Least Heat Moon's responses to Barbara Pierre's signals, with Walt Harrington's offer of a ride to young Michael, with Lars Eighner's move to "hitch" with a half-naked driver, with Proulx's Loyal Blood as he contemplates his own hitchhikers, or with Hill's Vic Messenger as he ventures into the brink for the as-yet unknown other Basil Belheumer (pp. 12–13), all at least tacitly and quickly require Lofland's "decision calculus" for connecting with the strangers. This holds for the innumerable chance encounters presented to other picaros and picaras. Some, like Waller's Vaughn Rhomer, in his agonizingly calibrated approach for three nights running in New Orleans as he toasts the "distant" and yet alluring woman, the dark exotic other, across the tables at the Cafe Beignet (p. 163), suggest that the calculus belongs to an even higher mathematics as some picaros assay the trespass of the social borders. Some others, like Nan in Berg's *The Pull of the Moon* as she sizes up the lonely man invited to her cabin, instinctively practice a more emotion-laden equation.

But if the picaro can skillfully trade in the conventional suits of social interaction, taking advantage of the accepted points of "permission" in meeting the strangers, he can as well regard as trump cards the possibilities his marginality, his unbondedness, his road-exile, allow him to bring to what Lofland terms the "unconventional games" the more daring cosmopolitan can play. First among these are "identity games." Since the adventurous urbanite or the acrobatic picaro approaches the unknown strangers as much "anonymous" to them as they are to him, the adventurer among strangers can deploy himself quite as he will, according to Lofland, by "passing," or "performing," or "pretending" (pp. 161–66) and, with these chameleon prospects, can play sporadically or extensively at whatever identity might best bring him into the stranger's ambit by putting cosmetic on his own desirability, or by "staging" prospects of "legitimate" interaction, or by striking a timely pose to increase the other's sense of the appropriateness of the situation. New American picaros and picaras, like their literary forebears, frequently display large and ingenuous appreciations for the requirements of a scene, and their capacities for role-playing, the general rubric for their forms of cosmopolitan identity feints and ploys, most often stem from picaresque loneliness, on the one hand, and the narrative mission of social inventory, on the other, as both impel them to meet the strangers out there the road inevitably crosses. Their small or large identity duplicities, used as means for getting started with or gaining access to the unknown others, are usually harmless—like Steinbeck pretending to be lost or Joe Buck in *Midnight Cowboy* performing as the cowboy he is not—but even their more sizable encounter-deceits are or at least can be narratively utile in broaching the others. After all, as characters in picaresque narratives, the "Steinbeck" of the autobiographical pages as much as the "Joe Buck" of the novel, they labor less under the ordinary constrictions on social behavior than under the necessity to bring human ways and means of encounter, however unusual, forward for fuller inspection. As the renewed form of the genre thus sponsors the American picaro's participation in such social gambits, at least at one level, the vital possibilities revealed for engaging the strangers, the additional "ways and means" of penetrating into the worlds of others, might surely be thought to outweigh occasional indiscretions or socially unconventional forms of self-presentation, especially since these picaresque forms of role-playing are often nothing other in any event than extensions of the more or less predictable "guises" or "pretense" practiced in the society at large. Without falsely posing as a numbers messenger, E. L. Doctorow's Billy Bathgate could not gain entry to Dutch Schultz's underworld cohort, and, without some pretenses about his saxophone abilities, Richard Hill's picaro, Vic Messenger, could not become the marginal "messenger" between black and white social worlds.

This appears pertinent as well for the second kind of unconventional social adventures of encounter, those Lofland calls "interactional games,"

chief among which are "haggling" and "hustling," as these are inter-
twined with the identity shifts, dodges, and deceptions in the repertoire
of the skilled cosmopolitan. Haggling in its pure form between complete
strangers involves complex labors of self-concealment and self-revelation,
at least with respect to the objects of desire, and, as the parties anonymous
to one another attempt to pierce each other's deceptions, this practice or
art can bring the unknown other into the realm of the personally known
stranger. Although Lofland suggests that such a practice might no longer
exist purely in the frame of late modernity, there can be little doubt that
certain new American picaros borrow of such an "art," sometimes com-
bined with barter, as they attempt to make their various ways through
the world. Loyal Blood "haggles" over the price of gasoline with the
woman proprietor at the isolated tourist stop, and this creates an "introduction" to her, by way of a self-disclosure by her, that leads to sexual
barter. Steinbeck haggles over the value of his stores, himself diminishing the costs and thus trading whiskey for company. Larry McMurtry's
"Cadillac Jack" follows the trail to secure fascinating objects fascinating
to his desire (like Rudolf Valentino's hubcaps), but the reader is soon
aware that his picaresque tour occurs far less for any acquisitive purposes
than for the opportunities for haggling, barter, and exchange, with the
"objects" continually trading hands and secondary in any event to the
matter of the picaro's forays into and out of new occasions for human
interchange. The play, not the possession, is the thing.

The other unconventional maneuver of interaction, hustling, the essential goal of which is to get the stranger to enter a "game" the cosmopolitan or picaro supposes he can win, involves forms of posing that invite the stranger to the same supposition, with the hustler all the while
enticing the "mark" onto grounds where he or she can be revealed or, in
terms of inventory, "taken." Related to the grifts of con-artistry when the
purposes are fraudulent, this game has the new American picaro retriev-
ing the delinquent arts of old picaros like Guzman de Alfarache, but the
hustle can work to other kinds of purposes as well, not the least of which,
in this context, is to bring the parties into forms of exchange and social
familiarity. En route, the picaro frequently meets hustlers, as when W.
Hampton Sides encounters the Justice of the Peace who wagers that he
can bite his own eyes or when Least Heat Moon meets the road-evangelist Arthur Bakke, who hustles for Jesus, or when young Vic Messenger
meets Ice, who pimps, peddles, and pushes, but the picaro too can take
a turn at this game, as when Herlihy's Joe Buck plays out on the social
edges at the world's oldest "hustle" or when Berger's Jack Crabb plays

the lost naif in white society or the expert "scout" to General Custer in order to gain a "place." As haggling and hustling occur in the social actions of the new American picaro, they are again marginal actions, in the sense that the picaro's life on the social peripheries gives him the advantage of employing such unusual means for moving into encounter, for gaining familiarity, for taking social stock wherever and however he might, for locating such virtues as devolve to the adventurous cosmopolitan navigating the seas of social anonymity. His "unbondedness," for all of its lonesome exile, provides him with a special margin of freedom, for he can float and move and sting and dodge, can adapt and camouflage himself, can even dissemble, all to gain encounter, and can do so without the binding constrictions of those who belong to and are obligated by the behaviors incumbent upon those resident in some social center. In mobility, the games are "on."

In many ways thus made for a life continuously among strangers, the picara and picaro, like their more localized counterparts spotted in the genuinely skilled urbanite, propose, as Lofland observes, that "we can live in a world of strangers only because we have found a way [or ways] to eliminate some of the 'strangeness'" (p. 176). Both the picaresque figure and the city adventurer, in learning the necessary codes and skills, in developing the pertinent attitudes, and in entering the games, answer to the requirements of the social reality each must confront. According to Lofland, the phenomenon of the city, with its congestion of strangers, "created a new kind of being—the cosmopolitan—who was able . . . to relate to others in the new ways that city living made not only possible but necessary" (p. 177). And, if the true urbanite is equal to his or her social situation in the city, the new American picaro can prove up to the task of negotiating his own broader world of strangers in an America filled with anonymous others, can indeed learn from even the most unconventional cosmopolitan, just as Joe Buck studies with Enrico "Ratso" Rizzo. For the most adept wayfarers, to develop the various skills, attitudes, and ploys of this shape of urbanity is not necessarily to lose the capacity for lasting, multifaceted, and deep personal and intimate relationships: it is, rather, to supplement them with new ways and means appropriate for wider social reaches into the spheres of unknown others; it is, as Lofland observes, to gain "the capacity for the surface, fleeting, restricted relationship" (p. 178), to possess an acumen for the life of movement in which departures are more or less continuous. For the picaro or picara at least, the lasting personal or intimate relationship is ordinarily not an option—not possible, that is, as long as the figure carries out his or her road work.

The New Civility: Arts of Inventory after Babel

As necessary as elements of such a "new cosmopolitanism" are for the picaro's own passages onto social turfs that are terra incognita to him, however, those capacities in and of themselves are not sufficient for the task of getting the natives from the natives' point of view. While the picaro's ability respecting the fleeting and restricted relationship is indispensable because it serves existence in a world of "others" and because it can help him rapidly cover a lot of social grounds, thus multiplying the numbers of shapes, stripes, styles, and sizes of "human-kinds" in the American inventory, this cosmopolitan finesse can only make for the quickest of encounters, and it must be accompanied by other capacities if the social stock-taking is to be or become anything adequate to the intentions of Peter Jenkins, Harrison Salisbury, David Lamb, Walt Harrington, Taylor Greer, Oedipa Maas, Joe Buck, Billy Bathgate, and others, to hit more than the glancing interactional blow of quick encounter, to be able to move more fully into engagement, to find out, as Jenkins, Moyers, and others define the mission, who the strangers out there really are, how they live, what they think, fear, hope, and how one might stand in relation to them. Unless the picaresque inventory should only result in the skinny items or the spare notations "Arthur Bakke: crazy road-evangelist" and "Barbara Pierre: employee at Ford dealership," Least Heat Moon knows further social arts must be cultivated. Unless the items entered by yet another picaro into the social encyclopedia are to read only, briefly, "Betty Boop: drug-addicted jazz singer" or "Tonto: alto-sax man" or "Ice: pimp, peddler, pusher," Vic Messenger knows that the engagements have to go further, that he must figuratively (and with Ice literally) grab the stranger's neck "in a headlock and hold on," that he must manage to move quite past initial encounters into somewhat more sustained interludes, at once more telling or disclosive of the other. Fleeting access alone, opened by cosmopolitan nimbleness, is not enough to conquer the picaro's loneliness, to quench his curiosity, or to fulfill the urge of the narrative genre for a deeper demography. Once access to the other has been achieved, by urbane tactic or by accident, the fuller connection with the person hitherto a stranger can occur only if the picaro or picara can muster additional arts of trespass, piercing deeper into the now-known stranger's point of view, even while such fuller "connections" must also lack permanence in the face of the call of the road, the need to move on.

These "additional" arts, which often aid the picaro or picara in finally superseding the quickest cosmopolitan hits or misses, serve him or her in taking roadside relations past anonymous encounter, past scant forms of familiarity and into fuller terms of engagement, and they flow more or less naturally from several of the picaresque figure's defining traits. For the Tonto of first meeting to become more completely apprehended by Vic Messenger, for the Jack Dawson of initial converse to be more "realized" by David Lamb, for the Arthur Bakke or Barbara Pierre of accidental meeting and greeting to reveal more fully to Least Heat Moon, the matter of simply gaining access must be completed by the picaros' and picaras' actions and attitudes of a "new civility" appropriate not only for approaching but also for beginning to decipher the myriad strangers in the American world after Babel. At once obvious and subtle, the fundamental terms for thus coming more thoroughly into the company of strangers depend on the picaresque figure's ability and willingness to be who, what, he or she is as picaro or picara, as a marginal figure whose "place" and corollary manner on the margins is, once again, instructive about the possibilities of achieving at least temporary and tolerable and, thus, significant human rapport in a socially discordant environment marked for the stresses and strains of its pluralistic anonymity.

A cornerstone of the "new civility," a rudiment required to convert a fleeting encounter with the stranger into an occasion for that other to disclose something of himself or herself, lies in the picaresque protagonists' usually sustained trait of a democratizing equanimity, their ability to approach and to engage all of the varieties of the human "other" out there without predispositions concerning who is high and who is low, who is right and wrong, important or unimportant, powerful or deprived, even interesting or boring, and so on. Hill's Vic Messenger, as a case in point, first approaches the local musician Tonto with the same kind of regard that he later brings to the encounter with "Satchmo," Louis Armstrong, and, for another, Thomas Berger's Jack Crabb, caught between social worlds in *Little Big Man*, practices the same kind of latitude with the crazy, "reverse" Indian as he displays at least for a time with General George Armstrong Custer. Such a trait, related to the picaro's affable "tolerance" and essential "coolness," is perhaps a function as well not only of loneliness and curiosity but of that marginal status he himself has in exile that makes him slow to judgment of others. In any event, when marshaled, such an attribute, such ingrained or learned forbearance, helps to extend interaction with the stranger when it also, beyond expansive courtesy, generates in the adept picaro or picara a characteristic manner of calm regard, neither fawning nor condescending (unless, of course, the "game" requires), neither aggressive nor taciturn. Tending to approach all with equal eye, unless the "codes" or "signals" alert him otherwise, the picaro or picara, in the mood, in effect "invites" the encountered stranger into fuller converse by giving that other a countenance, simultaneously, of interest and, ironically, of indifference. The self-presentation in this demeanor is not usually feigned: it grows, perhaps inevitably, out of the picaro's life "on edge," craving to come out of isolation but slightly wary of, or at least highly alert to, the prospect of rebuff. Nevertheless, signaling openness, even such casual interest might flatter enough to elicit a beginning, cordial responsiveness.

The accompanying "indifference" appears as a form of self-restraint, a measure of ego-control that, refusing temptations of self-assertion to fill the conversational "spaces" exclusively with the lonely, chattering picaro's views, allows the other to enter those communicative spaces with his or her views.[19] More a tolerant nonchalance than any callousness, like Lars Eighner's sculpted diffidence in *Travels with Lizbeth* when he accepts a ride with a man wearing only undershorts, it is not a brusque or uncaring aloofness and not a facile and unprincipled assent to any proposition but is, rather, a noncommittal shape of personal reserve, a self-presentational formality that can reassure the just-met acquaintance of a kind of operative detachment in this wayfarer. A posture that does not rush to evaluate and, so, does not insult or threaten or pry too deeply, is, of course, natural to the picaro's marginal situation. At least temporarily unbonded during his time on the road, he is also uncommitted when he arrives on any particular social scene, and, without investment in the dynamic of the scene, he appears before the others, the strangers, as one who is placidly unimplicated and, thus, implying no harm. As Georg Simmel's pioneering, if somewhat impressionistic, sociological work on the stranger concludes, this kind of figure arriving from the road, securely signaling what here is termed "a new civility," is just the stranger to whom any one or more of those there, in place, might possibly open up *most* completely, to whom they might indeed prove willing to reveal intimate aspects of their lives not to be shared with or even revealed to the others in the place.[20] The unimplicated stranger, the picaro, who will soon "go" in any event poses no danger by virtue of his hearing things of one's private life that one would not wish known by his or her neighbors, those who have "stayed" and whose continuing presence affects one. Thus coming as a kind of sounding-board, an affable, attentive, and civil ear, the picaro or picara as keen listener also becomes, or can become, a megaphone through which the others, the strangers, speak themselves into the reader's hearing. This picaresque receptivity, notable for its predilection against quick judgment, is also a virtue, of course, leading as it does or can in this context to the picaro's slightly more extended stay and to the possibilities of inventories in more depth than, for David Lamb, "Jack Dawson: Montana cattle-rancher" or, for Herlihy's Joe Buck, "Tombaby Barefoot: misshapened, half-breed pervert."

But to succeed in this deeper stock-taking, such simple and apparently undiscriminating receptivity must itself be accompanied by yet another feature the most engaging picaros and picaras seize upon in their practices of the "new civility" required to get to know the strangers— namely, a capacity abetted by life on the boundaries for what Ninian Smart calls "structured empathy," the suppleness of feeling and imagination to be able to walk a mile in the other person's moccasins.[21] To be or become merely "an open if indifferent ear" to the stranger invites only the most trivial talk in response, even if the weather or sports or "what breed of dog that is" gives an initial opening. For the relationship to move ahead even briefly, to quicken into fuller reciprocity, the picaro or picara must learn to be reassuring to the strangers not only about his or her interest and his or her non-judgmental temperament but also about a willingness at least for a time to enter the others' world views, to see things as they see them, to try out their values, to feel life as they suffer it, not just to get it, as Geertz puts it, "from the natives' point of view" but to enter as a cordial outsider into the natives' world and to participate in it with a measure of "fellow feeling." Signals of such empathy not only to engage but to be engaged with the other's outlook might well temporarily afford fuller "in-look" into the strangers' conditions and self-understandings, and the highest quality of empathy itself rides decisively on a key attribute of the picaro's nature, his heightened capability for sensory attunement to what or whom stands outside of him, to play the human scene as the scene presents itself, instead of surrendering to egotism or succumbing to a preformulated script.[22] As with the anthropologist, this empathy must be "structured" by firm holds on self-possession and critical senses of limits—the object is not, after all, to "go native"— but, again, the picaro's defining equipoise, that inner equilibrium that keeps him balanced if not "upright" in hard and tumultuous situations, can stand by him well. With the integrity of his own identity intact, he can participate fully, "see feelingly," not only allowing the other to speak but also, in deference for a time to the other's world, beckoning that now-known stranger's own integral life—high or low, empowered or deprived, noble or mean—to come to fuller disclosure.

In the brief affective and successive participations in "world view" after different "world view" during the picaresque journey, moreover, another of the picaro's standing assets can prevent that condition in which the quality of empathy is strained past breaking or dissipated by overwork. His life on the margins, in the social interstices, creates in him the remarkable narrative trait of being able, time and again, to start over, *volver nuevo*, to move himself from one episode to the next with fresh and ready and newly opened eyes, and this ability clearly anticipates the need of the road quickly to leave behind one stranger's "world" in order to enter just as rapidly yet a quite different stranger's "world" always looming up ahead and, in that new entrance, to conduce and allow the stranger to be himself or herself. For the ever-shifting empathies these multiplicitous worlds of strangers necessitate, the picaro or picara manifestly requires, indeed cannot in this framework do without, some form of what the anthropologist Hortense Powdermaker terms "the ability to be psychologically mobile,"[23] an ability, again, founded on and funded by the picaro's sensory alacrity and emotional resilience. For the sake of civil responsiveness, his inner disposition must be quickly and variously adaptable, prepared for the sake of his empathies to relinquish neurotic baggage and to come psychologically "clean" to his serial but serially heterogeneous work of social engagement. The fuller inventory of the American picaresque depends upon skills of empathizing, as these skills are dependent upon a "psychological mobility," itself in turn enabled or at least latent by virtue of literary and literal mobility through numerous and discrete social pockets.

A final crucial element of the new picaresque civility is a subset related both to the figure's receptive equanimity and to his or her empathetic adaptability, and it centers in a communicative expertise appropriate for the socially anonymous, pluriform, and often rancorous or opaque worlds of the American social "babble" the picaro and picara must traverse. In such a world or worlds, after the fact of "Babel," the confusions and conflicts of "tongues" can best be averted, George Steiner contends, by the fine and devoted arts of translation. Segregated into different "worlds" of outlooks, values, means and modes, customary behaviors, and the like, strangers to each other employ a multiplicity of manners of speaking that stymies social converse and complicates social existence, their very "languages" often seeming impenetrable to those who traffic in a different tongue, and the tricky business is to locate means by which those worlds can at least "correspond." As Steiner recognizes, with himself as a case in point, the people most fully equipped to translate such worlds to each other are the ones who belong fully to neither world, who belong partly to or can empathize with both or several worlds, and who, on such edges or borders, want to be honest and respectful to each world of encounter.[24] Again, the condition of exile or "unbondedness" becomes an asset for life in a world of strangers, and, albeit a much more rapid and extemporaneous action than Steiner envisions, the necessities of the picaro or picara can again turn into his or her virtues, if, that is, he or she can work from the margins to master the modes of communicative intercourse that allow hearing the strangers for what they in fact say and mean and that have the empathetic charge to make the picaro "conversant" with them in their own idioms.

Construed in this way, the feat of translative connection that might bridge the discrete worlds can be accomplished most completely by one who travels the several worlds, the stranger on the road whose dialogical acumen can not only establish civil discourse with one American stranger after another but whose very *forms* of conducting discourse in a world of myriad strangers might be a model for introducing those strangers to each other, as so clearly it is a narrative means for bringing them all forward for the witness of the reader, another stranger still. Flowing from highly tolerant curiosity, self-restraint, and equanimity, the picaro's finest art of dialogue, the effort of creating reciprocity and empathy, the operation of "translating" the other more fully into the picaresque inventory, follows, in scene after scene, some form of a non-intrusive but interrogatory mode in which the picaro poses questions, listens attentively if "indifferently" to the response, subdues the temptations either to assent or to rejoin, poses another slightly more probing question, and continues this communicative process as long as the other, the situation, the success of the exchange, and the call of the road will allow. In responding to the picaro's questions, when the queries are apt, gracious, and ever more empathetically inviting, the stranger, ideally, can be reassured about being ever-more forthcoming, revealing himself or herself in ways that enable the picaro to deal with him or her less in categorical terms, less as a specimen of a type, and more in terms of his or her singular, distinctive, and integral character. With such increasing self-disclosure by the stranger, under the encouraging guidance of the inquirer's gentle interrogations, the picaro or picara with conversive acumen might finally gain a fuller appreciation of the complex lexicon of the stranger's speaking and the world from which he or she speaks, thus enhancing the ability to translate this other to others (including the reader) without awkward intrusions or overweening and distorting interpositions. When this or that picaro or picara fully, if sometimes unwittingly, realizes or approximates such civil converse, it is clear that this dialogical, interrogatory, and translative art is less substantive than formal, depending at least to a point less on what is asked or said than on the manner of converse itself, but, though the picaro's manner in the inquisitive mode might well be a matter of attitude and form, it is also clear that the possible result is substantial, the newly known person of substance, enfleshment, depth, now replacing the "stranger" of category, preformation, broad type, scant outline.[25] Working on the social edges, crossing human borders, temporarily transgressing on the other, the picaros and picaras arrive on a socially troubled American scene "just in the nick of time." Their trespass is complete and completely forgiven when the translative discourse of the new civility has affect: the stranger is now "known," not utterly but more integrally, the inventory deepens as well as widens; the once-stranger indeed might well have increased his or her own social stock, expanded his or her own welcome and room for new company, by granting the picaro or picara some momentary narrative admission.[26]

With cosmopolitan approaches mastered and civil discourse learned, the cumulative inventory of the new American picaresque can include not only the quick and impressionistic sketches of those whom the picaros and picaras trespass rapidly en route, yet with whom nothing much develops, but also deeper realizations of those more fully engaged, those who become more than simply nameless, for whom fuller portraits are possible because of their own self-disclosures. There are, of course, literally thousands of American "others" who, on the pages of the new American picaresque, appear and disappear in sudden successions, those "met" but only to remain yet-anonymous and only categorically "known" even if the narrator can render the quickest of senses of them in passing: the nasty river-rat near Tomato rapidly fronted by B. C. Hall and C. T. Wood in *Big Muddy*, the fragile adolescent homosexual Joe Buck "encounters" briefly in *Midnight Cowboy*, the sorry and irritable tourist designated "Shirtless from Wisconsin" and quickly passed over by David Lamb in *A Sense of Place*, the "steely haired woman . . . [with] a bored look" in the Chicago personnel office who "wearily"[27] and brusquely dispatches the title picaro, Joey, in David Rounds's *Celebrisi's Journey*, the "young-ancient waitress" in the German restaurant in Minnesota in a chat so peremptory in *Travels with Charley* that Steinbeck cannot decide if she is "a young and troubled girl or a very spry old woman" (p. 130). But, in the accumulated human stock-taking, there are also, indeed, those whose names are never known or at least mentioned by the picaro or narrator but whose more fully re-vealed "selves," elicited by the wayfarers' urbane largesse and civil con-verse, enter the *galeria* in more dimension than such silhouettes. In *Blue Highways*, Least Heat Moon, with studied skill, empathy, and translative decorum, engages to a point of his own exasperation the character to be "known" by the reader only as "The Boss of the Plains," and this world-weary "stranger" divulges everything from his proctological status, his regrets about an earlier, ended marriage, his job troubles and worries about aging, even his horror that one of his daughters is a "model" on condom machines scattered around the city of Tucson (pp. 179–84). Or, in E. Annie Proulx's *Postcards*, Loyal Blood's naively "cosmopolitan" barter can yield a somewhat more faceted inventory item regarding the woman recorded on course only as "Mrs. Sweetheart Pinetree" (pp. 27–30) because he is able with instinctive, if innocent, dexterity to evoke her complicity in the "fun and games" of disclosure.

And, past these short but fuller portraits, the picaro and picara often stay long enough and succeed completely enough at the work of engage-ment and the arts of civility to be able in narrative retrospection to pro-vide those pictures of the strangers that push even deeper, range further, in delivering "studies" of the others' human dimensions and complexi-ties. Richard Hill's Vic Messenger gains a nuanced and empathetic sense of Betty Boop, the troubled black jazz singer, in part because she herself guides him, with a reassuring touch on the back, into a deeper introduc-tory realization of the possibilities of human relation (p. 87). Least Heat Moon returns a significant episode of his narrative to "Miz Alice" Venable Middleton of Smith Island, Maryland, "one of those octogenarians who make age look like something you don't want to miss" (p. 433) and who deepens his own growing capacities for a new civility by beginning to teach him that the most difficult things about living with others are "'hav-ing the gumption to live different *and* the sense to let everybody else live different'" (p. 442). Mort Rosenblum practices a thoroughly attentive equanimity in dealing with and in delivering to the reader both the Idaho tycoon J. R. Simplot and his "flip side" Carl Yanick, retired hobo, cattle-puncher, and chef,[28] just as Richard Reeves uses his interrogatory "indif-ference" to hear out and render not only Thomas Stachelek, a Philadel-phia assistant prison superintendent, but some of the "residents" at Graterford, Rexcell Cook (inmate F3925), Miguel Rivera (F4976), and James Charlton (F5265).[29] David Rounds's Joey Celebrisi, even in the midst of his own concentrated travail and a series of picaresque "stunts," overcomes a difficult start processively to invite one new acquaintance, Brother Stephen, to "breeze on" and discovers for the inventory one who "had outdone even a priest"—"His stunt was total; he had reinvented his entire life" (p. 71)—and, moreover, one who helps give Joey comparable prospects. Whether in fast and scant detail, when time or cosmopolitan failures allow nothing else, or more in fuller, deliberative representation, when the new civility works to affect, these and hundreds upon hundreds of Americans—high and low, generous and vicious, content and angry, healthy and neurotic—"people" the new American picaresque *galeria*, a veritable encyclopedia of American humanity constructed in the course of road exile and brought into view through the picaro's roving eye and attentive ear.

Now, obviously, not all of the new American picaros and picaras are equally adept at meeting the requirements of the new civility that the marginal life of the road presses on them, and, of course, even those most intent on meeting and knowing the American "others" cannot always sustain the attentive but studied indifference of engagement, the self-restraints necessary for structured empathy and psychological mobility, or the quickened arts of colloquy and translation. When they can be seen to fail at these subtle road necessities of social existence through some faults of their own, the picaresque inventory of the social motley will nevertheless appear on the pages: the numerous strangers at roadside will continue to come into view regardless, even if some several socially feeble picaros are only able or willing to enter them onto the pages and into the census books in spare notations. And, even with such failures of fuller engagement, these picaros' shortcomings work heuristically, symptomatic as they are in exposing to view the nature and toll of epidemic social incivility and, thus, signaling lessons yet to be learned.

When the picaro or picara succeeds, however, when he or she seizes upon the accidental virtues of exile and marginality to sate the craving created by loneliness and what Lofland regards as an intolerable anonymity, the picaresque presents those momentary episodes that reify in many narrative embodiments the urbane adventurer, the skilled cosmopolitan, the assiduous democrat, the capacious and mobile "empathete," the restless translator. In the glimpses the reader catches of this timely figure, commensurate with the times, none other than the new American picaro or picara, the fundamentals of a new civility, forged out of lives lived on the margins and adequate to the task of moving about in the midst of strangers emerge for inspection. Moreover, with some shifts and amendments, they appear in this work also for possible adoption by other people, quite beyond the picaro or picara, as all seek to cope with the congestions of strangers nearly all Americans, nearly inevitably must encounter in their own courses through contemporary life.

In one of its major contours, then, the new American picaresque accepts the challenge of a complex "social work" as the literary genre answers to some of the most significant and difficult dilemmas of the American times. By exposing the social-psychological malaises of the "self" suffered by the picaros and picaras and other Americans, it also proposes the therapies of the road as one vital, experiential means of individual self-recovery. In exploring a kaleidoscopic pluralism, it employs its narrative means to register the myriad and complex territories of American human "difference," and, in diagnosing "the pains of pluralism," it isolates those socially estranging maladies that discomfit the picaros and picaras and their countrypersons alike as each and all find themselves caught in a tumultuous world of strangers. By tracing out the possibilities created by the picaro's and picara's life on "social edge," life after the felt consequences of Babel, life in loneliness and need, the new American picaresque both posits the terms and requirements for coping in the congested world of strangers and poses lessons that might be learned in the curriculum of exile regarding a "new civility," a form of psychological and colloquial responsiveness to the social "other" that might suffice for deeper human stock-taking. In this work of detection and counter, diagnosis and possible cure, encounter and engagement, the American social inventory provided by this literary formation literally fills to brimming. Not only does the cumulative picaresque supply a demographic accounting, however, and not only does it deliver additional human "contents": it also explores the ways that the picaros and picaras grapple with the very acts and arts of taking such stock and seize upon the virtues of the margins. These narrative dramas perhaps issue a new kind of datum or extensive new human data for social-scientific reflection—to wit, a "personalized" collection of American strangers learning to cope with other American strangers, an anthology brought to the fore for inspection through the unanticipated medium of *Humaniora*. But if the social "world of strangers" entered by the new picaro and delivered by the American picaresque might possibly give the sociologists and anthropologists something new to consider in the contemplation of their own human "findings" and the terms of their own vocations "on edge," the general service of the social "road-work" in these narratives is to those American readers "out there" who themselves must wrestle with the problems of what to make of and how best to live in the pluriform human theater that is their country, indeed how to manage life in relation to their neighbors' stark othernesses.

At the least, the new American picaresque provides readers with a vicarious access to encountering "strange" other Americans and, in this, presents occasions for readers to stretch their own capacities for fuller receptivity and social translation respecting those others met on the pages. Indeed, the picaro's or picara's performance in civil forms of converse with those met might well afford the reader some tutelage, in the nick of time, in comparable communicative rituals of rapport to practice in dealing with strangers, perhaps even to locate through the reading experience momentary empathies with the "others" so shortly before considered unapproachably alien.[30] But the labor of the highways continues. The inventory finally to be compiled goes beyond the social varieties that must be counted and noted to approach some broader questions of American meanings and horizons. Thus, new American picaresque purposefulness and the roads it travels must extend into and across wider cultural terrain wherein, again, the picaro's and picara's marginality continues, if now in different ways, to play out vividly and importantly on the various and complex fields of the republic.

PART 3

The Cultural Work of the
New American Picaresque

7

Homo Viator, Homo Spectans:
Slants on the Size of America

The literary work and the social work presented in and by the new American picaresque narratives begin to inaugurate an even broader cultural work. In terms of the literary toil of the new picaresque, the genre accumulated out of its numerous disparate instances revivifies the potency of the old Anglo-European fictional form. By locating an expressive formation to surpass the limits or at least to supplement the vistas of the contemporary literature of alienated "interiority," works like Peter DeVries's *The Blood of the Lamb,* Mort Rosenblum's *Back Home,* Larry McMurtry's *Cadillac Jack,* and Walt Harrington's *Crossings* present a distinctive narrative means apt in several ways for exploring the "outside," American cultural existence "out there," in a time of tumult. The necessary character of such responsiveness to the cultural times pushes the picaresque into a situation of "blurred genres," into a shape that incorporates a variety of literary options—everything from modes of fiction, autobiography, and travelogue to the textual recourses of humanistic geography, social-psychology, narrative sociology, and interpretive ethnography. Thus, in terms of the social labor of the genre, the confluence of fictional and nonfictional tacks of representation signals a narrative struggle to achieve some presentational form adequate to the complexities and upheavals of the American reality. As the works in the genre cumulatively wrestle with the nature and terms of the social scene, they bring to exposure not only the scope of a complex pluralism and not only the tricky conditions for inhabiting this social realm but also, from the margins traveled by the picaros and picaras, some of the conditioning malaises and experiential "cures" of contemporary selfhood and some strategies and arts for locating what will suffice for tolerable social life in the midst of an America experienced at large as "a world of strangers."

As much as the literary and social thrusts of the new American picaresque might thus provide unaccustomed data, unanticipated evidence, and unspent resources regarding those cultural spheres of expressive arts and social matrices, however, the particular nature of the narrative formation, viewed in a certain light, also presents a "through street" into and across much wider and narrower terrains of American culture. The distinctive kind of "road work" enacted by the picaros and picaras and recorded in the cumulative picaresque moves obviously and concertedly into the country's large and abundantly variable stores of regional geographies, local topographies, shifting culturescapes, multiplicitous life forms, kaleidoscopic life-styles, works and days, men and manners, cabbages and kings. The trail ranges in its random and erratic course across virtually every imaginable aspect of American life and touches, in its careening and often accidental progress, practically every possible element of myriad different Americans' ways of "thinking" or "fashioning" themselves and of inserting themselves into their environments.[1] Such a gathered cultural inventory—made possible by the picaros' mobile tours in exile, their unfailing curiosity, their unflinching capacities for trespass, their fleeting rapport with the "others," their transitory connections to scenes, their highway empirics of detail and nuance, and their sheer intrepid ways through an endless series of "roadside attractions"— is indeed encyclopedic, a staggering total of "there" and "them," this and that and the other, a virtual "America" on the pages, the sheer size of which clearly requires numerous picaros and picaras "on the road" all the time.

In the context of concerns related to the general cultural work of the new American picaresque, however, the significance of the genre increases again just because—again—its numerous, disparate narrative texts, as they together approach the crucial chore of American inventory, labor at this task by operating on and from the cultural margins. As Giles Gunn has reminded the world of American cultural criticism, such vantages gained from the edges afford interpretation a special margin of freedom by supplying to it different viewpoints with which to think through the culture anew from directions and with perspectives that

crosscut the conventional grain.[2] The work of this chapter, then, is devoted to the ways the new American picaresque provides such vantages
on and from the margins and thus "advantages" the reader with new
possibilities for his or her possible re-envisioning of the American cultural stores. Not only with the size and diversity of American plenitude
gathered but also with the particular character and process of the work
of inventory, the new American picaresque performs the service of providing a significant interpretive leeway, this "margin of freedom," by
gifting the reader with fuller inventory, with neglected stock, and with
new slants on the preserves extant in the American hold.

The nature, dynamic, and potential effects of this cultural inventory
from the edges appear in three distinct ways. In a first matter of exposition here, the focus must necessarily widen to account for the size and
variety of the sheer stuff accounted by the genre. The huge and viscous
stock cumulatively taken *is* taken, of course, by way of picaros and picaras
in their road exile, a particular species of *homo viator* (the "human traveling"), and, thus, the items entered rapidly or more gradually into the
bookkeeping clearly include far more numerous and disparate things,
places, people, and scenes, than any individual reader, no matter how
extensively traveled or intrepid in spirit, could ever encounter directly.
In these travels, the picaros and picaras, en masse, naturally become narrative agents for the reader's vicariously covering vast, almost unimaginable reaches of American ground and thus amplifying his or her senses
of the "size" of the American place. But the marginality of these narrative agents leads to a second significant point of consideration—namely,
the picaro's views into ignored or neglected or at least less-traveled territories. Unaccustomed items for the inventory are tracked down on what
a reader might well have concluded are the peripheries of American culture, and such ignored or neglected areas are tracked down or fortuitously
encountered or blundered into by those picaresque figures whose own
mobile and peripheral situation in the culture presents them with points
of access to some marginalized areas not to be gained by people more
"normally" or conventionally situated in cultural terms. The picaresque
form thus occasions for the reader not only enormous range but often
unusual access, with one picaro or picara or another, to "people" and into
"places" the reader might not otherwise have encountered. But even
when readers find this picaro or that picara moving toward or into sites
and scenes altogether familiar or more or less predictable to public or
common view, the new American picaresque often manages to locate
other than the anticipated angles on these things, and this ability to ob-

serve "on the slant," another function of the picaresque figure's marginality, points toward a third important element of the cultural work of inventory. Tramping on life in road exile, the picaros and picaras work not simply as *homo viator*, covering broad ground, but, intermittently, with the special status of *homo spectans* (the "human seeing"), and, because they view America from the edges or peripheries, they frequently see on unexpected horizons, from odd angles, through singular lenses, with unique slants on things, enabled by the narrative witness from these margins. With each of these thrusts, the formations of the new picaresque, following their transitive characters on their haphazard courses, sometimes make provisions on behalf of readers for approaching the American experience through the perceptual life of these "others," these marginalized figures on the road, these wanderers free in their unbondedness to cut across the accustomed views. In this, seeing with and through the eyes of the picaros and picaras, the literary form invites the reader to enter occasions for his or her own defamiliarization, to risk those momentary episodes gathered here and there that entice or coerce the reader to see another thing or to see a common thing in another way. In this cultural work of cumulative inventory, then, the new American picaresque represents not only a transient struggle to seize hold of the size and variety of the country but also a narrative expedition to rediscover America by seeing the place anew.

"What They See": The Size and Scope of Americana

Interspersed throughout E. Annie Proulx's *Postcards*, whose protagonist's hapless and sporadic picaresque career spans the 1940s to the present all across America, there are short passages entitled "What I See,"[3] and these little interludes in narrative time, usually attached to Loyal Blood's consciousness, briefly interrupt a journey in narrative space already rich in the sights and sounds of Americana to compound the narrative catalog with additional entries. Early on, he finds, "sees," among many other things, "metal signs saying Nehi," "plaster ducks on withered lawns," "the steamy warmth of the Olympia Cafe [where] he eats thick pancakes with Karo," Pennsylvania vineyards (p. 31), "miles of snow fence," "southering geese," and, again, "the H&C Cafe" within which, "hunched over the cup of coffee, he wonders how far he is going" (p. 32). Later on the road or in the decades, what he sees includes "three girls standing at the edge of the woods, their arms encircling masses of red trillium," a sign for "Sigurd's Snakepit," "a man sleeping under a tractor in a black strip of shade," "a cow lying in a sea of grass like a black Viking boat, a table with a white cloth under an apple tree and at the table a shirtless man with a mahogany face and soft white breasts," "wet boulders along a lakeshore," and, in another diner, "painted wooden tables" (p. 62). In the uranium towns of Utah, he spots "dusty, dented jeeps," "bulldozers and backhoes," "stake trucks loaded with burlap sacks of ore," and everywhere "men in dusty, crumpled clothes putting nickels in red Coca-Cola machines" (p. 109). On the ancient native grounds of the northern tier he catches echoes and resonances of that older world as it "still booms with the hoofbeats of the horses of Red Horse, Red Cloud and Low Dog, the great and mysterious Crazy Horse, . . . [as] they come tearing out of ravines, rise up in killing smiles in the astounded faces of Fetterman, Crook, Custer, Benteen, Reno," and he also catches glimpses of the contemporary native moment by looking through "a box of discarded patient cards from an asylum in Fargo," with photographs and "a description of the subject's mania," including the case of an Indian patient, one "Walter Hairy Chin" (p. 250). In these ways, *Postcards* provides a quick indication of the energies of the new American picaresque in its surges to cover American ground. From the perfectly obvious Nehi sign to the mundane made into metaphor like the Viking-ship cow, from the aesthetically pleasing scene of the young girls holding their flowers to the gritty scene of backhoes, from the natural vistas to the constructed environments, from the past to the enjambing present, from the predictability of snow fences to the startling picture of the shirtless man seated at his white-clothed table under the apple tree, the world of American images swirls past, and the picaras' and picaros' best abilities for attending to this outside world—their innocent approaches, their reluctance to evaluate "high" and "low," their unflagging curiosity, their tutored attunement to scene, their finely calibrated empirical attention to detail, nuance, and the fortuitous moment, and, not least, their narrational capacity for "perfect memory"—all play out powerfully toward the effect of bringing this enormous inventory of the American scene before readers' eyes.

Without special, segregated sections on "What I See," numerous other texts in the new American picaresque add to the general store, comparably to Annie Proulx's novel, seeming fully intentional in terms of their general geographical sweeps across vast American "scapes" and standing similarly dependent upon the figure of the picaro or picara as a lens for the reader's vicarious possibilities in taking in what Steinbeck called "this monster land." In the gathering work of the genre, each of these works itself gathers broadly, capturing American images and scenes, sights and sounds, people and products, in intermittent moments of narrative repose, however short the stay or fleeting the picture. As George Meegan enters his North American ground in *The Longest Walk*, for instance, he successively and quickly encounters and represents several Texas towns that serve his beginning index to the shapes and varieties of American life. After splurging on his tramp's threadbare course for motel time, he remembers that, after South America, North "America only really began for me . . . in Room 112 of the Brownsville Ramada Inn" because "an American motel room is surely one of the wonders of the world: wall-to-wall carpeting; a banana tree outside the French windows; and beyond, sparkling through the foliage, a swimming pool; running hot water, with ice close to hand . . . crisp, spotless sheets, and heart-stopping, deep pillows . . . all this starched hygiene was heaven."[4] Such heaven disrupted by a series of obscene phone calls, however, he soon returns to the rougher road, whereon the inventory of Americana continues to mount out of his wayward course through other Texas towns. First, in Sinton, Meegan reports, "I slept on a judge's lofty bench, directly beneath a photo of LBJ" (p. 290). Then "in a shower of mosquitoes I hit Refugio, a town with a Spanish name just southwest of Calhoun County—an Irish name [—where] an American pilot with the Dutch name of Hans Vandervlugt took me home" and "I thought: this is America; America contains all the world" (p. 290). Next, however, "my idealism took a battering": "as I sat inside a general store in Colet Creek, seeking momentary escape from the sun and insects, the owner brought out a rifle and ordered me off the premises" (pp. 290–91). Then soon, again seeking overnight shelter, he finds in Victoria that "the church elders sniffed at my press clippings [about the journey] before declining to let me sleep on the Sunday School floor," and later, staying over as a recourse at the Salvation Army emergency center, he listens to the paupers' and dead-beats' amazement that one among their number "had been an extra in the film *The Alamo*" (p. 291). All of this—motel hygiene, cinema, obscene calls, church, names—appears virtually at the beginning of his journey through the United States, and, page after page thereafter, what Meegan sees in his long trek, south to north, across the country, narratively stores items of American cultural stuff to points of brimming over.

If a single picaresque text can collect such an amount and variety in so brief a narrative span, others multiply the store with their own comparable sweeps or reaches in generally canvassing the country, with their

own pages adding to the cumulative inventory. Joey Celebrisi, the picaresque lens in David Rounds's narrative, finds temporary work on the
conveyor belt in an East Chicago slaughterhouse, from which experience
he records some of his own sites, sights, and sensations:

> In rode the pigs' heads, looking waxy and solemn. Each person [along
> the belt] was assigned a certain bit of anatomy to rip out of each head as
> it passed by. The backs of the heads were gone when they got to me. Using
> a long pair of curved scissors with a blunt guard, I had to nudge aside
> the brains and snip-snip, pluck out the pituitary, a bright pink pea. Two
> peas a minute made . . . nine hundred sixty in an eight-hour day, till I
> ached with the burning stink of the place and my head was a blur.[5]

After this, it must perhaps seem only fair to the reader that Joey soon witness a more soothing venue of Americana, one he enters into the accounting about his passage of a week through rural Illinois, Iowa, and South
Dakota: there he finds "the plains . . . warm with crops, gold with the ripe
winter wheat and green with the unripe corn [as] the cornstalks waved
their tassels like cheerleaders in the wind" (p. 152), and later, around a
combine "harvesting at the edge of the round horizon, I could see the glint
of the sun on the window of the cab" and "I watched [the rising wind with]
its sweep across the surface of the wheat, bending down the top-heavy
stalks as it came, making a deep golden trough of a wave that sped across
the fields" (pp. 153–54). On one side of the continent, in Smoke Hole, West
Virginia, Geoffrey O'Gara locates the scene of an old woman who has
chosen for a half a century to live in mountain isolation: "in front [of Sadie
Kimble's house] sat the automobile she drove like a teenager, a green Ford
Fairmont" and "sheep grazed in a pasture across the road" from her "white
frame house, well kept, with a fenced lawn in front occupied by a mixture
of real and ceramic chickens."[6] On the other side of America, in Angeleno
Heights in Los Angeles, he surveys a more disparate scene of human residence in an urban neighborhood: "the Victorian houses along Carroll and
Kellam avenues have mostly been, or are being, restored. Parked in the
driveways of these stately Queen Annes were BMWs and Mercedeses;
right around the corner, a group of shirtless Hispanic teenagers tinkered
with an old Chevy in front of a graffiti-scarred apartment house, while a
radio roared" (p. 262).

Of course, no single example or several examples of the new American picaresque can begin to be a match for the sheer size of America—
indeed, even the accumulated works of the genre fall far short of any such

accounting—but, one by one and taken together, Andrei Codrescu's *Road Scholar*, K. T. Berger's *Zen Driving*, Mark Winegardner's *Elvis Presley Boulevard*, Mort Rosenblum's *Back Home*, William Least Heat Moon's *Blue Highways*, John Steinbeck's *Travels with Charley*, Richard Reeves's *American Journey*, Thomas Berger's *Little Big Man*, James Leo Herlihy's *Midnight Cowboy*, James Crumley's *The Last Good Kiss*, Peter Jenkins's *A Walk across America*, Laurel Lee's *Godspeed*, Bill Bryson's *The Lost Continent*, Larry McMurtry's *Cadillac Jack*, Katherine Dunn's *Truck*, Robert James Waller's *Border Music*, Harrison Salisbury's *Travels around America*, Bill Moyers's *Listening to America*, and many others, cover huge reaches of the American natural and cultural territories and send their own kinds of "post-cards" to readers by way of their more or less singular picaresque tours. Like the picaresque narratives of Proulx, Meegan, Rounds, and O'Gara, their movements are seven-league in stride, and together they return to the reader America from Bangor to San Diego, from Brownsville to Fairbanks, as they supply images of their own from the likes of little girls holding red trillium to the extraction of porcine pituitary glands, from Sadie Kimble's chicken-filled yard to the Queen Annes on Kellam Avenue, from the shimmering pool of the Brownsville Ramada Inn to the waves of South Dakota grain. What they see, singly and cumulatively, fills American ground from sea to shining sea.

Another shape of the new American picaresque similarly travels large grounds and, on course, takes natural and cultural inventory but devotes its transient way less to such vast or even continental ranges than to more particular territories. Jonathan Yardley's *States of Mind*, for example, treks an extended journey but confines its mobile narrative scope to the mid-Atlantic region, arriving to the reader through images, in downtown Philadelphia, like the "self-satisfied" character of an upscale enclave called "Shops at the Bellevue," designed to protect private investors, in its counterpoise with the area around Market Street, "a racial and ethnic jumble,"[7] the fully public sphere. Later, in the "academical village" of Chapel Hill, he finds a second deck added since his undergraduate days to Kenan Stadium, the University of North Carolina football field once nestled down among the towering pines that were visible from within, an addition now "compromising its unique beauty" (p. 163), and he revisits the Carolina Coffee Shop "where nothing had changed except that in the front room there was now a bar, liquor-by-the-drink having at last been approved" (p. 169). James Crumley's soft, cynical picaro/detective in *The Last Good Kiss*, one C. W. Sughrue, mainly travels a different region of America, the so-called Empty Quarter, the terrain of Lewis and Clark, and what Sughrue sees, among numerous other things, are "June in Montana, high enough up the steps of the northern latitudes to pass for cruel April . . . [when] blue skies ruled stupidly, green mountains shimmered like mirages, and the sun rose each morning to stare into my face with the blank but touching gaze of a retarded child."[8] Earl Thompson's *Caldo Largo,* with its picaro, Johnny Hand, explores the area of south Texas culture and the Gulf of Mexico, and he sees, among many other things, "up above Tampico near the place we call Twenty-four-ten or The Rocks . . . a whole long sparsely inhabited rocky coast . . . dangerous. . . . because of the submerged rocks and reefs."[9] The One-Eyed Mack in Jim Lehrer's *Kick the Can* follows his picaresque tour through the Great Plains to the Texas Gulf, and the narrative inventory of what is seen includes Armistice Day ceremonies in Adabel, Oklahoma, during which, in the midst of the pomp and circumstance, "the Spanish-American War vet was in a uniform I guessed was what he wore then . . . [with] medals on his chest . . . [who was] stooped when he walked but otherwise seemed healthy and with it."[10] As Pete Davies's subtitle indicates, his stock-taking in the country stays in those states comprising his particular venture at "A Journey through the Heart of America," and there, on the great rolling plains of the Midwest, in the midst of myriad other American images, what he sees, "dumped on the banks of the Arkansas," are "the Creek Nation Tulsa Bingo Hall [that] could take thirteen hundred people . . . [but was] slow tonight with only five hundred players (the great majority white) sitting hushed and intent over their cards at rank upon rank of long narrow tables"[11] and, later, in Wisconsin, the play of the Rio Softball Association, "a civilized affair . . . [for which] your team of ten had to be at least half women" and "the pitcher and catcher had to be of different sexes" (p. 204). Although confined to particular regions or territories, these and many other new picaresque narratives possess broad sweeps and nevertheless return with their more circumferenced American journeys countless items in the cultural inventory. Tony Dunbar tracks across Mississippi in *Delta Time,* John Grady Cole, Cormac McCarthy's picaro in *All the Pretty Horses,* skits along the Texas/Mexican border territory, Russell Banks's accidental picaro, Bob DuBois, bungles his way through South Florida in *Continental Drift,* Binx Bolling in Walker Percy's *The Moviegoer* follows mainly a Louisiana course, George Hayduke dashes around the American desert Southwest in Edward Abbey's *The Monkey Wrench Gang,* and B. C. Hall and C. T. Wood follow many others before them on their river trek in *Big Muddy.* Without moving from sea to shining sea, these and other slightly less expansive narrative travels take in their large entries of Americana, further multiplying the cultural storage the narrative genre accounts.[12]

Still other examples of the new American picaresque compile their American stock and contribute to the accumulated hold by following some more selective design that promises to yield decisive clues about "America" or by searching for some particular form of Americana that seems most telling. For instance, convinced like Least Heat Moon in *Blue Highways* that the "real" America is to be found off the main roads and away from the urban centers, David Lamb in *A Sense of Place*, and Bill Bryson in *The Lost Continent*, travel the rural and small-town course. Thomas H. Rawls, following his subtitle in *Small Places*, goes "In Search of a Vanishing America" and records on the way items as various as that of Tom Wolfe ("a dandy, dressed in a white suit and black-and-white shoes" who "struts his own") as he lectures on small-town America in Herrick Chapel at Grinnell College in Iowa,[13] that of the charcoal-making process at the Jack Daniels distillery in Lynchburg, Tennessee (pp. 109–10), and that of an article in a back issue of the Point Reyes Station newspaper, *The Light*, about the five historical waves of ethnic immigrants—Irish, Swiss-Italians, Portuguese, Yugoslavs, and Mexicans—who had settled in that area of west Marin in California (p. 192). The story of America for others, like the one for Frances FitzGerald, is not to be found in the rural likes of Grinnell or Lynchburg or Spivey's Corner but in the nation's intentional and enclave urban communal formations like The Castro (the gay area) in San Francisco, the "other" Lynchburg (Falwell's Liberty Baptist community in Virginia), the Sun City Center of retirees segregated on the outskirts of Tampa, and the Rajneeshee community of well-to-do New Agers in Oregon. In the journey from one of these to the next, of course, the proliferations of American images compound enormously and often clash utterly,[14] all the more when seen alongside another inventory of such intentional groups like that of Hampton Sides. For his part, Sides winds his way through another, somewhat less geographically fixed set of eight unusual American subcultures, cataloging groups from the Rainbow People to be found in the Jarbridge Wilderness of Nevada to acolytes in the Church of God in Christ in Memphis, and, along the way, he finds in Sturgis, South Dakota, the cohort belonging to the Harley Nation, devotees of the hog, the motorcycle: "Tens of thousands of bikers are out posing and profiling. Guys with names like Iceman, Lizard, Bandit, and Lurch. So much reverence [for the Harley] on the faces of so many bad seeds, all roistering in their riveted concho vests and latigo belts. Sultry mamas in leather chaps but no underwear, their bare cheeks exposed."[15] In another picaresque tour, David Lamb follows the trail of Americana to be seen in America's minor league baseball parks and locates, among much happier sights, images like those in the down and out town of Seligman, Arizona, along what had been one of the last passable patches of old Route 66, a town now bypassed by interstate highway: "Bud Brown's pool hall had collapsed. Frank Smith's convenience store was a pile of boards. The drugstore that held the high school graduation each June had been abandoned. All that stood in good repair was the Harvey House hotel" but it "had been boarded up since 1954, its grassy courtyard now weed dead."[16] And numerous other examples of the new picaresque narrative follow suit. Whether tracking down America by way of the icons of the Elvis cultus like Mark Winegardner in *Elvis Presley Boulevard*, seeking it by visiting landscapes inscribed by American "high" literature like Fred Setterberg in *The Roads Taken*, or encountering it by entering hick territory like Bo Whaley in *Rednecks and Other Bona Fide Americans*, they pursue their ways into and record their images out of the slice of American culture they happen to traverse.[17] In their more deliberate forms of looking, what they see also supplies a huge variety of items into the general picaresque "encyclopedia" of American culture.

At times, of course, the more singular path taken is, in fact, a singular path, a specific route that suggests somehow that that road will make a cut into or through the central stuff of the culture. For Michael Wallis, for instance, Route 66, stretching from the edges of Lake Michigan in Chicago to Ocean Avenue in Santa Monica, the thoroughfare Steinbeck calls the "Mother Road" of America, holds out the prospect of glimpsing the country's "Main Street," and he returns images from this road that turn out to be as various and disparate as America itself. There are the houses facing the highway in downtown St. Clair, Missouri—front-porch swings, yards "decorated with ceramic deer, windmills, wagon wheels, and whiskey barrel [flower pots]," with "bumper crops of marigolds and petunias and irises," where "kids still peddle Kool Aid from stands, swap baseball cards, and put captured lightning bugs in jars."[18] But there are also, in Amarillo, the somewhat less aesthetically pleasing venues—the gip-joint called the Inn of the Big Texan that promises free steaks if the meal can be completely eaten in an hour but invariably mounts up to $30 because the accompanying food makes the repast too huge (p. 133), the Cadillac Ranch (ten caddies nosedown in the prairie) on the land of Stanley Marsh 3 (pp. 135–36), and the old Cattleman's

Club, now in decline but still long on rules and pretense, wherein at the dining tables "by late in the day, most patrons—sad-looking men with mutton-chop sideburns and blank stares—settle for Mexican food or cheeseburgers with side dishes of fried okra" (p. 135).

Jim Lilliefors, as his title indicates, follows a comparably designated route, a single road, but all along *Highway 50*, from Ocean City, Maryland, to Sacramento, California, he ponders about what he sees, as his subtitle suggests in either an exclamatory or an interrogatory mode, "Ain't That America"—images ranging "edificially" from those stately ones observed in Washington, D.C., on "Constitution Avenue [also U.S. 50], passing the Washington Monument, the Vietnam Veterans Memorial, the Lincoln Memorial,"[19] to those functional ones going into Fairfax on the Lee Highway (also U.S. 50) found in "mirror-sided office buildings" (p. 17), to those tacky ones seen along the strip like "Hiway 50 Motel, All States Motel, Hy-Way Motel ('Color TV by RCA')" (p. 17), to those quaint ones approached on Route 29 (also U.S. 50) like Tastee 29, a diner wherein "the stools are chrome-rimmed, and the tabletops are a marblelike formica . . . [and] at each booth is a Tri-Vue wall jukebox" (p. 17). All of these buildings appear in quick narrative contiguity, all issued visually by American culture, all now registered in the amplifying picaresque catalog, there in the midst of a succession of many others to be joined near U.S. 50's end by two other kinds of American "monumental" structures, the beautiful house of Carol and Frank Bleus in Eureka, Nevada, "an old gothic church" that they have restored to live in, and an "old whorehouse" in nearby Ely that Frank is working to convert to a "bed and breakfast" (p. 207).

Or there are the American vignettes that appear by tracking on U.S. 40, another singular route, from Atlantic City to San Francisco. George Stewart's episodic narrative, a rolling tour dedicated to this highway, which, like Lilliefors's probes into Americana along U.S. 50, works on the conviction expressed in the subtitle, "Cross Section of the United States of America," that U.S. 40 will yield an indicative sampling of the country. On course, among hundreds of other scenes, Stewart comes across a "crippled melon-vendor [asleep in his wheelchair, who] has set up shop just east of the town of Brazil, Indiana," and who "has manufactured a sign . . . from the sides of a card-board carton, and written on it with black crayon, a curious over-correctness prompting him to insert [in the word 'melons'] an apostrophe where one is not needed."[20] Thomas and Geraldine Vale, for their part, want to get a grasp on "change" as a significant clue to America, and the narrative presentation of their career on U.S. 40 "is a look at the changing landscapes of America, through space and through time,"[21] that seeks as much as possible to revisit the exact scenes Stewart recorded slightly more than some twenty-five years earlier. The Vales do not, of course, find the ungrammatical, wheelchaired melon-vendor and some other items that Stewart had inventoried, but they do manage to capture the character of American mutability at some sites, as, for instance, in their observations on the Red Brick Tavern in Lafayette, Ohio. Earlier, Stewart had found the place, "storied" as the second tavern to be built in Ohio, "architecturally beautiful, ivy-grown, shaded by its magnificent sycamore, neatly fenced in white" (p. 131), but for the Vales "the scene is far less elegant": "the vines which once covered the front and part of the side are dead and gone. The great sycamore tree is likewise no more. . . . The sidewalk and curb are weedy, and the formerly neat fence has been broken" (p. 63). What they see on U.S. 40 is even more America, and their catalog supplements all the others. In its "elegant" charm or its seedy state, the tavern takes both of its places in the picaresque encyclopedia, along with the Kool Aid stands, the Cadillac Ranch, the Lincoln Memorial, the chrome-rimmed stools at the Tastee 29, the whorehouse "B & B" in Ely, and the melon-vendor, particular routes affording snapshots at least of the America to be gained and to be held up for the reader by way of staying on the one narrative road.

Even when the picaresque course concertedly tracks only one shape of Americana or devotedly travels only one highway, however, the picaro's or picara's traits of curiosity, attentiveness, and inveteracy frequently send him or her willy-nilly off to encounter something different from the intended thing, and the accidental and erratic movement that defines the wayward journey often steers them off the singular course, off that dedicated route of certain visuals and tactiles, and, thus, off the projected path. Mark Winegardner might very well pursue a nearly coast-to-coast thread of the varieties of "Elvisiana" as the American form revealing the country most and best (he repeats throughout "'give us this day our daily Elvis'"), but, "out there," he stumbles on, or is drawn to, much more than this. Of course, in Pigeon Forge, Tennessee, he finds the likes of the Heartbreak Motel, "U-shaped and vaguely Alpine in its architecture, with a bush-filled courtyard in the middle and the Elvis Museum at the base of the U" (p. 18) and the likes, in Santa Fe, of the young man, breathless in his excitement, to have been able to buy a limousine that had belonged to Elvis (p. 145). But Winegardner locates as well, for instance, "a family-style Sunday buffet [in Des Moines] at a restaurant featuring Bavarian decor, a waitress with an Australian accent and steaming piles of roast beef and green beans" (pp. 118–19) and Fremont Street in Las Vegas, "an auxiliary corridor of decadence," where he spots "the Golden Nugget, and a huge neon cowboy I'd seen in a movie" (p. 177). Or, for another instance, although picaros like Least Heat Moon, David Lamb, and Bill Bryson want to confine their careering picaresque way to the small towns, they nonetheless respectively discover the skyline vistas and street images of America's cities. And, in another work, *Stolen Season*, David Lamb's single-minded tour of the country's minor-league baseball fields nevertheless brings him onto other scenes and sights and sensations, as, among other such "accidents," when he stumbles upon the Jesus Festival being held at the stadium in Baseball City near Orlando, Florida, when he arrives there seven hours before game time (pp. 134–35). Similar detours befall even those like Lilliefors and Wallis and Stewart, and, knocked narratively—if only slightly—off route, they also find, away from the unitary course, many more American images than anticipated.

It is not the road itself, after all, but what is at roadside that presents America to the picaro and picara. An academic, Stewart finds himself not only stopped at roadside but narratively pulled into the histories of many of the locales he encounters: as an English professor he is thus alert not only to the writing error by the vendor of "MELON'S" but to the stories behind the visual aspect of the Red Brick Tavern, keen not only to catch the ranges of topographical variety and beauty of U.S. 40's course through the Sierra Nevada but also to move off route for a time to recount the origins and history and plotting of the ultimate road (pp. 270–74). And Wallis might well confine his progress to Route 66, but America is to be found in the interrupted course, during those brief pauses, as when his passage through Commerce, Oklahoma, includes a chat with Mickey Mantle about his boyhood spent there (pp. 93–94). Or Lilliefors, however committed to travel his particular road, nevertheless makes a brief detour, "just off Highway 50" (p. 114), in the town of Times Beach, Missouri, now with only a few scattered trailer homes and virtually a ghost town because of dioxin contamination of the soil (pp. 114–15). Elements of the huge American cultural mosaic—the Jesus Festival, the Heartbreak Motel, industrial pollution, and neon cowboys—continue to be entered in the reckoning despite any projected unitary courses. Whether the journey is general and random, bent on some thematic, or spun along some specific route, a hallmark of the inventory taken by the new American picaresque narrative is that its "items" or images or sites are often gained by the odd chance, the accidental discovery, the fortuitous encounter. As the picaro or picara winds his or her way, quite intent or simply meandering, the inventory comes best when even the temporary itinerary yields to the picaresque coincidence, the momentary enticement, the sheer blunder. Those picaros or picaras who discover America most are those whose picaresque traits—mobile alacrity and resilience, disarming narrative curiosity and forbearance, and finely tuned approaches and senses—alert them to the welter of American stuff to be gathered at these "roadside attractions."

In one degree or another, then, the cultural stock-taking in this formation requires another element of the picaro's fine "indifference." For the genre's style of inventory, the more or less indiscriminate picaro's eye—refusing to sort out kitsch from high culture, the ordinary from the prepossessing, the trivial from the commanding[22]—must be accompanied as well by a kind of carelessness respecting destination. No matter how much one is aimed, like Lilliefors in Ocean City, Maryland, toward some arrival in Sacramento, the picaresque tour requires its vagabondage, its central character's quick willingness, even the unchecked impulse afforded by the freedom of road exile, to go slightly off course in Times Beach to "count" the industrial damage or down sideroads in Midwest farm areas to see "Kansas Skyscrapers" (grain elevators). For nearly all of the new American picaros and picaras, the nature of the travel and the resulting inventory is the one articulated by John Steinbeck, in his selection of a Spanish term as much applicable to Mark Winegardner and George Stewart, to John Kennedy Toole's Ignatius Reilly and E. L. Doctorow's Billy Bathgate, to Bill Moyers and William Least Heat Moon as ever it was to Lazarillo de Tormes, Guzman de Alfarache, Jack Wilton, or Gil Blas: "it is the verb *vacilar*," Steinbeck writes, "present participle *vacilando*. It does not mean vacillating at all. If one is vacilando, he is going somewhere but doesn't greatly care whether or not he gets there. . . . Let us say we wanted to walk in the streets of Mexico City but not at random. We would choose some article almost certain not to exist there [or clearly existing everywhere there] and then diligently try to find it."[23] But it is far more important for the picaro to see on his route a large sample out of the plenum that can be seen than it is to find that specific thing or place he set out to find. If "Maine was my design, [and] potatoes my purpose" and "if I had not seen a single potato," Steinbeck concludes, "my status as *vacilador* would not have been affected" (p. 63) and he would have seen Maine nonetheless. On the contours of the course, on and off the road, following the sightlines of the picaro's roving eye and recording the accidental, gratuitous, and ostensibly limitless images of America scattered all about, the new American picaresque takes in its cultural stock from coast to coast, and what the picaros and picaras see includes everything from metal Nehi signs, to combines in wheat fields, to Elvis souvenirs everywhere, to the Carolina Coffee Shop, to Tom Wolfe in a midwestern college chapel, to the conveyor line in a slaughterhouse, to Queen Anne houses in Angeleno Heights, to Kool Aid stands on a small-town main street, to the Creek Nation Tulsa Bingo Hall.

What Else They See: Odd Stock, Roads Less Traveled

In large measure, of course, what the picaresque inventory returns from America to the reader, or records of American culture for the reader's perusal, turns on those myriad sights and signs, people and productions, natural vistas and human venues, perfectly familiar to Americans who have themselves traveled some around the country, watched television, and imagined *other* American images on the bases of their local life. A reader need not have witnessed a combine in South Dakota or ceramic yard-chickens in Maine to be able to muster up those images, nor even have entered the Tastee 29 in Fairfax or the Carolina Coffee Shop in Chapel Hill to picture those scenes, nor indeed have labored in an East Chicago slaughterhouse to connect with Joey Celebrisi's sense of the "ambience" of such a place. The reader's comfort of recognition of these and other more or less "usual" images naturally helps posit a connection with the reader respecting that America "out there," even as the narrative presentation marshals its own plausible life by delivering these ordinary sights.

Moreover, because the picaro's or picara's "innocent eye," unbonded in exile from customary or conventional viewpoints, is the lens through which the reader catches the explosion of images and scenes the narrative inventory involves, even the most familiar American "stuff" can often come in for refreshment, for re-vision, or for a refurbished look that can have the effect of defamiliarizing the attentive reader. The altogether mundane or ordinary or even trite object or scene, however quickly passed and left behind, when seen through the singular eyes and rendered through the idiomatic sensibility of this or that picaro or picara, can have the effect of the reader's pausing briefly to reconsider the customary cow, with Loyal Blood, to find it anew as its prone state in the field makes it look like a black Viking boat and makes the scene around it into a grassy sea, or to reimagine the common cornfield, with Joey Celebrisi, as the stalks in the wind wave their tassels like cheerleaders, or to think again about Fremont Street in Las Vegas, with Mark Winegardner, as "an auxiliary corridor of decadence" (p. 177). As Geoffrey O'Gara recognizes, the transient passer-by cannot hope to compete respecting all those familiar American scenes and objects "with the credibility of witnesses who have known these places [and things] for a lifetime," but the traveler-narrator has his or her own kind of advantage and can perform a special job of work, "like the aerial photographer who flies over at a considerable remove and gives us a useful new view of a landscape we know, but still might know differently" (p. xix). Just so, the glimpses of American life caught by the various picaros and picaras, at least temporarily unfettered by conventional outlook, can frequently result in possibilities for the reader to take in the inventory in ways that make the commonplace scene more exotic, the customary thing rife with additional facets, the familiar converted to something different, perhaps a "useful new view." Marginalized in road exile, the picaro and picara always have at least the possibility of seeing from that "considerable remove" and, thus, disconnected or largely unimplicated with regard to the scenes they observe, might have views not constrained by those who are there "in place," long accustomed, and who might have turned the ordinary scenes and things around them into the stuff of habit.[24]

Still another form of picaresque work goes quite beyond the stuff of accumulating items of the staple or familiar or at least recognizable variety, quite beyond the task of gaining a plausible footing with respect to the external world "out there," and quite beyond the effort to brush the dust off some "accustomed" elements and to propose renewed images of how those things might belong to the country's cultural stock. The narrative genre, formed as it is, also possesses and enacts the capacity to exceed such customary limits, to veer off the usual routes into territories far less known to readers, even to stumble across that place or thing so long hidden off the beaten path or so well camouflaged within the welter of American images that it has been lost to general view. Again, the very marginality of the picaro and picara helps to confer this capacity. Because the central figures of the genre generally traverse the "edges" of American existence, liberated while on the road from the seats and centers of cultural authority, convention, and even at times "normalcy," they often have far shorter distances to travel in order to detour from the familiar and worn paths of many a reader. Because their road-lives take them away from the middle of things, push them to the peripheries of settled existence, the picaresque venture has them, like Robert James Waller's Texas Jack Carmine and Vaughn Rhomer, forever hearing a little "border music," perhaps not always audible to every reader. Because the picaro and picara have ineluctably in them the itch to move on, the sense of not having any particular place to be, the responsiveness to the pure allure of the next place, the constancy of curiosity, the willingness and adeptness to trespass, their extravagant travel often pulls them across boundaries and into the range of alien, odd, neglected, or hidden American stock to be accounted on the strange course as they go and as readers go vicariously where they themselves might not or could not, apart from the reading experience, have ventured for the sake of any elaborated American inventory or, for that matter, anything else. In the accumulative work of the genre, the mobile and wafting narrative ways bring the picaros and picaras across people, places, situations, and sights some readers might well recognize but many others might not even have imagined. While no full accounting is possible, a number of texts suggest such prospects, even as they enter more arcane Americana, "odd stock," into their various books.

In some examples of the new American picaresque, for instance, the reader crosses the borders, with the purposeful or accidental routes of the picaro or picara, into those venues of American human shapes that belong to the inventory but that, without the picaresque tour, might lie hidden from view. In *A Walk across America*, Peter Jenkins follows his nose into the recesses of the Virginia Blue Ridge near Saltville, goes off road, and delivers to the reader the old hermit, Homer Davenport. Seeking him out, Jenkins tells the old man, "'because I wanted to find out if you were for real,'"[25] the young picaro finds mountain-man philosophy lodged in the wild terrain. Wilderness comfort and cuisine within the old man's home, "made of hand-hewn logs and roughly cut bare boards . . . [with the front outside] shingled with old metal saltine cans that had been beaten flat" (p. 72) finally gives Jenkins reason to think "what amazing differences we were discovering in America" (p. 80). Decidedly more discomfiting than what Jenkins finds on Homer's mountain, however, are some of the "odd stock" in American human forms Joe Buck discovers in New York City in his trespass of social borders. Among others, Joe is at first allured by the ostensibly gender-interchangeable twins, Hansel and Gretel MacAlbertson, and their young, urbane, camp friends in a world of demented chic,[26] whom he will later think emblematic of many American children, born "loose and alien and unconnected" (p. 204) and, shortly thereafter, he runs upon a man on Seventh Avenue, one Townsend "Towny" Pederson Locke from Chicago, symbolically "a musical comedy American," presented by this "red [complexion], white [hair and silk muffler], and blue [eyes and overcoat] person of about fifty" (p. 210) whose chatty and jovial countenance is soon enough replaced by the terrified pathos to be seen in his life of homosexual liaisons with complete strangers. Or, again, among others encountered, Bill Moyers turns up for the reader another odd American bird, the self-undecipherably-made Winston F. Bott, a poor-born transplanted Ohioan, unassuming in appearance, and now mayor of Mathis, Texas, who has (apparently) taken the Chicanos' part, alienated the Anglos, practiced his own powerful ambition with both parties, passed as both greedy and altruistic, ruthless and generous, become both a "hero" and a "nut" even to his few friends, "'Garibaldi or St. Francis of Assisi'" or an "inscrutable, stubborn, singleminded Quixote," all in one, and who, even for the clear-eyed Moyers, remains an eye-widening question: "To the Anglos he is a nemesis, to the Chicanos an ally or at least a useful instrument, to the traveler an enigma."[27] Then, for another kind of American form, there is Greta Wigbaldy, the sexually zesty but practical, self-satisfied in life but conspiratorially anti-parent Dutch Reformed girl, who temporarily attracts Don Wanderhope. Indeed, she lures him into a tryst in a subdivision built by her wealthy father ("an expansive man typical of what we mean by Dutch *gemoedelijkheid*") where they wind toward their lair (the Model Home) through "the pillared gateway of Green Knoll, under a shingle reading 'The American Dream,' and striking up dark Willow Lane"[28] to the empty house, all of this before "the discovery of a bond with Greta beyond the physical" so fills Don with a picaro's apprehension that his heart is immediately set on "how I could possibly extricate myself from such a muddle" (p. 76).

No less improbable in form and moving than any of these, but likewise emphatically cases of the *rara avis Americanis,* such unusual stock is turned up everywhere in the new American picaresque. There are, for instances, the incidental figure Jack Crabb recollects out of long picaresque memory in Thomas Berger's *Little Big Man,* the man called Little Horse, a gay Cheyenne who, despite a life and manner clearly marginal in the nineteenth-century American setting, is fully accepted by his native tribe; the figure dredged up in passing by David Lamb in Bayfield, Colorado, named Gene Jordan—no one "gets more quizzical looks than a cowboy who comes out of the closet and admits he is a practicing poet"—who reports that his wife, embarrassed by his "garbage," is "'my ex-wife now'";[29] and the highly unusual, because so far-from-taciturn, bartender encountered only briefly by Mark Winegardner in Central City, Colorado, a man named "Rabbit," a sixties drop-out, with expertise in every area, especially triviality, who "one-ups" every statement, and who, like Forrest Gump, seems always to have been "there" at *the* significant moment, and whose garrulous and objectionable conviviality is exceeded only by his capacity for egregious self-inflation (pp. 135–40). In the survey of these and hundreds of other more or less singular American "embodiments," an individual reader, perhaps more familiar with some figures among such odd stock than with others, can sift out the fully alien from the merely quaint, but, for the most part, that reader will judge the stock without much help from the picaro and picara, whose most general tendency, working at a "considerable remove," is a highly calibrated diffidence, the trait in them that allows them to encounter, to observe, and to move on, now having tucked the person or thing or scene or situation into the accounting, often by simply noting "how odd" but most frequently without evaluation or any commentary whatever.[30]

Along with a fair amount of derring-do and the permits of the marginal status, it is just such a trait of a subjectivity ordinarily untempted by judgmental dispositions that enables the picaro's or picara's entry to those characters and cadres that, in broad accumulation, can pull this reader or that even further beyond his or her wonted experience of America. With this remarkable capacity, the picaro or picara slides in and out of scenes, gathering inventory after having made temporary fits or at least having tuned into the work of picaresque stock-taking. Among a great many others, Geoffrey O'Gara's *A Long Road Home* supplies a telling instance. Traveling in the 1980s, O'Gara might well be following the general courses of the guides to America created by the writers in the 1930s Federal Writers' Project, but only his capacity to develop rapport for a scene, to tune to a situation, can move him into the world of pick-up basketball in East Los Angeles, a world certainly beyond the survey of the Writers' Project, clearly beyond the direct witness of most people even now, and perhaps completely hidden from many contemporary readers. Penetrating into the scene, O'Gara utilizes his marginal status, refuses to discriminate, and proves that he has an instinct for how to "get into the game." In the midst of the mingled ethnic and racial dynamics of the players in their interplay—some business-like or "workaday" Anglos, numerous happy-go-lucky Hispanics, and a few intense African-American players—at a point when no guidebook could suffice to help him, he manages with a look to connect with his only non-Hispanic teammate, a young black man who would "accept me as another minority and agree fleetingly with his eyes to make common cause," to establish a "limited contract" for the sake of winning (p. 274). Only with these picaresque capacities can the scene and situation, this little stratum of Americana, be accounted in this way: nothing less than such an entry could give O'Gara, and then the reader, the sense of the game and more at stake in the young black man's lonesome refuge in the gym, his "glory" in going to the goal, his desperation to win, his prideful despair in losing, all delivered to the reader without judgment (pp. 272–76).

But other kinds of worlds, mostly hidden to readers' views, are also entered and gathered, also made accessible by the picaro's character and mobile mission. If O'Gara's brief gymnasium interlude helps the picaresque inventory gather in what might be for some a largely hidden slice of American cultural life in an accidental episode, some other wayfaring picaros and picaras carry the reader along on more extended tours into and through what for many or even most readers might be uncharted territories. Bill Terry's road narrative follows the careening existence of an archpicaro, "the Kid," one A. J. Poole, one who was not "lazy or unimaginative or without enterprise . . . but all of his energies, and they were considerable, were directed toward the avoidance of what you might call permanent labor, a thing he found totally irreconcilable with his restlessness."[31] Following this picaro "on the old roadhouse circuit, mainly in Arkansas, back in the 1950s," is to get what is for most readers a largely unknown element of Americana, "along the river roads that ran into U.S. Highway 70 when it was fast and narrow and dangerous" and into the "sweat and howl . . . places like Flossie's and the Shake Loose Club and the Silver Moon" where they came to dance and brawl and drink "enough beer and whiskey and set-ups to wash a train" (p. 1). In such a world, A. J. Poole, full of easy equanimity, insouciance, and charm, comes and goes at full tilt, and, through his trafficking, the inventory of the new American picaresque gains for the reader access to hitherto "untried" scenes and still more odd characters like Rainbow and Doodle Socket. Or, again, in a somewhat similar vein, there is the more updated road work of Bo Whaley, he who navigates "redneck culture" in order to locate such people: "you gotta go south to find pedigreed rednecks, the real thoroughbreds." For him, these folks are some signal elements of authentic America, and "the best place to find them," he claims, "is in juke joints" on Friday and Saturday nights.[32] Those who know only the worlds of "night clubs, supper clubs, cabarets, or social halls" stand with Whaley's rowdy picaresque tour to come upon new inventory in a juke joint, "one of those down-yonder, roll-up-your-sleeves, bring-me-another-beer, every-man (and woman)-for-himself, three bucks to get in $37.85 to get out, Willie Nelson-Conway

Twitty-Loretta Lynn establishments where they stamp your hand when you spring for the three and suck up your $37.85 like an Electrolux" (p. 5). Near the Altamaha River, in one such joint (Daisie Mae's Place—Cold Beer and Fish Baits), he encounters one Rooster Roberts, "the cock of the [particular] walk," at whose permanently reserved table Whaley has mistakenly seated himself. Clearly marginal in this scene, he must exercise to full advantage the tactics of picaresque approach like arriving on a motorcycle ("credentials, man, you gotta have 'em"), like the traits of picaresque alacrity ("moved to another table," "didn't pass Good Judgment 101 at Georgia Southern by taking foolish chances"), like high charm ("'Excuse me, sir, but do you have a match?'" to Rooster with a wooden match stuck in the corner of his mouth), and like intrepid spirit (chatting with Rooster about "that ol' gal" on the other side of the room Rooster continues to send beers). Within a brief time, Rooster is calling him "Hoss," and, by evening's end, the splendid redneck, fully disappointed, amorous designs on "that ol' gal" completely thwarted, has his portrait in the American inventory, present and available and unevaluated for readers unfamiliar with "the well-worn longneck Bud and Red Man trail" (p. 7) on which Whaley executes his narrative travel.

But the tracks of the new American picaro and picara are not always or only into the hidden or neglected grounds that might be found in American rural or "hick" culture. While McMurtry's title picaro, "Cadillac" Jack McGriff, can zoom across the Western plains and can soak up the forms of life in the best flea market in the world in California, he also courses through areas of wealth and political influence in the District of Columbia, plunges into the lower forms of hot-tub culture in a nearby suburb (with two dropouts from secretarial school, Lolly and Janie Lee, who think him as "normal" as they are [pp. 188–93]), and shortly lands in the quarters of one Bryan Ponder who has one of the largest nest collections in captivity (pp. 194–201). Disclosing the "hidden" world of the Dutch Schultz mob, E. L. Doctorow's *Billy Bathgate* follows its title picaro not only into his temporary interlude with the gang in small-town, upstate New York but into his adventures in the mean city streets around Bathgate Avenue, whereon the reader meets, among others, the collector "Arnold Garbage," into his quick picaresque sallies through Manhattan high society, where the reader gets the odd "other" life of Schultz's erstwhile girlfriend, Drew Preston, and even into the chic setting of Saratoga in racing season, where money and menace meet. Frances FitzGerald and Hampton Sides pierce into their respective sets of those several intentional, alternative community enclaves to deliver to the reader's view stripes and styles of social existence quite off the beaten track. Richard Farina's Gnossos Pappadopoulis pulls readers into the groves of and around Athene wherein he charms his erratic course through an academic motley peopled of straight and strange characters—coed Betty Kneesox types, the paranoid black artist Calvin, zombies, Asian gangsters—in a world, presented for the reader's inventory, just short of "dropping out" altogether. B. C. Hall and C. T. Wood explore the often hidden recesses of American river culture, inventory the different styles of life it contains, and return to the reader several sets of "odd" characters like, for instance, the sad, toothless woman they encounter on the streets of Vicksburg, who sits, cries, and gobbles Moon Pies while awaiting a husband, Roy, who has abandoned her.[33] Tom Robbins's Sissy Hankshaw, she of the outsized thumbs—one reason she stands as hitchhiker extraordinaire—penetrates into the alternately unusual realms on her picara's way of mobile sexuality, of New York fashion modeling, of life on a western women's ranch, all the while collecting an odd assortment of American people, places, and styles as a part of narrative stock-taking. Some picaros and picaras blunder upon this or that odd item for the inventory, while others seem especially drawn to them. After Andrei Codrescu, a former champion, visits the little-known venue of the World Heavyweight Poetry Championships in Taos,[34] a summer event of spontaneous poetry competition run by his friend Peter Rabbit, no less, the "road scholar" encounters in typically rapid picaresque succession three American characters who might notably count as "odd stock" for many readers—Chris Griscom, "a past-life reader, a death worker, and an all-around psychic healer" (p. 146) who converts Codrescu into a herbivore; Alan Olken, "an astrologer's astrologer who counts among his clients politicians and movie stars" (p. 149) and who "reads" that, beyond giving up meat, Codrescu should abstain from sex; Sheila Lowry, who is a channel for an entity called Theo, an impatient and even irritable amalgam of spirits, that speaks (through Sheila) "with a ponderous German accent" (p. 151); and, among many others, in the elderpolis of Sun City, Arizona, one Jo-Dina Errichetti, "ex-mortician" and now lead vocalist for "One Foot in the Grave, Sun City's punk rock band," who leads the band through a song called "'Menopause,' a pathos-filled, jarring ditty about the evils of old age" (pp. 163–64). Hundreds upon hundreds of such quaint, odd, bizarre, hidden, or neglected people, images, scenes, and situations are recorded in the cumulative inventory of the new American picaresque, their entries made possible by the willingness, even necessity, of the picaros' and picaras' having taken the roads less traveled, having become *homo spectans* out on the edges of American life, having utilized their own temporarily marginal status in road exile for trespassing into the peripheries to count the odd stock in the American cultural inventory.

Respecting this very strange accumulation, a few readers might recognize many items in the inventory, and many might be familiar with a few items, but the odds are against most readers' being familiar with or sufficiently introduced to all or most of them. Thus, many can add to their own senses of the size and diversity of American culture by way of this "odd stock" in the category, gathered by the picaros and picaras out of "what else they see" and what readers see now through picaresque trespass. While the border-jumpers follow out the new American picaresque tour, one function of the general cultural inventory they take is to reclaim the ordinary sights and sounds and scenes of Americana and often to *defamiliarize* them for the reader by seeing them through the picaro's or picara's singular kinds of views of them. But another function or possible effect of the narrative form in its frequent treks along roads less traveled is to carry out, at least in initial terms, the task of *familiarizing* readers with those strange or hidden or camouflaged or neglected human territories—everything in the cultural array from the MacAlbertson twins to the Sun City punk rock band, from the woman who channels Theo in Santa Fe to a gorilla nest in Riverdale, Maryland, from Arnold Garbage to Rooster Roberts, Homer Davenport, Lolly and Janie Lee, and, yes, Peter Rabbit—that the reader might never have seen quite so up close or, consequently, have imagined to include among the elements of American cultural existence. This work performed by the new picaresque genre of reaching into odd pockets of the culture to retrieve the "loose change" that can be found there surely depends on the kind of narrative life the picaro spends on the peripheries, and it just as surely increases the size and variety of the American inventory.

But the marginal status of the picaro and picara in road exile not only introduces him or her to possible occasions with odd "others" and, thus, not only opens opportunities to diversify the inventory for the reader. When the picaros and picaras practice the arts of both *homo viator* and *homo spectans,* their work on and from the edges can put new slants of vision on America, can put the American scene in a different relief, and all the more when some of those picaresque voyagers are socially and culturally "marginal," in ways quite beyond road loneliness.

How They See: American Culture on the Slant

In an "Author's Note" preceding the picaresque narrative to unfold in *Back Home*, Mort Rosenblum observes that, after two decades as a foreign correspondent "reporting from 145 other countries," he felt he could return to America "to look at my own [country] with the same optic."[35] His sense of a now unfamiliar America stems from a late-night conversation in France:

> a French reporter [a correspondent to the United States] told me about a city at the edge of a desert. Its inhabitants lived on grease and plastic; they decorated themselves with blue rocks and chokers made from scorpions encased in Plexiglas. Its stark hills and rare cacti were fast disappearing under bulldozer blades. The place, in what he called *le Far West*, seemed strange enough for me. What difference did it make if it was Tucson, Arizona, where I had grown up and gone to school?

Now that America had come to appear to him as strange "as if it were Burundi," now that "time and absence had made me an outsider insider," Rosenblum suggests, he needs to take to the course of the roads in his own land for the purposes of rediscovery. As alien and exiled as he will sometimes feel in the picaresque journey that follows, he nevertheless operates throughout the tour as "an outsider insider," one who though tracking grounds perhaps grown unfamiliar nevertheless tracks *his* own home grounds. In this, his marginality, his picaro's condition, consists in his always being the arriving stranger, the unknown person approaching the scene, with all the risks attending the picaresque venture, but his recovery of America when once again at home—even upon the roads less traveled—has a kind of centrist cast, delivered by one who rarely doubts his social and cultural standing. Only the road life temporarily undertaken puts him on the peripheries, a kind of Tom Jones for a time but, unlike Fielding's character, who is ignorant of his birthright, one aware and confident all the time of a denouement that will secure him where he belongs. And, despite intermittently afflicting senses of exile experienced because of solitary travel in what is perceived as a confusing, cacophonous, or "monstrous land," an alien America, a number of other new American picaros and picaras share Rosenblum's sense generally of belonging, of having "insider" status, even as each also sometimes feels an "outsider" in their various picaresque interims. Bill Moyers, David Lamb, Frances FitzGerald, Hampton Sides, Mark Winegardner, Richard Reeves,

Jim Lilliefors, Harrison Salisbury, Jonathan Yardley, Geoffrey O'Gara, Bill Bryson, John Steinbeck, Thomas Rawls, Douglas Brinkley, and some others, including even Peter Jenkins, Bo Whaley, and even more fictionalized picaros like Jack McGriff and Don Wanderhope, can all take to the highways, venture the work of trespass, dance to a little "border music," all the while comforted by the recognition that their "home-berths" of success, status, fame, position, or at least prospects of these things more "central" to American cultural life await them at journey's end.[36]

But there are other new American picaros and picaras who are not white, adult males, or who possess no culturally centering empowerment, or who lack entitlement or even a "place" altogether, and indeed whose utter marginality in American life was for them a felt "fact" of their lives well before being pushed to the new cycles of peripheral status that occur in road exile. These disenfranchised figures of the journey, now doubly marginal on the road, take cultural inventory on behalf of the reader just like Rosenblum, Moyers, Steinbeck, Lamb, and Salisbury: they cross over the usual and familiar highways, and they broach the strange, hidden, or neglected byways; they might well refurbish the commonplace and domesticate the alien along the way in their picaresque service to the reader. For these picaros and picaras on the margins, however, American culture is often seen on the bias conditioned by the terms of their more radical marginality. What is usual or commonplace for a Moyers or a Salisbury might well be quite the rarity for a Joe Buck, Herlihy's long-neglected, penniless orphan in the world, or a Lars Eighner, casting about in poverty and homelessness. A majority cultural world seen from a white position of centrality might appear customary enough inventory to John Steinbeck, even in those episodes when he takes stock of some of its most outrageous racial prejudices, but the same world is bound to look different and to enter the record accounted in a different way to the young black narrator of Ralph Ellison's *Invisible Man* and to seem different still to Eddy L. Harris in taking inventory in his picaresque journey of a black man through the *South of Haunted Dreams*, both of whom were pushed to the edges of American culture before their picaresque tours even began. That very same white-centered world will be accounted in hues and tones altered further still by Richard Hill's young, white jazz saxophonist picaro, Vic Messenger, after his having defamiliarized the black world of Tonto and Betty Boop, just as Walt Harrington, white man married to a black woman, will learn to see it anew, take its stock on an altered bias, during and after his picaresque crossing into black America.[37] In contrast to the inevitably centrist bearings of those of Rosenblum's "outsider insiders" who are more "in" than "out" in one frame or another, Joe Buck, Lars Eighner, Ellison's protagonist, Eddy L. Harris, Vic Messenger, and Walt Harrington all feel decidedly more outside the pale of American culture than they feel pulled by some important centrifugal experience toward it, and their roving picaresque eyes, seeing the culture from their marginalized angles of vision, take their American inventories in decidedly "eccentric" ways, perhaps defamiliarizing the culture further still for those readers who might be prepared for a time to look at disparate elements of the country in one or another or several of such "off-centered" ways. While all picaros and picaras become "situationally disadvantaged" just by virtue of the highway isolation that has them forever appearing as the stranger at the gate, some travel on even more radical margins just by virtue of gender, race, age, social status, and so on.[38] For all that this hampers them on the picaresque course, these deeper "disadvantages" give them sometimes highly unconventional sightlines, a clear advantage for seeing elements of American life in a different way, and these picaresque figures thus also provide for the reader lenses that work from unaccustomed vantage points in surveying the country's cultural stock. What such doubly marginalized picaros and picaras see also becomes a part of the picaresque inventory, but *how* they see what they encounter, how their angles of vision record the stock, can give readers newly disclosive cuts across the customary American grain.

Some picaros, clearly marginalized beyond only road alienation, return scenes to the reader that can startle to unexpected insight. When the picaro's very disadvantage gains him not only access to a situation, however much usual or odd, but also grants him an eccentric view of that situation, the reader might well be forced to a revision of understanding or at least to a pause for some reconsideration. In S. E. Hinton's *The Outsiders*, for example, the reader, late in the book, moving along with the young narrator-picaro, Ponyboy, arrives at the edges of a teenage street rumble between a coalition of two eastside crowds labeled the "Hoods" and the "Greasers" and a group they call the "Socs," short for the "Socials," a well-off bunch of westside kids. Without having traveled with the particular likes of Ponyboy to this point, the "centrist" reader would probably have a preformulated idea of this scene, of who is who, this portion of the stock in the American inventory already well-decided. But this young picaro—orphaned, cobbling together a life in the world, "officially" a greaser, not only essentially innocent but bright and thoughtful, an eager learner, and quite unpredictably well-read—has by now defamiliarized readers by way of the marginalized slants on things he supplies out of his own off-centered disadvantages, and the impending fight scene thus takes some turns not to have been anticipated without what Rosenblum would call Ponyboy's "optics":

> [The Socs] looked like they were all cut from the same piece of cloth: clean-shaven with semi-Beatle haircuts, wearing striped or checkered shirts with light-red or tan-colored jackets or madras ski jackets. They could just as easily have been going to the movies as to a rumble. That's why people don't ever think to blame the Socs and are always ready to jump on us. We [the Greasers] *look* hoody and they *look* decent. It *could* be just the other way around—*half* of the hoods I know are pretty decent guys underneath all that grease, and from what I've heard, a *lot* of Socs are just cold-blooded mean—but people *usually* go by looks [emphasis added].[39]

The carefully qualified language, of course, suggests Ponyboy's pica-resque reserve about evaluation, his form of unimplicated remove from the scenes through which he passes, and this extends even to letting cen-trist readers (certainly *not* the "people" he mentions) off the hook of judg-ment. In this way, as picaro turned retrospective narrator, he cajoles those relieved readers to consider his quite particular narrative slant, one that invites them to reverse their conventional perceptions of "Hoods" and "Socials" and, therefore, to revise the customary inventory. Disabled by his youth, his social status, and his orphaned condition, as well as by his picaresque exile, he only wants to belong somewhere and cares not a bit about the "social" divisions: "what difference does the side make?" he asks himself as the gangs align themselves (p. 151). And, after achieving that still more remote vantage point on things, akin to Geoffrey O'Gara's "considerable remove," Ponyboy delivers as well on O'Gara's "new view of a landscape we know, but still might know differently." As the lead-ers of the gangs approach, "sizing each other up," the young, bookish, greaser picaro distances the scene again in a still different way: "the rest of us waited with mounting tension. I was reminded of Jack London's books—you know, where the wolf pack waits in silence for one or two members to go down in a fight" (p. 151). As picaro, he has no need to develop the tactics of Least Heat Moon's "skewed vision" in order to see the world anew or differently for himself or for the reader. Ponyboy's own forms of "peripheral vision"—less those glimpses from the corner of the eye than those viewpoints grown out of a life lived on the cultural peripheries—propose additions to and re-visions of the American inventory at practically every turn.

In the new American picaresque, such examples are abundant. Picaros and picaras pushed by the country to the cultural edges, dismissed to the points of being beyond recognition, are enabled out there on the fringes not only to witness "peripheral" America, those areas far away from the centers of authority or influence or even normalcy, but to provide altered slants on centrist American life when it is seen through the eyes of such marginalized people. At one level cast out from the seats of cultural power, Winston Groom's Forrest Gump can reel in well-known American roads and utterly familiar American scenes, but, gathering the experience of the country through the lenses of that mental disadvantage dislocating him from the regular order, *Forrest Gump,* both picaresque narrative and contemporary fable, also imagines new, sometimes outrageous slants on the national life. Disadvantaged by sex and gender constructions and seduced in their nearly Gumpian innocence by American male authority, Thomas Pynchon's Oedipa Maas and Tom Robbins's Sissy Hankshaw also find themselves on the fringes of American existence—the stuff of W.A.S.T.E. and the lesbian ranch respectively—and *The Crying of Lot 49* and *Even Cowgirls Get the Blues* not only follow these picaras out to those edges for the sake of the additional inventory to be found there but also, through the perceptual "optics" of Oedipa's paranoia and Sissy's newly awakened and newly quickened sexuality, put the dominant America of male construction into new relief, enable the reader to see it on a different bias. From a narrator so made marginal by his blackness in America that his picaresque recounting occurs from a subterranean perspective, Ralph Ellison's "invisible man" takes stock of South and North, fringe-life and structural center, affectless existence and political rage, and, through it all, cuts deeply across the American grain, exposing both the unthinkingly vicious and right-mindedly benign forms of cultural "normalcy" to significantly altered understanding. Tripping America on paregoric, weed, alcohol, and purposed disaffection during a time when, as Norman Mailer observed, college students had become "the new niggers" in American political culture, Richard Farina's Gnossos Pappadopoulis crosses the lines of normal recognition and, from out there, beyond the pale, takes an inventory of the university, the military, the government, and the society that literally turns the country on its head by one whose marginality creates those idiosyncratic forms of vision suggested in the title, *Been Down So Long It Looks like Up to Me.* With Forrest, Gnossos, Sissy, and others, what might otherwise stand as a culturally hegemonic take on things can come in for a different look, a revision, a different way of accounting for the inventory.

In one of the most apparently determined permutations of the new American picaresque on this score, Marilynne Robinson's *Housekeeping* presents the case of the picara temporarily held captive in terms connoted by the title of the novel. While most picaresque narrators work in stasis, at last in stand-still, retrospectively rehearsing an earlier period on the move as picaro or picara, Robinson's narrator-picara, Ruthie, mainly records *from* the road her earlier life in a small town on the northern plains as that life—and her Aunt Sylvia Fisher—led her eventually *to* the road. The final catalyst for Ruthie's embarking on the life of the picara is "Sylvie," the aunt whose own remarkable picaresque itinerancy is interrupted only when she is called upon to return to Fingerbone, to the old family home, for the sake of the young girls, Ruthie and sister Lucille, who have no other family to care for them. Though Sylvie in Fingerbone worked hard at and "talked a great deal about housekeeping,"[40] Ruthie informs the reader, her habits remained those of transience. Making herself stranger to all in town, Sylvie appears on the pages as the picara "held captive": she wanders the local precincts day and night, tells Ruthie and Lucille about the stock to be taken in her tales of the road, keeps house as if suddenly to flee, inadvertently inspires her charges in small-town truancies of all kinds, and ultimately returns to the life of the road, now with Ruthie in tow. As Sylvie roams the edges of town and as the girls in their make-believe games train in ways of the picaresque—"too old for dolls, we played out intricate, urgent dramas of entrapment and miraculous escape" (p. 86)—it grows ever clearer that Fingerbone itself, the life of constricted normalcy, is the most biting trap, that Sylvie and Ruthie are being kept by the house and not vice versa, and that "housekeeping" itself, the regularized routine of settled life for the American woman, has to be seen in a new relief, taken stock of on a different slant. When viewed through the eyes of a Ruthie, who, having with Sylvie made a "miraculous escape" to the road, the report comes toward the end of the narrative that "at first our trail was intricate so that we could elude discovery, and then it was intricate because we had no particular reason to go to one town rather than another, and no particular reason to stay anywhere, or to leave" (p. 216).[41] In this case of Marilynne Robinson's entry into the new American picaresque, as with a great many others, inventory is not the only or even the major item on the narrative agenda so much as it is simply a function and result of a peripatetic and restive form of vision. As an operation of the genre, however, the stock-taking occurs nevertheless, and, when the picara or picaro is for whatever reason doubly "eccentric," more fully off-centered because pushed away in human status from cultural centricity by age, gender, race, circumstance, or outlook, the forms of *homo spectans* featured in such cases of the picaresque narrative slice into America in ways virtually bound to provide a crosscurrent to the mainstream.[42]

For some such more radically marginalized picaros and picaras, of course, the slanted inventory, the "skewed vision" is a much less tacit matter or incidental effect of the narrative labor. In the recounting that makes up Lars Eighner's picaresque tour, for instance, the view of the American scene from the slant of the peripheralized and homeless narrator of *Travels with Lizbeth* becomes for the reader a main enticement, an angle on things not to be gained from Harrison Salisbury, John Steinbeck, David Lamb, Bill Moyers, from even a Texas Jack Carmine, a Sal Paradise, or a Phaedrus in Robert Pirsig's *Zen and the Art of Motorcycle Maintenance,* or indeed from any of those only erstwhile picaros who, all the while on the road, fully know they have a home to which to return. Like Sylvie Fisher's gendered status, Eighner's homelessness doubly marginalizes him on the road, and this fringe status gives him access to neglected American stock, like the general world of alcohol, drugs, and insanity in the camps of the dispossessed and the more particular woman, Matilda Temple, once a part of a well-to-do family but now psychotic by any measure—speaking a language that "mental-health workers call *word salad*"[43]—on the streets of Austin, Texas. But both easy access and peripheral angle give Eighner as well idiosyncratic perspectives on these and other aspects of American life. Viewing such social edges from his own edge, he observes that hard-drug usage is not nearly as prevalent among the homeless as among university students, that, given his or her condition, a homeless person sometimes cuts down on legally prescribed medications "so that he can get the good feeling of being a little bit crazy" (p. 162), and "that the vices of the homeless do not much differ from the vices of the housed, but [for the fact that] the homeless, unless they become saints, must pursue their vices in public" (p. 165). Such notes, recorded among other such accountings on course, collect the likes of a Matilda Temple into the inventory in a way that invites the "housed" reader also to move at least temporarily "off center," away from home.

For another kind of example, John A. Williams and Eddy L. Harris are not marginalized in their road exiles by that social status of homelessness that pushes Lars Eighner to the fringes, but, like him, the situational disadvantages of being a stranger on the road are compounded, in their cases, by being black Americans. As they are thus further pushed to the edges, however, their perspectives thus further afford eccentricity of view for readers. For John A. Williams, in *This Is My Country Too*, the exhilaration of picaresque autonomy is clearly present, but the sheer character of the anxiety he candidly records of his feelings on course, his fear about going into certain places and encountering some people, simply and inevitably alters the America returned on the pages to the centrist white reader: "I do not believe," Williams writes, "white travelers have any idea of how much nerve and courage it requires for a negro to drive coast to coast in America."[44] Though daring the tour nevertheless, the stock-taking occurs on the bias by making the view of the country more restrictive or at least more circumscribed, by approaching many of its various venues in foreboding, by seeing America through an "optics" tinted with a sense of danger not to be felt by Bill Moyers or Mort Rosenblum or Cadillac Jack McGriff even in the worst moments of trepidation during their road times. For a somewhat less nervous because perhaps more angry Harris, in *South of Haunted Dreams*, the stock to be taken, decided in advance of the picaresque tour, is an inventory of southern bigotry,[45] but the survey he actually takes on course is refracted through an increasing astonishment about the people and places, malignant and benign, that can make readers alternately flinch or smile in recognition. Of course, he encounters those who despise him as a matter of course, thus confirming some altogether familiar perspectives on the white South, but he also finds Andrew in Raleigh, who befriends him (pp. 115–32), finds Peter and Jacob on Okracoke Island, who offer to put him up at home when there is no room for him at their inn (p. 182), finds Jack and Greg in Wrightsville Beach, who open their house to him (pp. 186–93), finds white owners of a motorcycle repair shop in the Florida panhandle who stay past closing to fix his bike and who then arrange accommodations for him in a place called Niceville (p. 220), and finds James Anderman in South Alabama, who converses with him through their mutual pain, black and white (pp. 221–24). In these ways, the different inventories of America taken by Williams and Harris are all the more different by virtue of the fact that the generic road marginality of the picaro, shared with the likes of a Moyers or a Lamb, collects Americana through lenses radically "skewed," slanted, biased, by the more radical disadvantages they bring to and suffer on the picaresque trail, a condition they share in their disparate ways less with Rosenblum, Moyers, and Lamb than with Forrest Gump, Gnossos Pappadopoulis, Oedipa Maas, Lars Eighner, Sylvie Fisher, and other picaros and picaras comparably and decisively forced to work from the cultural fringes.

At the last, in the enormous accumulation of the sights and sounds, people and places, scenes and styles, all assayed by the new picaresque, the "America" gathered by the picaros and picaras, whether centrist or eccentric in their narrative lives as *homo viator*, presents to the reader a cultural landscape of "monstrous" proportions, ranging from the rock formations of southwest mesas taken in by many of the texts to the "rock formation" found by Codrescu in the Sun City punk band One Foot in the Grave. As traveled and observed and delivered to readers by any one picaro or picara, either a Bill Moyers or a Sissy Hankshaw, it is a land of wild diversities and often stunning contradictions, supplying even on its face huge challenges to thought about what such a culture might mean or even portend. When the stock-taking of the cumulative new American picaresque spreads before the reader in all of its multiple human forms and features, acts and artifacts, outlooks and modes—from Bo Whaley's record of the Saturday-night society of redneck Rooster Roberts to Hampton Sides's depiction of the preening citizens of the Harley Nation, from Peter Jenkins's survey of the Blue Ridge "mansion" of Homer Davenport to Geoffrey O'Gara's participant-observer log of the social drama of L.A. pickup basketball—the terrific welter of Americans and Americana, the sheer size of America trespassed by the picaros and picaras, gives the reader every reason to think that the culture itself provides innumerable borders to cross, alternate centers of human meanings everywhere, and, thus, in, around, and between those multiple centers, plenty of leeways remaining for cultural creativity. And when the picaros and picaras operate "on the slant" in their mobile stock-taking, when they become *homo spectans* in ways that familiarize "the alien" and defamiliarize "the ordinary" stuff of American existence, when their ways and means of observation crosscut the grain of American conventions, then the new American picaresque itself becomes a special form of cultural criticism.[46] Performing the crucial service with its modes of inventory of assuring Americans that stock remains yet to be taken and that margins of interpretive freedom not only still exist but are required for any full cultural reckoning, the narrative form simultaneously exemplifies some of those numerous creative ways—in its varieties of picaresque "optics"—that remain possible, indeed altogether necessary, to travel through such an abundant, yet ambiguous culturescape.

8

Road Work:

Detours into the Renewal of American Meanings

In taking to the road for purposes of creating an American inventory, of course, many of the new picaros and picaras are animated in strictly individual terms by nothing so much as nostalgia or hope, even as their particularized personal tours frequently crosscut more general patterns of cultural desire. Their meandering courses might be random or haphazard, but their general narrative designs, understood in retrospection if not always while on the road, appear in often-expressed concerns to locate a country, a culture, in which they can feel genuinely "at home." For a few, like a Lars Eighner or a Laurel Lee or even a Sylvie Fisher in Marilynne Robinson's *Housekeeping,* this might mean simply a specific place that can fully and finally and literally be called "home." Even for them, however, as for many others, the far-ranging picaresque courses taken suggest—even when the narrators themselves do not—an unfulfilled need for some broader, more containing meaning of America that will include "home" but refer as well to "homeland," the stuff not only of a comforting "place" but of a coherent and compelling cultural mythos, a framework for "belonging." Picaros and picaras as different from each other in many respects as Walt Harrington, Joe Buck, Richard Reeves, Laurel Lee, Cadillac Jack McGriff, Harrison Salisbury, Oedipa Maas, and Mort Rosenblum, among others, take their various stock in the struggle to find the "real" America "remembered" from childhood, or a "vanishing" America still partly to be recovered in rural or small-town life, or a "core" of America now camouflaged by tumultuous and alienating change, or a hoped-for America somehow hidden within confusing appearances. Often too, the reader suspects that, even when the narrators are not overt about the matter, the retrospective presentations themselves have the purpose of recovering for readers' eyes, perhaps even restoring for them in changing and opaque times, some essential or unifying American cultural meanings, some defining national identity and community, or at least some confederacy of common character, constituted out of all those disparate elements in the human plenum discovered on the picaresque tour. John Steinbeck's *Travels with Charley* expresses the craving straightforwardly enough, as the musing narrator proposes that, despite ethnic, religious, or racial backgrounds, regional styles and outlooks, generation gaps, class structures, and the like, "the American identity is an exact and provable thing,"[1] an assertion he makes even having earlier recognized how, on course, "every safe generality I gathered in my travels was canceled by another" (p. 157).

Even for those like Steinbeck most strenuously bent on the new American picaresque way to locate that univocal populace of common identity and meaning and loyalty, the country to correspond to the residual myth, the contemporary road ordinarily turns out to be rocky. While they might here and there locate remnants of Americana matching their nostalgic desires, or small and intermittent pockets of American attitudes and values commensurate with their senses of earlier American social and moral life, Salisbury, David Lamb, Reeves, and others usually come to the recognition upon taking their inventories that the American cultural reality is too huge, too diverse, too variegated, too utterly contradictory to be contained by anything beyond the utterance of "safest generality," the most clichéd interpretive efforts to find the lowest common cultural denominators.[2] Again, Steinbeck himself, perhaps the most ardent of all such seekers after the meaning of America, has to own up at last that his claim for the "exact and provable" character of the American identity cannot be borne out in any significant terms: it is simply another generality dashed on the rocky realities of America, that "monster" land. Even before entering the South, the region that will put to final rout his conviction about any "generalized characteristics" of Americans, as real and certain as his hope might have been, he confesses his own doubts about the plausibility of that earlier conviction. Toward journey's end, the lessons of the road having withered such conceits about any such staple cultural identity, he reports that "the more I inspected this American image, the less sure I

became of what it is. It appeared to me increasingly paradoxical, and
. . . when paradox crops up too often for comfort, it means that certain
factors are missing in the equation" (p. 242). For Steinbeck, as for many
another American picaro and picara, the nostalgic drive to locate the essentially defining character of the Americans, the hope for a core of experience common to them all, the quest for a singular and sustained and
containing meaning and substance of American life, finally fail to obtain.

But the road leads elsewhere in any event, at least for those picaros
and picaras who learn to care more for what lies ahead and how to get
there than for what lies behind, already receding into the past even as they
themselves forge forward. For these voyagers the picaresque motion of
the tour is itself or becomes the objective, and the detours along the way
become as important as the main way. Even as they apparently surrender the possibilities of a univocal and codified idea of America or Americans, however, the argument here is that the forms and movements of their
"detours," one metaphor for picaresque travel, has the ironic effect of
reinventing some other decidedly American traits, outlooks, and modes.
These picaresque figures commit themselves to the processes of the journey and relish the present tense, the active verb, quickly dismissing nostalgic satisfactions and unwarranted hopes or more gradually learning
that their lives on the road are not for the sake of revivifying what they
recall as old (and better) American cultural authority or reconsolidating
what they fancy were traditional (and superior) American values or spy-
ing out just how the old myths of the American character and destiny
might still convey or even confer some special cultural essence.

The charge here, then, is to examine the ways in which the new picaresque narrative, in addition to its other functions, effects, and implications, struggles with the cultural question, the question of American
meanings and values, and the working agenda of the exposition is to
trace out how in three disclosive forms of response promoted and sustained by the new American picaresque the objective is not any America
in codicil, everlasting in meaning and universal in effect, but, rather, a
dedication to the *processes* of being American and thus of being always
"in transit." As the picaros and picaras exhibit some of the characteristic road habits that define their literary formations, they move, wittingly
or not, to renew and reaffirm some longstanding American habits of
mind and traits of heart having to do with spatial freedom, with experiential deliberateness, and with improvisational acumen. These habits and
traits, signaling attributes of loyalty to processive life, refer much less to
hard fidelity to received tradition, to cultural stasis, to uniform identity,

than to the work of committed transience, empirical fluidity, studied mutability. In these three major and requisite attributes for the work of the road, there appears cultural work that answers to a time of confusion. Renewing these *ways* and *means*—not any one way or one meaning—of living in America, the new American picaresque posits, often involves the risky work of the detour, the challenge of forging forward even while shifting course, advancing even while altering objective, in an America whose possible meanings seem always up for continuous amendment, always "under construction."[3]

Thus, if many of the picaros and picaras enter onto the road seeking the terms of a unified culture "redisovered" by way of the highway or a country somehow "recovered" by way of narrative presentation, what they tend actually to discover or what their readers find renewed through them is not some essential "America" common to all or a sustained and static set of "American" beliefs and values compelling for all. The contemporary experience of American culture simply turns out for them to be too unapproachable in those terms, too messy for all of that. What most picaros and picaras manage to locate or somehow to express through their narrative self-presentations is, rather, the abiding importance of some distinctively American theaters of opportunity, habits of mind and imagination, and modes of living, just when the turbulences of cultural existence apparently require them most. When deepest hungers for cultural unity have gone unsatiated in a feeding frenzy of contentious power struggles, when efforts to consolidate old values have been crushed under the weight of new pluralities, when appeals to the old American mythos seem impotent or backward nostalgic gambles, when attempts to codify traditional symbols and meanings fizzle out in the fires of new and discordant expressive forms, the picaro or picara might well, like a Steinbeck, despair about being lost in his own country or, like Bill Bryson, seek stable interpretive repose through a tutored cynicism or, like Thomas Pynchon's Oedipa Maas, suffer a deep anxiety that the "core" cannot finally be dug out for scrutiny. But the most nimble picaros and picaras, those best equipped for the twists and tumults of the cultural road, also manage even so to work past any cravings for fixed cultural substance, any chimerical longing for standard and stable meanings, and to relocate and reinvest long-standing American commitments to the high priority of *process* as a stratagem of meaningful existence. Especially in a time when matters of common cultural identity are under dispute, when the very idea of a hegemonic cultural identity is under siege, the reflexive tactics of processive being do not lead to a univocal "substance" of American being. They work, rather, substantially and substantively to renew some old ways of being American that are perhaps more deeply, culturally, ingrained in Americans in any event than any perduring code of values or canon of meanings or unitary identity.

Freedom in Space: The Renewal of an American Calisthenics

Americans from the outset have often acted out, writers have expressed, and critics have noted, the penchant in American life to locate the terms of individual freedom in the more or less unfettered capacity for personal mobility afforded by, indeed beckoned by, the expansive "space" of the continent.[4] Such a disposition appears at least implicitly in William Bartram's naturalist entries into the wildernesses of the American Southeast in *Travels* (1791), in Benjamin Franklin's curriculum of self-making in early parts of the *Autobiography* (1793; 1818), in Timothy Dwight's itch for the next scene in *Travels in New England and New York* (1821–22), in Henry David Thoreau's volumes on going to the New England woods, in the "restless analyses" of Henry James in *The American Scene* (1907), in the compelled character of John Muir's *A Thousand-Mile Walk to the Gulf* (1916), and in the exhilarated "ride" of Theodore Dreiser in *A Hoosier Holiday* (1916). It comes to the fore at least figuratively in James Fenimore Cooper's Natty Bumppo in the Leatherstocking tales as that worthy attempts to stay a step ahead of the settlements, in Herman Melville's Ishmael, who requires some "sea room" in *Moby-Dick* (1851), in Thoreau's metaphors that seek mythic status in the famous essay on "Walking" (1862), in Mark Twain's depiction of the several "flights" from Hannibal and the closing musings about escaping captivity by "lighting out for the territory" embodied in *The Adventures of Huckleberry Finn* (1884), and, later, in the educational, cultural, and political voyages of Saul Bellow's title character in *The Adventures of Augie March* (1953). The itch to cover ground displays itself more explicitly in actions as various as the journeys of Lewis and Clark, as the frontier jumping of Daniel Boone, as the migrations of "Johnny Appleseed," as Americans pioneering westward, as folk-action in Woody Guthrie's *Bound for Glory* (1943), and as social and political performance in Henry Miller's *The Air-Conditioned Nightmare* (1945) and Clancy Sigal's *Going Away* (1961), among many other individual proclivities, social notions, and cultural venues. For good or ill, and quite apart from the phenomenon that was Jack Kerouac, the idea of freedom in spatial mobility is expressed mythically in the American "classics," enacted literally as an American trait, embedded deeply in the American bone-marrow.[5] As Ralph Waldo Emerson, the source of so many aphoristic "takes" on American life, once observed, "there are three wants that can never be satisfied: that of the rich, who wants something more; that of the sick, who wants something different; and that of the traveler, who says 'Anywhere but here.'"[6]

This American fancy for liberating mobility, then, can well be thought not only a habit of mind and experience but also always to have been double-sided. For Emerson, the cravings for "more," for "different," for "elsewhere," are in some forms at least of a piece, possible signals of a cultural dis-health rooted in what Emerson considered a fundamentally adolescent dissatisfaction with life, and this American notion of freedom, revealed in traits of restlessness in spatial terms, often discloses itself in negative forms—"moving on" as an action of acquisitive materialism, as a form of escapism, as a symptom of personal irresponsibility or antisocial behavior. In this context, when the desires for "beginning again," for "starting over," for "getting away from it all," seem possible to be fulfilled simply by moving to another place, the next place, those desires might also express facile remedies for personal failures, or immature repudiations of the claims of the past, or "primitive" refusals of social restraints. These kinds of actions, of course, are all abetted in part by other cultural patterns (the quick fixes of cosmetic cure, easy declarations of bankruptcy, instant therapies of "self-making," finances of social mobility, even efforts at "going straight"). Such actions are surely enabled by the expansive spaces of American geography with their "promise" that in a new place one can become a new person, live a new life.

In a less suspicious view, of course, the stuff of spatial freedom is surely part and parcel of crucial elements of the American dream. America as "the land of opportunity" in individualistic and personal terms has often been predicated on the amplitude of American space. America as the place wherein creative character and hard work displace privileges of birth and inheritance has frequently been attached to locating one's patch of land, carving out one's own "place," achieving one's personal space. America as the theater for achieving new moral identity has often been associated with, even dependent upon, the opportunity to "move on," "begin again," "start over." The compelling idea of American freedom in space, then, flows from and through original immigrant experience, economic autonomy, a democratic polity, a westering frontier, a psychic and social need. Whatever its sources, however, it appears over and over not simply as a reification of dream or wish but as a fact of American life rooted in the realities of America's open spaces, abundant size, expansive landscape, long vistas, far horizons, willing populace.

In at least relative degrees, the Emersonian identification of the itches for "more," for "different," and for "elsewhere" and the "promissory" American space unfolding on the road appear quite prominently for many a picaro and picara, indeed inspiring or requiring just that movement in space that in so many ways defines the figure. For the picaro or picara, impoverishment and not wealth might elicit the want for the "more" possibly to be found in the motions of the road, as readers are reminded again of the old form of the picaresque narrative as an "epic of hunger." As much as for Lazarillo de Tormes or Gil Blas or Jack Wilton, this is clearly the case for E. L. Doctorow's title character in *Billy Bathgate* as he travels about New York with the Dutch Schultz gang in quest of his fortunes, for Joe David Brown's "Addie Prey gang" in *Paper Moon* as father and daughter search for the "big score," for James Leo Herlihy's Joe Buck in *Midnight Cowboy* as he blunders west then to east then to south trying out his chosen trade, for Lars Eighner in *Travels with Lizbeth* as he sallies about to improve his relative prospects, for Barbara Kingsolver's Taylor Greer in *The Bean Trees* as she sets out from rural Kentucky toward the promise of more, better, in the West, for Mona Simpson's picaras, Adele and Ann, in *Anywhere but Here* as they hit the road, thereon making do with little, in answer to the call of riches and glamour in Hollywood, for Laurel Lee in her *Godspeed* as she scrimps and saves and struggles northward toward some "home," and for Russell Banks's Bob DuBois in *Continental Drift* as he enacts the dark underside of the American Dream in his noir version of "starting over," from snowy Pennsylvania to sunny Florida, seeking to "get ahead." In these and other instances, the want for "more," the material character of the *rota Fortunae*, the sheer hunger and hope for something better, and the freedom of movement in American space, all operate in compelling reciprocity.

For other picaros and picaras, the illness creating a "want" for something "different"—except in a case like that of Ratzo Rizzo in *Midnight Cowboy*—ordinarily refers less to physical ailment than to emotional despair or yearning, remedies for which, again, seem to such "sick" to attach to freedom in space, to movement toward the next place. Such psychic disease clearly plays its role in the spatial restlessness found in both Texas Jack Carmine and Vaughn Rhomer in Robert James Waller's *Border Music*, as their personal forms of sadness lead them to seek that "different" thing in another place, and, of course, in various and disparate ways, it goes to the very heart of "Phaedrus" in Robert Pirsig's *Zen and the Art of Motorcycle Maintenance*, of Ralph Ellison's protagonist in *Invisible Man*, of Joey Celebrisi in David Rounds's *Celebrisi's Journey*, of Jed Tewksberry in Robert Penn Warren's *A Place to Come To*, and, as the Dream implodes, of Rojack in Norman Mailer's *An American Dream*. Comparable "sicknesses unto death" are propelling as well for the more restricted spatial ventures of Saul Bellow's urban picaro Tommy Wilhelm in *Seize the Day*, of Binx Bolling in Walker Percy's *The Moviegoer*, of Ignatius J. Reilly in John Kennedy Toole's *A Confederacy of Dunces*, and of Don Wanderhope in Peter DeVries's *Blood of the Lamb*, just as such "disease" can be discerned in the vividly restive despair of Sylvie Fisher in Marilynne Robinson's *Housekeeping* as this picara, in her sad captivity to the responsibilities of the house, prowls the edges, the outer limits, of the small town like a caged tigress until her next break to somewhere, something "different" can finally be accomplished. Perhaps less dramatically, or at least less overtly, the psychic disabilities of the yearning heart or the impaired emotion also occasionally come to the fore in nonfictional examples of the new American picaresque, and, again, the promises of health or wholeness attach to the actions of taking to the road for Peter Jenkins in *A Walk across America* as he seeks to get past his youthful disaffection for his country, for William Least Heat Moon in *Blue Highways* as he rolls across the landscape in "Ghost Dancing" after suffering deep disintegrations of personal life, for Walt Harrington in *Crossings* as he travels black America to resolve his emotional afflictions, for Eddy L. Harris in *South of Haunted Dreams* as he moves through what are for him the troubled territories of America's racial legacy, and even for Harrison Salisbury in *Travels around America* as he retraces a personal past he gnawingly fears might be vanishing. In these and other cases, American picaros and picaras, from Don Wanderhope and Sylvie Fisher to Least Heat Moon and Eddy Harris, answer to the call of the road, to the "different" prospects of life to be located by moving through American space, in ways that connect their health to this "freedom." If personal "health" or "recovery" by way of the road is an idea clearly without warrantee in every case, the idea of freedom in American space just as clearly continues to compel the American picaresque imagination.

For most of these and for many other new American picaros and picaras, however, Emerson's third American "want," the sheer desire of the traveler, the craving to be "elsewhere," the itchiness to move along, is surely the superseding habit of mind, even as it often folds wishes for "more" and "different" into itself. This urge to be "anywhere but here,"

prompted and accommodated by the prospects of another vista, the call
of the far horizon, in the spaciousness of the American landscape is a
distinctive American attribute as even that newly "naturalized" American picaro, Andrei Codrescu, recognizes. Caressing old roadsters as he
prepares for his own new trip, he muses, "The old cars gave off an exu-
berant giddiness, a musk of eternal youth, a Huck Finn feeling off their
shiny huck fins. They said, 'You're an American, you can start over again.
The mystery of America has barely been touched'" (p. 26). Although
recognizing that for many Americans "moving on" has frequently meant
only relocating to the suburbs and leaving garbage behind, Codrescu is
entirely alert to the fact that the old idea of freedom in space still runs
with the American grain. The cars, old and new, "gave off the feeling—
which is also the secret birthright of every American—that if things didn't
work out where you lived you could always get in your car and go someplace else" (p. 26).[7] Especially attached to its corollaries in the American
imagination, to new prospects, to hope and desire, to the budding opportunity to begin again, this idea of freedom in space is not simply an
invitation to drift. However much it might in some enactments imply an
evasion or refusal of the past, however much it might in many cases be
followed out without certain destination, it responds to promise, if not
sure purpose: it answers to longing, if not to certitude. For Codrescu as
for generations of Americans before him, the idea of freedom in spatial
terms, if not a birthright, is at least latent and enduring, always possible.[8]

It is, of course, a centrally animating idea of the new American picaresque, therein to come to fuller measure in narrative life than it ever could
for most Americans, to be extended quite beyond the ordinary course the
idea could take, and, with those measures and extensions, not only to
duplicate the old American trait but to renew it. The picaro or picara, by
definition, can scarcely resist the idea of free motion in space, the picaresque, of course, cannot exist as a narrative form without it, and, for figure
and form, of course, the idea is never temporary: the form elicits the idea
continuously; the idea sustains the form thoroughly.[9] For the picaro or
picara, it is a matter of course that he or she stay in motion, never simply
a matter of moving to the next place only to stop there. He or she cannot
take up or be propelled by the idea, as many or most Americans are, only
to find the repose in that space Codrescu refers to as "their suburban plan-
ets" (p. 26). The very moment the picaresque wanderer stops moving, or
at least stops feeling and acting upon the need to move along, the life as
picara or picaro is ended. As an ineluctable and controlling habit of her
or his narrative existence, the reiterated idea of free movement for the new

American picaro might well be a search for "home," but, once entirely at home, with no further "want" or capacity for elsewhere, the road hits a dead end or a final cul-de-sac, the picaresque venture truncates, the figure goes sedentary, and the narrative form withers into closure. Saul Bellow's Augie March might well end his adventures in America with the vow to remain "a sort of Columbus of those near-at-hand,"[10] but, despite the promise, his life as a picaro is over as soon as he locates that hearth and home from which emotionally or psychologically he will never stray very far for very long. Whether it is with Steinbeck in *Travels with Charley* as he winds his way back toward home in Connecticut, David Rounds's Joey in *Celebrisi's Journey* as he finds a stationary calm in the Buddhist monastery, E. L. Doctorow's title character in *Billy Bathgate,* disguising himself from his earlier picaro's existence, as he now narrates from the status of high station, Laurel Lee as she finds the homestead, the place she was "meant" to be, Elizabeth Berg's Nan in *The Pull of the Moon* as she returns to Martin and home, or Thomas Berger's Jack Crabb in *Little Big Man,* now enfeebled, no longer mobile, as he recounts his 111-year-old life in American space from the confines of the old persons' home, the journey always comes to an end because, for whatever reason, the picaro or picara ceases to move in space, because, some denouement reached or sensed, the story is ripe for closure, or because, somehow, the "want" of the traveler for "anywhere else" is now ensconced in "this place." At this moment, fixed in this place, the picaro or picara goes "out of character," recedes into the past tense, now becoming or giving way to a narrator.[11]

Until that time, however, while yet on the road, the new American picaro or picara not only lives out at full tilt the general idea of mobile freedom in space but cultivates to full term its several corollaries. The picaro's movement may sweep from "sea to shining sea" in the highly various accounts provided in Codrescu's *Road Scholar,* Steinbeck's *Travels with Charley,* Larry McMurtry's *Cadillac Jack,* or Mark Winegardner's *Elvis Presley Boulevard.* The reader can "ramble" around in broad regional territories with new American picaros as different as a John Grady Cole in Cormac McCarthy's *All the Pretty Horses,* a David Lamb in his *A Sense of Place,* a "One-Eyed Mack" in Jim Lehrer's *Kick the Can,* a Jonathan Yardley in his *States of Mind,* a C. W. Sughrue in James Crumley's *The Last Good Kiss,* or a Tony Dunbar in *Delta Time.* Or the picaro or picara may bump about on city pavements, narrower terrain, more concentrated venues, or a watery course like, respectively, Toole's Ignatius J. Reilly and Jay McInerney's narrator in *Bright Lights, Big City,* Percy's Binx Bolling in *The Moviegoer* and Richard Hill's Vic Messenger in *Riding Solo with the*

Golden Horde, or Thomas Pynchon's Oedipa Maas in *The Crying of Lot 49* and David Lamb again in his *Stolen Season,* or Raban in his *Old Glory* or B. C. Hall and C. T. Wood in *Big Muddy.* The length of this or that trek matters little. Continuing motion in space is the thing, and, in that motion, what matters most is the next place, the need or desire to be elsewhere, even as "then and there," with arrival, only spurs as usually it does the picaro's *new* itch for, curiosity about, and heightened anticipation of, what now lies ahead. Beyond some form of quick glancing into the rear-view mirror, the picaro and picara only occasionally look back to the last or some earlier scene: departures tend to be fast and clean in the narrative presentation as transition becomes nothing so much as "rapid transit," full speed ahead, to the next place, wherever or whatever it is or might become.[12]

Thus, in quick transit, with all of the free and forward, if usually haphazard movement in space, the new American picaros and picaras manage, moreover, not only to elude the past in broadest terms while on the road but also, just as an element of a picaresque definition, to revivify that important corollary of such spatial freedom. They also pick up the accompanying notion of "beginning again" or "starting over," by playing out this possibility not simply once or once in a while but more or less continuously in the smaller, daily contours of their road movements. Convinced that it "seemed like the time to make a clean break,"[13] Barbara Kingsolver's Taylor Greer in *The Bean Trees* makes one grand flight in the effort to strike out anew, as she removes herself from Kentucky to Arizona, but even stuck for a time in Tucson she remains in motion, within this tighter sphere, as she bumps from episode to episode, one day to the next, forever expectant of a fresh start. Struggling toward something "different," Elizabeth Berg's middle-aged picara Nan, in *The Pull of the Moon,* literally runs away from home, a desperate action to achieve a new kind of life. Her first letter home to her husband says "'I needed all of a sudden to go, without saying where, because I don't know where.'"[14] Once on the road, however, the turn of every day for her is a matter of continuously starting over from the previous day. Jim Lehrer's "One-Eyed Mack" in *Kick the Can* also kicks the traces of Kansas and, seeking an expanse of water to match his resolve for starting a new life as an adventuring buccaneer, heads for the Gulf of Mexico: "there was no way to be a pirate in Kansas."[15] But life on the road for him forces him, and enables him, to zoom from one place and situation to another, with each and every new adventure a new revolution in his young life.

Luck, detours, timing, curiosity, new horizons, all alter courses and change itineraries, and cycle after cycle of new starts in new landscapes is the defining life of the picara and picaro. Following out and flowing along in more or less steady motion, enacting abrupt transitions from site to site and scene to scene, pausing only occasionally to muse about the last scene, the picaresque life turns on the primacy of the episode immediately to the forefront, at least until another quick departure need be performed. In this disjointed course, each and every new episode represents, if need be, the occasion to begin again, *volver nuevo*, to start anew, as again the picaro rejuvenates this American habit by enacting it, by definition, in the extreme and with frequency.[16] The ending of every episode or the beginning of any new one becomes the occasion to start from scratch, as if yesterday did not exist or at least matter, and this is all the more the case when an episode demoralizes or batters the new American picaros or picaras. If remaining in character, they display just that trait of intrepid resilience and hopefulness depicted in old picaros and picaras like Lazarillo and Gil Blas and Moll Flanders: they pick themselves up, dust themselves off, and declare their forward movement, beginning again with the idea that the next day is a new day, that the next scene or place holds out better prospects. When bullied by the callow, teenaged manager of the Burger Derby where she works, Taylor Greer, having "lasted six days" (p. 66), throws her cap in the Mister Miser trash compactor (p. 67), walks out, and more or less immediately concludes that "the want ads every day gave new meaning to my life" (p. 68). Nan in *The Pull of the Moon*, after an uncomfortable but self-discovering overnight in the woods, meets the new day with comparable hope: "I am sore and creaky, and a thin line of pain runs from my shoulder into the middle of my back. But I am exhilarated. I can roll up my bed, and go back to the cabin for coffee and then I can drive to a new place. And then to another new place. I am only fifty" (p. 218). The One-Eyed Mack's first miscreant adventures on the road make him think often about returning to Kansas. His new life seems to be turning on the wheel of misfortune, pulling him into untoward and even criminal hijinks, and three early chapters end with his concluding that "It was an awful life I was leading" (p. 16), that "It really was an awful life I was living" (p. 23), and that "I could always plead insanity" (p. 45). But the opening sentences of each succeeding chapter in each case restore him for a better day, propose a new horizon, another prospect, a different opportunity, as the picaresque drive to begin again takes over from his doubts and difficulties. One picaro or picara after another follows such a continuing cycle of small and daily new beginnings when the freedom of movement in space refreshes the picaro's hope, when the road requires a new course, and when the picaro's and picara's own defining habit of life answers to the call of the next place, the looming future, the promise of "something different."

In these and other ways, then, the new American picaresque not only reasserts the continuity and power of this particular idea of spatial freedom for the contemporary American imagination but also reinvigorates the old idea by rehearsing it through characters, picaros and picaras, usually up to—even somehow born for—the demands and detours of the road. Although many picaros and picaras encounter from time to time this or that other person who, wistfully, expresses the "wish that I could come along," not every American, of course, can stay in such motion, much less enact on the way those other facets of the American commitment to processive life that the road entails. Even for those who could put down their everyday responsibilities, not everyone can for long resist the comforts of "home," not many can withstand the episodic need to begin again continuously, and few indeed can sustain the required feckless and intrepid picaresque manner on a rough and tumble course, as indeed some new American picaros and picaras themselves quickly or slowly learn. Some, however, indeed sense themselves not only equipped for but somehow inherently built for this form of being American. Codrescu, for one, after some brief uncertainty about getting more than a pedestrian's view of the country, declares himself ready for the long haul in just such terms as a matter of personal temperament and style: "Here was a chance for me to transform myself once more, to begin again. I love being born again, and I practice it. It's my passion, also my *métier*, my specialty. Changing names, places of residence, body shapes, opinions . . . what endless delight. America was set up for this kind of thing, a vast stage for projecting images of self that Europe had made impossible" (p. xiv). Or there is Mona Simpson's picara, Ann in *Anywhere but Here*, who remembers staying home "then" with her mother from their "now" on the road and who concludes that she was and is still to the picaresque "manner" born: "My mother and I should have both been girls who stayed out on the porch a little longer than the rest, girls who strained to hear the long-distance trucks on the highway and who listened to them, not the nearer crickets. We would have been girls who had names in their heads: Ann Arbor, Chicago, Cheyenne, San Francisco, Portland, Honolulu, Los Angeles; girls who looked at the sky and wanted to go away."[17] For those in the new American picaresque mode like Andrei and Ann—and their numbers are plentiful—space becomes the medium for a style of free movement, and this spatial liberty becomes both career and calisthenics. Being on the road *is* the picaro's or picara's job of work, and being on the road in the picaresque style is to practice a set of physical exercises and motions involving, leading to, and extending the continued health and vigor of certain traits of American processive outlook and temperament.

In the linear life of continuous motion, for these practitioners, the regimen of the road cultivates a craving for "difference," creates a desire and sponsors a capacity to move forward, generates refusals to settle for the status quo, points them always toward the future, forces them to cast off excess baggage and to "travel light," equips them to seek change, steels them with fecklessness, and steers them in hope. While surely not the only habits of mind and heart to be found in Americans, these would decidedly seem some distinctive and long-standing and oft-prized forms of American outlook or disposition that come in for reinvention in the new picaresque style, a renewal apt and timely as the narrative form answers to the confusions and vagaries of contemporary American experience. If the earlier American drive to move unfettered through space was an impulse promoted by the largely "unpeopled" and "unstoried" character of the open landscape beyond the settlement or the frontier, the new American picaro's or picara's recovery and renewal of the reflex pulls him or her into a different, more humanly congested terrain, but the new motions of freedom and hope and their entailments in necessary style and attitude nevertheless correspond to the processive nature of being in American space, of being American in spatial terms, no less than those old travelers Emerson described who wanted more, different, elsewhere, committed as they were to change, to the future. And this picaresque fidelity to movement and change, always resistant to any long personal repose, arguably serves as well as a broad narrative reminder about the dangers to cultural health that come with nostalgic stagnations, about a needful readiness for those changes in America that will come willy-nilly, and about the need for some form of calisthenics, exercises for process, in order to stay in American cultural trim.

Deliberate Life: Experience and Self-Possession

If Waldo Emerson helped detect the certain and long-standing American itch for freedom in spatial terms, he likewise identified—perhaps even helped to create—another element or proclivity that was or would become a distinctively American habit of approaching life. His call in the essay entitled *Nature* (1836) for his countrypersons to seek "an original relation to the universe" was nothing less than an appeal to his age to engage the world in immediate terms, to plunge past tradition and convention in order to seize immediate experience directly and fully, and to wrest from the world in personal terms what it surely offered for meaning and insight. Often since interpreted or misconstrued as a charter for a kind of trite self-reliance or "rugged individualism," the most decisive thrust of this appeal in Emerson's own outlook was to insist on an ideal form of American self-definition radically rooted in the primary data of the experiential domain: the authentic person came to full integrity by virtue of that person's possession of his or her experience in the most heightened ways. In one form or another ever since, if usually without any of Emerson's visionary casts of mind, some such idea of the "experience-made" person has often had a prevalent place in American cultural self-understanding. In order to get "the meaning of it all," the cipher for which is the great whale, Melville's Ishmael in *Moby-Dick* needs to go into the low boats, whose proximity to the whales in their own proper element will ensure his firsthand encounter. And this sense of the priority of a personal "original relation" for Melville was not only one to be acted upon by the character he created but one that Melville himself felt forced to follow—to swim, as his poetry expressed it, "'Twixt the sharks' black flukes." For the integral character of Walt Whitman's own knowledge, to sing any "Song of Myself," that worthy needed also to walk among the low and oppressed on city streets, to roam among the country's populace, to put his hands on the wounded in field hospitals. To possess the most fundamental insights, Ernest Hemingway's "old man" must suffer the bloody hands and bone-biting fatigue that come as he struggles with the elemental forces of life in *The Old Man and the Sea*, while Hemingway, for his personal part, needed to participate in the war, in the safari, in deep-sea fishing, in boxing, in the bull-fight scene, and so on. Again and again, the primacy of immediate personal experience becomes the predicate of both the right conduct of living and the fullest measure of existence in this particular American way of conceiving the terms and conditions of a life.[18]

As with some other aspects of the rhetoric of Emerson's theoretical agenda, Henry David Thoreau perhaps best supplies the rhetorical echo of this course of experience in practice. Among the most famous passages in American literary expression, in the chapter of *Walden* entitled "Where I Lived and What I Lived For," Thoreau marks out his own version of what Emerson's "original relation to the universe" might be, and, as a part of his account, he clearly reiterates a necessary saturation in experience radically understood that makes for a fully realized form of the American self. As he recalled:

> I went to the woods because I wished to live deliberately, to front only the essential facts of life, and see if I could not learn what it had to teach, and not, when I came to die, discover that I had not lived. I did not wish to live what was not life, living is so dear; nor did I wish to practice resignation, unless it was quite necessary. I wanted to live deep and suck out all the marrow of life, to live so sturdily and Spartan-like as to put to rout all that was not life, to cut a broad swath and shave close, to drive life into a corner, and reduce it to its lowest terms, and, if it proved to be mean, why then to get the whole and genuine meanness of it, and publish its meanness to the world; or if it were sublime, to know it by experience, and be able to give a true account of it in my next excursion.[19]

Recognizing all the while that most people cannot or will not pursue experience in such radical terms, Thoreau nevertheless provides a commission in this passage for those Americans for whom a "deliberate life" involves encountering the world directly as if it were brand new, being seen for the first time (the vocabularies of "being awakened" and "waking up" shoot through *Walden*). Such a course curves away from resignation or despair, and, as with American spatial freedom, corresponds to hope. Above all else, the commitment is to approach life in immediacy, "to know it by experience," and, thus, for Thoreau the term "deliberate" does not refer to anything prudent or even gradual: it combines experiential intensity with certain intentionality in the effort, for the sake of the self, to front the facts out there, to corner the fundamentals of things, in order to learn what the world has to teach. Although not a style of existence for everyone, Thoreau's challenge to himself certifies in its way what for many Americans has been a persistent trait of mind at the level of their requisite self-reckoning—namely, again, that need for individual and personal possession of the facts of life as the only valid test of satisfactory meaning.

As with the mobile response to the expansive character of American "space," the new American picaresque flourishes in answer to the demand for such "deliberate life."[20] For the most part, the picaro or picara follows no precisely intentional itinerary, of course, because the maps provide only the conventional course. He or she realizes that the detours and the roadside attractions present the raw, experiential "facts" of life far more, far better, than any pre-mapped course and in their novelty or compelling character do so in ways that "wake" the figure up to the promises of possession. As this picaresque narrative or that tracks along the jumbled way with its central figure, the intentional commitment to the experience of the "site" or episode to the immediate forefront and the degrees of intensity with which these sites and situations are entered make clear from one case to the next that the picaros and picaras both cherish and embody this American mode of cornering life for what it can yield. Their ways and means are not necessarily, much less always, Thoreauvian in style or rhetoric—his, after all, is only one form of living deliberately, his only one set of "facts" from which to wring the fundaments. In tenor and tone, however, the picaresque figures display just that intrepid spirit of getting the "meanness" or the "sublimity" or the simple authentic feel of and grasp on the scene, the continuing hope against resignation, the altogether personal terms for locating original relation and meaning, in ways that resonate with Thoreau's own forms of this American cast of mind and mode.

In this sense, if the new American picaresque is reminiscent of the old "epics of hunger" proposed in the figures of Lazarillo, El Buscon, and Moll Flanders, it is also clear that, like those forebears, the new picaros and picaras enact forms of the "epic of individual experience." E. L. Doctorow's young title picaro in *Billy Bathgate,* for instance, simply cannot observe from afar, cannot go unimplicated: he must be in the middle of the risky, criminal, and violent business with Dutch Schultz, must witness the murder of Bo Weinberg, must take up with Drew at his own peril. In Thoreauvian terms, he seeks to suck the very marrow out of every novel venture he enters. Narrating from his "maturity," from the angle of his subsequent success, he fully recognizes himself as the experience-made man, and, in closing "this story of a boy's adventures,"[21] he says of his impoverished, complicated, and dangerous picaresque youth, "I drop to my knees in reverence to think of it, I thank God for the life He has given me and the joy of my consciousness, I praise Him and give all reverent thanks for my life of crime and the terror of my existence" (pp. 321–22). His gratitude for his life extends past his current wealth and station because, for him, "the joy of my consciousness" and what he calls "the fount of all my memory" reach back into the sheer vibrancy of his youthful experiences, however miscreant, and, while later corrections don't "exonerate the boy I was" (p. 321), he knows fully now that he managed then "to cut a broad swath and shave close" in "this bazaar of life" (p. 323). But beyond those dramatic intensities of illicit episode that vitalize the young Billy Bathgate, the "deliberate" approach to life occurs in a number of other forms, and many another picaro and picara both crave and enact their own, different modes. They take the radical turn into experience, make the effort to front the "essential facts" as they find them, seek to move past or to cut through "what was not life," all in order to serve a will to empirical possession that, they believe or learn, has everything to do with their constructions of themselves out of the accumulations of what "happens" and what "matters" to them.

For some, the intention to live deliberately by taking to the road flows out of senses of omissions or regrets, out of feelings or sudden discoveries that, until now, they "had not," as Thoreau put, "lived at all." This is just the case for Elizabeth Berg's picara in *The Pull of the Moon*, who, before taking off, had lost her sense of herself and recognized that she was full of regrets after having relented for years to a husband who has told her, "Nan, ever since I've known you, you've looked for meaning and excitement in life. But life is by and large meaningless and dull."[22] The road for her becomes a voyage of discovery of experiences that can belong, finally, exhilaratingly, only to her and that vitiate earlier omissions and regrets as she learns how "this trip has made me aware of so much I'd kept hidden from myself" (p. 227). As she plunges into her second chances to respond to life and to grasp the essentials, in ways and forms much quieter than Billy Bathgate's tumultuous ride, she sleeps naked in the woods, intercedes for a woman verbally assaulted by her husband, plops herself on the porch of a stranger's farmhouse to carry on intimate conversation, and, withal, plunges in at the level of her deepest capacity to secure her claim on what happens and matters to her. "'This doesn't feel like travel to me,'" she writes to Martin at home. "'It feels too much my own to be like travel, if you know what I mean'" (p. 141). Later, still recovering herself in her experience, still locating her individual integrity in "the scheme of things," she writes in her journal of her night in the woods, in terms that resonate with Billy Bathgate's closing vocabularies, "I could feel my own longing for my own self return, my insistence on my own importance, at least to myself," as this depth-episode makes her "feel as though this was a holy and personal event I will never share with anyone" (p. 218). For Nan, as for other picaras and picaros, the exclusive character of the individual's experience is a matter of taking personal possession of what stands in "front" of him or her, soaking it in in deepest ways, and calling it his or her own.

Often, given the accidental character of the focal figures' various "progresses" in the narratives of the new American picaresque, what "fronts" them might very well detour them into experiences neither anticipated nor desired. Even in these episodes, however, the timbre of the scene, the measure of the events, the feel for the life contained therein, are there to be taken up deliberately, taken in for the sake of experience itself. In *Anywhere but Here*, when the child Ann grows petulant in the car and mother Adele discards her temporarily on the roadside to "teach lessons," Ann displays that, even at a tender age, she trains well at the picaresque venture of seeking "an original relation" to the universe immediately around her. When the car "was nothing but a dot in the distance" (p. 3), she stops her crying and takes the empirical measure of what is there. Even feeling alien in the landscape and sensing that "it had nothing to do with me" (p. 4), her dedicated senses nevertheless take it all in:

> I don't know if it was minutes or if it was more. There was nothing to think because there was nothing to do. First, I saw small things. The blades of grass. Their rough side, their smooth, waxy side. Brown grasshoppers. A dazzle of California poppies.
>
> I'd look at everything around me. In yellow fields, the tops of weeds bent under visible waves of wind. There was a high steady note of insects squeaking. A rich odor of hay mixed with the heady smell of gasoline. Two or three times, a car rumbled by, shaking the ground. Dry weeds by the side of the road seemed almost transparent in the even sun. (pp. 3–4)

Mother returns, Ann enters the car, the trip continues, now with a new store of sights and sensations absorbed by the young picara as her own, not to be relinquished because now it has become part of who she is and is becoming.

Other wayfarers in the new American picaresque comparably find themselves detoured into unwanted but, finally, still necessary experiences of which to take possession. Surely even less desired than Ann's brief roadside punishment is the abandonment in the forest suffered by the manically adolescent picara Jean Gillis (called "Little" by her mother and "Dutch" by her friends) in Katherine Dunn's *Truck*. Already a runaway, she has been made even more a fugitive by her callow and delinquent consort, Heydorf, and then stranded by him for days to survive in the California wilderness with virtually nothing to sustain her. Like Ann and many other picaras and picaros, Dutch seizes the situation, and, in this case, is literally forced "to live so sturdily and Spartan-like" that her experience is crowded into its lowest, most fundamental terms, Thoreau's "essential facts." Also like Ann and others, this Jean Gillis nevertheless works to front her experience deliberately even in its full, grubby, and fearful "meanness," soaks it into herself, and, when finally "rescued" by her lower-middle-class parents, refuses to allow the experience to be other than exclusively her own. As the family packs the car to return the young *picara* to home, she does not want them even to touch the things that, for her, now stand for the experience:

> It's my stuff. My things. I worked and scraped and stole and cadged to get it. All of it. I want to jerk it out of their hands and scream. It was all with me out there. The canteen still has water in it. I grin and shuffle and take the bow from [brother] Nick. Sound eager and remorseful and cheerful and glad to see them but I want my things. I don't want them to look into my packs and touch the stuff and talk about it and ask me questions. . . . Dad tries to help me with the stuff and I pull it away and grin stiff and put it on. Can't bite him. Spoil it. "Naw, I'll take it. I carried it this far." (pp. 209–10)

From the outset of the narrative, before high-tailing it out of Portland to California to meet Heydorf, she has worried that she might end up in her life with "what was not life," in Thoreau's terms: she has feared that "I'll marry a service station attendant and never see or go or know anything or do anything or ever feel myself all over full of possibility" (p. 12), and has troubled in the thought that it was "already too late for me" (p. 13). By journey's end, her accumulated experiences in low, Dutch, Jean, simply cannot now imagine herself apart from those moments into which she has plunged, so vital are these episodes of life lived directly and authentically to who she is and is becoming in her "possibility."[23]

Not all of the episodes of deliberate intensity recounted in the new American picaresque occur in primal encounters with the natural world, of course, and most have less dramatically presaging power than Jean Gillis's days in the wilderness, but the focal figures are remarkable for their consistent efforts to try out the "new," to dive in deeper, and, through it all, to operate as if an equation between "experience gained fully" and "life lived best" were a paramount matter. From text to text, picaros and picaras seize self-consciously or not on the occasions that arise "to cut a broad swath and to shave close," to do and feel more intensely, to drive into the unwonted possibility. Just as much as Doctorow's Billy Bathgate follows the allure of that world not yet known but there to be learned with the Dutch Schultz mob, Joe Buck in *Midnight Cowboy* can no more resist the novelty of the twisted and curious twins' party than he can turn away finally from the life "on edge," in its fundamentals, with Enrico "Ratso" Rizzo. Andrei Codrescu's intrepid "road scholarship" pulls him ineluctably into episodes he then often and willingly pushes to extremity, participating in them to the extent that he "becomes," however temporarily, just the character called for by the experience, all in a very deliberate, highly intentional, effort to suck the marrow out of the life-forms presented him.[24]

The examples multiply in the new American picaresque of this craving for the intense personal experience. Walker Percy's Jack "Binx" Bolling in *The Moviegoer*, for all of his world-weariness and for all of his second-hand experiences by way of the "silver screen," recognizes a good "rotation" when he encounters one and seizes upon one with his present girlfriend and his crippled young cousin Lonnie at the drive-in where they have gone to watch *Fort Dobbs* again: "Lonnie likes to sit on the hood and lean back against the windshield and look around at me when a part comes he knows we both like" (p. 143), and, on this particular evening, with Lonnie "beside himself" with joy, "My heart sings like Octavian and there is great happiness between me and Lonnie and this noble girl and they both know it and have the sense to say nothing" (p. 144).[25] Or, again, there is Peter Jenkins's fighting down his fear of southern blacks when, down and out, he is invited to become for a time a part of a rural African-American household on Texana Hill in Smokey Hollow near Murphy, North Carolina. This invitation he finally accepts because of a presentiment he has had, because of the black mother's insistence that this is a divine test of faith, and because, after concluding "My dream and Mary Elizabeth's God were too much to ignore,"[26] he senses what he comes ultimately to learn after three months, that this portentous episode will stay with him significantly forever. Looking in the mirror toward the end of his stay, he sees himself briefly as black, but "No, I was white. At least my skin was. I had been through so much with my family here, and all I had seen was black faces, that I forgot for a split second that I wasn't black too. For weeks . . . I remembered the morning I forgot my skin color. The memory still lives in my mind. It always will" (p. 167). In case after case on the road, with eyes cocked for the ways to crowd "life" into a corner, the sojourners of the American tour discern or discover or devise those experiences to be plumbed in their fullest possibility. Some are more adept than others in this effort, and, at times, of course, most grow weary and downcast and refuse such willed empirics. More often than not, however, the hunger for "more" and "different"—more and more different experiences—directly and personally absorbed and "saved" is a hallmark of the American picaresque turn of mind.

The new American picaros and picaras must—by definition and by virtue of their own various, idiosyncratic senses of necessity—travel through American space, and, in their very narrative "actions," they reaffirm the long-standing cultural value of mobility as that motion in space becomes the medium through which, for them, life comes to be realized. Whether on the road in flight, in drift, in curiosity, or in some vague objective, however, the medium conduces naturally to the reassertion in this form of American letters of that experientialist drive also deep in the cultural bone-marrow as a primary value. Indeed, in some cases it seems clear that, if the picaro or picara craves movement and motion, he or she craves "reality" even more and that American space simply becomes the avenue into a possibly fuller experience of the realities of things, the route toward and into a life of one's own forged out of the singularity of one's encounters. This is surely what sends Nan to the road in *The Pull of the Moon* as it is what impels "Dutch" Gillis in *Truck* and Taylor Greer in *The Bean Trees*, the desperate sensation each has that she has been living "what is not life," what is not real, just as much as Oedipa Maas in *The Crying of Lot 49* goes deeper and deeper or at least further and further into her journey as her anxiety increases about a "real" world hidden behind, beneath, within the apparent world of "normal" habitation. In different terms, this is what drives figures as different in other respects as a Steinbeck who wants to get a hold on the American reality out there beyond suburban Connecticut, or an academic picaro like Robert Penn Warren's Jed Tewksberry, who comes quickly in adolescence to think of a life beyond Dugton, Alabama, and to understand his mother's observation about their hometown ("'Ain't nothing here for you,' my mother would say. 'Yores is waiting for you, somewheres'"),[27] or a Peter Jenkins in his efforts to penetrate into that African-American world hitherto hidden from him, or an Andrei Codrescu, who wants the authentic experience of the road, his "reality" of the road, even in the face of his suspicion that even "roads aren't real anymore . . . [only] now metaphors about the road . . . [of] people [who] would rather stay home . . . [and] feed on lots of clichés about the road" (p. 30).[28]

As with Jed Tewksberry's dark ride and Oedipa Maas's anxious journey and Jean Gillis's "survivalist" episode, not all of this seeking after broader experience, more reality, introduces picaros and picaras to an unmingled realm of good fortune, warming sunshine, and happy circumstance. Indeed, some discover in their wayfaring what Thoreau ostensibly only half-supposed might turn out to be the case, that life might be "mean." For instance, Russell Banks's hapless but compulsive picaro, Bob DuBois, finds his course increasingly opaque and ever more desperate, but, committed by his text and driven in character, he has to push on in his "mean" picaresque venture, deeper into this life, this set of events and encounters, in order as Thoreau would say "to get the whole and genuine meanness of it and . . . to know it by experience." In different terms, forms, and degrees, quite a number of new American picaros and picaras—from John Steinbeck and William Least Heat Moon, Bill Moyers, and Harrison Salisbury, to Jim Lehrer's One-Eyed Mack, Don DeLillo's David Bell, James Crumley's C. W. Sughrue, James Leo Herlihy's Joe Buck, Richard Hill's Vic Messenger, Norman Mailer's Rojack, and Walker Percy's Binx Bolling—travel in whole or in part through rough and mean terrain as they meet on occasion or by and large the seedy, vulgar, lurid, vicious, delusional, or violent elements of the "realities" their picaresque tours bring them to front.[29]

As with Thoreau's injunction to himself in the chapter "Where I Lived and What I Lived For," then, the commitment of the new American picaresque to deliberate life, to fuller experiencing, is a charge the picaro or picara cannot put down, and the charge is to experience itself, not simply to fortunate experience. Even when the road entails the dark, dismal, or disastrous course, the primary characters' needs and the demands of the narratives pull those focal figures forward toward the next episode and the next, and, as this drive into experience is enacted over and again, the narrative form itself reiterates the continuity of that sustained American idea of "the experience-made person" and renews the values promoted by Thoreau and others of grasping life in its immediacy, going "out far" and "in deep," cornering the real in its fundamentals, and finding a "true account" in personal terms.

If the picaresque mode answers naturally enough then to the primacy of physical motion in space in the American cultural imagination, if such tales illuminate again that particular calisthenic of possibility, the narrative formation recalls and revives as well that old American insistence on plunging in with full intensity and intentionality, on wresting the most from things for one's life: if the present episode is tacky or vulgar, dreadful or vicious, the picara's capacity to start over, to move on, fills her with expectancy about a next, better rotation. Even after being brought back into a world of comforts and caring after the wilderness sojourn alone, "Dutch" Gillis, true to her picara's nature, thinks almost immediately that it "Feels like I ought to be goin' someplace. The Missouri, New Orleans, China" (p. 209). Thus, again, the experientialist requirements of the American self, at least in this particular pantheon of cultural values, are pinned on those assumptions and emphases about the processive nature of existence. Self-definition, indeed "character," arrives from the *cumulative* terms of the picaro's or picara's experience, and one's identity is never static, always processive, changing to meet the variety of experiences confronted on the American scene and responsive to the ever-changing nature of that scene. Thus, again, as the new American picaresque emphasizes and dramatizes the requirements of the term on the road, its radically detouring figures promote some older attitudes in the American tradition, their road lives driven as they are by the work of "deliberate life" as they career into America "to know it by experience" and to know themselves. If the American "realities" and the experience of America prove vexing or difficult or dangerous, then that only issues in the need for the picaro or picara to call forth yet another of his or her defining capacities, another trait and style that echoes with some continuing American traditions, the capacity for spontaneous response.

Contemporaneity and Improvisation: American "Riffs"

If nineteenth-century thinkers like Ralph Waldo Emerson and Henry David Thoreau provide certain clues to and promote the importance of the primacy of spatial mobility and the priority of firsthand experience as values distinctively American in tone, cast, and performance, Albert Murray—that twentieth-century "renaissance person" (working as cultural critic, musicologist, novelist, public philosopher, aesthetician)—helps to identify yet another sustained and powerful constellation of ideas and meanings often exhibited and valorized in American life. Murray describes and wants to vaunt what he calls "skill in the art of improvisation."[30] Exemplified for him perhaps most impressively and directly in the African-American traditions of jazz and blues, as players extemporize their own variations on and within the scores or "scripts" immediately to the musical fore, Murray believes also that "improvisation" is a trope for a style of creativity in resistance to rigid codes, in resilience under confining contexts, in ingenuity with the conditions at hand, in alertness and alacrity to avenues of temporary escape from various kinds of captivity, in dexterity and adaptability in preserving the individual, even, given all of this, in a kind of non-heroic heroism. The jazz/blues artist "lives" musically constrained by his or her circumstances, the codified idiom of the sheets, but he or she also "plays," follows the adventurous path, moves off into those "riffs" that provide variations in exercising the tunes in non-scripted ways, asserts the unique character of the player in radically personalized terms, insists, according to Murray, "that experience is for the most part what you are able to make it" (p. 106). Again, just as the new American picaro and picara are in some respects "born" for movement in space and are committed by their road lives to wring experience for as much as possible of what it contains, that broad vocabulary of "improvisational skill"—alacrity, resilience, adaptability, dexterity, freedom, ingenuity—plays surely to one of the strongest suits embodied in the picaros and picaras on their various "adventurous paths."

That Murray finds the most visibly manifest examples of this tenacious improvisational tradition among African-American jazz and blues figures is not surprising—their lives are lived in a difficult and confining idiom, they are the source of the "riff" per se, and it is definitive for their art—but this does not prevent Murray's insisting as well that this blues tradition is, much more generally construed, a decidedly American trait of temperament and response when encountering a world of obstacles and frustrations. As he describes what he considers the American "roots" of this trait, he seems to be describing the new American picaro as well:

> So much is obvious if only by inference, and in addition much goes to show that the blues tradition itself is, among other things, an extension of the old American frontier tradition (which, incidentally, was always as applicable to the city and the plantation as to the wilderness, the mountains, and the plains). There is, for instance, the same seemingly inherent emphasis on rugged individual endurance. There is also the candid acknowledgment and sober acceptance of adversity as an inescapable condition of human existence—and perhaps in consequence an affirmative disposition toward all obstacles, whether urban or rural, whether political or metaphysical. In all events, the slapstick situation [a world of continuous difficulty and ambiguity for a solitary figure] is the natural habitat for the blues-oriented hero—who qualifies as a frontiersman in the final analysis if only because he is a man who expects [hopes for] the best but is always prepared, at least emotionally when not otherwise, for the worst. (pp. 106–7)[31]

Although Murray here refers to "the slapstick situation" as a generalized understanding of the wearying difficulty of life understood as farce, as fundamentally absurd, there to be faced by the singer of the blues and to be survived only by the dexterous and nimble, he elsewhere recog-

nizes the natural affinity of this "blues-oriented hero" with the central
figure and situation of the picaresque narrative: "the confusions and
insecurities of the ancient Greek mortals," he writes, "were all too often
[for the gods] only a matter of capricious concern at best. It was not for
nothing that the wily Odysseus was a picaresque hero [broadly under-
stood] whose nimbleness was his fortune" (p. 103). In continuity and
reaffirmation of this ancient Aegean delight in and need for "improvisational skills," in the lineage of all sorts of American "frontiering" experience, now as then, whenever "flexibility or the ability to swing (or
to perform with grace under pressure) is the key to that unique compe-
tence," more recent masters of the art of the "riff," according to Murray,
are probably required as examples to teach contemporary people "to be
at home with [their] sometimes tolerable but never quite certain condition of *not* being at home in the world" (p. 107).

Virtually by definition, of course, picaros and picaras, old and new,
inhabit this condition of felt homelessness like Lazarillo de Tormes's recognition, "Yo soy solo." If not literally like Lars Eighner in *Travels with
Lizbeth,* they are displaced more or less as a result of their being at least
temporarily unmoored, cast away and about, by the sensations of the road,
full of its "confusions and insecurities" and requiring "nimbleness" for best
"fortune." Thus aligned with the old forms as epics of hunger and epics
of individual experience, the new American picaros appear also, as do most
of their forerunners like Lazarillo, Gil Blas, Moll Flanders, and Tom Jones,
to perform as prime players in their "epics of ingenuity." In a world often
of the nature of farce, whether it be Pynchon's Oedipa Maas caught in the
episode with "The Paranoids" or Bill Moyers in the hostile diner in Dime
Box, Texas, or Jim Lehrer's One-Eyed Mack in *Kick the Can,* they are forced
to play through, to see the avenues out of the constraining script at hand,
to understand that rhythm and timing are everything. In a world of apparent caprice, the new American picaros feel most "at home" (in character) in the full exercise of one of their most valuable traits, that asset of
improvisational dexterity, the capacity for the riff, which helps them manipulate the prescribed scores, the given conditions. Binx Bolling's ways
of coping with the despair of sameness in *The Moviegoer* point up just this
ability to be alert to the new possibility, to locate the extra measure, as he
tracks out the variations possible in a world, for him, of numerous "rep-
etitions" and "rotations" that help him unfold the scripts of his life in
unanticipated ways. Andrei Codrescu regards his own capacity for continuous re-invention not only as an American craving but a "style," certainly as his own "métier." Just as the forward but erratic movement of jazz

lives or dies according to "the art of the riff," he works the road by play, altering himself, his responses, by tuning in to the opportune facets of the situations he enters. In a series of dark riffs, designed or at least entered to escape the given "score" of suburban predictabilities in Wakefield Estates, an "engineered community"[32] wherein even "the vegetables are lined up like good little soldiers on the cutting board" (p. 5), Steven Wright's Wylie Jones runs, drives, through American space, dives into experiences different, advances, escapes again and again, through a series of improvisations entailing total overhauls of identity, and, thus, as the novel's title indicates, plays out a number of variations on American existence by *Going Native*, absorbed completely into the life-ways of otherness he adopts in contemporary experience. In this respect, his is a more recent noir version of the comic shifts, dodges, adaptations, and maneuvers, played out through nineteenth-century scripts by Thomas Berger's Jack Crabb in *Little Big Man,* he of Great Plains improvisations, he the master of various and temporary *personae* adapting for survival. Bright or dark, enticing or repugnant, again as with jazz, some of the most significant elements of play in the art or skill of improvisation appear in the vagrant wanderings away from the sheets, in the adventurous, opportune "detours" from the maps, in the capacity for trying out another alternative or finding a different route that John Steinbeck calls "vacilando" (p. 63).

In this framework, of course, a decidedly convenient example of the picaro as a kind of jazzman in the new American picaresque appears in the figure of Richard Hill's Vic Messenger in *Riding Solo with the Golden Horde.* Vic is never so much "at home" as when he practices at his skill as a fledgling saxophonist: as he plays, even when he knows he is only pretty good "for a white kid," he "experienced a kind of surrender in which the important part of him had retreated behind the other part that was doing what the [white] crowd demanded, giving just enough signals for the remote parts to keep working while he watched from there."[33] For developing the more complete art of the player, however, he knows he must "go native," to play out with Tonto and Betty and the black band, to learn from Tonto's African-American sense of the riff, the lessons about that creative ingenuity born of fighting against obstacle and constraint. As Tonto had told him, "'That why [God] made the horn so hard to play, life so hard to live. But you don't go 'round cryin' about it. Keep it inside for fuel, don't spill it sittin' at no bar. Think of it as a gift you can do somethin' with. That's soul'" (p. 33). Under Tonto's instructions and Vic's own absorption into the band, his ability grows to go solo in his music, to spring reflexively with his horn to the sudden possibilities of the opening found in the score, but it is difficult to determine whether his increasing artfulness in improvisations with his saxophone is a result of his gorgeous picaresque riffing in the school, on the streets, in the precincts of nighttime St. Petersburg, to make more than anticipated out of what is available to him, or, on the other hand, whether his skill in picaresque adventures and maneuvers, acrobatic adjustments to the moments, as he jumps back and forth among cultural worlds, has translated into new capacities with his horn. Both realms of his life are deeply informed by his skills of improvisation, his gifts in dealing with the blues, and, even eventually off to college to play in the Florida State University marching band, he continues to "ride solo," for the reader and the crowd can see that "nothing seemed able to make that boy march in step" (p. 140). In either case, and in any event, Vic's jazzed life and his life in jazz provide him with that special equipment Murray describes as necessary for a rough and tumble contemporary life, requisite for the traits and processes of adaptability and resilience as a non-heroic sort of hero struggling to get along in the world. His marching solo in the midst of the "golden horde" might well be thought repaid by the new discoveries he makes on course as he enters a new world for him of racial complexity.

If Murray believes the skill of improvisation seeded in the American character by the frontier experience was reinvested in American cultural tradition by the jazz/blues traditions, he would also surely recognize other distinctively American forms that, in their various ways, both express and require "the art of the riff" and that might refine and hone this special talent for the non-heroic picaro and picara. While the narrative formations of the picaresque and indeed the road itself insist on the quick reflexes, that alacrity and dexterity, that make for the picaro or picara who would most rise to the challenge of the adventurous or unavoidable detours, the intricate cadences of road life, the figures themselves frequently call upon other training or backgrounds to display these hallmarks of their characters in a variety of ways.[34] They are not all jazz/blues practitioners like Vic Messenger, of course, but many have found, or calibrated, their own talents for quick flexibility, rapid adaptation, pace and movement, spontaneous nimbleness, as they train eyes eager for the new opening, exhibit gifts for maneuvering the script and making "more" out of what is available, and, withal, deliver on those extemporaneous decisions and actions that allow them to advance through creative actions. The finely tuned skills for the riff, so important on the road, appear in a number of ways in the central figures of the new American picaresque. For some, it is simply the skill or education that both founds and nurtures imaginative freedom and an intrepid will to advance to further, deeper experience. As a poet, Andrei Codrescu is forever in training to improvise the language to make it open onto new semantic horizons, and this dexterity, imagination against constraint, extends to new uses on the road as he keens on the latent possibilities of situations and scenes. William Least Heat Moon uses a number of shifts and feints, several variants of social nimbleness, to gain access to further dimensions of the experiences he fronts, a skill developed out of his capacities for alert observation, of course, but also out of his abilities in reading and interpretation, just as John Steinbeck here and there displays a quick sense for the ways to seize the opportune openings, surely a consequence of his lifetime spent in expressive alacrity and in creative imagination of scenes and people.

For some others, another indicative trait or talent seems to be foundational, funding as it does the skill for detouring, for massaging the "givens" of a situation, or for posing a break with the containing script. David Rounds's title picaro, Joey, in *Celebrisi's Journey*, for one instance, has a dis-reputation in his hometown, before the road cannot be resisted, for being something of an expert as a "stunt man," not because he substitutes for others in performing physical actions but because he "pulls stunts," plays practical jokes, designed to manipulate the usual and ordinary situations of the town to make them play out in surprising ways. This disposition and ability translate into comparable tendencies when he is pressed by obstacles on his later road, if occasionally with comparably disastrous results, as he maneuvers his constraining circumstances. For some several others, at least dormant improvisational skill is signaled clearly by some athletic prowess found and practiced in youth. E. L. Doctorow's Billy Bathgate juggles, the very activity in fact that brings him to the attention of Dutch Schultz, as he handles the given materials with the kind of skill that makes them yield in unanticipated ways, an ability, of course, he also uses to cope with and emerge resiliently from the tricky situations he encounters in his "mob" life. Jed Tewksberry notes his football backgrounds early on in Warren's *A Place to Come To*, sure means to teach him to shift and dodge on the fly, spot openings in the face of obstacles, anticipate on-rushing hazards, and these physical and mental abilities calling for alertness, nimbleness, and expectancy are indications on the field of the same kinds of quick "riffs" off the field that help him deal with childhood poverty, teach himself Latin (doing Caesar "on the sly"), cope with schoolyard bullies, wrangle admission to graduate studies at the University of Chicago, and "invent" himself again there as a Southerner for social purposes. Geoffrey O'Gara's basketball acumen—displayed in an important scene in *A Long Road Home*[35]—has not only made him skilled in the gymnasium at nimble footwork, at spotting openings, at mid-air changes of plans, but also obviously in exercising comparable traits off-court, on the road, as he proves himself expert in shifting tone and cadence, changing pace, massaging possibilities, extemporizing for the opportune moment, in order to find paths into experiences not otherwise usually to be located.

In some notable cases, the training or instinct for improvisational life comes clearly into triangulation with the American craving for continuing movement in space and with the call to enter experience with immediacy and deliberate intensity. Like Jed Tewksberry, Larry McMurtry's "Cadillac Jack" McGriff goes to college by way of athletics, and, like O'Gara, basketball is his youthful forte, but Jack's particular assets for the road have also been cultivated by other forms of physical pursuit in his youth. He recalls:

> it was a basketball scholarship that took me to college, though I was tired of the sport even before I got there. My real passion was gymnastics: I loved the clarity, the precision, and the utter loneliness of it. But of course it was a hopeless passion since I was six feet five inches. One day I was watching an amateur rodeo when it occurred to me that bulldogging was just a form of applied gymnastics. You jump, you grip, you swing, and you twist, and if the timing of the four actions is precise the running animal will throw himself with his own weight, rolling right across your body and whopping himself into the ground with a satisfying thump. (p. 14)

"When I started dogging," Jack reports, "I was looking for a passion" (p. 14) to replace gymnastics, and the search for new and exhilarated adventures, the requirements of dexterity and precision and timing, the solitary pursuit of opportunity within the scripts, this urge to make more of the materials at hand, the feckless insouciance and the unending hope for more, all suggest, even for Jack, that he used "the stimulus of sport" as early means in the quest after "deliberate experience" and in development of the art of the riff that subsequently translate into his narrative life's road work of tracking around, with frequent changes of course, undaunted by the detours, after objects of "quality" and people of "beauty" (p. 14). It shortly becomes clearer still that, remembered years later, long after his having been a "crackerjack bulldogger" (p. 14) for a time, that third American disposition, freedom in spatial mobility, was early on entered into the equation as well: "I was honestly fascinated by bulldogging, but apart from that what I really liked about the [rodeo] life was the opportunity it gave me to drive across vast, lonely American spaces" (p. 16). While many new American picaros and picaras remain much less direct in their calculations of their own traits and temperaments or much less disclosive about those activities or backgrounds that schooled them in improvisational erudition, those who most qualify for the picaresque way, like McMurtry's resplendent "Cadillac Jack," turn out to prove themselves on the road quite capable indeed of "detouring" toward new horizons provided by the episodes to the fore in their travels, and they stand, in their varying ways, as Murray's jazz-men or -women, prepared to go solo, fearless about veering off the given maps, poised for the opportune timing, and spontaneously ready for the experiential riff.

Whether earlier trained through some roughly equivalent form or whether simply taught by the curriculum the picaresque road always entails, the high acumen for improvisation is an ineluctable element of the picaros' and picaras' best and most necessary equipment for living, and, as with the ideas and virtues of spatial freedom and experiential deliberateness, their commitment to make more of the given circumstances, to exercise creative ingenuity, to go the rugged solitary way, to cope against obstacle, all signal and signify again just those decisively American habits of mind and disposition rooted in loyalty to the notions of beginning again, advancing to another condition, changing what seems necessary, seeking more or better in the next place or episode, finding new prospects and resources for living. As before, the ideas are grounded in hope, fueled by intrepid spirit, shored up by a certain innocence, and altogether founded upon a sense that contemporary life means a life in process, always on course, forever meeting detours, always undergoing change.

Thus, the new American picaros and picaras continuously perform their highway "riffs," following out the promising impulse, whether seen in the small improvisations in *The Pull of the Moon* as Nan alters her itinerary to sleep in the woods or to allow a lonely stranger into her cabin or to stop for a talk with the old woman she spots on the farmhouse porch, or observed in the larger change of course in *Going Native* as Wylie Jones veers away from the script of suburban existence to enter another realm on the road. As the figures move and shift, advance by taking the detours, change pace, their actions in playing out sudden variations are definitive marks of their literary character. The picaresque narrative form, of course, not only fully accommodates but in its nature relies upon just these plays of the picaro and picara, these extemporaneous actions, rapid movements, almost instinctive timing, quick changes of direction, and abrupt transitions to achieve its apparently "unscripted" possibilities in cultural expression. In these and other instances and ways, then, the new American picaresque reiterates and renews several older styles and some traditional "virtues" of spatial mobility, of experientialist approaches, and of improvisational skills, along with certain corollaries of the three like hopefulness, intrepidity, adaptability. The narrative form, through its central figures, broadly reaffirms their importance and necessity as distinctively, even emphatically, American traits of character and as values still required—if not now even much more significantly—in the midst of contemporary experience.

Even so, as important as the prose form might propose such elements of the American self to be under the conditions of life in the late twentieth century, it is easy enough to critique these ostensibly happy traits of character and casts of mind, especially when they run to excess, and indeed, again, the accumulated texts present examples from one to another that supply the terms of such criticism. Unfettered movement in space might be a well-spring for the American imagination that nurtures hopes of new beginnings, heightened expectancy, commitments to advance, as it serves to sustain and recreate Barbara Kingsolver's Taylor Greer in *The Bean Trees*, Peter Jenkins in his trek cross-country, or Least Heat Moon on the *Blue Highways*. At least occasionally, however, and more often when completely unchecked or exercised intemperately, it can also lead to a pathological kind of drifting, or to the unmoored, disorienting, and dangerous experiences of Rojack in Norman Mailer's *An American Dream*, to the adolescent escapisms of "Dutch" Gillis in *Truck*, or to the lonely fearfulness of John Williams in *This Is My Country Too*. Likewise, while the drive to experiential immediacy might lead to new, deeper, healthier senses of self for Nan in *The Pull of the Moon*, or for Eddy L. Harris in *South of Haunted Dreams* and Walt Harrington in *Crossings*, or for Binx Bolling in *The Moviegoer*, such plunges into experience, pursued too recklessly, too innocently, or, often, too unreflectively, can eventuate in some of the nightmarish episodes endured by Joe Buck in *Midnight Cowboy*, in the chaotic and debilitating series of tumults "fronted" by Bob Dubois in Russell Banks's *Continental Drift*, or, at best, in the deep confusions encountered in varying degrees by both John Steinbeck in his travels and Ignatius J. Reilly in the midst of his *Confederacy of Dunces*, as these picaros attempt to corner life in its fundamental terms but learn little from their experiences or, worse, suffer personal disintegrations in the face of them. Even the high capacity for the "riff" cannot always salvage such experi-

ences, and, of course, that fine art of improvisation, which can sometimes
open new vistas for the likes of a Steinbeck, a Least Heat Moon, or "ad-
epts" like Richard Hill's Vic Messenger or Larry McMurtry's Cadillac
Jack McGriff, can also be pushed to such extremity that it results in those
"renegade" disregards for the containing "scores" seen from time to time
in Richard Farina's Gnossos Pappadopoulis when that worthy insists too
much on immediacy of sensation as the object of the riffs, in the altogether
complete "solo" that Robert James Waller's charming Texas Jack Carmine
finally has to play out when his creative resilience leaves all others behind not knowing how to accompany his complex and continuous improvisations, or in those devised absorptions by Wylie Jones into so many
various personae that Wright's erstwhile picaro disappears into his own
riffs to the point that any sustained personal identity for him evaporates
completely into a psychopathic state.[36] Now, as earlier in American life,
these key traits and virtues have their obvious limitations as well as their
advantages and can have their dark undersides as well as their bright-
ening prospects, and these facts are not blinked away by the new American picaresque.[37]

Nevertheless, as the new American picaresque carries out this element
of its cultural work, as it detours into the realm of traits and values, styles
and meanings, it points toward the continuing utility of certain decidedly
American strains of character seeded in older traditions and arguably still
necessary in contemporary existence. While the "spaces" to be traveled
now by a Joe Buck or a Peter Jenkins are surely different from those tra-
versed by earlier Americans, those spaces continue to beckon, both elicit-
ing and corresponding to an essential hopefulness about new beginnings,
sustaining processes in the face of unending change. The contemporary
elements of life to be "fronted" might in some respects be more complicated, or at least radically different, than those of earlier decades and centuries, but the commitment to "deliberate experience" by both a David Bell
in *Americana* and a Harrison Salisbury in *Travels around America* testify to
the ongoing necessity of that inveterately individual need and desire to
take personal possession of the complex "facts" of life as they are forever
changing, to gain more and "more meanings" when any singular meaning seems slippery and elusive. Through space, into experience, the "frontiers," of course, are constantly moving and taking new shapes, but the new
American picaresque spirit of pioneering improvisations, with its American insouciant derring-do, as exemplified both by McMurtry's "Jack" and
by Andrei Codrescu in their big Cadillacs, posits the ongoing need for the
"player," the person capable of the riff, and the attributes of ingenuity,

alertness, nimbleness, still unspent in the "tradition" of improvisation and still necessary for resisting given conditions, finding the new way, following out the tutored impulse. Indeed, as the narrative form proposes for contemporary American culture the available vitalities yet latent and useful in these standing American traits and virtues, even the darker journeys and the excessive picaros and picaras have their own kind of instructiveness for the culture. They too provide exempla, if not of appropriate responses to the vagaries of contemporary existence then of what can go quite and vividly wrong when those vagaries become so extreme, for some Americans, that open space answers only to drift or fugitive escape, that any new experience becomes only more dark or vicious experience, that sensations become substitutes for thought, that arts of improvisation also apply easily enough to several sizes and shapes of duplicity, the "grift" (or sting or scam) as well as the "riff," the criminal as well as the creative impulse.

Still, for the most and best of picaresque possibility in contemporary America, the new form suggests resources in the deep grain of some American characters that flow from and answer to hope, that commit to processive life, that look to the next moments, and that anticipate new beginnings. Moreover, as deeply connected and continuous as the new American picaresque might be with some older American ways and means and indeed as fully aligned as it is with the old narrative form as an epic of hunger, of individual experience, of ingenuity, the new narrative form and its figures not only point toward those past values but seem to aim at future enactments. In the cultural work of reckoning with its own time and place, in its labors to revivify some older and still requisite American values, the new American picaresque—"traveling hopefully," as Jonathan Raban puts it—points up its figures' equipment for dealing with detours, for overcoming obstacles, for finding ingenious byways, and, thus, seems also to be formed for a cultural epoch in general caught in the wash of a "sea change" at a moment of tidal-sized transitions. As Joe Buck understands this situation, scaled down to his own felt existence in his reckoning with *his* time and place, the art of the "new angle" is required simply to stay in the process: "Of course, living by one's wits was just as problematical in its own way as legitimate work: competition was overwhelming, one had constantly to be on the lookout for a new angle and, finding one, to be ready for its sudden obsolescence."[38]

9

Postmodern Religious Conditions and Picaresque Gifts

In the closing pages of Pagan Kennedy's *Spinsters*, the often recalcitrant picara Frannie recalls the sentiment her now-dead father had repeatedly observed to his daughters that "'the world has just gone and changed on us,'"[1] saying this "as if he had been betrayed, as if sometime in the thirties the world had promised him it wouldn't change and here it was cheating on him again" (p. 158). By the end of her cross-country trek, however, Frannie has found inspiriting vitalities in the life of change and motion, the surge into experience, and the ability to adapt, and she knows full well that the lessons of the road have given her "evidence that my life would never be its sleepy self again" (p. 157). As she and others among the new American picaros and picaras follow courses that make them responsive to change and that have them restore to view and reinvigorate certain values, outlooks, and styles, they perform in their narrative behaviors and temperaments in such a way as to present to the culture assets (and limits) imbedded in standing American traditions that might yet have utility and potency. In the cumulative example of these figures, ways and means come to the fore for dealing with life "under construction" and "in process," as these ways and means in turn come in for cultural reckoning in the midst of the tests and trials of the narrative road. For them, the picaresque tour becomes both the occasion and the medium for the recovery of some notions of the Americans, and, for the reader, their lives in spatial freedom, their drives into the experiential realm, their capacity for the inevitable "detours," and, above all, their animating if sometimes innocent hopefulness, all feature what for many might be thought among the best attributes of "being American," even indeed requirements of authenticity for simply being in America, that "monstrous land" of continual change.

As the picaras and picaros embody these potentially valuable traits and thus invite some American renewals, however, the cultural work of the new American picaresque is scarcely done. Their inventories of their "home grounds" taken, their "American" ways and means established, they provide, with these and other forms of reinventing the picaresque narrative, not only some services for an interpretive reconnaissance on American life, the culture in and of this place, but also some signposts for cultural existence during a period of radical and unsettling transitions into a new age, cultural life in and of this time. As Western culture hovers on the brink, caught between the final throes of its three-century-old project in modernity and the incipient appearance of the so-called postmodern era, the new American picaresque can also be thought to move quite beyond its retrieval of what has been funded by the American past toward the further work of exemplifying, under a particular line of interpretive reasoning, the shapes of human sensibility that might now be required to move into the cultural future. In this framework of critical attention, the traits and character of the picaros and picaras and the more general facets of the narrative mode are fraught with religious implications. As the figures and their form remain inveterately, even stupendously, secular, shaped just as they are by the nature, terms, and conditions of modern cultural life, they nevertheless operate most frequently, like their picaresque forebears, on the edges, on the margins, in counter-response to the controlling elements of their culture, and, in this, they appear as harbingers of certain styles of mind and imagination that seem to open to fresh spiritual prospects.

The concentration on the "road work" here, then, shifts attention slightly and temporarily from the nature of the "American-ness" of the narrative phenomenon and its central figures in order to inquire more broadly into the wider cultural labors the form and its protagonists might be thought to perform in clarifying some of the conditions for locating religious meanings in a time of radical trials and profound transitions. It is not that the new American picaresque stops being a decidedly, even concertedly, American formation—only, rather, that its particular shapes and dynamics as an American form of cultural expression adumbrate prospects that extend beyond the immediate context.[2] As a first task, then, this chapter takes up a brief and pointed examination of the character of those postmodern conditions that bear on religious life and outlook and that, in a number of accounts, indicate a certain set of necessities for a spiritual authenticity adequate and appropriate to the times. In their depictions of this contemporary religious situation and in their proposals regarding the nature of the new human "shapes" that will be not only commensurate with but full of virtuosity in the postmodern setting, these accounts arrive in terms that at least portend the importance of something like the new American picaresque life as a frontrunner into the new era. This in turn leads to consideration of the ways in which the new American picaresque represents a perhaps unanticipated cultural resource in this framework of concerns as it presents certain surprising "gifts" for those persons feeling and projecting the need for the emergence of a postmodern religious sensibility. Finally, then, the nature of these gifts suggests, prompts, invites a closing reconsideration of the cultural significance of the new American picaresque, a concluding recounting of the imaginative and interpretive yield of the "gathered" narrative form, and the parts and places, advantages and limits, this expressive form might generally be thought to possess for those seriously intent on their own interpretive roads, those yet bent on exploring American character and possibility again as the millennium turns.

Postmodern Religious Conditions and the Required "New Person"

One of the most perspicacious thinkers and writers about the turbulences for human sensibility in an age of "sea-changes," one indeed who seems to anticipate in broad terms what others only later will encounter in their own experience and thought, is Walker Percy, whose novels and essays often sift through the human predicament in ruinous situations of emptiness, despair, and confusion in the late days of modernity. Percy raises the issues and suggests the needs abruptly and powerfully in musing on the question of "why does man feel so sad in [the closing decades of] the twentieth century . . . [now that] he has succeeded in satisfying his needs and making over the world for his own use?"[3] The questions he raises are fundamentally pointers to spiritual malaise in the midst of the distresses of modernity, and his answers arise from yet another question:

> What does a man do when he finds himself living after an age has
> ended and he can no longer understand himself because the theories of

man of the former age no longer work and the theories of the new age are not yet known, for not even the name of the new age is known, and so everything is upside down, people feeling bad when they should feel good, good when they should feel bad?

What a man does is start afresh as if he were newly come into a new world, which in fact it is; start with what he knows for sure, look at the birds and beasts, and like a visitor from Mars newly landed on earth notice what is different about man. (p. 7)

The name so far assigned to Percy's "new age"—"postmodern"—confirms that its character, its exact nature, is not yet determined or at least not yet clear, but what has become quite clear for many another thinker along with Percy is that things are much different at the level of human self-understanding and that the former age no longer suffices at the level of affording spiritual fulfillments. "Where does one start with a theory of man," Percy continues, when "all the attributes of man which were accepted in the old modern age are now called into question: his soul, mind, freedom, will, Gulliverness?" (p. 7).

As with Percy, a number of cultural analysts and critics understand that the trials and turmoils of a postmodern form of seeking flow from the very conditions of modernity, even as those conditions must be surmounted by any emergent postmodern style, sense, and sensibility, a fact especially presaging in the world of traditional religion. For those feeling the anguish of the "lost" world of spiritual meanings and the tugs of postmodernity, that traditional world seems simply to have run out of solutions or even recourses that people can regard as adequate to their needs in the intractable world of modern secularity in which their lives must be lived out. Driven over by the engines of modernity, the old religious myths did not survive well their collision with modern history: their truths have eroded; their authority has been displaced by science; even their "poetic" explanatory powers have withered in the face of other machineries for the location of understanding. Religious responses have not served adherents well, according to this line of thinking. On the one hand, to the extent that some enclaves of traditional religions have retreated into fundamentalisms—a species of anti-modernism—those groups have simply abandoned the field, beseeching their people to play with rules anachronistic for the altogether modern game that is, willy-nilly, underway. Or, on the other hand, to the extent that the religion of the traditions has adjusted itself to or been absorbed by the modern project, to that same extent, according to the theorists, it has become complicit in creating the problems of identity, relation, community, and meaning people suffer by placing them in those modern equations of pain that result from insipid humanism, desiccated rationalism, gross economic determinisms, commodified human relations, spiritless bureaucracies, uncontrolled technology, artificial communities, social alienation, domination politics, unrelieved narcissism, psychic fragmentation, and the like, that suggest life's erosions, entropies, general "shrinkage." From its brave and hopeful Enlightenment origins that promised so much progress to advance the estate of humankind, the work of the modern venture has for many apparently run its course to the point of stranding human beings in what they experience as an inhospitable and often inhumane environment. The result has been what Peter Berger and others describe, in detailing "Modernity and Its Discontentents," as "the homeless mind."[4]

In such a situation, according to those thinkers in the streams of theological and religious studies concerned about this matter, the struggle of the postmodern religious sensibility begins precisely at the point Percy identifies—with the effort to start afresh as if newly come into the world, with the hopes of restoring to human beings ways to reintegrate themselves genuinely into the world they experience on the pulses, as "felt" in the times and places they inhabit, as met daily in the modern era, as irrevocably tied to secular existence. Even in the midst of the modern malaise, then, postmodern religionists are to begin where they are, and, from there, seek to find their places and identities anew in terms consonant with the realities they experience. They look to find significant axes of coherence in their personal lives and in the strata of general experience, to discover or invent meanings with which to orient themselves fully, faithfully, in relation to nature and history, to locate the well-springs of their spiritual health and integrity, and to root out the resources with which life might yet, for them, be redeemed. In short, the cravings of the postmodern religious person are essentially the same cravings long identified in traditional *homo religiosus,* indeed in *homo Christianus,* albeit now pursued in and through their secular existence, the bequest of their modernity, the "place" they start. Not yet full-fledged, however, postmodern religion arrives in multiple, loose, viscous shapes and sizes.

Without any full recourse to traditional religion, especially in its institutional forms, and now forced to "begin anew," the character and situation of postmodern religious life put it under some decided pressure to explore the grounds of spiritual possibility in fundamentally different terms. The early, tentative appearances seem to arise in those counter- or sub-cultural quarters, ideas, and movements that plant themselves squarely in the midst of secular culture but that stand in opposition to its most distressing or destructive patterns and courses. Different students of the phenomenon see these stirrings in ecological movements, goddess cohorts, Wicca, various self-realization groups, feminist theology, and the like, as these movements attempt to meet the demands of modern life in ways more effectual for them than the equations structured into the modern project at large. In such postmodern ideas and groups, one can often discern a restoration of some element out of the religious traditions come in now for reinterpretation, but, in such cases, it is always an element out of the past, as in the present, spurned by the religious and cultural "majorities." Now, as then, these elements taken up by postmodern religion are most often regarded as "marginal," all the more once modern institutional religion has comfortably made its bed in modern cultural terms. Most often recognizing its own marginal status, then, postmodern religious sensibility seems less intent in its religious desires to seize *the* ultimate truth than it is bent on finding the *ways* in the maculate realm of secular existence not only of surviving but of harmonizing the turbulent fragmentations of modern life, ways for human beings to feel spiritually at home again after the syndrome of "the homeless mind." Regardless of the particular channels through which the postmodern energies flow—whether through some new communalism, some personalized pastiche, or some revision of the social construction of gender—those compelled by religious desires seek the rubric, the controlling metaphor, the over-riding image, that will allow them to make the disparate and fragmented forms of life cohere and that will give them orientation, discerned or devised, in the new, pluralistic *ecumene*.

The business of postmodern religion, of course, remains unfinished: its presiding rubrics as well as its appropriate forms remain indistinct or at least unsettled. But some have begun to isolate various facets and attributes of this cast of mind beyond its inescapably secular context, its disposition toward the margins, and its efforts to locate alternative forms of sense-making and devoted commitment to survive modern fragmentations and anomie. H. Paul Santmire, in describing what he calls "the birthing" of postmodern religion, locates a key trait of this sensibility in its drives to posit the terms of a new "immediacy" of persons to the environing world—including their own feelings, minds, and bodies—from which modernity has so alienated them. Instead of fleeing the distresses of modern culture, he observes, these new religionists make ingressions more deeply into it "in order to enter into that experience [of doubt, uncertainty, emptiness, disintegration], explore it, and wait faithfully for signs of a new beginning."[5] The contemporary theorists, gurus, or exemplars are people like Thomas Merton, John Cage, Norman O. Brown, and Sam Keen, who, all repudiating the exclusive rule of "the rational" in modernity, want to recover mystical interior worlds, cacophonous sounds and visceral sensations, the visuals and tactiles of ordinary moments of life, as these in turn might be restored, apart from the mindsets of overweening reason, to disclose resources in the very midst of secularity for new "religious" vitalities and meanings. An important image is that of "the child," the creature who arrives to experience full of innocent hope, without codified predispositions, and brings to the givens of life reflexive sensation, spontaneity, and imagination, just the form of vibrant responsiveness that can make a self more than what Christopher Lasch calls "the minimal self" conditioned by modernity.[6] With the restoration or reinvention of the self as "child," there might follow discoveries of the sacred in the realm of the secular, a new way, in short, to think about the immediacies of spirit in a world thought utterly depleted by the long career of rationalism. The injunction to reconstitute the self with the attributes of the child connects surely with Paul Ricouer's recommendation of a new kind of postcritical consciousness that would surpass the exclusively rationalist mode. Realizing that the self resides in the world instead of vice-versa, Ricoeur thinks, could lead to the attitude of a kind of "second naivete," an attitude toward the surrounding world that might locate new, unsuspected horizons in it.[7] Like Percy's man forced to "start afresh," to become childlike in naming the "birds and beasts" all over again, the beginning point is immediately at hand in the "givens" of experience, not apart from them in some other world of inherited meanings, but where people "are."

Along with this drive to achieve a new immediacy, a retesting of secular resources that the restored self might bring to experience, Harvey Cox, among others, finds in the postmodern religious dynamic the pursuit of new senses of community or, more specifically, an urge to discern or devise those experiences in which peoples' affective lives can cross the interspaces created by modernity between them and their fellows. Thus, Cox insists on the validity not only of the new immediacy—the sensate life that might rehabilitate the forlorn self—but of the prospects for a renewed sense of the relational self. The grounds for this special form of other-directedness and the possibilities for genuine community that are its issue appear for Cox in what he calls "peoples' religion,"[8] in the informal secular stuff they practice to celebrate their common life in terms of social bonding, in images and situations of play, of carnival, of festival, of concert, for in these metaphors (which are also actual situations and events in the experiential realm) he perceives forms of special relationship among people in which participation is joyful not guarded, in which the highest stakes are celebration and sharing not power and domination, and in which social barriers are temporarily abolished in liminal moments to promote equalities among the participants quite past the maintenance of usual reserves and hierarchies. Such small centers of possible "community"—available in life in situ, even in late modern circumstances—pull the self away from alienation toward other selves and invite people to imagine the wider affective possibilities of *communitas,* not on the basis of rationalist social planning, Cox adds, but on the bases of these very real "democracies" of joyful experience. For Cox, *The Secular City,* the title of an earlier book, will remain irretrievably secular, but that does not mean that that selfsame city cannot hold out instances, imbedded as they are in secularity, rife with spiritual implication and religious import.

Finally, however, as postmodern religionists seek the new rubrics for spiritual life that will reorient the self in reality and discover those experiences that promise fuller community in these and other ways, it is apparent that the postmodern charter is scarcely begun, that the exploration of secular life in search of new religious possibilities is incomplete business, proceeding as it must through vast, intricate, complicated regions as yet untried in these terms. As Mark C. Taylor notes in his excursus on "a postmodern A/theology,"[9] the postmodern religious person is, in the meantime, one who must necessarily be viewed as a "wanderer" across strange modern terrains and one whose key metaphor, working rubric, must be, at least in the meantime, the life of "exile." He or she shall feel caught in history in such a way that the religious past no longer obtains (the old gods are dead) and the outline of the spiritual future is opaque. For such as these who go looking for "amazing grace" in the ruins of late modernity, Taylor points out, they will travel without the presiding authority of ancient religious guides or stable itineraries formed out of inherited religious doctrine: their courses will have to follow the mazing, frequently bewildering, always labyrinthine paths of life as lived, felt, sensed, and suffered in the contemporary secular age. These persons will be "knights errant," on a journey to perform an errand, but, as well, maneuvering the etymologies further, perhaps willingly or inevitably "erring" along the way all the while, as they transgress the tried, prove extravagant in their vagrancy, blunder along with the hope of discovering new continents of experience, some places of grace.

Also with at least faint echoes of Percy's sense of "starting over," Richard R. Niebuhr's *Experiential Religion,* surveying the prospects for Christians in the postmodern world, refers to this form of starting out, of tentative seeking, and of religious desire, as "new-mindedness" or, as he develops it, a synonym for faith in a dramatically altered world of radical uncertainty. For Niebuhr, as for other students of the phenomenon, moving into the possibilities of a spiritual "territory ahead" means, first, moving more deeply into the nature and terms of the secular here and now. What is most sorely needed, he argues, is something like Taylor's knight of faith on his errant and erring course, but Niebuhr's key image is the "mapmaker," one who charts not the place but the times.[10] The figures and offices of traditional religion are too much committed to holding their present ground and cannot move ahead effectually in this quest, and the one who would serve best, according to Niebuhr, is the one who can map anew the secular terrain without bringing traditional predispositions to the work. This secular vicar, this maker of new maps, then, must be one into whom the age, including its deep doubts about itself, has entered most profoundly. Indeed, Niebuhr points out, "what the presence of doubting does signify is the penetration of the saeculum into all the recesses of the individual's soul" (p. 14). Only such a person can develop a sympathetic imaginative possession of the experiential realm in its entirety, only he or she can take a full inventory of the character and resources of a diverse, multiplicitous, and competitive cultural scene, and only this person, this "new citizen" not of a place but of the age, can practice that form of "new-mindedness," saturated in secularity, that might locate the religious territory ahead by containing, embodying, its very nature and character within himself or herself. As Niebuhr calculates the needs, this labor requires a new, imaginative re-entry into the world and the world into the person:

> the [authentic] citizen of the present age has a vocation he cannot shun to define for himself the relations between the different spheres of interest and power that [also] inhere in his own being. Specifically, he has to map anew the changing shapes of the religious and the other great fields of human thought and action. He must become the cartographer of the times [as held turbulently] in his own mind. And if we recognize the propriety of imagining him as a mapmaker whose mission is to survey

the religious and other territories of the human spirit in his times, it follows that in projecting the map he will significantly determine the fall of the land in his own being. He has no external guides he can implicitly trust to advise him [about] what is "lower" and profane and what is "higher" and holy. He himself is both the terrain and the scale of projection. This is enough to make any man uneasy. (pp. 16–17)

When the landscape of modernity appears inchoate and debilitating in spiritual terms, when the old religious maps no longer suffice, when the felt sense of the times is one of "exile," and when a new cartographer is called to begin anew to map out the age he or she is within and *has* within, the postmodern project of religion is not only daunting but presents the need for a style of hopeful advance for him or her who would enter the territories.

As Robert Jay Lifton has noted in a somewhat different vein, however, the question of postmodernity even prior to the question of discovering new spiritual resources and possibilities is a query squarely enough about survival, about what it might take at the level of human resilience simply to maintain some sustaining sense of personhood in a world of incredible flux, fragmentation, and few guides for a right conduct of life. In the face of huge historical dislocations, extreme media saturations, and a nearly unspeakable potential for global annihilation wrought by modernity, he argues, "we have little knowledge of the overall consequences of this combination [of factors]: indeed, we are just learning to ask a few pertinent questions . . . [about] the capacity of the individual self under such circumstances" because "there are no precedents for the situation in which people find themselves today, at the end of the twentieth century."[11] In determining the best resources for surviving and locating life-enhancing prospects, Lifton recommends what he calls "proteanism," a form of the self fashioned on the model of that old Greek god Proteus whose divine distinctiveness lay in his abilities to assume myriad shapes, a self capable of and understanding itself as living a life "as one of 'rolling configurations,' which retain 'serial equipoise' in the constancy of change" (p. 30). Such a postmodern self is best and most deeply funded, in Lifton's view, by America itself, "the protean nation," whose most significant collective insights and attributes have to do, borrowing from Ralph Ellison, with "America's 'rich diversity and almost magical fluidity and freedom'" and "'its diversity and swiftness of change'" (p. 33). "American self-invention and shapeshifting," according to Lifton, "are prominent" (p. 33) in the origins and modes of the nation's cultural history and are not only required but abetted by the terms of contemporary existence—everything from immigrant origins to the frontier experience, to African-American styles, to electronic acts of "channel grazing," to even the threat of annihilation—calling for and contributing to continuous rebirths, identity simulations, sudden alterations, serial shifts in relations to the world.[12] To each of these things, including the most threatening ones, one can relent in despair of self-loss or can "bring to it various forms of protean malleability and capacity for transformation. Indeed, precisely those tendencies may be called forth by the threat itself" (p. 47). By meeting these challenges steadily and continuously, by proving out as resilient in recourse to "shapeshifting," Lifton suggests, "we [Americans] have never been other than protean," a fact providing a sense, even in late modernity, "that transformation may be just around the corner" (p. 49).

In these efforts of diagnosis and remedy with respect to the ailments of modernity, to the spiritual "territory ahead," and to the incumbencies upon a religious life authentically postmodern, there is clearly a call for a new or largely reconstituted form of personhood required for the arduous entrance into a world not yet clear in what it might provide to sustain such a self. This new person must possess the capacity for "shapeshifting" to be able to dodge the hazards hurled his or her way and must in this protean style prove resilient, malleable, and prepared for vast transformations. This "new citizen" of the turbulent age must be saturated in the total secular milieu in order to create new maps of the times and must come to this labor without old or conventional predispositions regarding its as-yet unrealized spiritual possibilities, perhaps camouflaged yet in secular garb. As a denizen of the transitional period, working without the aid of presiding religious authority, he or she must be a knight of faith and hope, caught in historical exile, whose errant way is the mazing, serpentine path, whose errand is to spot out in the given world new forms of felt "grace," whose erring and vagrant journey can be no other than filled with trials and tribulations and "blunders," all of which just might disclose the object of the errand. In approaching the experiential realm, he or she must be prepared to work on the margins in order to develop alternative vantages, to trespass boundaries in order to surpass alienations, to enter enclaves of "otherness" in order to locate what might be there for human communion.

For all of this, the new "mapmaker," bent on an altered inventory of what is perhaps significantly latent in ordinary life, must approach experience with innocent eyes, with chastened self-consciousness and spontaneous instincts, with alert senses, in the drive to achieve a new immediacy of the self to its containing environment. Above all else, the testimony seems to be, the new person of the new "borning" age must be one who is prepared to "start afresh as if he were newly come into a new world" and to begin there, at the beginning, to take a new "look at the birds and beasts." In order to clarify the possible spiritual grounds ahead, this secular creature must be willing and able continuously to "start over," the tactic of beginning again as if for the first time now having been isolated as his or her special métier. In these accounts, then, surmising the beginning necessities of the postmodern religious man or woman and depicting the character of him or her who would first and most authentically enter the new epoch, what seem most especially called for are a lifestyle of "rolling configurations," a tolerance for contingent life, a full temerity about beginning again brand new, a craving for immediacy, a relish for the "detour," a democratic attitude about experience, and the like—only a few of the attributes that these new persons of spiritual craving would seem even on the face of the matter to share with the figures centrally cut by the narrative lives "on the road" followed and featured in example after example of the new American picaresque.

Postmodern Sensibilities and Picaresque Gifts

To suggest that the new American picaresque accumulates figures, patterns, and styles of existence that might stand as possible resources and forerunning exemplars for an emergent postmodern religious sensibility is not in the least to suggest either that the narrative form devolves out of some incipiently religious drive or intentionality or that the new American picaras and picaros can be "baptized" by some marauding religious activity bent on scooping up unsuspecting converts wherever it can. For any integral approach to them, the figures and the form, first to last, remain intractably secular. Even when the road ultimately yields spiritual insight, as in the cases of the closing pages of E. L. Doctorow's *Billy Bathgate* and William Least Heat Moon's *Blue Highways*, and even when this or that picaro or picara finds that his or her particular road has led to a compelling religious locus to call "home," as happens with David Rounds's Joey Celebrisi and with Laurel Lee,[13] the picaresque form per se possesses no generic structure or automatic attribute with religious dimensions, and the picaros and picaras, of course, simply cease and desist as picaros and picaras at the very moment any "home" in *any* form replaces the road as defining for their lives. In fact, the narratives and their focal characters, including Billy, William, Joey, and Laurel, have whatever interest and significance they have as picaros and picaras precisely because their various roads are roads into the general milieu of the times, drenched as they are in the secular character of the age.

Ironically, however, the sheer secularity of the figures and their highways represents, according to the theorists of postmodern religion, the very point of departure that is the necessary beginning, and, if the new American picaresque and its central characters can be thought to withhold "gifts" for postmodernity, it is in part because the form and figures satisfy this preliminary criterion. The formal task, as Niebuhr suggests, is to travel the territories for the sake of a new cartography, and the person who represents the best candidate for the mapmaking venture is the one who can survey the most of the saeculum, indeed the one who has had the most of it penetrate into him or her. Inveterately secular, then, the cumulative new American picaro and picara appear as a kind of secular harbinger, frontrunners, fully equipped—because most in it and of it, in all of its distresses and possibilities—to take a full inventory, to provide a new set of maps and new principles of mapmaking, for those who might later follow and use this gathered "store" for religious sustenance. In this context, moreover, the possible gifts of the new American picaresque scarcely end there: in situation, in style, in strategy, and in substance, the new American picaros and picaras seem more or less fully to qualify as those "new citizens" arrived on the scene who might function to clarify the terms for living and the grounds on which any postmodern religious sensibility will have to make its halting, errant, and erring way.[14]

If feelings of "exile," "homelessness," or "dislocation" must be the presiding sensation of those experiencing the difficult beginning conditions of postmodern life in general, then, one after another, the new American picaros and picaras enter such a life of contingency, either willingly because "made" for it or unwillingly because thrust somehow into it. In either case, and even in those cases wherein the figure might know he or she has a home "back there" to which a return is ultimately possible, the time they spend "loosed" into the road life itself unmoors them, dislodges them from any comfortable repose, removes them from any existence within which they can simply stand pat on their old and customary ways, and, willy-nilly, spins them off into relative isolations as they become the strangers arriving to and departing from the various centers of social and natural existence through which their roads happen to pass. Their exile, their at least temporary "homelessness," in whatever degree it is experienced, is actual and literal so long as they remain on the picaresque way. Lars Eighner in *Travels with Lizbeth* offers up precisely a narrative of homelessness, of course, but his condition of "exile" from the past in the face of an opaque present and an uncertain future, his narrative life of historical contingency, is no different except perhaps in degrees and particulars than that of a John Steinbeck while on the road in *Travels with Charley,* who knows he has a home in Connecticut on his return. To be on the road in the picaresque manner is to experience exile, to feel oneself in transit, to move toward an uncertain future, no less for Steinbeck and David Lamb and Harrison Salisbury than for Robert James Waller's Jack Carmine in *Border Music* who has his Texas "home," for Doctorow's Billy who always has his Bathgate Avenue, for John Kennedy Toole's Ignatius J. Reilly who always knows where his mama's house is in New Orleans, or for some of these and numerous others—like Robert Penn Warren's Jed Tewksberry and Pagan Kennedy's Frannie—for whom the old "home" is only now a memory, faint, receding, and no longer quite possible. Their sense of felt "exile" while on the picaresque trail is not a "symbolic" sensation, much less a *trope* for life; it is not usually or even often felt or understood by them in the "epochal" terms Mark Taylor and others describe. They certainly do not think of themselves as harbingers of some postmodern sensibility. But for all of that, their isolation, separation, and unrootedness in narrative life are no less real or powerful or felt less acutely: indeed, for the conception of the unmoored and transient self proposed by the theorists of postmodern religious sensibility, the daily, palpable, and more or less continuous sense of estrangement from the past and nervous entries into the future might be regarded as even more presaging in understanding the conditions of postmodern sensibility just because, for the picaros and picaras, exile is felt so often on the pulses, in the forlorn heart, instead of cognitively regarded as "symbolic."[15]

Just so, in the cumulative patterns of the new American picaresque, in the unconnected life of exile, in the transitive existence of an inchoate time, the picaros and picaras respond to the felt exigencies and ambiguities, the constant mazes and detours, in ways that put flesh on and "flesh out" Taylor's postmodern, errant, "erring" Knight of Faith on his errand by embodying the work of the road and by doing so in worlds of narrative facticity, in the sense at least that those "worlds" are replete with the chaotic, turbulent, multiplicitous forms and "feels" of life that broadly characterize the stuff of late modernity. This world, according to the critical witness, requires the errant knight *and* his faith. In an astonishing way, after looking down into the valley at Hat Creek, a sight of "a wild, mad, silent, spectacular descent of green iridescence," William Least Heat Moon, surely one of the most articulate of the new American picaros and picaras, virtually duplicates Taylor's abstract vocabulary of "erring": "Again on the road, I drove up a lumpy, dry plateau, all the while thinking of the errors that had led me to Hat Creek. The word *error* comes from a Middle English word, *erren*, which means 'to wander about,' as in the knight errant. The word evolved to mean 'mistake.' As for *mistake*, it derives from Old Norse and once meant 'to take wrongly.' Yesterday, I had been mistaken and in error, taking one wrong road after another. As a result, I had come to a place of clear beauty."[16] If Taylor's Knight Errant is a heuristic "emblem," the new American picaros and picaras bring it at least to narrative embodiment. On the errant and mazing road, then, Least Heat Moon locates a special scene of natural beauty, a gift of mazing grace, and believes that "if a man can keep alert and imaginative, an error is a possibility, a chance at something new; to him, wandering and wondering are part of the same process, and he is most mistaken, most in error, whenever he quits exploring" (pp. 239–40).

Virtually made for such an "erring" life or remade by it, the new American picaros and picaras, whatever the personal "errands" of each, go on their ways animated always by the hope of starting over, day by day, from one cycle of experience to the next.[17] Moreover, as the course "hair-pins" and rolls and tumbles, as obstacles appear, as the inevitable detours arise or beckon, they prove over and again to be full not only of a sustaining hope about the future and not only of a faithfulness to their experiential autonomy but also of the resolute stuff of creative resilience.[18] Intrepid in their advance, they err, they blunder, they fall, and they begin again, and their mazing paths are met by their sometimes amazing capacities for the protean shapeshifting, the gift of the improvisational "riff," the eyes for the avenue "out," the ability to devise for the moment at hand, that the reader spots in figures as various as Doctorow's Billy Bathgate, Richard Hill's Vic Messenger in *Riding Solo with the Golden Horde*, Thomas Berger's Jack Crabb in *Little Big Man*, Least Heat Moon in *Blue Highways*, Walt Harrington in *Crossings*, and Geoffrey O'Gara in *A Long Road Home*.[19] Of the secular world as well as in it, they are sometimes its full measure, and their "erring" movements, their practiced vagrancy, sometimes has them extravagantly burst beyond conventional routes, trespass old boundaries, follow their noses along extraordinary "detours," and, so, take a full survey of the territories and an inventory of what they contain. Even in this world of exigency, risk, and confusion they make their maps, exercising their cartography of the age like Loyal Blood in Annie Proulx's *Postcards* by delivering to narrative account plenary versions of "what they see."[20] As the new American picaros live and move and have their narrative being in the difficult "spaces of the times," errant in exile and persistent in faith and hope, they in these ways bring to view for any burgeoning postmodern religious sensibility a more or less fully formed example of the kind of "new mindedness" to characterize the "new citizen" Niebuhr identifies as the appropriate figure to enter the new era, namely the one into whom the penetration of the saeculum has occurred most completely. In all of the distresses and prospects that late modernity might present, Texas Jack Carmine and Cadillac Jack McGriff, Gnossos Pappadopoulis in Richard Farina's *Been Down So Long It Looks like Up to Me*, Oedipa Maas in Thomas Pynchon's *The Crying of Lot 49*, or even Bill Bryson's altogether jaded persona in *The Lost Continent*, among many others traveling in the new American picaresque mode, appear on the scene as carriers and prospectors, bearing within them some of the malaises to be surmounted and, thus, themselves belonging fully to the pitfalls and the potentials of the "frontiers" they explore.

In the approaches to and drives into the experiences they front along the roadsides, the new American picaros and picaras seem further yet commensurate with the casts of mind and response required of those who would be forerunners of the postmodern religious way of entering the "new" territories or old territories seen anew. In answer to Niebuhr, Percy, and Cox, they put on full display their various intensities with respect to entering all episodes of their experience in deliberate terms designed to wring from the experience directly at hand all of the possibilities it might disclose for those who encounter it fully.[21] Whether spied out in Elizabeth Berg's Nan in *The Pull of the Moon*, Katherine Dunn's "Dutch" Gillis in *Truck*, David Lamb as he surveys the people of the "Empty Quarter" in *A Sense of Place*, or Jonathan Yardley's efforts to get the "feel" of the Mid-Atlantic in *States of Mind*, the experientialist drives of the new American picaros and picaras resonate with the calls for a postmodern sensibility dedicated to take up anew, as if for the first time, the firsthand encounter with the world, to test ordinary experience again in attempts to detect the possibilities of coherence, of meaning, of reimagined "grace" it might reveal, or at a minimum in late modernity, as Least Heat Moon might put it, to determine if history had always to mean "ruin." Discovery or rediscovery of the experiential realm—of the multitudinous sights, sounds, and scenarios—leads to or derives from originating curiosity or learned road "attentiveness" in the picaro or picara. Regardless of sources, however, their headlong plunges into ever-amplifying worlds of experience, sought out for the figures' own health, can be heuristic examples for those birthing postmodern outlooks that call for alert pursuits of what Walker Percy, via his Binx Bolling in *The Moviegoer*, identifies as "good rotations," those moments that present something far more than any anticipation of the moments might ordinarily have expected.[22] The pull toward the fullest possible empirical hold on the surrounding life-forms, the renewed effort to "look at the birds and beasts," the full employment of the sensory approach, come vividly forward in the new American picaresque to provide instructive "case studies" for postmodern approaches to the prospects of the territories of experience when entered without the charts of exclusive rationalism, without the pre-perceptive maps generated by a modern form of reason predisposed to "anticipate" the world or to see it in already settled terms. The picaros and picaras, as Niebuhr notes is necessary, work quite without any such charts or guides, and, as they approach the world, they are stunning examples of the prospects for his idea of "new-mindedness," that "democracy of experience" to be practiced by those not preconditioned to understand beforehand what is low and what high, what is profane and what, astonishingly, might be a vehicle for the sacred.

For this form of work to be effectual for postmodern men and women, however, the first lesson to be learned is how to avert the old maps of modernity, the charts of conventional response, and, again, the central characters of the new American picaresque follow road curricula that stand to school them utterly in what it means to "start afresh," to become "like a visitor from Mars," in approaching the world. Just as a matter of their characters as picaros and picaras, of course, they possess a finely alert set of senses to begin with: they tune into scenes in apparently instinctive ways; they are full of sensory alacrity; they employ their wide-open nerve endings as a feature of their ability to survive, even to thrive, rough and tumble episodes of life. Moreover, responsive to Santmire's observation about the needs of postmodern sensibility to develop a "new immediacy" to the human and natural environs, the picaros and picaras not only display intrepid attempts to "front" as fully as possible the irreducible "thereness" of the world, not only seek out those Thoreauvian encounters that "cut a broad swath and shave close," but also learn on the road to approach experience with tactics natural or learned that often allow them to see it "afresh," without the intermediating codes, con-

ventions, and habits that could stand between them and the raw encounter, thus preconditioning their immediate responses.[23]

The effort to see anew appears over and over again. While few can
entirely elude the claims of preconception, almost all of them relish the
"detours," those off-the-beaten-path moments that take them quite beyond the routes followed by customary usage of the maps, and a number of picaresque figures manage strategies and styles of response along
the way that give them heightened attentiveness to novel features of the
landscapes and culturescapes. They exhibit over and again their capacities for extemporaneous maneuvers, their rather large gift for quick improvisational actions, designed to open new avenues out of the old constrictions and into new facets of the experience at hand. In *Blue Highways*,
Least Heat Moon has his tactic of "skewed" or "peripheral" vision, seeing things on the slant in ways that cast them in new lights. Jim Lehrer's
"One-Eyed Mack," of course, gets different, new views of things because
of his visual condition in *Kick the Can*. Steinbeck devises the strategy of
vacilando, that style of ambling about looking for one thing in order to
discover something other. Barbara Kingsolver's Taylor Greer in *The Bean
Trees* learns from the two old women—the blind Edna Poppy who uses
her friend to see—and presents to readers the advantages of seeing the
world through Turtle, the child, who *in fact* encounters the world as if it
were "brand new."[24] Geoffrey O'Gara attempts to go beyond the conventions of local knowledge of any locale he enters by achieving a "remove"
from it, a "new and idiosyncratic perspective," like an aerial photographer, not to compete with the witness of those who live there but to realize the place as one that even they "still might know differently."[25] In
these and other instances, whether as intended objective or as simple,
surprising upshots, the picaras and picaros labor to see with those "innocent" eyes through which might appear novel possibilities, and, as
they do so, they provide postmodern religious craving with what are at
least rudimentary examples of Ricoeur's notion of "second naivete," after
the project of rationalism. With chastened consciousness, they approach
the world with childlike eyes, understanding with a "studied" innocence
that they exist in the world of palpable meanings and not that the world
of meanings resides only in their rational possessions of it, and they
sometimes find that this faithfulness to the external world, approached
in empirical "immediacy," can repay them with gleaming insights into
the redefined locations of grace. At the last, now possessing eyes tutored
by the road work, Frannie in *Spinsters* can fully "re-vision" as spiritually

rich even the old family home, that tired, emptied-out place in New England she had thought by now quite left behind: "We [had] sat in those same chairs almost every night, four square . . . [and] content and forgetful, we lived nowhere but in our New Hampshire town, a place that was as prim as an unsullied woman but nonetheless visited by the miracle of red-etched leaves falling in patterns of extraordinary significance" (p. 158). As with others, the erring, mazing picaresque way leads Frannie not only more widely into the realms of the experiential territories but more deeply into the possibilities of experience arrived at in these styles of "new immediacy."

Indeed, as they push their ways along, it might be thought that the only shortcoming of the new American picaras and picaros in answering by example to the needs of postmodern people entering a postmodern world is in that area identified by Harvey Cox having to do with the location of "peoples' religion," those spontaneous or unintentional "communities" that spring up at least temporarily among disparate peoples when, gathered, they celebrate the joys of their common life and realize perhaps unanticipated "communion" one with another, another form of grace, another kind of miracle. Such "natural" communal moments, alternatives to artificial social existences promoted by modernity, obliterate the learned "distances" to be maintained respecting strangers and bridge those chasms between human beings the modern world has constructed, but, on the face of the matter, the picaresque way, full of solitariness and constant movement, would seem to veer away from any such possibility. The picaros and picaras, in social terms, are always marginal figures in relation to the human preserves they enter, living touch and go, hit and run, away from containing relationships that would go to stymie the need always to be in motion ahead. They are loosed by definition from any bonding ties to communities and, at least on first scrutiny, would seem completely cut off from such social solidarities.

Even in this framework, however, the new American picaresque presents its "gifts" to burgeoning postmodern charters—not by "settling" its central figures into any sustained participatory communities but, rather, by having them be simply who, by definition, they are "on the pages."[26] By recording just how their continuous arrivals into new, multiple, and discrete human "centers" cultivate in them styles and shapes of a certain picaresque "cosmopolitanism," the new American narratives, in many of the focal figures, portray how some might move with facility among far-flung enclaves of human otherness, how they manage to imagine themselves as "strangers," in exile, in order to achieve quick rapport with others, how, again, they call up the art of the "riff," the skills to improvise, in order to break social ice, how their guilelessness, an insouciant innocence, enables them to trespass social boundaries without affront, how they display a certain instinct for locations of human conviviality, how their sustained democratic equanimity helps them enter into and participate for a brief time in alien social contexts, and even, indeed, how on occasion they themselves enrich with their own brief, participatory presence those scenes of common-life celebration they chance upon. Whether found in Peter Jenkins's temporary "adoption" by an African-American mountain family in North Carolina in *A Walk across America,* or in Nan's first somehow knowing and then fully nurturing the receptivity of the woman on her front porch spotted from the road in *The Pull of the Moon,* or in Andrei Codrescu's charming his way into the enclave of the geriatric rock band in *Road Scholar,* the stuff of sustained, full community is not accomplished for any great length of time, but there is achieved the preliminary work of meeting the other, of crossing boundaries of social artifice in moments of rapprochement among perhaps distrustful strangers, and even in the hit-and-run manner of the picaro and picara of emerging realizations of authentic human connection, not forced but found, that would not perhaps have been "inventoried" without the picaro's or picara's social virtues. When Texas Jack Carmine in *Border Music* stumbles into the fortieth anniversary party of Mr. and Mrs. Thorvald, he comes across one of those moments Cox might think a locus of "peoples' religion," one of those occasions wherein folks are gathered in common in celebration of life, and, though Jack is not and will not become for long a member of this standing community, his vital, open, spontaneous, participatory "trespass" on this human scene leaves it clearly more vibrant and joyous than before. As he tells his partner, Linda Lobo, as they dance at the party they are crashing, "'We could create endurin' legends here tonight.'"[27] The stout, middle-class Thorvalds are in fact smitten with Jack and Linda, but it is clear that they have only added to the scene, not created it: "He and Linda moved around the floor in waltz time with the others who had come to honor the Thorvalds and the night and all things caring and patient and loving in a world that was moving otherwise" (p. 37). The work of Texas Jack and other picaros and picaras is, of course, only a first step—the one of finding or enhancing those communal centers of "peoples' religion" Cox identifies. But that predictable picaresque work, the identification of and entry into such temporary centers of celebration, no matter how preliminary it might be to the longer work of sustaining such communities, is made possible by the picaro's and picara's capacities for ingress into "other" social scenes, wherein on behalf of readers they might spy out, as do Jack and Linda, at least a quick and quickened sense of possibilities, even in the face of modern erosions of community. Even if as picaro and picara they themselves cannot stay for long, they see for the reader while there, along with the other celebrants, "how the Thorvalds smiled at each other, saw on their faces all the years of working it out and making it work. In a world getting more and more used to losing, Mr. and Mrs. Edward Thorvald had won big" (p. 38). Dozens of picaros and picaras locate on course comparable such "stores" of vivid or quiet communal possibility, locations they are able to identify and sometimes enter in large part because of their own defining traits. Thus, while the picaresque form might pull its central characters away from "belonging" to such communities, the travels of the solitary way nevertheless have them often trespassing, for readers' eyes, these common grounds.[28]

In all of these ways, then, the new American picaresque enters the world in ways that hold out "gifts" not only for the cultural "space," America, that comes in for exploration and some "renewal" but for the "times," late modernity, as people labor to enter a new kind of world. Saturated in secularity, the new American picaro or picara might very well be thought to qualify as something like Niebuhr's "new vicar," not one bearing a particular religious outlook in service to a particular community of belief but one through whom limited vicarious explorations of the fullest terms of the saeculum might be undertaken by struggling postmodern sensibilities in general.[29] Among others, the narrative lessons include those, construed at least in the picaresque fashion, of how to cope with exile, how to "start over," how to venture outward into the untried territories, how to see again things already "tried," how to work with wonder and faith, how to be creatively resilient, how to take new possessions of experience, how to seize the prospects of the "detours," how to go without the "guides" of authority, how to make use of "erring," how to find permeable those hard social boundaries, how, in short, to learn to live in a difficult and trying time, in a world of altogether maculate existence. Even when the picaros and picaras fail in their narrative deliveries of these things, they nevertheless aid Niebuhr's new cartography of the times, if only by pointing up the faults of the blundering mapmaker or the sheer difficulty of charting certain tricky terrains. Most often just by definition canny and "gifted" in these arts and skills, however, the picaros and picaras, without a whiff of religiousness about them, can in preliminary ways prove instructive for postmodern strivings to locate remaining resources for faith and hope, to recenter selves vitally in the intractable world, to reconceive the loci and dynamics of community, to reimagine the "nature" of things in general and the terms of spiritual possibility more immediately at hand.

Nor are such "gifts" in service to the work of postmodern selves to be thought any less "American" for the fact that they also prove responsive to the times in general of modernity in its distresses. If it is American culture that has elicited the broad phenomenon of the reappearance of the picaresque form, with its distinctively American permutations, then it is surely because, as Frederick Karl, Albert Murray, Lifton, and others have noted,[30] the very nature of American existence has so decidedly required, funded, and nurtured in space and time—from immigration, frontiering, malleable political and social forms, rapid historical advances, diversities of cultural styles, and the like—some of the habits and traits that suit the picaros' and picaras' forms of life in motion. If those forms of life provide heuristic resources and prospects for another, postmodern generation, it is in large part because of the renewals by the new picaresque of distinctively American facets of freedom in space and time to move on and begin again, to drive into the unexhausted experiential realm for the sake of the self's authenticity, and to cultivate the high and resilient art of the riff, that deep faith in improvisational performance always to be able to find a way out, a new opportunity appearing, even when all about the "scripts" of life seem most closed and containing. If Steinbeck's "monster land" was born in many ways of Proteus, as Lifton contends, the new American picaros and picaras would seem now the rightful descendants to introduce the requirements and terms of American inheritance for moving, *always* moving, into the future.

Glaring Defects, Grand Effects: The Significance of the New Picaresque

Remarkable for the individualistic character of the sojourner, every picaresque journey appears as finally and decisively different from others, of course, and no one picaro or picara brings to narrative "embodiment" every nuance and facet or trait and capacity that might be thought to belong to the figure in generic terms, any more than any single new American picaresque narrative can reasonably be expected to deliver all of the literary, social, and cultural "work" that appears in the general, accumulated form. Still, in accumulation, interpreted along the lines followed out to this point, the new American picaros and picaras, always by definition highly marginal figures in the culture of their appearance and frequently quite idiosyncratic in relation to broader cultural patterns, nevertheless serve the cultural time and place just by dint of their road work, their labors "on the margins," and their eccentric, erring, and extravagant ways. They are highly disclosive in their symptomatic character of some of the deep maladies of contemporary American life, and they are at once instructive about some forms for cure and recovery in the measure that many find their health again by way of the prescriptions of the road. Moreover, these figures are pushed forward for inspection by a narrative form, itself a reinvention of an old literary form, that in turn arrives on the scene both poised for an exploration and inventory of the place, a rediscovery of America, and peculiarly suited for probing and testing the possibilities of "renewal" in the midst of the complex struggles of the cultural moment. But, at the last, in sizing up the cultural significance of the new American picaresque, critical interpretation must also reckon with the very nature of the figures and the form themselves, not least with respect to the way the new picaresque form, while delivering to readers its very real assets as "cultural work," also exposes and magnifies its own very real limits and liabilities as a potential resource for American self-understanding in contemporary culture and as a possible model for American imitation in this time of transitions. Thus, while not losing sight of the considerable "gifts" the gathered picaros and picaras come bearing, those gifts, in short, have no utility or advantage—indeed can have a disabling effect—if they are not understood finally as so securely tied to their originating framework that unfastening them for broader uses is delicate interpretive work indeed.

In assessing just how the picaros and picaras provide heuristic possibilities for American life in the very nature of their narrative "lives," part of the accounting must attend to the fact that many of their traits, skills, and styles, were they to be employed at large by people in the culture, are full of glaring defects. Because the picaros and picaras travel American "roads" in several senses familiar or at least recognizable, because they attend to an exterior world "out there" that most Americans realize as a highly probable "America," because, among other reasons, the picaresque figures bear what might be thought some of the malaises pervasive in the common life, and because, in short, their experiences ordinarily seem credible, the continuing temptation is to "suspend disbelief," to regard the figures themselves as "real people," and perhaps to think their finest and most effectual traits, skills, and styles entirely imitable by others in the ordinary runs of experience. Such a temptation is full of hazard. As the narratives themselves often propose the matter, the picaros' and picaras' successes on the road occur within and are affixed to the broader condition of their exile and marginality. Pulled out of this containing context and pursued as a totalizing course of existence, this is a life full of lonely itinerancy, cut away from the virtues, graces, and restraints of ordinary responsibility, loosed from identity-sustaining commitments, that can easily fall into drift, callousness, and emptiness. As a desirable and meaningful full-time vocation, undertaken as a career, the stuff of continuous motion, of hit-and-run relationships, of uncommitted transience, is not only impossible for most people but also, most would think it reasonable to conclude, best reserved for characters in books. The critical point, of course, is that the picaresque "life" is just that, a life in stories, fictional or not, accumulated out of the "lives" of narrative characters whose depicted road careers always end, if not by their finally settling in somewhere then by narrative closure itself. A life-long highway jockey, full of picaresque capacity, paid handsomely, and finally tuned to the joys of the roadside attractions, even Charles Kuralt, in narrative ending, concludes where he is that "I love this place. When I am here, I think I would be happy never to leave it. Every trip has to end."[31]

Even if the temptation is resisted to consider the picaros' and picaras' *general* lives as more than metaphorical, as somehow directly translatable, whole-cloth, into a possible form of life outside of their containing narrative confines, certain particular assets, virtues, and modes exhibited and practiced by these figures might, at first blush, seem sufficiently worthy of adoption, right and ripe for imitation in a troubling time and confusing place. Indeed, inculcated and exercised in moderate ways, the picaros' and picaras' insouciant advances, sustaining hopefulness, resilient faith, fine social equanimity, and some other qualities are admirable on the face of them and could surely be appropriately and usefully assumed in ways that might revitalize many American lives. But there are other habits and characteristics that, while situationally functional and even enviable given the narrative "worlds" in which they live and the tumults they must face, appear as defective and even dangerous, especially when enacted in extremity. Again, then, some critical circumspection needs to be exercised, and again the narratives themselves provide the surest cautionary clues. Without reciting all such defective elements nestled in among the picaresque figures' various assets, it is apparent, for several instances, especially when pushed to the hilt, that the picara's intrepid curiosity, exceeding openness, and eager readiness to trespass conventions and boundaries can eventuate in intrusions into others' desired preserves of privacy and even in violations putting her in harm's way, that the picaro's studied innocence can play out as stupidity, his practiced tolerance as callous indifference or moral paralysis, his carefully maintained neutrality as smug superiority or irresponsibility, that the picaros' and picaras' plotted and defining marginality and eccentricity can go radically awry with "detouring" leading into deviance and "off-centeredness" shading into aberration, and that even those perhaps most "American" of his or her virtues—freedom in mobility, deliberateness of experience, improvisational skills on the hoof—can have dark and destructive undersides.[32] It is not that these "defects" always or even very often appear in the new American picaresque figures, only that, mixed as they are at least potentially into the very virtues of some of the picaro's ways and means, a guarded response needs to be mustered against thoughtless or hasty admiration or adoption of them. When the limits on the values and assets are lifted, when the traits and styles are removed from context, and when the picaro's or picara's necessary attributes for survival careen along in extremis and without necessity, the virtues seen as virtuosity recede, the defective responses inevitably appear, and those picaresque "gifts" that would serve the culture in turbulent and confusing times only exacerbate the difficulties of the cultural period.

Beyond the fault-lines and stress-cracks to be seen or at least anticipated in potentiality in the traits and styles of the picaros and picaras, the new American picaresque form itself, just by virtue of its particular nature as a form of narrative, also calls attention to its own formal limits as a literary formation and to the limitations on its utility for broader cultural purposes. To the extent that any particular case in point genuinely operates to fulfill the requirements of the picaresque form, then to that same extent it surrenders some other, valuable possibilities. As an expressive vehicle predicated on the sheer, rapid movement of its picaro or picara, the new American picaresque as narrative ordinarily has little time or patience for lingering with the possible "depth" qualities of the experiences through which its figures speedily pass. While any such sensed qualities might be quickly noted, the main narrative need is for the picaro or picara to push on, impelled not only by his or her own temperament but by formal picaresque criteria, a narrative characteristic that makes the depiction of experience seem often only a matter of surfaces slid over, of one-dimensional postcards or snapshots, or, at worst, of hasty superficiality. Likewise, because the exhilarated transience of the central figure in most respects controls the form, characters encountered along the way never come in for extended "characterization." The picaro's or picara's extraordinary capacity to develop instant terms of rapport with "strangers" is, in this light, rarely matched by any comparable capacity he or she displays to locate the possible depths of the other, much less fuller, deeper relationship with the other, a capacity quite forfeited to the larger narrative need of moving to the next encounter and the next. The result is a kaleidoscopic social run through multitudes of "others," and, as vivid or memorable as the rapid brush portraits of some of those characters turn out to be, literally dozens of such characters and "lesser" ones in any sampling of the new American picaresque will each loom up for the first time two-thirds into the narrative, will thereupon be enticed into some three-paragraph rapport with the focal figure, and will then literally disappear on the next page, never to be beckoned forth again for narrative reappearance. Again, one of the picaro's or picara's defining traits, his or her "unbondedness," combines with the narrative necessities of the form, and again the result can frequently be a gallery of human beings, a huge gallery indeed, in which most of the hundreds of hanging portraits are generally "flat," much less than fully realized, quality ostensibly defaulted upon for the sake of quantity, depth apparently sacrificed in the effort to enlarge the gallery's collection. Like other roadside attractions, characters encountered by the picaro or picara most often become "fleeting images," left quite behind in narrative flight.

If the picaresque form cannot often satisfy this or that reader's irresistible itchiness for depth, just because it only scratches the surface of things, it cannot either, by definition, be especially responsive to cravings for order, pattern, and resolution. Even if the picaros and picaras sometimes hope for the emergence of such forms of orientation in their narrative lives, the picaresque narrative trail seldom provides them. Insistent as this literary formation is—in John Steinbeck's locution—that trips take people and not vice versa, the picaresque form commits itself to the witnessing and record of picaresque trips, thus to follow out in narrative sequence whatever happenstance befalls its central figures, figures whose mobile, contingent, haphazard, errant and erring, and often tatterdemalion lives operate without presiding overall itineraries, without controlling maps or guides, and often without even immediate plans. The result is an "episodic," often apparently "formless," form in which scene follows rapidly upon disconnected scene, without apparent conjunctions among them except by chronology and, often, without any transitional means except the picara's own catalyzing need to move on down the road. As the picaros and picaras maze their erratic ways along, bumping and blundering from one disjointed episode to the next, things do *not* most often fall into place, the fabric of their experience is too unraveled, with too many loose threads scattered about, and, though the figures and even the narrators might ponder from time to time whether patterns might not appear among their experiences or whether their journeys might not, underneath the confusions, have some ordered character, the authors most often stubbornly refuse to trick out some controlling structures from it all. If "plot" refers to that authorial creation of a collusion of characters, actions, and forces to animate a causal order and pattern of narrative "progress" toward some discernible resolution and closure, then the new American picaresque gives up on plotting in about the same way Steinbeck finally gives up on "generalizing" about the Americans. The jumbling of disparate experiences, the discrete character of the apparently countless episodes, the flight of multiplicitous and competitive images, the zigzag nature of the picaro's "progress," all conspire against a picaresque "plot." The tale simply goes where the focal character, for whatever reason, happens to go.

Moreover, if the picaresque formation most often spurns any but linear plotting in advancing narrative movement, conceding altogether to the random and haphazard and "formless" advances of the picaros and picaras themselves, it also usually disdains any crafted denouement and satisfying closure. Unifying narrative resolutions, after tracking the picaros' and picaras' erring and happenstance courses, would in any event probably seem spurious. Unloosed as the narrative threads turn out to be by virtue of the focal figures' inchoate road experiences, any effort to reweave them in the end, to somehow make the episodic narrative render some discernible unity and order, ultimately to represent the jumbled course as having all along contained some executive principle of coherence, would necessarily play false with the foregoing tale. The tale usually, simply, quickly, closes where the picaro or picara, for whatever reason, happens to leave the life of the road. While the picaresque narrative promises the reader that the road itself stretches on— its unresolvable nature, its endless and disparate episodes, all now confirmed for readers to think of it in no other way—the narrative in question ends when the picaro or picara who has catalyzed it no longer takes up such a promise. If that particular road life has come to no final, cohering shape, readers with a rage for order might well feel cheated of such satisfactions by a narrative form that, given its very nature and limitations, most often promises only the road looming up ahead.

In these and perhaps other ways, then, the picaros and picaras—and indeed the picaresque narratives wherein they exclusively reside—supply on their various ways their own cautionary tales about the extent that these "literary lives" can be imitated and the scope of what they can deliver. Still, for all of the problems, the potential fault-lines, and the rather clear limits to be acknowledged respecting the picaro and picara and the narrative form that "follows" them and follows from them, the new American picaresque arrives on the cultural scene bearing "gifts," and those gifts would seem considerable in a time of American trials and transitions. If no one ought to or even can select such a life as the new American picaros and picaras most frequently have to live out just as characters in narrative, that is only to say that these "lives" of even temporary exile, contingency, confusion, and loneliness themselves argue against anyone's choosing such a course. Nevertheless, as narrative lives, they can posit the field and "feel" of such sensations and can do so in ways that invite readers to recognize comparable such feelings, however momentarily felt, in themselves in the midst of late modernity. If the picaros and picaras experience alienation and estrangement, the sense or the reality of "homelessness," in extended and often desperate ways, then they can indeed stand as "vicars," suffering in broad and intense terms what many another American in the age also suffers, if only intermittently and less intensely, while quartered at home. If the picaros and picaras often enter onto the highways of the land with a nagging and troubling sense of "self-loss" and then an inevitable recourse to play Narcissus, then the conditions creating or leading to these psychic distresses are simply the same ones, perhaps magnified, pressing on and debilitating others in the culture comparably, if in smaller degree, backed into situations of minimalist prospects and few resorts. If the picaros and picaras, faced with pluralistic, contradictory, and contending American social formations, have often to feel the pains of strangers wary or fearful in meeting other strangers, it is, after all, the American social reality they feel and must learn to cope with along with all those other Americans who, at some point or another in some scene or another, feel themselves pushed to the margins, made peripheral by some form of human "otherness." If what spurs the road lives of the picaros and picaras is often an anxiety that they have lost "America" or have somehow become "lost" in it, then their action in going on the road only reacts more radically to what seems an endemic feeling in the American populace more generally. Understood in these ways, then, some of the "gifts" of the new American picaros and picaras consist in the unusual extremities to which their lives on the road often run: they reveal in themselves in enlarged terms some of the distresses felt most acutely in the culture; they suffer in full public view for readers, on the pages, ailments that might have hitherto gone unspoken for readers; they display the symptoms of these malaises in expanded expressive terms; and, through all of that, by pulling the "diseases" under a bigger, more powerful microscope, they might well abet the search for cures. The very extremes to which they go, then, those things that make them induplicable, serve also the work of broader cultural diagnosis and perhaps remedy.[33]

The gifts of the new American picaros and picaras extend further, however, quite beyond the amplified attention they call to American maladies and predicaments. If they hugely and vicariously suffer American cultural ailments in their narrative lives, they also propose possible cultural solutions. Indeed, though again their ways and means cannot be entirely or heedlessly adopted, these figures often themselves locate or devise possible prescriptions, sources and forms of treatment designed to cure themselves, that might benefit broader cultural recuperations. Even as they often doubt the power of the world exterior to them to sustain life in rich ways, they nevertheless muster the kinds of intrepid faith and hope that have them advancing into that world at full tilt, prepared to discover the assets and resources the world might yet contain, skilled in the improvisational arts that help them find ways out when the road runs to apparent cul-de-sac or dead-end. They display along the episodic way an amazing resilience, an enormous capacity to get up again, to start over, when the haphazard terms of experience knock them down and buffet them about, and this capacity, enabled by the "innocent" eyes with which they attempt to enter experiences and apparently flowing from a commitment to processive existence, accompanies their effort to rediscover the world "out there" in fresh terms. For this, they draw upon or develop the necessary temperaments to operate without settled presdispositions regarding the scenes they enter, to marshal for the most part a studied reserve with respect to evaluating what they see, and, while maintaining this asset of equanimity, to develop and enhance their empirical skills in those finer calibrations allowing them to "tune" themselves to the immediacies of what is at hand. In all of this, the new American picaros and picaras school themselves on how to live in a world of fluidity, of astonishingly rapid successions of images and appearances, of detours and reversals. Their road curriculum, nothing other than American existence itself, is clearly one in which all of their countrypersons have to study to some extent and one in which many of the skills of the picaros and picaras might prove not only imitable but sustaining. Even if the full adoption of the life of the picaro or picara seems quite ill-advised, many of his or her attitudes, traits, and "arts" can come in for employment by others who feel themselves sent "back to school" by the difficult conditions of contemporary American life.

If some of the picaro's and picara's assets in approaching the world at large can be adopted at least in part to cultural advantage, his and her specific, if peculiar social skills would also seem effectual for people who traffic in and yet find themselves bewildered by a dazzling, pluralistic framework of human "others" out there in America. While the new American picaros and picaras, by the nature of their errand as narrative figures, cannot ordinarily exemplify the stuff of depth relationships with others, they do often enjoy some notable virtues for living in and coping with a world that presents an endless succession of strangers. Again, their picaresque equanimity, openness, and "innocence" can come into play as they themselves, working from the social edges, learn to see how quickened senses of their own marginal status can help overcome a disabling xenophobia, how their own peripheral slant on things can abet their seeing others in renewed terms, how loneliness can catalyze them to develop facility in crossing boundaries. In moving into discrete enclaves of otherness, in learning to "translate" the lexicons of alien voices, their risky road work of establishing connections when they are always the "strangers at the gate" can be instructive in demonstrating how the terms of social approach might be undertaken, how some quick rapprochement with the other, dreaded stranger might be achieved, how even some obvious facts of road "civility" and some innocent tricks of cordial duplicity might serve the possible social engagement in genial acts of trespass. Forced either to develop some such forms of improvisational, shapeshifting "cosmopolitanism" or else to suffer as a tormenting, continuous confusion the omnipresent, pluriform presence of disparate, suspicious, and even hostile human shapes and sizes, styles and outlooks, they learn to keen in instantly to social scenes by drawing on their sensory alertness, to practice a kind of calm indifference by calling upon their defining inner equilibria, to exercise a high degree of controlled "empathy" respecting the integrity of the "other," by pushing their "brakes" on hasty evaluations and preconceived judgments.

Perhaps ironically, then, these socially "unbonded" characters even introduce the possibility of a broader and more containing American "community" as they present access to "fellow Americans" of all varieties page after page after page. By gaining momentary entrance to these "others" on behalf of readers, the picaros and picaras not only fill up the American social *galeria* but also exhibit the requirements for gaining access to this extended and disparate national cohort. As the new American picaros and picaras introduce themselves to the American world of myriad "social worlds," in short, they adumbrate at least some of the supple forms of approach and engagement that must be plied to broach the encounters with strangers. Even when they fail in these social terms to achieve even some momentary interpersonal relation, their cumulative "example" nevertheless serves to map the gorges that must be jumped, the mountains to be climbed, in the difficult terrain of the social territories in contemporary American life. When they succeed, with their social "gifts" vividly offered up to readers, they stand as ready models for reasoned and appropriate imitation in a world, inhabited or at least recognized by most Americans, filled with countrypersons not *yet* known as more than "strangers."

At the last, then, just as these wandering picaresque characters can be understood to present certain benefits in their styles, skills, and motions, perhaps to be measured for their possibly broader cultural application and utility, the narrative form itself also invites consideration of its own "gifts" beyond those of simply putting the picaros' and picaras' best "lessons" on full display. In the accumulation of the numerous examples, in the various, gathered instances that constitute the form, the new American picaresque proposes its service to cultural self-understanding just in fulfilling its narrative conditions and capacities. Dedicated as a representational and expressive form to follow its focal characters' unbonded and solitary courses into a world "out there," the narrative beckons readers temporarily at least to get the feel of such an exilic life and the dramas of contingency it entails and to cultivate this imagination for the sake of illumining their own, perhaps less stringent, situations of sensed or "felt" exile. Whatever the form forecloses upon at the level of finally securing a containing, comprehensible pattern of experience in the midst of late modern tumults, it more than repays. By featuring that serial, episodic line of rapid, haphazard, often ambiguous or opaque, and apparently countless images and appearances, scenes and situations, the form presents to the picaros and picaras a world, the world, to which readers also feel the tie. Devoted to the witnessing and recounting of the picaros' and picaras' large trials and small triumphs in such an experiential realm, moreover, the form promotes the ideas not only that contemporary conditions have created a difficult and confusing course but also that there is indeed a world "out there," however unapproachable it might seem, to be grappled with anew, after alienation. Thus veering away from the deep explorations of complicated or tortured inner life that entice other kinds of contemporary narrative formations, the new American picaresque sets up for its own kinds of explorations. Through the media of its central figures, in the numerous, complex journeys of rediscovery, inventory, and errant stock-taking that they take into an enormously various American world out-side of themselves, they learn that this is the world of their fullest pros-pects as well as of their troubled situation. In its testimony about the contemporary conditions to be faced, then, the new picaresque clarifies some fundamental terms of the predicaments of American selfhood chal-lenging picaros, picaras, and all others, most especially the daunting task of driving deeper into such experiential territory.

But the narrative form begins as well to present at least one form of accounting about remaining resources and possibilities. In this cultural reckoning, which occurs through its narrative requirement or mission of inventory—as the picaros and picaras work to glean the large and small, gorgeous and vulgar, trivial and presaging images of life—the pic-aresque form presses forward some standing American traits and val-ues and modes, retrieved or reasserted and represented for the reader's inspection regarding the ways such locations of freedom, commitments to experience, and styles of extemporaneity might yet be useful in a time and place demanding a processive understanding of life. Moreover, the itemized inventory itself, accumulated from all of the examples of the new picaresque, posits an "America" in plenary terms: it delivers to read-ers image upon image, place upon place, a long run through the social kaleidoscope, an encyclopedic enumeration and annotation of Ameri-cans and "Americana," multiplied in variety and nuance by the idiosyn-cratic slants on things brought by each picara's unique "lenses," more than enough to sustain the picaro's continuous hope, enough perhaps to begin to convince even the wariest reader that the place, America, might not yet have met its "dead end," might not yet be only a matter of pestilence and ruin, might yet yield a rich harvest. As the form records with its figures the sheer abundance of "what they see," the cumulative picaresque rendition simultaneously works to reassure readers that, in America, for every appearance of a vicious madam in a worn-out bor-dello there is also the presence of that old woman at roadside dispens-ing free lemonade and cheer because she wants to be a friend to human-kind; for the sighting of every dusty, exhausted strip-mine there is also the vista of wind-waved golden wheat all the way to the horizon or the fortuitous glance catching the deer slipping into a shadowy, wooded glade; for every obnoxious encounter with a petulant tourist's child wearing Mickey Mouse ears there is also the quickly glimpsed image of white-dressed little girls, before a dark forest backdrop, with their arms full of red trillium. Always departing, the picaros and picaras flee the ugly scenes, and even the vibrant and alluring images quickly recede, rapidly disappearing in rear-view mirrors, but, though the fugitive picaro or picara only seldom lingers for very long with even the most radiant such moments, the new American picaresque suggests that comparable images and scenes, for those with readiest hopes, innocent eyes, and intrepid hearts, might be found everywhere. Even in those spots ordinarily thought most empty or exhausted, sustaining "graces" are located in the most unanticipated quarters, hints that well might give the reader pause to linger for a time, after the picaro or picara has quite flown the scene, in order to imagine and test the spiritual qualities resident, "in place" there.

Finally, however, according to its own necessary structures and to its own dictum that "no one can make a journey for anyone else," at least in the picaresque way, the form insists both that any picaro's or picara's trip into America is induplicable and, thus, by implication, that no reader can fully, vicariously travel the American road through this medium. No matter how much the new American picaresque might work to serve a restoration of cultural confidence about the validity of some American ways of being American, no matter how much this shape of narrative expression might instill in readers hope about American experiential terrain out there to be discovered anew and taken up in process in its fresh possibility, the form insists also on a necessary "new immediacy," on individual trials at cartography, on fronting experience in personal terms. Built deeply into the narrative attitude of the new American picaresque, this aversion to the vicarious road is perhaps its last, best gift of all, its implicit vehemence about the reader's having to conduct his or her own road work in some scope on some scale, perhaps buoyed at the start by picaresque narrative restorations, perhaps employing on course the picaros' and picaras' best ways and means. Just because the roads into America cannot be followed out merely by reading about them, as the form asserts, does not mean that the roads are not there or that America does not need continuous rediscovering.

NOTES

1. Some might immediately conclude that this huge wave of road narratives is simply a post-Kerouac following, imitators trailing in the wash of books like *On the Road, The Dharma Bums,* and *The Vanity of Duluoz.* As subsequent chapters will make clear, however, these more recent road books often display an awareness of Jack Kerouac's grand American adventures, but they are more often bent toward a different way of being on the American road than the one depicted in Kerouac's autobiographical novels. Whereas Kerouac's characters speed across America, often late at night, bent on catching up to the next counter-cultural "event" or enclave so promising to their "beat" cadre, whereas Sal Paradise, Dean Moriarity et al. zoom across America without much interest in it beyond getting "there," these more recent "road workers" are far more inclined to stop to witness what is at roadside, to locate what can be found on the promising pathway, to determine what can be experienced of the palpable stuff of American life in general. Their journeys are usually more leisurely, slowed by sights and scenes, in thrall to detours, wayward, without quick itineraries. Hence, Kerouac, by now an abundant resource for a small scholarly industry, does not figure prominently in this study.

2. In the chapters that follow, it should become clear why other forms of travel literature cannot serve the same functions as what here is called "the new American picaresque." While the new picaresque might occasionally share a "family resemblance" to the literature of tourist guides, trip journals, travelogues, *gazetteers,* travel diaries, pilgrimage accounts, mythic and/or psychological "journeys," and the like, its own particular shapes and drives move toward a cultural accounting not to be afforded by any of these other forms. Perhaps this is also

the point at which to observe that contemporary American road movies like *Easy Rider, Thelma and Louise, Rainman,* and others, might well be further illumined by this study of new American picaresque narratives, but they fall outside the scope of the inquiry here, broad enough in any event.

3. Not everyone is completely happy to see the *cultural* reprise of the picaresque narrative. In a kind of half-lamenting tone, Annie Dillard, for one, thinks such narratives deal only in surfaces, that depth of characterization is lost, that the "picaros reflect the general flattening of character" in contemporary literature. See the chapter entitled "Two Wild Animals, Seven Crazies, and a Beast" in her *Living By Fiction* (New York: Harper & Row, 1982), pp. 38ff. But, apparently distressed by a literature of "surfaces," she quite neglects what the picaresque narrative *can* offer, and, as subsequent chapters argue, its possible contribution, while quite different, might also be quite significant. A broader and more devoted lament about the voluntarily "mobile" character of American culture in general appears in William R. Leach's *Country of Exiles: The Destruction of Place in American Life* (New York: Pantheon Books, 1999), as he bemoans the dislocations, the "placelessness," part and parcel of transient existence as everywhere destructive of community, of patriotism, of common identity and stable meaning. At one level, the present study seeks to rehabilitate at least the *narrative* possibilities of transience found in the new American picaresque by proposing how these are responsive to a world of conditions and necessities quite as much as choices and how they, in turn, illumine new possibilities in social and cultural terms for living in an America that, as Leach irately sees it, is open to "continual amendment."

CHAPTER 1: THE PICARESQUE OLD AND NEW

1. E. L. Doctorow, *Billy Bathgate* (New York: Random House, 1989). Hereafter, page numbers in parentheses following quotations from this novel will refer to this edition.

2. Actually, it should be noted early on, efforts to include Miguel de Cervantes's *Don Quixote* in the tradition of picaresque narratives are generally spurned by the Hispanists and many in the field of comparative literature as gross errors. While acknowledging that it has a few picaresque elements and that it also worked to bring an end to the chivalry books of the age, they think the book too closely resembles comic and satirical romance to qualify as picaresque. On this, see Ulrich Wicks, *Picaresque Narrative, Picaresque Fictions: A Theory and Research Guide* (Westport, Conn.: Greenwood Press, 1989), p. 14. Wicks's work is an extremely useful compendium of the scholarship on picaresque narratives, on which this study draws generally in various sections of this chapter and quite heavily at a point noted later.

3. Wicks understands this but recognizes as well that some literary-critical "fundamentalists" (his term) have been and are steadfast in their resistance to the idea that a genre can expand and contract, can prove mobile, and can extend

itself to include even imaginative texts that press the generic limits. He describes these critics as "closed" (pp. 21–25) and himself subscribes to and recommends a more "open" sense of the genre (pp. 25–32) that yet balances off the demands of "generic purity" with such possibilities of "generic plenitude" (p. 37). This study concurs with Wick's recommendation but the *suspicion* here is that Wicks could well be dismayed by or at least would not agree completely with the extent to which, here, the limits are stretched to include hitherto ignored texts.

4. Practically every book that deals with the emergence and character of the picaresque tradition of narrative begins with this cautionary note. See, for instances, Peter N. Dunn's *The Spanish Picaresque Novel* (Boston: Twayne Publishers, 1979), pp. 11–16; his *Spanish Picaresque Fiction: A New Literary History* (Ithaca: Cornell University Press, 1993), pp. 3–9; Stuart Miller's, *The Picaresque Novel* (Cleveland: Press of Case Western Reserve University, 1967), pp. 3–5; and, for a "gathering," Wicks, pp. 17–34. For some, the classic Spanish originators of the sixteenth and early seventeenth centuries apparently represent the only "true" picaresque. For others, the genre is sufficiently ample to include French, German, English, and even North American texts. Others define the tradition in a way that excludes satirical thrusts or third-person narration or outlooks rooted in the comic sense of life. A. A. Parker, for instance, insists that hard "delinquency" and "realism" are the presiding criteria and, thus, fairly dismisses *Lazarillo* out of hand as but a "primitive" precursor, finds the pinnacle in the early period represented by *Guzman*, and altogether repudiates *Don Quixote* (*Literature and the Delinquent* [Edinburgh: University Press, 1967], especially pages 2, 3, 6–7). An earlier study by Frank Wadleigh Chandler, on the other hand, gives only the scantest credit to the Spanish origins and, preferring picaresque narratives flavored by the possibilities of "the *romance* of roguery" (emphasis added), decides that the prototype is *Gil Blas*, which "in short . . . outdid the Spanish picaresque tales in art, morality, humanity, and breadth of appeal" (*The Literature of Roguery*, 2 vols. in 1 [1907; repr. New York: Burt Franklin, 1958], pp. 21–22). See also note 3 above.

5. This is basically Parker's point in *Literature and the Delinquent* (see note 4), but most others, thinking that vagabondage and anti- or non-heroism are more important, would not be nearly so adamant about the requirement of even small "criminalisms" by the picaro. At the other extreme, especially with Robert Alter and R. W. B. Lewis, while maintaining the matter of necessary "outsidership," there is a tendency quite to ameliorate the figure's delinquency in favor of a more generous understanding of his or her "touch and go" relationship to the social scene (see, respectively, *Rogue's Progress: Studies in the Picaresque Novel* [Cambridge: Harvard University Press, 1964], and *The Picaresque Saint: Representative Figures in Contemporary Fiction* [London: Victor Gollancz, 1960]). It should be noted, however, that Lewis is completely heedless of the tradition and structures of the picaresque genre; he is concerned only with some contemporary characters in fiction whose "drift" is picaresque only in the very broadest sense of the term.

6. Harry Sieber, *The Picaresque* (London: Methuen, 1977), p. 24.

7. This phrase originated in Francisco Javier Garriga's *Estudio de la novela pica-resca* (Madrid: Hernandez, 1891), p. 22, perhaps the first full-length study of the picaresque narrative. The phrase has since become, as Wicks notes, an epithet for the picaresque novel.

8. This was the title of Frank Wadleigh Chandler's Columbia University doctoral thesis of 1899. Also see note 4 above.

9. For the most pointed account of the ways picaresque narratives assume the world view of romance while concomitantly inverting and countering it, see Barbara A. Babcock,"'Liberty's a Whore': Inversions, Marginalia, and Picaresque Narrative," in *The Reversible World: Symbolic Inversion in Art and Society,* ed. Babcock (Ithaca: Cornell University Press, 1978), pp. 95–116.

10. On the matter of the retrospective narrator's reliability in rendering the picaresque account, see William Riggan, *Picaros, Madmen, Naifs, and Clowns* (Norman: University of Oklahoma Press, 1981), pp. 38–78, which explores eight "key" cases in his view. Riggan is one of those critics for whom only the first-person narrator will do for picaresque, but he errs in this with his assumption of "an older *picaro* who actually performs the narrative function" (p. 40, n.2). In the view operating here, even in the cases of first-person narrators, it is only the younger self, on the road, who can be regarded as a picaro: the older, retrospective narrator has quit the picaresque life if only to stop to tell the story, and, having quit, he is only—like the settled Lazaro—an autobiographical storyteller, not a picaro, and might as easily be a third-person narrator-biographer of some young picaro. Moreover, although also disposed to require first-person narration, Claudio Guillen points out that there is some real distance between even the once-picaro, now first-person narrator and the picaro he once was: "The [first-person] picaresque novel is a *pseudo*-autobiography" (emphasis added). What is important is that the narrator—whether first- or third-person—participates in what Guillen calls the picaresque novel's "self-saturation of the style . . . [in which the] life is at the same time revived and judged, presented and remembered" (*Literature as System* [Princeton: Princeton University Press, 1971], p. 81).

11. Some critics, perhaps most notably Parker, reject satire as a possible structure of the picaresque, another reason perhaps for the dubious status of the Cervantine masterpiece *Don Quixote* in the tradition. It seems clear, however, that satirical treatments of figures in the gallery can appear intermittently, though often the rapid narrative movement of the picaresque pins its satirical moments on caricatures of figures on the social scene and, thus, arrives more in parodistic jibes than in extended satire. Indeed, this penchant for parody—in the control of the retrospective narration—can even appear in episodes of self-parody as the narrator sometimes zanily exaggerates attributes of the young picaro he was or to whose consciousness he attaches. This can occur with third- as well as first-person narrators. See note 10.

12. This suggests that, at least in the first century or so of picaresque narratives,

authors were aware of the work of their predecessors. In fact, there are cases of direct intertextuality—that is, of references in the narratives to earlier picaresque narratives. *Guzman* is clearly cognizant of *Lazarillo*, and the picara in *La Picara Justina* claims marriage to Guzman de Alfarache, while throughout executing complex parodies of the picaresque genre itself. Perhaps the most well-known of these intertextual allusions occurs in the twenty-second chapter of *Don Quixote*, wherein the would-be author Gines, in conversation with the man of La Mancha, mentions Lazarillo de Tormes. See Wicks, *Picaresque Narrative*, pp. 7–13.

13. By "comic sense of life" here, the reference is not to hilarity in episodic adventure or outrageous caricatures of social types or vaudevillian staging of scenes or even funny incidents but, rather, to that perception of, conviction about, and confidence in the world to right itself, to work out, to reach resolution, even though—from time to time—things run afoul, "gang agley," fall apart.

14. Celine's *Voyage au bout de la nuit* could well present the darkest picaresque world ever traveled, infused as it is with unrelenting squalor, scatology, viciousness, and despair. Apparently the only person ever to think it in possession of elements of comedy was Allen Ginsberg, who described the book as "the first genius international beat XX century picaresque novel written in modern classical personal comedy prose by the funniest & most intelligent of mad Doctors whose least tenderness is an immortal moment" (as quoted by George Steiner, "Cry Havoc," *The New Yorker* 43 [Jan. 20, 1968]: 109).

15. In moving toward a definition of picaresque, Guillen provides a point of balance between "generic purity" and "generic plenitude" when he writes that "no [one] work embodies completely the picaresque genre. The genre is not, of course, a novel any more than the equine species is a horse. A genre is a model— and a convenient model to boot: an invitation to the actual writing of a work, on the basis of certain principles of composition" (*Literature as a System*, p. 72).

16. This and the preceding paragraph are heavily indebted to Wicks's survey-catalog of the elements that go to constitute "the nature of the picaresque narrative," pp. 53–67.

17. This is a phrase used by Gustavo Pellon and Julio Rodriguez-Luis, eds., *Upstarts, Wanderers or Swindlers: Anatomy of the Picaro, A Critical Anthology* (Amsterdam: Rodopi, 1986) in their introduction to indicate that not only exemplary imaginative texts but some key critical texts help to isolate or deduce the executive principles of the picaresque narrative (p. 10).

18. John Kennedy Toole, *A Confederacy of Dunces*, with "Foreword" by Walker Percy (Baton Rouge: Louisiana State University Press, 1980). Percy sponsored this novel through to publication after Toole's mother brought it to his attention several years following her son's suicide in 1969.

19. Wicks, *Picaresque Narrative*, pp. 7–8, and Babcock, "'Liberty's a Whore,'" pp. 96–97, provide quick surveys of the semantic and etymological debates.

20. This "materialism" is also a matter of the realistic style of the picaresque narrative. Even at its most farfetched moments, the style has to maintain for the

reader a sense of the empirical validities of the scenes, without which the counter to romance represented by the picaresque "delivery" would be lost. Of course, this or that impoverished picaro might also be "materialistic" in acquisitive behavior but rarely, it seems, for the sheer sake of possessions, at least until he stops being a picaro to become a retrospective narrator.

21. Christine J. Whitbourn argues that the question of the picaro's morality is complicated by two thrusts in the tradition—one strongly realistic, that presents the vagabond's life as morally debilitating, and the other more romantic, that sees the wanderer's experience as morally edifying ("Moral Ambiguity in the Spanish Picaresque Tradition," in *Knaves and Swindlers: Essays on the Picaresque Novel in Europe,* ed. Whitbourn [London: Oxford University Press, 1974], pp. 1–24). For another view of the narrative "virtues" of the so-called amoral style of the picaro, see Babcock, pp. 95–96, who sees this style as a trick of the unreliably "regenerate" narrator and as a function of life in a moral vacuum. The following paragraphs outline still another view, supplementing Babcock. But one wonders in any event why such scholarly attentiveness is given to the moral life of the picaro, a character that, after all, lives only in narrative, not next door. It could simply be argued that, full of moral probity or not, any literary character, including the picaro, justifies his or her fictional existence not by some standard of rectitude imported by the reader or critic but by bringing some possibility to illumination through imaginative rendition that would not otherwise have come to the fore.

22. Thus, with reference to the picaro or picara as a "democrat of experience," the suggestion is that not only does he or she level (or sometimes invert) high and low social types but also that he or she tends broadly in approaching and regarding life to level (or sometimes invert) experiences themselves, a fact signaled by the proportionate "spaces" given to them in the narrative presentation. At this or that narrative point, what the reader might suspect is a highly significant experience by dint of its explicit potential for dramatic seriousness or its implicit freight for heightened insight can be blown through narratively in a couple of sentences or a quick paragraph (always on the move). At other moments, the most self-evidently mundane or trivial experience can take up pages of presentation. Respecting *most* experiences, the picaro or picara regards them, deals with them, as of approximately equal worth, with none (except in the inversions) overwhelming others by receiving disproportionate attention.

23. As quoted in Wicks, *Picaresque Narrative*, p. 64.

24. The picaro or picara does not, in short, love or desire the life of chaos and ambiguity found "on the road" but endures it in seeking order and meaning, the actual objects of his or her craving. Most critics of the picaresque narrative agree that the retrospective telling of the story indicates just that craving, an attempt to find order and meaning in the *vida* that the movement on the road, while on the road, did not yield.

25. Jay McInerney, *Bright Lights, Big City* (New York: Vintage, 1984). Hereaf-

ter, page numbers in parentheses following quotations from this novel will refer to this edition.

26. This again is a feature of the moral balance—not necessarily moral seriousness or moral rightness—of the picaro described above, or what Robert Alter understands as "the incorruptibility of the picaresque hero" (Alter, *Rogue's Progress*,
pp. 11–34). These thoughts of Billy Bathgate are remarkably similar to musings
about himself by Gil Blas upon leaving the sordid debacles of theater life: "a rem-
nant of honor and religion, which I did not fail to preserve amidst such corrup-
tion, made me resolve to leave Arsenia. . . . [and] I quitted the house where I had
breathed nothing but the air of debauchery; and I had no sooner performed such
a good action than Heaven rewarded me for it" (*Gil Blas*, trans. Tobias Smolett [New
York: Appleton and Co., 1854], pp. 212–13).

27. Perhaps still the best introduction to the anti-hero, his character, place, and
significance in contemporary American literature, is Ihab Hassan, *Radical Innocence: Studies in the Contemporary American Novel* (Princeton: Princeton University Press, 1961).

28. The fullest and most convincing account of the impetus toward the modern novel created by the earliest Spanish picaresque narratives and, later, by *Don
Quixote*—both seen as new "counterfictions" of different kinds—is that of Walter
L. Reed in his *An Exemplary History of the Novel: The Quixotic versus the Picaresque*
(Chicago: University of Chicago Press, 1981). Reed's arguments surely ought to
displace those critical views still held in thrall by Ian Watt's earlier assertions that
the origins of the novel are to be found in the British eighteenth-century fictions
(see Watt, *The Rise of the Novel: Studies in Defoe, Richardson, and Fielding* [Berke-
ley: University of California Press, 1957]).

29. These attempts of cultural codification in the late medieval, early Renaissance Anglo-European setting should not be surprising, even as they appear in
the efforts of highly thoughtful and creative people who in many other ways
advance their cultures. After all, in an earlier period of transition and turbulence,
Virgil's *Aeneid* sought the cultural encoding of "authentic" Roman virtues through
the presentation of the heroic ancestor, and, in a slightly later period, the British
romantic poets' celebration of the values of pastoral existence stemmed at least
in part from their senses of and nostalgia for what was fading under the onslaughts of urbanization and industrialization.

30. Dunn, *Spanish Picaresque Novel*, p. 9; Wicks, *Picaresque Narrative*, p. 232.

31. For the "thicker" account drawn upon generally in the preceding depictions, see Dunn's "new literary history" in *Spanish Picaresque Fiction*. He provides
a nuanced exposition of the "outer" or external worlds in *Lazarillo* and *Guzman*,
how those fictional worlds correspond to the actual historical, socio-economic,
and political circumstances of the age, and of the "inner worlds" of Lazarillo and
Guzman, how their "psychologies" are commensurate with life in the age.

32. In the adjustments here to picaresque genre theory in this and subsequent
chapters, this study is guided by Alastair Fowler's recognition that genres are

mutable. He writes: "genres are actually in a continual state of transmutation. It is by their modification, primarily, that individual works convey literary meaning. Frequent adjustments in genre theory are needed, therefore, if the forms are to continue to mediate between the flux of history and the canons of art. Thus, to expect fixed forms, immune to change yet permanently corresponding to [new] literature, is to misunderstand what genre theory undertakes (or should undertake)" (*Kinds of Literature: An Introduction to the Theory of Genre and Modes* [Cambridge: Harvard University Press, 1982], p. 24).

CHAPTER 2: THE PICARESQUE BORROWED AND BLUE

1. Critics have from time to time noted picaresque features of pre-twentieth-century American narrative fictions, especially with respect to Mark Twain's *The Adventures of Huckleberry Finn* and Herman Melville's *The Confidence-Man*; and, of course, Hugh Henry Brackenridge's *Modern Chivalry* (1792) was an earlier, consciously studied attempt at the form. And, without detailing the matter in any extended ways, a number of critics have observed that the nature of the picaresque narrative makes it "correspondent" with elements of American experience and cultural habit. Among the first of these, perhaps, was William Dean Howells. With a somewhat peculiar understanding of the form, he suggested in 1895 that the Spanish picaresque could provide authors in the United States with "one of the best forms for an American story . . . [because] each man's life among us is a romance of the Spanish model, if it is the life of a man who has risen, as we nearly all have, with many ups and downs" (*My Literary Passions* [New York: Greenwood Press, 1969], p. 143). Few have followed through on this matter since, however, and none have tracked out a full-blown collection of the American picaresque in the second half of the twentieth century. While Saul Bellow's *The Adventures of Augie March* has received a fair amount of attention as a picaresque novel, contemporary criticism—with some exceptions, to be cited in due course—has not ventured a full treatment of the numerous texts of an emergent picaresque renewal in contemporary American literature, much less grappled with its literary and cultural significance. Respecting American picaresque literature since mid-century, Robert Alter's *Rogue's Progress: Studies in the Picaresque Novel* (Cambridge: Harvard University Press, 1964) attends in a few brief pages only to *Augie March*; R. W. B. Lewis's *The Picaresque Saint: Representative Figures in Contemporary Fiction* (London: Gollancz, 1960) gives brief mention to Steinbeck, and offers a full chapter only on William Faulkner (a dubious inclusion); Stuart Miller's *The Picaresque Novel* (Cleveland: Press of Case Western Reserve University, 1967), mentions Nelson Algren, Bellow, William Burroughs, Ralph Ellison, Joseph Heller, and Thomas Pynchon, but gives no more than a page of attention to any of them; and William Riggan's *Picaros, Madmen, Naifs, and Clowns* (Norman: University of Oklahoma Press, 1981) discusses in the case of his picaros only *Augie March*. Attempting a broad catalog of picaresque, even Ulrich Wicks, while noting "a con-

temporary American picaresque as an assertive strand of twentieth-century narrative," lists only ten such fictions, only one of which was published after 1960 (*Picaresque Narrative, Picaresque Fictions: A Theory and Research Guide* [New York: Greenwood Press, 1989], p. 15), and later in the "guide" through sixty "prime" or "basic picaresque fictions" touches on ten American cases, only three of which appeared after 1960.

2. This sentence rearranges the title of Stanley Cavell's *This New Yet Unapproachable America* (Albuquerque: Living Batch Press, 1989), and, of course, Cavell himself is borrowing it from Ralph Waldo Emerson's essay "Experience." Unpacking the phrase, Cavell asks "what about America is forbidding, prohibitive, negative— the place or the topic of the place? Is the problem about it that it is uninhabitable or that it is undiscussable— -and the one because of the other?" (p. 92). For Cavell's provocative exploration of Emerson's sense of being "lost" in his America and of contemporary America as an interpretive and philosophical problem, see especially pp. 88–98.

3. While this might seem overdrawn on its face, the testimony of foreign visitors to America in the second half of this century suggests otherwise. See, for instance, Jonathan Raban's *Old Glory: An American Voyage* (New York: Simon and Schuster, 1981), which attempts to decipher the country by way of a trip down the Mississippi, or his *Hunting Mister Heartbreak: A Discovery of America* (New York: HarperCollins, 1991), which, playing in its title with the name of J. Hector St. John de Crevecoeur, takes up Crevecoeur's old question "what, then, is the American, this new man?" Or see John Williams, *Into the Badlands: Travels through Urban America* (London: HarperCollins, 1993), a British inquiry into American territories and meanings that follows the trail of cities marked out by the author's favorite American crime writers. As Raban and Williams and others encounter a hugely difficult America to decode, one is reminded of Stephen Spender's observations about such contemporary trans-Atlantic literary crossings ("England and America," *Partisan Review* 40:3 [1973]: 349–69). "The America that has to be imagined is," he writes, "almost uncontainable" (p. 368). Thus, the American writer goes to England, Spender suggests, because America is too much, too overwhelming, and the British scene helps the writer restore imagination in a setting less taxing and more scaled and manageable in terms of human proportion; the British writer turns to America, on the other hand, to avert inertia and provinciality, in order to replenish his or her work out of American size, vitality, and tensions, "drawn to the United States by its immediately contemporary energy" (p. 355). For another kind of view of the difficulties America poses for the British imagination, see Peter Conrad, *Imagining America* (New York: Oxford University Press, 1980).

4. Waller, *Border Music* (New York: Warner Books, 1995), p. 111. Hereafter, all page numbers in parentheses following quotations from this work refer to this edition.

5. Now, all examples of the picaresque narrative do not have to travel across

huge landscapes, only to pass through terrain that has somehow become "alien" or ambiguous or exotic for the picaro in question. As with John Kennedy Toole's Ignatius Reilly in *A Confederacy of Dunces*, the "road" might well be confined to the streets of a city like New Orleans, as the city poses the life of vagabondage the picaro must enter. Other examples of a kind of "local picaresque" will be discussed in later chapters.

6. On the confusion and rapidity of contemporary American "signal systems," see Marshall Blonsky, *American Mythologies* (New York: Oxford University Press, 1992), and see the next three notes.

7. For this particular piece and this kind of evidence, one can turn to W. T. Lhamon Jr., *Deliberate Speed: The Origins of a Cultural Style in the American 1950s* (Washington: Smithsonian Institution Press, 1990), p. 78. Lhamon's study of the wildly accelerated pace of life since mid-century, as this is both signaled and created by the forms of popular culture, is a full-length treatment of the points made in this paragraph. Of course, Lhamon in many ways simply exposes the current popular "lore cycle" of the old Henry Adams "feeling," as *Deliberate Speed* documents anew in its more general terms the personal sensations recorded in *The Education of Henry Adams* that the sheer rush, change, and energies of American existence were outside of one's capacity to keep up with. In another way, Lhamon's analysis of the popular sense of life's rapidity confirms the insights, if not the droll approaches, one can glean from Alvin Toffler's *Future Shock* (New York: Random House, 1970), about the arrival of the future so quickly and overwhelmingly that practical, intellectual, psychological, and emotional life are not, cannot be, prepared for it.

8. According to Miles Orvell, the problem of "authenticity" in an American world filled to brimming with confounding images and increasingly filled with simulacra, began to emerge in the mid-nineteenth century. See his *The Real Thing: Imitation and Authenticity in American Culture, 1880–1940* (Chapel Hill: University of North Carolina Press, 1989). For other, different kinds of accounts of the manufacturing of images, see Daniel Boorstin, *The Image: A Guide to Pseudo-Events in America* (New York: Harper & Row, 1964); Paul Fussell, *Bad; or, The Dumbing of America* (New York: Summit Books, 1991); Thomas Stritch, "The Blurred Image: Some Reflections on the Mass Media in the 60's," in *America in Change: Reflections on the 60's and 70's*, ed. Ronald Weber (Notre Dame: University of Notre Dame, 1972), pp. 206–19., and Blonsky, *American Mythologies*.

9. For an exceptional account of the new social propinquity created by the high technics of simultaneity and the consequent social tensions this produces in an extraordinarily pluralistic society, see Joshua Meyrowitz, *No Sense of Place: The Impact of Electronic Media on Social Behavior* (New York: Oxford University Press, 1985), especially part 3, "The New Social Landscape."

10. One of the earliest critical works on the Spanish picaresque actually concludes that such an inventory, or encyclopedia, of the social realm is the *primary* function of the picaresque narrative. Fonger deHaan's 1895 doctoral dissertation

argues that it is a "mine of information concerning the habits, customs, ways of thinking, of dressing, of eating and drinking, of seeking diversion . . . of all classes of Spain during the time of the Habsburghs" (published as *An Outline of the History of the Novela Picaresca in Spain* [The Hague: Martinus Nijhoff, 1903], p. 66). While this view is disputed by other critics, it does call attention to the work of the picaresque narrative in giving realistic rendition of the environment through which the picaro passes, and few would disagree that the picaresque approaches the broad human gallery as a staple of its narrative operations.

11. Ulrich Wicks coins this term to distinguish the old picaro from the "Everyman" of the medieval morality play. See his "Onlyman," *Mosaic* 8 (1975): 21–47. The point to be made and enforced in subsequent discussion is that the contemporary American picaro represents a shift even from "Only-Man" to a more democratically understood kind of "Anyperson."

12. Patrick W. Shaw begins to hit the mark, then, in his notation about the contemporary picaresque that such a novel represents "the literature of voluntary alienation," centering on a picaro that is not "an outsider by birth, providence, or circumstance," but Shaw's assertion that the picaro is, therefore, "a conscious rebel" simply does not follow ("Old Genre, New Breed: The Postwar American Picaro," *Genre* 7 [1974]: 208). As the discussion in this and subsequent chapters will demonstrate, while the life of the rebel remains a picaresque possibility, it is also—and perhaps much more often—the case that the new American picaro or picara can willingly elect marginality, discover himself or herself alienated, not as an action of rebellion but as a function of his or her sudden or gradual sensation that the surrounding scene has become an "alien" one in some way. But this is a catalyzing sensation for the figure's life on the road more than it is any perduring trait of rebellion in him or her.

13. It is interesting to note that R. W. B. Lewis's first book, *The American Adam* (Chicago: University of Chicago Press, 1955), which sketched out the charter of the American "party of hope" as over against the "party of memory" in the period of the early republic, followed this exploration of the cultural sources of American innocence and hope constituting "Adamism" with a later book, *The Picaresque Saint* (see note 5 to chap. 1). Although the latter study plays "loose" with the picaresque as a genre category and only scantly touches American instances, Lewis might have had an instinct for the ways an Adamic character and a picaresque structure might converge in contemporary literature, though nothing is made of such a convergence in either book.

14. Frederick R. Karl, one of the critics thinking the picaresque—*very* broadly conceived—a cogent literary form for the expression of the American experience past and present, points emphatically to this matter of spatial freedom as an American precedent for the defining "mobility" of the picaresque narrative and understands how it conjoins with the American Adamic idea and the impulse always to be "starting over" ("Picaresque and the American Experience," *Yale Review* 57:2 [December, 1967]: 196–212). Although there is much that is intelli-

gent and provocative in Karl's perspective and although one wishes he had had more to say on this subject, he probably overstates the extent to which a kind of frontier "escapism" plays a part in any contemporary configurations of the picaresque.

15. As Alastair Fowler has pointed out, the numbers of genres fully available or "active" in any era—that is, suitable and functional, given the general outlook of the age and its literary artists—is probably small: formerly effectual genres recede as other, newly cogent genres appear with "affect." See the section "Available Genres" in his *Kinds of Literature: An Introduction to the Theory of Genres and Modes* (Cambridge: Harvard University Press, 1982), pp. 226–28.

16. See, for instance, Reed, *An Exemplary History of the Novel* (Chicago: University of Chicago Press, 1981), which traces the history of the novel through the picaresque tradition, on the one hand, and the alternative stuff of the "Quixotic" tradition, on the other.

17. Erich Heller provides a fuller discussion of this matter in his *The Artist's Journey into the Interior* (New York: Random House, 1965). See especially the title essay.

18. Codrescu uses this phrase in reference not only to the penchant of the computer age to replace the "window" on the world with a "window" (monitor) only into one's own propositions—a window through which one elects interiority—but also to what he regards as an outside world of sensate experience that is being obliterated by restricted zones, by electronic simulacra, by forms of "mediaspeak" replacing the language and thought with which to engage the world, and so on. See the title essay in *The Disappearance of the Outside* (Reading, Mass.: Addson-Wesley Publishing, 1990).

19. J. Hillis Miller's *Poets of Reality: Six Twentieth-Century Writers* (Cambridge: Belknap Press of Harvard University, 1965) explores this condition of what he regards as a new romanticism, as the artist—after the disappearance of God and, thus, the sanctioning of the created order—gobbles the external world into him or her as nothing other than a function of his or her own consciousness. Miller discusses the nihilistic limits of such a literary condition and proposes how his six "poets of reality" venture to allow that world external to the imperial ego to reassert itself. The present study proposes that the new American picaresque represents another means than those described by Miller for narrative expression to engage the "outside world" again after the literature of interiority has held the day. See also Heller, *Artist's Journey into the Interior.*

20. Marcus Klein, *After Alienation: American Novels in Mid-Century* (Cleveland: World Publishing Company, 1964). Klein's question, of course, refers to the issue of the writer's engaging society at a point beginning in mid-century when it was becoming clear that sublimely elected exile, self-consciously studied alienation, and literary-social rebellion had become dissipating arts for the American writer and intellectual, and he points to the emergence of new fictions after World War II that begin to renegotiate the "tricky distance" between the self in its free-

dom and the society in its sheer facticity. He refers to these novels as fictions of "accommodation," not in the sense that they surrender easily to outlooks belonging to social conformity but in the sense of an emerging mood, "after rebellion had exhausted itself," in which some writers attempt to locate the terms with which "to meet the small, bitter necessities of engagement" (p. 29). Pertinent to the present discussion, the "hero" of such novels, Klein notes, typically works at the "simultaneous engagement and disengagement" with society that, after alienation, represents his condition: "the hero exercises his wits and thereby lives within his dilemma, and managing to live within it he proposes the possibility of living" (p. 30). At least three of the "accommodationist" writers Klein treats as in active career at mid-century—Saul Bellow, Ralph Ellison, and Wright Morris—had by 1964 utilized the picaresque form to re-engage American society, although Klein makes nothing of this. As the social reality has become increasing complex in ensuing decades, however, it could well be thought that the new American picaresque arrived more fully to take up the work of "accommodation" in some aspects of Klein's sense of the term.

21. These terms—"exhaustion" and "replenishment"—are borrowed from John Barth, but both are being used here in ways somewhat different than Barth's cultivation of them in his famous *Atlantic Monthly* essays. See "The Literature of Exhaustion" (August 1967: 29–34) and "The Literature of Replenishment: Postmodernist Fiction" (January 1980: 65–71). Part of the latter essay seems to recant the former. In the first Barth suggests that the new anti-novels, and other projects in "mixed-means" art, signaled an "exhaustion" of the possibilities of the novel tradition in general to continue to create anything genuinely original. Thirteen years later, however, he claims to have meant *not* the end of the novel but the desirable end of the aesthetics of high modernism, and he holds out bright new hopes for creativity, for originality, and for significance, in the replenishing examples provided by the postmodernist fictions of Italo Calvino and Gabriel García Márquez. Needless to say, perhaps, that the present study finds another, American form of "the literature of replenishment" in other narrative formations.

22. Saul Bellow, *The Adventures of Augie March* (New York: Viking Press, 1960), p. 536.

23. The language of this paragraph, though altered to slightly different purposes, is heavily indebted to Paul Ricoeur's essay "The Symbol Gives Rise to Thought" in his *The Symbolism of Evil,* trans. Emerson Buchanan (New York: Harper & Row, 1967). Ricoeur's argument about the problem of the immediacy of belief as an element of the distresses of modernity posits the necessity of a postcritical "second naivete" that will restore the world to the interpreting self, a form of fresh approach to experience predicated on the prior realization that the self is in the world and not vice-versa. See also notes 17 and 19. This thematic is "revisited" in chapter 9.

24. Thomas Pynchon, *The Crying of Lot 49* (New York: Bantam Books, 1967), p.

137. Oedipa is pondering, more exactly, if her continuing to be at all relevant to America means she has to be "an alien" to it.

25. Like several other matters in this chapter, this point, only touched quickly here, will come in for more extended treatment in later chapters as the social and cultural work of the new American picaresque receives more detailed attention.

26. "The Life and Death of Literary Forms," *New Literary History* 2 (1971): 201. In this essay, of course, Fowler is not concentrating only or even mainly on the picaresque genre or mode, but the points made in the essay on genre theory and history, and utilized in this paragraph, are nonetheless important and applicable here.

27. On genre evolution, see Fowler, *Kinds of Literature*, especially chapters 10 and 11, and Fowler, "Life and Death of Literary Forms."

28. Geertz's "Blurred Genres: The Refiguration of Social Thought" appeared first in *The American Scholar* 49 (Spring 1980): 165–79. It is reprinted in his *Local Knowledge: Further Essays in Interpretive Anthropology* (New York: Basic Books, 1983). Hereafter, all parenthetical page numbers following quotations from this essay refer to *Local Knowledge*.

CHAPTER 3: THE PICARO IN FICTION, THE PICARESQUE IN FACT

1. William Least Heat Moon, *Blue Highways: A Journey into America* (Boston: Little, Brown and Company, 1982). Hereafter, all page numbers cited in parentheses following quotations from this book refer to this edition.

2. Clifford Geertz, "Blurred Genres: The Refiguration of Social Thought," in Geertz, *Local Knowledge: Further Essays in Interpretive Anthropology* (New York: Basic Books, 1983), p. 21.

3. John Steinbeck, *Travels with Charley* (New York: Bantam Books, 1962). Hereafter, all page numbers in parentheses following quotations from this book refer to this edition.

4. David Espy, "The Wilds of New Jersey: John McPhee as Travel Writer," in *Temperamental Journeys: Essays on the Modern Literature of Travel*, edited by Michael Kowalewski (Athens: University of Georgia Press, 1992), p. 164.

5. Some comparable elements appear slightly after mid-century in Langston Hughes's *I Wonder as I Wander: An Autobiographical Journey* (New York: Hill and Wang, 1956), for instance, but the journey motif is just that for Hughes, a motif in this stricter autobiography, as he recounts his life, and not for the work of a travel narrative per se. Before mid-century, of course, among others, Henry Miller had published his mild diatribe, *The Air-Conditioned Nightmare*, 2 vols. (New York: New Directions Books, 1945, 1947), a travel narrative of America stemming from his temporary return from self-imposed "exile." "I felt the need," he writes in opening, "to effect a reconciliation with my native land. . . . I wanted to have a last look at my country and leave it with a good taste in my mouth. I didn't want to run away from it as I had originally" (I, p. 10). The title of Miller's work indi-

cates the "taste" he was left with. Earlier still in the century, Henry James had effected a similar return that led to the publication of *The American Scene* in 1907. James's own "written" history as a traveler, with the question America finally posed for him, is interesting in the framework of a study of the American picaresque. His major biographer, Leon Edel, drawing on the author's own sense of himself in his evolution, describes James as traveler on the Anglo-European scene successively as "the sentimental traveler," "the observant stranger," and "the brooding tourist"—all of this before the reckoning with his own enigmatic country in *The American Scene*, wherein James becomes "the restless analyst." See Edel, *Henry James: A Life* (New York: Harper & Row, 1985).

6. Bill Moyers, *Listening to America: A Traveler Rediscovers His Country* (New York: Harper's Magazine Press, 1971), p. vii. Hereafter, all page numbers in parentheses following quotations from this book refer to this edition.

7. From the originating era in sixteenth-century Spain forward, picaresque narratives have often contained accounts of one "horrible incident" that seemed to portend the nature of the whole world. *Lazarillo de Tormes* has an episode of suspected priestly cannibalism in the "old" picaresque, and, nearer at hand, there are Billy's witnessing Dutch Schultz's murder of Bo Weinberg in E. L. Doctorow's *Billy Bathgate* and Joe Buck's being sexually plundered by Tombaby and Juanita Barefoot in James Leo Herlihy's *Midnight Cowboy*, both of which incidents establish a narrative "world" of confusion and danger. For Habe to revolve his travel narrative around the event of the Kennedy assassination, therefore, is for him to adumbrate with this incident the character of the American "world" his picaresque journey encounters. Then there is the "Battle Royale" scene in Ralph Ellison's *Invisible Man*, a betrayal of assumed privileged status that forever then marks the picaresque protagonist. On the "grotesque or horrible incident" in picaresque, see Ulrich Wicks, *Picaresque Narrative, Picaresque Fictions* (New York: Greenwood Press, 1989), pp. 65–66.

8. Richard Reeves, *American Journey: Traveling with Tocqueville in Search of Democracy in America* (New York: Simon and Schuster, 1982), p. 15. Hereafter, all page numbers in parentheses following quotations from this book refer to this edition.

9. David Lamb, *A Sense of Place: Listening to Americans* (New York: Random House, 1993), p. 3. Hereafter, all page numbers in parentheses following quotations from this book refer to this edition, unless otherwise noted.

10. Lamb's travels presented in this book are actually composite, several discontinuous trips collected in the one volume. It scarcely matters, however, because *as presented* the travel narrative takes the form of the picaresque whether the actual travel did or not. See the final section of this chapter on fictional elements in the literature of travel.

11. Some other travel books that practice in the elements of picaresque push into other "microcosmic" American spaces in their efforts to find the keys to "unlock" huge, puzzling America. As Lamb travels the "Empty Quarter" in search

of clues and as Reeves follows Tocqueville's path, Jim Lilliefors simply takes a certain, long road in *Highway 50* (Golden, Colo.: Fulcrum Publishing, 1993); Mark Winegardner tracks through American pop-tacky-land in *Elvis Presley Boulevard: From Sea to Shining Sea, Almost* (New York: Atlantic Monthly Press, 1987); Dayton Duncan travels New Hampshire's political season in the national primaries in *Grass Roots* (New York: Viking Penguin, 1991); Tony Hiss pushes into ecological predicaments across the country in *The Experience of Place* (New York: Knopf, 1990); Phillip Berman goes to collect ordinary Americans' "stories" in *The Search for Meaning* (New York: Ballantine Books, 1990); and Pete Davies traces "storms" and "lives" through America's heartland in *Storm Country* (New York: Random House, 1992). Frederick Turner, Fred Setterberg, and Alfred Kazin move into those places both actual to hand and "storied" in American literature in, respectively, *Spirit of Place* (San Francisco: Sierra Club Books, 1989), *The Roads Taken* (Athens: University of Georgia Press, 1993), and *A Writer's America* (New York: Knopf, 1988). In each case, however "narrow," the "road taken" seems to the narrator of each of these texts of travel to have promised revelations of the "broader" meaning of America.

12. Eddy Harris, *South of Haunted Dreams* (New York: Simon and Schuster, 1993). Hereafter, all page numbers in parentheses following quotations from this book refer to this edition.

13. Harrison Salisbury, *Travels around America* (New York: Walker and Company, 1976), p. 4. Hereafter, all page numbers in parentheses following quotations from this book refer to this edition.

14. Attention to this matter here is necessarily abridged because more thorough investigation is reserved for the second section of this study, "The Social Work of the New American Picaresque."

15. In an essay mainly devoted to excursions of American travel writing into areas of "hyperspatiality"—the fake, the inauthentic, the illusion, the simulacrum—as well as into the contrasting perdurable natural landscape, Terry Caesar suggests that the burden of recovering the external world, in a culturescape of hyperrealities, has become quite difficult and that the charge of postmodern American fiction in this regard, "the responsibilities for representing the real *as* real have to some extent fallen upon American travel writing [which, though also unavoidably entangled with hyperreality]. . . . cannot be easily severed from the real without losing its cultural function" ("Brutal Naivete and Special Lighting: Hyperspatiality and Landscape in the American Travel Text," *College Literature* 21:1 [February 1994]: 76–77, endnote 4). Compare this also to the literary "place" the new American picaresque seeks to wedge open for itself when other forms of contemporary literature have defaulted on the external world (see chapter 2, the section entitled "The Cultural Place of the New American Picaresque"). The stuff of hyperreality also relates to that whirling confusion of the American "images" that fly by on the picaro's way (see chapter 2, the section entitled "The New American Setting and Permutations of the Picaresque"). Moreover, although Caesar does not discuss the

travel text as a form of picaresque, his article calls important attention in other ways to the maze of dilemmas the interpreting self confronts, a topic to receive more detailed attention later.

16. Bill Bryson, *The Lost Continent: Travels in Small-Town America* (New York: Harper & Row, 1989), pp. 29–30. Hereafter, all page numbers in parentheses following quotations from this book refer to this edition.

17. This point comes in for further discussion in the next section of this chapter, but for now it should be noted that lengthy and extended descriptions of any particular thing or place or person—that is, renditions that go on for pages and pages—are infrequent in the new American picaresque. The rapid narrative movement, forever forging ahead to follow the picaro's mobility in spatial terms, precludes lingering over every detail of a scene, but the point here is not that descriptions must be exhaustive, only rather that they catch the disclosive visuals and tactiles in order to represent a strongly recognizable "sense" of the thing or place or person. The pause need only be momentary to communicate such a sense, for the picaresque must "move on," intent on a broad, not a narrow, inventory of American variety

18. As discussed in the preceding chapters, it is important to remember that no single text can either exemplify or exhaust all elements of the nature of the picaresque genre. The narrative category is broad and malleable, evolving with each new entry into its fundamental formations.

19. Needless to say, perhaps, the contention that certain American texts of American travel belong to the narrative form of the new American picaresque is not at all to argue that all nonfictional travel narratives take the shape of the picaresque or that all contemporary pieces of American travel literature belong to the new American picaresque. There are those narratives of travel that work in the stuff of metaphor ("the road of life"), tourism ("the road of collection"), pilgrimage ("the road to Mecca"), colonial expansion, utopianism, scientific and social-scientific expedition, crusade, foreign missions, military strategy, and the like. From time to time, any narrative of any of these other types might intersect briefly with the picaresque form, but, for the most part, such narratives depict much more purposeful travel, pre-planned routes, directed ends, tighter schedules, clearly pointed objectives, certain destinations, and so on, than the loose itinerancy, the random course, the rebounding movement of the picaresque narrative. On travel and travel literature in general, especially on the psychology and social-psychology of the traveler, Eric J. Leed provides a stunning study with his *The Mind of the Traveler: From Gilgamesh to Global Tourism* (New York: Basic Books, 1991). Given the range of interest and erudition of Leed's book, it is interesting that it does not treat—indeed does not mention—the picaresque form.

20. Lars Eighner, *Travels with Lizbeth* (New York: St. Martin's Press, 1993), p. 29. Hereafter, all page numbers in parentheses following quotations from this book refer to this edition.

21. This is not to say that these books do not judge that which passes before

view in the narrative travel—only, rather, that "judgment" remains subservient to the larger purposes of taking inventory on the picaro's part. While the narrational "memory" might well cast this or that matter in such a way as to elicit evaluations from readers, the picaro or picara usually practices a kind of studied and composed "neutrality," given his or her established temperament, this to inculcate the innocent approach to and the open engagement with the experiences of the road. Occasionally, of course, the reserve of the picaro is strained past the breaking point.

22. The question of intentionality here is a difficult one, and it seems most reasonable, in general, to suppose that the writers of these "nonfictional" travel narratives, at the level of composition, do not so much consciously set out to duplicate the nature and structures of the picaresque form as they happen, willynilly, to locate and utilize a form that seems commensurate with the experiences they want to represent, a form that critical readers, ex post facto, can identify as the picaresque. But see note 32 below on some texts whose authors appear to be more self-conscious about the picaresque form as a narrative strategy.

23. There are two important points here. First, of course, the point of view of picaresque narrative does not necessarily or always have to be "first-person"— either in the new American picaresque fictions or in the older Anglo-European examples. The requirement is that the point of view of the retrospective narrator must be securely associated with, attached to, the picaro "being remembered." Indeed, in a case like *Midnight Cowboy,* it would work to cross-purposes to have a Joe Buck narrate his own story: as inept as he is in the ways and means of social connection, he could scarcely establish any "converse" with readers superior to his communication abilities with other characters; as inarticulately innocent as he is, he could not render his travels except as bewilderment without the aid of a more "knowing" narrator to guide the reader. In the cases of the autobiographical and "nonfictional" travel text, of course, the point of view remains in the first-person. Second, however, it should be kept in view that these are not "autobiography" in the strict sense of a person's narrating his or her own life story but are, rather, travel texts narrated "autobiographically." They neither propose to present the story of the person's whole life to the time of writing nor pretend that *la vida* in question is the only center of concern. Rather, they limit their narrative duration mainly to the period of the life spent "on the road," and they indicate that the "travel" is as much a narrative concern as the "major character" that is its vehicle. *Listening to America,* for example, is not Moyers's autobiography; it is an instance of the new American picaresque presented autobiographically.

24. Walker Percy, *The Moviegoer* (New York: Knopf, 1979), p. 3.

25. Respecting the work of fiction, these are standard points since Wayne C. Booth's *The Rhetoric of Fiction* (Chicago: University of Chicago Press, 1961). Here the contention is that, in the scrutiny of strategies of narration, Booth's distinctions among author, implied author, first-person narrator, and "his" or "her"

character apply fully as much to autobiographical work as to fiction, in regard at least to discriminations to be made and maintained in critical theory even if they cannot always be verified in this or that autobiographical text by critical practice. On the question of the "reliability" of the picaresque narrator, see, further, William Riggan, *Picaros, Madmen, Naifs, and Clowns* (Norman: University of Oklahoma Press, 1981), pp. 38–78.

26. Peter Jenkins, *A Walk across America* (New York: William Morrow & Company, 1979), p. 23. Hereafter, all page numbers in parentheses following quotations from this book refer to this edition.

27. For a perceptive treatment of this inadvertent and "advertent" fabricating in travel literature, most strictly attentive to the eighteenth century but useful in thinking about all travel narratives, see Percy G. Adams, *Travelers and Travel Liars, 1660–1800* (Berkeley: University of California Press, 1962). Adams deals in everything from distorted perceptions and memories, conscious and unconscious plagiarisms, and willful duplicities, to the creations of false topographies.

28. Purported "memories" allow completely rendered and extensive dialogue, notations of the smallest gestures, features of countenance, changes of facial expressions, recollections of colors, clothing styles, and automobile models, vivid representations of scenes, billboards passed, songs heard on the radio, food eaten at particular ordinary meals, and so on. With respect to such "perfect memory" indeed in travel writing, Terry Caesar refers to it as "romancing the facts" in a chapter of his *Forgiving the Boundaries: Home as Abroad in American Travel Writing* (Athens: University of Georgia Press, 1995), and he explores the interpenetration of "fact" and "fiction" in that chapter (5) and in his seventh chapter, entitled "To Make This Place Another: Fictions of Travel, Travel of Fictions." Although Caesar's study deals almost exclusively in the texts of travel of Americans abroad and although he does not attend to the picaresque narrative, his contention that "contemporary travel writing has been required to know itself as fiction" (p. 128) is obviously important in a critical consideration of the new American picaresque, as are others of his insights that can come into play in later chapters. See also note 15 above. Jonathan Raban, a travel writer himself, is also keen to the admixture of fact and fiction in his view of travel literature: "Much of its 'factual' material, in the way of bills, menus, ticket-stubs, names and addresses, dates and destinations, is there to authenticate what is really fiction; while its wildest fictions [thus] have the status of possible facts" (*For Love and Money: A Writing Life, 1969–1989* [New York: Harper & Row, 1989], pp. 231–32).

29. Indeed, a travel writer succeeds best who, like Paul Theroux, manages his or her narrative throughout with the kind of imaginative subjectivity that makes the road work interesting and potentially significant just because it is filtered through potent imagination. As Paul Fussell has observed, Paul Theroux writes authentic travel literature because he is poised for the unexpected. His travels are interesting because *he* is interesting. See Fussell's "The Stationary Tourist," *Harper's* (April 1979): 31–38. The point is that, as committed as the picaro is to

"objective" encounter with experience, narrational memory of the picaro's travels cannot simply deteriorate into recounting the "facts." If Harrison Salisbury's *Travels around America* can make a significant claim on a reader's attention, it is not because Salisbury delivers the "facts" but because that reader has been persuaded about the importance of participating in Salisbury's subjective imagination of the road in "looking at *my* continent, *my* America." If Jonathan Yardley's narrative course through the American mid-Atlantic region merits a reader's responsiveness, it is not because the author "facts and figures" Pennsylvania, Maryland, the District of Columbia, Virginia, North Carolina—most of the state Chamber of Commerce tourist brochures and atlases would do nicely to survey those states—but because Yardley manages to give them to the reader, as his title suggests, as "states of mind," as places recollected through Yardley's droll subjectivity.

30. As represented, "Tombaby Barefoot was a light-haired, pale, oddly constructed halfbreed. He had a small head and no shoulders to speak of, but from his stomach to the ground he was big and thick and heavy. He wore a gray sweatshirt with HARVARD printed on it, faded and torn levis, sneakers, and a pair of golden earrings." This man, called "Princess" by his mother, "moved like a cow with loose knee joints and seemed always on the point of collapsing into a pile of thighs and elbows" (Herlihy, *Midnight Cowboy* [New York: Simon and Schuster, 1965], p. 77).

31. As represented, the "Judge" is "an ornery old billy goat with a glass eye . . . [who] speaks in riddles and half-answers and generally likes to get a rise out of people who pass through town. Ask him where he fishes and he'll answer 'In the river.' Ask him where in the river and he'll say 'Sometimes upstream, sometimes down.' Once he made a public bet that he could bite his own eye. A skeptical visitor plunked down twenty dollars, whereupon the Judge popped out his glass eye and "bit" it in front of the speechless man. The Judge then wagered the man another twenty dollars he could bite his *other* eye. Figuring this was a truly impossible feat, the man agreed to the bet. The Judge promptly removed his dentures and 'bit' his real eye" (W. Hampton Sides, *Stomping Grounds* [New York: William Morrow & Company, 1992], p. 78). Compare this to the preceding note.

32. In terms somewhat like the intertextuality of the old Spanish picaresque— *Justina* incorporating "Guzman," *Guzman de Alfarache* alluding to *Lazarillo de Tormes*—some of these contemporary American picaresque narratives reveal awareness of earlier travel literature, picaresque and not, and of each other. As a medievalist by learning, Ignatius J. Reilly in John Kennedy Toole's *A Confederacy of Dunces* follows out a course amply sprinkled with references to the old literature of romance that would be supplanted in part by the picaresque narratives like Reilly's own. In the brief prefatory to Billy Terry's *The Watermelon Kid* (Baton Rouge: Louisiana State University Press, 1984), the author remarks how this narrative follows A. J. Poole ("the Kid") and his roadhouse gang, who "were the pilgrims" around the "sweat and howl roadhouses . . . [that] were

their Canterburies" (p. 1). And, in what seems a direct allusion to the picaresque hero, a teacher denominates Vic Messenger, the young picaro, in Richard Hill's *Riding Solo with the Golden Horde* (Athens: University of Georgia Press, 1994), a "rogue and peasant slave" (p. 133). In the "nonfictions" of the new American picaresque the inter-allusions among texts are even more direct. Reeves, of course, follows Tocqueville; Steinbeck names his camper "Roscinante" (Don Quixote's horse); Jenkin's travel text refers to John Muir's *A Thousand Mile Walk;* Least Heat Moon carries "Song of the Open Road" in Walt Whitman's *Leaves of Grass;* Mark Winegardner's *Elvis Presley Boulevard* refers at least obliquely to Least Heat Moon's *Blue Highways,* as does Michael Lane, much less obliquely, with the title of his "gay romp" through America, *Pink Highways,* and so on. And Reeves, in passing through Canandaigua, New York, follows not only Tocqueville's course but stops in the narrative to quote observations about the town from Salisbury's *Travels around America* when that traveler had passed through it in 1976. For one last example, Jim Lehrer's *A Bus of My Own* (New York: G. P. Putnam's Sons, 1992) refers not only to his own "fictional" picaresque narrative, *Kick the Can,* but also to the "road books" by "William Least Heat Moon, Charles Kuralt and others who travel the back roads of America" (p. 224) and offers up to all such wanderers some "Rules of the Road" decidedly in the picaresque vein: "Stay at Best Westerns" (because, locally owned, they are not all the same); "Stay off Interstates" (because the matters of interest are elsewhere); "Go alone" (to get to "another world"); and, among others, "Don't travel by itinerary" (because it prevents the "impromptu") (pp. 224–26).

CHAPTER 4: THE PICARO'S RECOVERY OF THE SOVEREIGN SELF

1. Harrison E. Salisbury, *Travels around America* (New York: Walker and Company, 1976), p. 2. Hereafter, all page numbers in parentheses following quotations from this book refer to this edition.

2. Peter Jenkins, *A Walk across America* (New York: William Morrow & Company, 1979), p. 24. Hereafter, all page numbers in parentheses following quotations from this book refer to this edition.

3. Robert James Waller, *Border Music* (New York: Warner Books, 1995), pp. 88–89 and passim. Hereafter, all page numbers in parentheses following quotations from this book refer to this edition.

4. Kenneth Gergen, *The Saturated Self: Dilemmas of Identity in Contemporary Life* (New York: Basic Books, 1991), pp. 49–53.

5. Ibid., p. 49.

6. Ibid., pp. 72–80. Gergen's point would seem largely to override the idea of John P. Hewitt that the central issue facing the self in contemporary America is the one of "staying" or "leaving," conformity or rebellion (*Dilemmas of the American Self* [Philadelphia: Temple University Press, 1989], pp. 99–107). Those choices are reduced in either case to the same predicament Gergen cites of the "cadre of

social ghosts" within one, quite regardless of whether one stays *or* goes. At a fundamental level, of course, Gergen's analyses of the claims of others on the self might simply rehearse in different terms the ascendancy of the "other-directed" over the "inner-directed" human being, as David Reisman et al. describe this in *The Lonely Crowd: A Study of the Changing American Character* (New Haven: Yale University Press, 1950). But Gergen's depiction of the "overpopulation" of the self gives renewed cogency to the work of Christopher Lasch (see notes 14 and 23 below).

7. Walker Percy, *The Message in the Bottle* (New York: Farrar, Straus & Giroux, 1975), p. 47.

8. Ibid.

9. Joshua Meyrowitz, *No Sense of Place: The Impact of Electronic Media on Social Behavior* (New York: Oxford University Press, 1985), p. 146.

10. Daniel J. Boorstin, *The Image: A Guide to Pseudo-Events in America* (New York: Harper & Row, 1964), pp. 7–44.

11. Meyrowitz, *No Sense of Place*, p. 181.

12. The depictions of the obstacles confronting contemporary selfhood presented in the preceding several pages first appeared elsewhere in a slightly different form and in a different context of exposition and argument. See Rowland A. Sherrill, "American Sacred Space and the Contest of History," in *American Sacred Space*, ed. David Chidester and Edward T. Linenthal (Bloomington: Indiana University Press, 1995), pp. 328–31.

13. On this matter of how a surplusage of stimuli, the emergence of the sense of affectlessness, and a resulting consequence of apathy, might relate to, lead to, the defensive mechanism of relinquishing the self's sovereign will, see Rollo May, *Love and Will* (New York: W. W. Norton, 1969), especially the introduction entitled "Our Schizoid World." May contends that "apathy is the withdrawal of will and love" and, as a self-defense, only makes the self even more vulnerable (p. 33).

14. See Christopher Lasch, *The Culture of Narcissism: American Life in an Age of Diminishing Expectations* (New York: W. W. Norton, 1978), and *The Minimal Self: Psychic Survival in Troubled Times* (New York: W. W. Norton, 1984).

15. Thomas Pynchon, *The Crying of Lot 49* (New York: Bantam Books, 1967). Along with the predicament of being overpopulated by the voices of the cadre within her, this incident in which Oedipa Maas cannot locate her reflection in the mirror—a signal of her own growing loss of self—alludes also, if indirectly, to the problem of narcissism, in this case the narcissism of Pierce Inverarity who has, Oedipa fears, built the whole of America in his own brutally consuming image. The mirror-episode occurs in a place called the Echo Courts Motel, into which she has come because a sheet-metal nymph on the motel's sign reminds her of herself. In classical mythology, of course, Echo is that figure whose caprice has led to a punishment by the gods to the effect that she cannot speak unless first spoken to and, then, only to repeat what she has heard—a curse, in short,

making her nothing other than a function of others' "voices." Her love for Narcissus is thus doomed to nothing because she cannot speak to him and, trapped in his own self-love, he cannot be responsive to her. See Pynchon, pp. 14–26.

16. David Lamb, *A Sense of Place: Listening to Americans* (New York: Random House, 1993), pp. 4–5. Hereafter, all page numbers in parentheses following citations of this book refer to this edition.

17. James Leo Herlihy, *Midnight Cowboy* (New York: Simon and Schuster, 1965), p. 55. Hereafter, all page numbers in parentheses following citations of this book refer to this edition.

18. Bill Bryson, *The Lost Continent: Travels in Small-Town America* (New York: Harper & Row, 1989), pp. 174–75.

19. Bill Moyers, *Listening to America: A Traveler Rediscovers His Country* (New York: Harper's Magazine Press, 1971), p. 44.

20. This problem of other voices within, of preprepared attitude, of "packaging" is especially cumbersome for those travelers who, like Reeves, follow the itineraries, the records, the "production" of places, left by narrational predecessors of all kinds. See, for instance, Mary Durant and Michael Harwood, *On the Road with John James Audubon* (New York: Dodd, Mead, and Company, 1981), in which the autobiographical records that appear are so thoroughly entangled with Audubon's own reports that any unpredisposed response becomes quite difficult for Durant and Harwood. Of course, all of those who want to float the Mississippi narratively—like Jonathan Raban, *Old Glory: An American Voyage* (New York: Simon and Schuster, 1981), or B. C. Hall and C. T. Wood, *Big Muddy: Down the Mississippi through America's Heartland* (New York: Plume, 1992)—must grapple with the ghost of Mark Twain via *The Adventures of Huckleberry Finn* and *Life on the Mississippi* in order to avert turning their own integral experiencing into mere responses to those earlier texts. All the more difficult journeys, in this respect, are those set on and following into the "literary" landscapes—the "Oxford" imagined by William Faulkner, the "Nebraska" of Willa Cather, the "Keys" of Ernest Hemingway—by virtue of the inevitable discrepancies between the "places" as encountered and the "storied places" as read, with the reading having created Percy's "preformed symbolic complex" that stands between the self and the immediate experience of the places. See, for instance, Fred Setterberg's *The Roads Taken: Travels through America's Literary Landscapes* (Athens: University of Georgia Press, 1993), which "revisits," among others, the Texas of the writers of "Westerns," the Maine woods of Thoreau, and the rural South of Zora Neale Hurston, and see, for a British example, John Williams's *Into the Badlands: Travels through Urban America* (New York: HarperCollins, 1993), that moves through those cities "precedented" for Williams by American crime novelists. Not all of these narratives converge with the picaresque form, of course, but each is indicative of the threats to the self's sovereign responsiveness, and, as argued below, those that locate means to evade the "intermediations" of experience frequently do so be-

cause their trips take picaresque turns, moving away, that is, from testing sites against the measure of "the sight-seer's satisfaction" preconditioned by earlier writers' productions of the places.

21. John Steinbeck, *Travels with Charley: In Search of America* (New York: Bantam Books, 1963), p. 115. Hereafter, all page numbers in parentheses following quotations from this book refer to this edition.

22. The retreat into self exemplified in the creation of Lonesome Harry out of what he has left behind is not the only such case of Steinbeck's default in *Travels with Charley.* There are other, intermittent displays of Steinbeck's claim of and pride in his ability to read the "spoor" of human beings—an odd recourse for one who had wanted and has ample occasion to encounter the people themselves. Moreover, the very action of stopping at the Ambassador East, putting himself off the road and in comfort, importing his wife for connections with home, runs against the picaresque grain. And, beyond what is revealed in this episode, Steinbeck's flawed efforts on the picaresque course can also be seen in his resorting to conversations with Charley when he—as picaro—ought not to be evading human encounter. See note 29 below.

23. As defenses against self-erosion, Lasch would remind, the behaviors of imperious arrogance and utter narcissism can follow predictably from a state in which one perceives the "minimalization" of one's self. Of course, the results are the obverse of those in which the atrophied self simply relinquishes its own authority to convention, to the crowd, or to the expert: in extremity, the imperial or narcissistic self becomes its own sole authority, preens itself only on its own commanding views, and, thus, stands pathologically beyond any "correctives" that might arrive from dissonant experiences or other voices. Thereby asserting its "sovereignty" with a vengeance, such a self nonetheless truncates the possibilities of encounter and responsiveness just as much as that self with no capacity at all for respecting its own integrity. Surely one of the most "dis-eased" picaros of all in this context is Ignatius J. Reilly in John Kennedy Toole's *A Confederacy of Dunces* (Baton Rouge: Louisiana State University Press, 1980). Reilly, sensing his own "minimalism," falls into continuous masturbatory self-absorption, authorizes his "educated" superiority over all others, props himself up with self-deluding powers, resorts to narcissistic attitudes of seeing the outside world only as a function of his own will and desires, and, withal, until the very end of the narrative, displays very little possibility of approaching others with some regard for their integrity. Needless to say, this form of "sovereignty," the overweening variety, is not of the order Walker Percy recommends or the picaro ought to seek if he is to restore himself to the possibilities of the external world.

24. As Terry Caesar suggests in his quick notes on Bryson's book, the visible and witty arrogance and cynicism with which Bryson works his narrative way are "comedic" camouflage for a self not fully certain of itself and its operations: for the writing of his travels, Caesar observes, Bryson "just doesn't feel the authority of his own experience to be enough justification" ("Brutal Naivete and

Special Lighting: Hyperspatiality and Landscape in the American Travel Text," *College Literature* 21:1 [February 1994]: 66). The points for present purposes are that Bryson's picaresque intention to bump around in America are not always— or even very often—matched by the requisite authority or sovereignty of the picaro and that he, like others on the picaresque course, bears and is symptomatic of the afflictions that beset contemporary selfhood.

25. William Least Heat Moon, *Blue Highways: A Journey into America* (Boston: Little, Brown, and Company, 1982), p. 4. Hereafter, all page numbers in parentheses following quotations from this book refer to this edition.

26. Because he is so callow, however, this new form of Joe's self-possession— with Ratso, at least—quickly, if temporarily, runs to another extreme, one no less likely to preclude integral encounter and response: "For the first time in his life he felt himself released from the necessity of grinning and posturing and yearning for the attention of others. Nowadays he had, in the person of Ratso Rizzo, someone who needed his presence in an urgent, almost frantic way that was a balm to something in him that had long been exposed and enflamed and itching to be soothed. God alone know how or why, but he had somehow actually stumbled upon a creature who seemed to worchip him Joe Buck had never before known such power and was therefore ill equipped to administer it. All he could do was taste it over and over again like a sugar-starved child on a sudden mountain of candy: cuss and frown and complain and bitch, and watch Ratso take it. For that's the way power is usually tasted, in the abuse of it. It was delicious and sickening and he couldn't stop himself" (pp. 164–65).

Though perhaps ridding himself of his inner ghosts, Joe's imperial responses to Ratso run parallel to the ways others had earlier treated Joe himself. But compare this transition in Joe to Lasch's points (note 23 above) as he moves from no sense of self to this state of "empowerment": neither will do for the picaro's vocation.

27. Richard Reeves, *American Journey: Traveling with Tocqueville in Search of Democracy in America* (New York: Simon and Schuster, 1982), p. 61. Hereafter, all page numbers in parentheses following quotations from this book refer to this edition.

28. Walker Percy, *The Moviegoer* (New York: Alfred A. Knopf, 1979), pp. 214– 16. Hereafter, all page numbers in parentheses following quotations from this book refer to this edition.

29. In many ways, Least Heat Moon, at least in his narrative persona, either possesses or learns to inculcate a heightened instinct for the picaresque life—often learning from his own mistakes as well as from others' notably falling short of the picaro's defining modes. Thus, while he might well falter from time to time, as when he languishes temporarily in the self-absorption that only returns the world to him in the "blue sparks" of his own image, he usually is able to ply the picaro's trade, to devise tactics of approach, engagement, and response in order to stay the picaresque course. His ways are corrective—and could be instructive—

for faults like those displayed by "the Boss of the Plains" and by others more intent on the picaresque life like Steinbeck, for example (see note 22). While Steinbeck retreats into the hotel for recognition, comfort, and "home," for instance, Least Heat Moon has learned on the road that, after a brief stint at the home of his cousin, "the wanderer's danger is to find comfort. A weekend in Shreveport around friends and security had started to pull me into a warm thrall, to enfold me, to make the wish for the road [seem] a craziness. So it was only memory of times in strange places where the scent of the unknown is sharp that drew me on to the highway again" (p. 145). Answering to the call of "times in strange places," of course, is the new American picaro's modus vivendi. Or, again, when he is asked by a new acquaintance why he is not carrying a dog along for company, Least Heat Moon's responses seem a direct challenge to Steinbeck's penchant for talking with Charley instead of the people on the roadside: "'It isn't traveling,'" he tells the man, "'to cross the country and talk to your pug instead of people along the way. Besides, being alone on the road makes you ready to meet someone when you stop. You get sociable traveling alone'" (p. 31). He or she who runs fast may learn. And, as the narrative indicates, he has from early on learned to spot the connection between the picaro's inveterate "curiosity" and the possibilities of self "cure": "Etymology: *curious,* related to *cure,* once meant 'carefully observant.' . . . Maybe the road could provide a therapy through observation of the ordinary and obvious" (pp. 18).

30. Eddy Harris, *South of Haunted Dreams: A Ride through Slavery's Old Back Yard* (New York: Simon & Schuster, 1993), p. 94.

CHAPTER 5: THE PICARO IN SOCIAL SPACE

1. This chapter thus picks up again, here from a different angle, some of the structures and thematics associated with the "social gallery," one of the defining traits of the picaresque narrative, old and new, discussed above in the third section of chapter 1, the first section of chapter 2, and the first section of chapter 3. In those earlier explorations, the emphases are on the requirements of the literary genre and the treatments rendered in literary presentation. Here the concentration is on the social and social-psychological predicaments of the matter as the picaro sees them, as he embodies them, and as the narrative formations of the picaresque supply a certain kind of evidence about contemporary American social existence.

2. The observations in these paragraphs about the issues of *Harper's* and *Esquire* are derived from an earlier treatment in a different context. See "Recovering American Religious Sensibility: An Introduction," in *Religion and the Life of the Nation,* ed. Rowland A. Sherrill (Urbana: University of Illinois Press, 1992), pp. 3–8.

3. There are numerous primary documents and secondary accounts of the rising tide of public militancy among "divided" Americans during the 1950s and 1960s. Prior to this point in mid-century, a "movement" among African Ameri-

cans existed, of course, but with the highly visible appearance on the scene of Elijah Muhammud, Malcolm Little (Malcolm X), Martin Luther King Jr., Eldridge Cleaver, Huey Newton, Angela Davis, and others—all of whom wanted in their ways to contest the nature and meaning of the society—the intramural lines began to be drawn in fully public ways and the debates to be pitched with increasing vigor. Likewise, while there has perhaps long been an American youth culture (at least since the nineteenth-century invention of "childhood"), the generations coming of age in the decades after mid-century were not simply different but visibly and vociferously in possession of a different set of ideas about American life than those of their elders and those of more "traditional" young people. Of all of the accounts of this emergent cohort, the one that perhaps best interprets the *public* difference is Todd Gitlin, *The Sixties: Years of Hope, Days of Rage* (New York: Bantam Books, 1987). What was then referred to as the publicly discernible movement for "women's liberation" had a significant, early catalyzing moment with the publication of Betty Friedan's *The Feminine Mystique* (New York: W. W. Norton, 1963), and, since then, the quarrels of feminists with American society, of feminists with other styles of womanhood, and indeed of feminists with other feminists have proceeded apace. A signal of just how vocal these and other groups contending with America and within themselves had become as early as the first years of the 1970s was given off in then Vice-President Spiro T. Agnew's appeal to a "silent majority" he fancied was out there, one whose "traditional" values, as he construed them, needed to be mustered to counter the other, sometimes strident groups' claims on the public square.

4. On the new American social and cultural admixture created by recent immigration, the literature is copious. For an important view on the heightened sense of and need for ethnic association among Americans, see Michael Novak's *The Rise of the Unmeltable Ethnics: Politics and Culture in the Seventies* (New York: Macmillan, 1972).

5. On the increasingly fractured and fractious worlds of religious life, Will Herberg's interpretive triumvirate of the American way of religion in *Protestant, Catholic, Jew: An Essay in Religious Sociology* (Garden City, N.Y.: Doubleday, 1955) seemed quite soon not to obtain even after it was thoroughly revised for republication in 1960. The divisions within those main camps of tradition continued to widen in sometimes openly hostile ways, and soon the scholarship on American religion began to acknowledge more fully all kinds of "others" only tangentially related to them or not to be considered as belonging within the standing traditions in any event—everything from older groups newly ascendant like Baha'i, the Latter-Day Saints, and Jehovah's Witnesses, to highly visible new groups and movements like those of Bhagwan Shree Rajneesh, EST (Erhard Seminar Training), Hare Krishna, The Way, the Unification Church, Transcendental Meditation, Scientology / Dianetics, and Eckanar. Writing in 1967, Martin Marty observed: "In search of spiritual expression, people speak in tongues, enter Trappist monasteries, build on Jungian archetypes, go to southern California and join a cult, become

involved 'where the action is' in East Harlem, perceive 'God at work in the world,' see Jesus Christ as the man for others, hope for liberation by the new morality, study phenomenology, share the Peace Corps experience, borrow from cosmic syntheses, and go to church" ("The Spirit's Holy Errand: The Search for a Spiritual Style in Secular America," *Daedelus* 96:1 [Winter 1967]: pp. 99–115). Subsequently and quickly, of course, even Marty's recitation would have to be amplified to make room for the likes of Focus on the Family, Promise Keepers, the new "Satanism" and the new "angelology," Iron John, the new Wicca, Gaia, other forms of goddess religion, the Church of the Holy Laughter, ersatz American shapes of Santeria and Rastafarianism, Scriptures for America, and so on. And the point is that these and other forms of spiritual choice and devotion sometimes create out of their inflammable religious passions not "the peace that passeth all [mis]-understanding" but intensely conflictual attitudes and actions with respect to other religious and cultural outlooks and commitments.

6. See James Davison Hunter, *Culture Wars: The Struggle to Define America* (New York: Basic Books, 1991), and Todd Gitlin, *The Twilight of Common Dreams: Why America Is Wracked by Culture Wars* (New York: Holt, 1995).

7. These include everything from national, well-organized "communities" of interest like Greenpeace, EarthFirst, the National Rifle Association, Promise Keepers, Focus on the Family, and Scriptures for America to more loosely or locally connected groups and movements like Skinheads, local and regional militias, the Posse Comitatus, the Order, the Covenant, Sword, and Arm of the Lord, and so on, to separationist enclaves like the Branch Davidian, the Freemen, and many others.

8. With the publication of E. D. Hirsch's *Cultural Literacy: What Every American Needs to Know* (Boston: Houghton Mifflin, 1987), a book grown out of Hirsch's earlier essay ("Cultural Literacy," *The American Scholar* 32 [1983]), and William J. Bennett's *To Reclaim a Legacy: A Report on the Humanities in Higher Education* (Washington: National Endowment for the Humanities, 1984), a significant episode of the "culture wars" opened in university life as some in academic culture defended the pleas and plans of Hirsch and Bennett for a consensus-America while others repudiated their work altogether as nothing more than coercive efforts of social and cultural management on the part of elitist white males.

9. The biblical myth of Babel, the beginning of multiglossia or the confusion of tongues, appears in Genesis 11. The babble of languages, the linguistic pluralism resulting from God's action on the plain of Shinar in blocking the tower construction symbolic of human autonomy and pride, clearly connects in the biblical account with divisions among the people leading to social and cultural pluralism and its possible pains. In Genesis 10, the sons of Noah disperse themselves and their families into separate "nations" or tribes, with the loss of a universal language soon to follow. These stories provide a beginning, heuristic metaphor for the inquiries into problems of social and cultural discourse in George Steiner, *After Babel: Aspects of Language and Translation* (New York: Oxford University Press,

1975). These problems, of course, are also central for the fields of sociolinguistics and ethnolinguistics. For a "starter set" on the more technical work in these areas, see Nancy Bonvillain, *Language, Culture, and Communication: The Meaning of Messages* (Englewood Cliffs, N.J.: Prentice-Hall, 1993).

10. This depiction is founded on Christopher Lasch's understanding of how the contemporary "self," sensing or perceiving the forces that make for its own minimalization, wraps itself in a protective narcissism. See his *The Minimal Self: Psychic Survival in Troubled Times* (New York: W. W. Norton, 1984), and *The Culture of Narcissism: American Life in an Age of Diminishing Expectations* (New York: W. W. Norton, 1978). This view of the situation and character of the defensive self corresponds to the view of the self playing out in social space for many practitioners in the sociological school of symbolic interaction following on the work of Erving Goffman. See his *The Presentation of the Self in Everyday Life* (New York: Doubleday, 1959) and *Encounters: Two Studies in the Sociology of Interaction* (Indianapolis: Bobbs-Merrill, 1961). For Goffman, the self in social encounter is an actor or performer, covering with masks and role-playing a hidden set of complexes grown out of suspected treacheries in the other selves it encounters.

11. While one might be tempted to conclude that electronic media like television might ameliorate some of the fractious or conflictual attitudes among the contending Americans—just by virtue of technological capacities to bring up-close and potentially familiarizing images of the once more distant and different "strangers" into one's presence in nonthreatening ways—there is reason to think that the opposite frequently occurs, that such electronic familiarity only breeds additional fear or contempt, that the images of the "others" now appearing in one's private territory are only felt as obtrusive, that the "social" propinquity with the alien forced on one by way of the television and other technics of simultaneity only repels. For astute analysis and interpretation of this phenomenon, of the contemptible "other" no longer confined to his or her or their "place," see Joshua Meyrowitz, *No Sense of Place: The Impact of Electronic Media on Social Behavior* (New York: Oxford University Press, 1985), especially Part 3: "The New Social Landscape."

12. Bill Moyers, *Listening to America: A Traveler Rediscovers His Country* (New York: Harper's Magazine Press, 1971), p. vii. Hereafter, all page numbers cited in parentheses following quotations from this book refer to this edition.

13. Walt Harrington, *Crossings: A White Man's Journey into Black America* (New York: HarperCollins, 1992), p. 2. Hereafter, all page numbers cited in parentheses following quotations from this book refer to this edition.

14. James Leo Herlihy, *Midnight Cowboy* (New York: Simon and Schuster, 1965), p. 45. Hereafter, all page numbers cited in parentheses following quotations from this book refer to this edition.

15. John Steinbeck, *Travels with Charley* (New York: Bantam Books, 1963), p. 242. Hereafter, all page numbers cited in parentheses following quotations from this book refer to this edition.

16. During an earlier, more formal trip in 1962 to this same Legion Hall, Moyers reports, he had found it even more contentious, then with *himself* as the target of antagonism. There "to refute charges that the Peace Corps had been infiltrated by Communist provocateurs," Moyers remembers, "several veterans hooted and hissed and laughed as I spoke, and one huge man with a broad forehead descending down a concave face into a long narrow chin kept picking his nose and flicking the fruits of his labor at my feet" (pp. 22–23). The opportunity to reconnoiter the place and attitudes several years later was one reason Moyers chose to return.

17. Mort Rosenblum, *Back Home: A Foreign Correspondent Rediscovers America* (New York: William Morrow, 1989), p. 236. Hereafter, all page numbers cited in parentheses following quotations from this book refer to this edition.

18. W. Hampton Sides, *Stomping Grounds: A Pilgrim's Progress through Eight American Subcultures* (New York: William Morrow, 1992), pp. 64–98. Hereafter, all page numbers cited in parentheses following quotations from this book refer to this edition.

19. Bill Bryson, *The Lost Continent: Travels in Small-Town America* (New York: Harper & Row, 1989), p. 199. Hereafter, all page numbers cited in parentheses following quotations from this book refer to this edition.

20. B. C. Hall and C. T. Wood, *Big Muddy: Down the Mississippi through America's Heartland* (New York: Plume Books, 1992), pp. 123–24. Hereafter, all page numbers cited in parentheses following quotations from this book refer to this edition.

21. Harrison E. Salisbury, *Travels around America* (New York: Walker and Company, 1976), p. 128. Hereafter, all page numbers cited in parentheses following quotations from this book refer to this edition.

22. David Lamb, *A Sense of Place: Listening to Americans* (New York: Random House Times Books, 1993), pp. 72–75. Hereafter, all page numbers cited in parentheses following quotations from this book refer to this edition.

23. Peter Jenkins, *A Walk across America* (New York: William Morrow, 1979), p. 34. Hereafter, all page numbers cited in parentheses following quotations from this book refer to this edition.

24. This is the title of the third chapter in Geertz's *Local Knowledge: Further Essays in Interpretive Anthropology* (New York: Basic Books, 1983).

25. William Least Heat Moon, *Blue Highways: A Journey into America* (New York: Little, Brown, 1982), p. 291. Hereafter, all page numbers cited in parentheses following quotations from this book refer to this edition.

26. There is, for another instance, the case of the ordinarily irenic, professorial Douglas Brinkley, who cannot finally resist, very deep in the narrative, one-upping the political talk he overhears in a pool game in Wall, South Dakota, among some socially reactionary fellows dressed in cowboy gear. After listening for a brief time, he raises a toast in their faces "'to Senator George McGovern, Senator Ted Kennedy, and the Reverend Jessie Jackson—true patriots of this great nation" (*The Majic Bus: An American Odyssey* [New York: Anchor Books, 1994],

p. 479). This little piece of self-assertion quickly makes him think "for a fleeting moment . . . I had gone too far and that they might lynch me" (ibid.). Although the incident ends harmlessly, Brinkley admits to his breach of diffidence: "I had previously tried to avoid this sort of argument" (p. 480). The picaro's self-restraint is a hard-won lesson, about which vigilance is necessary. A quite pointed lesson taught by one episode apparently does not prevent the picaro's committing the same mistakes in later cycles of experience on the tour. Ironically, Least Heat Moon's corrective instruction at the hands of the father of the handicapped boy about the life preparations that difficulty can yield has on that occasion to be learned all over again since it is a lesson the picaro claims already to have learned. In the *immediately* preceding episode of *Blue Highways*, the picaro has uttered a responsive "'I believe you,'" to the Royal Priest of the highway, one Arthur O. Bakke, a hitchhiking evangelist, who tells the picaro that "Hardships are good. They prepare a man'" (p. 291). In cases like this throughout the new American picaresque, the narrative evidence frequently suggests both that the picaro's faults run deep, are not easily rooted out, and simultaneously that this necessity to relearn matters from one experience to the next is a persisting result of the picaro's defining innocence and openness as he enters each experience "brand new," *volver nuevo*, fresh starting.

27. Simply as one out of many possible cases in point, Steinbeck's account of his sense of the proper timing for leaving the road, ceasing and desisting from the picaresque life, indicates just how the picaro's weariness or dread or fear of the all-too-numerous strangers looming ahead can be a factor making one quit the tour. Whelmed by America, he confesses, he simply stops taking social-stock or, in other words, refuses the encounter with the strangers. Camped during a chill overnight in New Mexico, he remembers that "I sat in the seat and faced what I had concealed from myself [about logging more miles than meeting the people]. I was driving myself, pounding out the miles because I was no longer hearing or seeing. I had passed my limit of taking in or, like a man who goes on stuffing in food after he is filled, I felt helpless to assimilate what was fed in through my eyes. . . . For the last hundreds of miles I had avoided people. Even at necessary stops for gasoline I had answered in monosyllables and retained no picture. My eye and brain had welshed on me" (p. 219). In narrative memory, this set of musings occurs with Texas and the Deep South still stretched out ahead of Steinbeck, one reason perhaps he approaches these territories with more than his usual attitudes of dread.

28. For one among a number of notable instances of this kind of picaresque "on the slant," see Richard Farina's *Been Down So Long It Looks like Up to Me* (New York: Viking Press, 1983 [1966]), with an "Introduction" by Thomas Pynchon. Like Pynchon's own *The Crying of Lot 49*, Herlihy's *Midnight Cowboy*, and a number of other examples in fiction, and like Bill Bryson's *The Lost Continent* and others in nonfiction, Farina's permutation of the picaresque narrative covers a heterogeneous social stock, to be sure, but it is less concerned to attune carefully

to the ways and means of the quite particular strangers out there encountered by the picaro (and Gnossos Pappadopoulis encounters a number of *very* strange "others") than to allow the episodic unfolding of the narrative to expose and then to take advantage of the perspectives filtered through the biases, limitations, even neuroses, that are the picaro's peculiar trademarks. If Oedipa Maas increasingly insulates herself in paranoia (a radical form of xenophobia), Farina's picaro re-treats from the strange and threatening "outside" (his "demon monkeys") into a protective self-segregation he attempts to maintain with his late-fifties, early-sixties "cool," a studiously designed and declared "exemption" from or "immu-nity" to social and cultural claims on people that he enacts to secure himself from contemporary madness. Thus in many ways similar to the slanted "outlook" arriving through the anxieties of Pynchon's Oedipa Maas, the "road-epiphanies" Pynchon recognizes in Gnossos Pappadopoulis's picaresque career (p. viii) reach the reader as vistas refracted through the picaro's symptomatic life. The social-psychological work of diagnosis remains intact, but the picara or picaro is clearly the pathological interest. This does not disqualify this or comparable texts from the genre in any measure: indeed, the gathering of social types in the old Anglo-European picaresque was frequently much less intentional than consequential when compared to the often much more purposeful social inventories to be found in the new American picaresque. In the cases of the "slanted" picaro in the new American picaresque, it is simply that, as discussed in chapter 6, the social in-ventory becomes subsidiary to other structural elements and possibilities of the picaresque genre.

29. This is not to obliterate the distinctions achieved and maintained in recent social-scientific understanding among degrees of "strangerness"—that is, the differences among the far off aliens never or not yet encountered, the nearer-to-hand or visually available but anonymous or unknown strangers, the biographi-cally known but personally unknown strangers, the met or named or personally recognized others, the biographically known familiars, and so on—as these have been constructed from Georg Simmel, Arnold Van Gennep, Erving Goffman, to more recent studies. And of course, depending on the *relative* strangeness of the "other," the encounter shifts in timbre, tone, kind, character, and level. For a more recent treatment, with such finer calibrations, see Lyn H. Lofland, *A World of Strangers: Order and Action in Urban Public Space* (Prospect Heights, Ill.: Waveland Press, 1973). These distinctions are real enough in the new American picaresque. Even after being duped and thus angered by Ratso Rizzo on first engagement, Joe Buck, adrift in New York, within what Lofland calls "a multiplication of strangers" in the urban territory, is not furious but relieved, even delighted, when by happenstance, passing through the anonymous throng, he recognizes and encounters again the stranger Rizzo: "Seeing Joe, Ratso closed his eyes quickly and remained as motionless as a person praying for invisibility. But Joe, having wandered homeless and a stranger for three weeks, a long time by the clocks of

limbo, was thrilled to see a face that was known to him. His whole being stopped short, accustoming itself to this keen, unexpected pleasure, and it took more than a moment to remember that Ratso Rizzo was an enemy" (p. 155).

30. Hortense Powdermaker, *Stranger and Friend: The Way of an Anthropologist* (New York: W. W. Norton, 1966). Powdermaker's reflections occasionally pass quickly over the facts that, short of endogamous joining of the natives under view for a lifetime (a form of "going native"), the anthropologist is not likely ever to be more than a marginalized figure in relation to the social center under study and that, in any event, to persist in relation ultimately to enter into friendships with "the natives" is in effect to forego the necessary balance between involvement and detachment that is the stock in trade of the participant-observer method. Deep involvements, implications with the subjects that truncate or alter the field, change the vistas of field work and simply shift the terms away from anthropological inquiry. Much of subsequent ethnographic theory, it seems, is quite decidedly more candid about the anthropologist's status so long as he or she remains an anthropologist, as is revealed by the title of a recent introductory textbook, Paul Bohannan's *We, the Aliens: An Introduction to Cultural Anthropology* (Prospect Heights, Ill.: Waveland Press, 1995).

31. Most of the picaros and picaras, of course, never consciously pose as sociologists or anthropologists amateur or otherwise, even as their rambling surveys often present, in any event, a kind of sporadic social encyclopedia or an inadvertent ethnography. Nevertheless, one significant element of "the social work" of the new American picaresque is that its accumulated coverage of the social gamut and its myriad examples of the faults, false starts, diseased tactics, limits, and predicaments of the picaro's encounter with the pluriform "natives" of America propose to the purview of humanistic social sciences forms of "evidence" it might well consider seriously. For sociology, the admittedly rapid, "unscientific," and slanted social "sampling" of the new American picaresque, anecdotal though it may be, can still provide a form of American "data" to theorists not cowed by opaque evidence or bent on statistical reduction. For the sociologists of symbolic interaction and for forms of anthropology more accustomed in recent years to the stuff of symbolic anthropology, locating dramaturgical elements in the field of observation and in their own modes of exposition is no longer a quaint tactic, and the narrative theater of the picaro's episodic encounters with other American players supplies ample and vivid instruction by way of its dramatic exempla of the complex work, the difficult human conundra, of engaging the stranger in a pluriform social world. See Goffman, note 10 above, and Victor W. Turner, *Dramas, Fields, and Metaphors: Symbolic Action in Human Society* (Ithaca: Cornell University Press, 1974), and *From Ritual to Theatre: The Human Seriousness of Play* (New York: PAJ Publications, 1982). And, as discussed in chapter 6, the problematical or marginal status of the picaro or picara as he or she invariably arrives as "a stranger at the

gate" might well be or become a crucial viewpoint for social-scientific perspectives, just because of the particular placement on the margins through which to see the social reality in unwonted ways.

CHAPTER 6: THE PICARO IN THE NICK OF TIME

1. In many respects, the picaro's life on a more or less continuous series of social borders, the concern of this chapter, makes him very much resemble that "marginal man" described in Everett V. Stonequist's somewhat dated but classic study of figures caught between the conflicting outlooks and claims of two (or more) rather different societies or trapped between an ending past and a significantly altered but not yet born future in a moment of cultural transitions. Belonging nowhere fully in particular but several possible social "places" in part, the figure has *some* loyalty to both (or several) of the discrete social worlds he travels but no complete fidelity to or captivity by any one such world. As Stonequist understands the matter, then, the "marginal man" is not so much a particular, staple "personality type" as he is a "situational character," a figure in whom certain traits emerge as results or effects of living in or moving between—indeed embodying within himself—conflicting societies or severe cultural transitions. The primary "data" for Stonequist are racial and cultural "hybrids," on the bases of whose social situations and potential attributes he first builds his conceptions, but he understands that these are simply the most "vivid" or extreme kinds of cases of people more generally who live on and travel across social margins, boundaries, or borders. See *The Marginal Man: A Study in Personality and Culture Conflict* (1937; New York: Russell & Russell, 1961). Still, Stonequist's work on the "hybrids" will be important for the kinds of considerations in chapter 7. Hereafter, all page numbers in parentheses following quotations from this book refer to the 1961 edition.

2. Thus, if chapter 5 concentrated on the picaro's afflictions in the midst of a painful world of social pluralism, ailments themselves importantly exposed to view as a part of the social diagnoses of the new American picaresque, this chapter takes a focus on some elements of what might be termed the picaro's "social successes" in such a world. As the narrative form also illustrates some attitudes, tactics, and styles for negotiating difficult passages through successions of strangers, it contributes another element to fuller American social self-understanding. Of course, the achievement of these picaresque social skills no doubt depends in large measure on the picaro's also accomplishing the kinds of curative or recuperative road work that enhances his self-integrity, the subject of chapter 4.

3. James Leo Herlihy, *Midnight Cowboy* (New York: Simon and Schuster, 1965), p. 92. Hereafter, all page numbers in parentheses following quotations from this book refer to this edition.

4. Richard Hill, *Riding Solo with the Golden Horde* (Athens: University of Georgia Press, 1994). Hereafter, all page numbers in parentheses following quotations from this book refer to this edition.

5. Robert James Waller, *Border Music* (New York: Warner Books, 1995). Hereafter, all page numbers in parentheses following quotations from this book refer to this edition. The only human "presence" Texas Jack maintains throughout his career on the road is with his old friend, country music artist Bobby McGregor, and this friend "stays" with Jack only through the tape deck in his truck. Bobby McGregor is himself a bit of a picaro, describing himself in the book's epilogue in terms of his leather boot heels that "have clicked across the tiled floors of more airports than I care to think about, fast-fading echoes of a life on the road" (p. 233), and being described in a review of one of his concerts as bearing "'some harbinger of tragedy, something about rain on lonesome highways and gray on the soul'" (p. 239), just the sort of lonely *isolato* companion through music fit for a Texas Jack Carmine in his picaresque exile.

6. Walt Harrington, *Crossings: A White Man's Journey into Black America* (New York: HarperCollins, 1992). Hereafter, all page numbers in parentheses following quotations from this book refer to this edition.

7. William Least Heat Moon, *Blue Highways: A Journey into America* (Boston: Little, Brown, 1982). Hereafter, all page numbers in parentheses following quotations from this book refer to this edition

8. John Steinbeck, *Travels with Charley* (New York: Bantam Books, 1963), pp. 59–62. Hereafter, all page numbers in parentheses following quotations from this book refer to this edition.

9. A powerful case in point appears in *Travels with Charley* when Steinbeck returns after many years to his old friends, his old haunts, on California's Monterey Peninsula, prepared after many miles on the road of confronting complete strangers to hope now for familiar faces. When the time comes, however, he only finds "others" in their places. He does spend some bar time with his old friend Johnny Garcia, who implores him to "'come home,'" but Steinbeck can only reply that this old place is not home, is not the same: "'I will tell you true things. . . . Step into the street—strangers, foreigners, thousands of them. . . . Today I walked the length of Alvarado Street and back to the Calle Principal and I saw nothing but strangers'" (p. 201). Then, later, making his way out of the bar, he reports that, "the double door swung to behind me. I was on Alvarado Street—slashed with neon light—and around me it was nothing but strangers" (p. 203). Later still, he recognizes that he himself is now the "stranger" here, even to those old friends still alive and still "in place" as much as to the unknown others now in the streets: "it was true what I had said to Johnny Garcia—I was the ghost" (p. 205). Most other picaros and picaras have disconcerting moments of such recognition of themselves as strangers. For instance, there is Phaedrus in Robert Pirsig's *Zen and the Art of Motorcycle Maintenance* (New York: Bantam Books, 1975), who has such an overt sense as he and his son enter a cafe in Hague, near the Missouri River, wherein "everything is different except one another, so we look around rather than talk . . . [and listen to] people who seem to know each other and are glancing at *us* because *we*'re new" (pp. 47–48). Or there is Broughton Coburn's recog-

nition as he travels with Aama, the old Nepalese woman. As Americans stare at the old woman, Coburn remembers and tells her about his feelings in Nepal: "'Everyone there looks at *me* just as people here look at you'" (*Aama in America: A Pilgrimage of the Heart* [New York: Anchor Books, 1995], p. 73). Or, for a final instance here, there is Geoffrey O'Gara's entrance into a family reunion he encounters near Smoke Hole, West Virginia: "I could not help feeling a little out of place, since I lacked the long, straight nose or the long, slanted mouth or the circle of chatting friends that marked most family members . . . [and] these people knew at a glance that I was not family" (*A Long Road Home: Journeys through America's Present in Search of America's Past* [New York: W. W. Norton, 1989], p. 59). In the mobile life, the picaro or picara always arrives as the stranger on the scene.

10. For one among a number of literary critics who emphasize the delusory exhilarations of the old picaro's "freedom" and who understand his coming late or soon to a sense of his solitariness and social marginality, see Barbara A. Babcock, "'Liberty's a Whore': Inversions, Marginalia, and Picaresque Narrative," in *The Reversible World: Symbolic Inversion in Art and Society,* ed. Babcock (Ithaca: Cornell University Press, 1978), pp. 95–116.

11. The vocabulary here alluding to road exile and loneliness in pedagogical terms of "curriculum," "lessons," "courses of instruction," "autodidacticism," and so on, is metaphorical, but it should be noted that some new American picaresque narratives do "travel" quite studiously and quite metaphorically within schools and universities. Among others, Richard Hill's Vic Messenger follows his singular journey, as well as into other spheres, through the various disconnected "episodes" of school periods (Art, home room, English, study hall, Music Theory, Band, phys. ed., even detention) at Boca Chica High School in St. Petersburg, Florida; Richard Farina's Gnossos Pappadopoulis in *Been Down So Long It Looks like Up to Me* is an erstwhile if estranged "student" at Athene University (a faintly disguised Cornell); S. E. Hinton's Ponyboy Curtis in *The Outsiders* tracks his orphaned and solitary course in and out of school and even has an assigned English theme figure prominently in the course of his experiential transcript; and, of course, John Barth's title picaro in *Giles Goat-Boy* pursues his alien and surreal studies in a university microcosmic of the world of experience that the subtitle labels "the revised new syllabus." Still, for virtually all of the new American picaros and picaras, in school or not, the "road" is a course of highly individualized instruction.

12. E. Annie Proulx, *Postcards* (New York: Charles Scribner's Sons, 1992), pp. 28–30. Hereafter, all page numbers in parentheses following quotations from this book refer to this edition.

13. Bill Moyers, *Listening to America: A Traveler Rediscovers His Country* (New York: Harper & Row, 1971), pp. 278–80. Hereafter, all page numbers in parentheses following quotations from this book refer to this edition. Such "retreats" as Moyers makes are frequent in the new American picaresque. For the picaro and picara, leaving one episode behind to take again to the ways of mobility is often

a matter of escape when this or that social encounter has soured, proved threatening, or run its course. The sudden awareness of an ending for such encounters is spurred by the picaro's finely tuned senses, the feel for the tenor and dynamic of a situation, that empirical alertness in which the picaro has of necessity been tutored. At times, the scene, as with Moyers, simply comes to seem "unpleasant," and, at other times, the picaro displays a reflex, an instinct, even an allergic reaction, prompting closure, as when E. Annie Proulx's Loyal Blood experiences breathless, choking sensations when too much intimacy seems forthcoming in moments that would compromise his mobile life (pp. 29–30, 52). Less dramatically, Steinbeck remembers in leaving the Monterey Peninsula after seeing himself the ghostly stranger (see note 8 above), "my departure was flight" (p. 205).

14. The more experienced picaros and picaras acquire a kind of knack for spotting those signs or signals telling them that access is possible, that some settings or situations will allow entrance into the strangers' worlds. "I soon discovered," Steinbeck writes, "that if a wayfaring stranger wishes to eavesdrop on a local population the places for him to slip in and hold his peace are bars and churches. . . . A good alternative is the roadside restaurant where men gather for breakfast before going to work or going hunting" (p. 33). And occasionally the figurative "signs of welcome" are, in fact, literally signs of welcome, as Least Heat Moon discovers in Ida, Kentucky. There, in front of a church, the sign reads "'Welcome All God's Children: Thieves, Liars, Gossips, Bigots, Adulterers, Children.'" There, he says, "I felt welcome" (p. 27).

15. One among a number of certain cases in point occurs early in the picaresque career of Richard Hill's Vic Messenger as the school tough, Mickey Moran, has cornered a new student, a "hipster" type, but one Vic does not know, who has found himself in trouble because he is "innocent of local ritual." Into the brink between the two, Vic leaps, making jokes and playfully lying in order to ease the tensions and to extricate the "new guy" from the situation (pp. 12–13). Vic's own "marginal" situation at Boca Chica High—he is himself implicated in "hip" culture but sufficiently proved out in "tough" culture (among others)—has "schooled" him in dealing with collisions between clashing social worlds, and in this, in part connected to both worlds, he exemplifies what Stonequist identifies, in a slightly different context, as the intermediating function best served by the "marginal man": "In such [conflictual] situations, the marginal man is more likely to evolve [if he cares to serve] into some intermediary role which leads to an accommodation and rapprochement between the clashing cultures: he often becomes an interpreter, conciliator, reformer, teacher" (p. 177). This shape and function of the picaro's marginality, associating him with more than one "culture" or dividing him among several cultures and thus opening intermediary prospects, will figure prominently in the next chapter.

16. Lyn H. Lofland, *A World of Strangers: Order and Action in Urban Public Space* (Prospect Heights, Ill.: Waveland Press, 1973). Hereafter, all page numbers in

parentheses following quotations from this book refer to this edition. While one ought not completely to ignore the fact that Lofland writes about the congested sphere of strangers pressed into *urban* settings, there seems little doubt either that the world her sociological work depicts and analyzes is ever more increasingly the *American* world, urban or not. As subsequent expositions will demonstrate, moreover, the new American picaresque—in both its city treks and countryside travels—wrestles in its own way, through the dilemmas of the picaro and picara, with the challenges to social existence posed by the vista of strangers everywhere. In any case, Lofland herself understands that the situation of encountering continuous successions of strangers is not only an urban phenomenon: "In short, while the world of strangers may be particularly characteristic of great cities and their surrounding metropolitan hinterlands, it is not limited to them. The necessity to cope with large numbers of personally-unknown others, the emotionally painful, wrenching shift from tribalist to cosmopolitan, is part of the texture of modern life" (p. 179) in general and at large.

17. Lofland's term "hero" in this framework, of course, is not meant to associate this urbane adventurer with traditional ideas of the hero. In smooth and easy movements among strangers, this cosmopolitan's heroism seems to consist not in his stalwart defense or rescue of a community in tumult and need but mainly in his being able to be the best individual player in the "games" of social tumult and, thus, in his bringing to (idealized) illumination a fuller idea of how the games can be played, itself no mean feat at all.

18. Beyond the acrobatic cosmopolitan, Lofland acknowledges, there are two other figures who are also able to move successfully through the world of strangers, albeit in much more accidental ways. Both "hicks" or innocents and "eccentrics" seem to be able "to operate amidst strangers with minimal risk" and even to evoke response from others just because the former, protected by ignorance, often goes with impunity or even sympathy where more knowledgeable people (including the cosmopolitan) might reasonably fear to tread, and the latter, protected by alarming appearance or behavior, seems to be able to cut a wide swath among strangers who often defer to this obvious oddball among them. The new American picaresque, of course, counts among its picaros a number of hicks/innocents like the title character of Winston Groom's *Forrest Gump,* Joe Buck in Herlihy's *Midnight Cowboy,* and the "One-Eyed Mack" in Jim Lehrer's *Kick the Can,* and, for eccentric picaros, few can match John Kennedy Toole's Ignatius J. Reilly in appearance and behavior in *A Confederacy of Dunces* or John Steinbeck in appearance in *Travels with Charley.* The crucial point, of course, is that such waifs and eccentrics often accomplish a kind of accidental access to strangers when other, more knowing or deliberate types fail at it. Innocent or oddity can alike appear "lost," as Steinbeck is aware, and can thus elicit a stranger's willing responsiveness.

19. The kind of "indifference" remarked here is comparable at least to Walter Lippmann's term "disinterestedness" when he points out the need for a recog-

nition of the ideal of a person's objectivity, his or her unimplicated, or detached, or non-personalizing approach to conflicting issues and values in a modern world wherein the authoritative moral centers have been eroded by "the acids of modernity." It does not mean "uninterestedness" in the world, only, rather, a form of engagement with experience in which, in at least prefatory ways, the personal passions are rendered innocent or, that is, stripped of totalizing self-interest and in which "disinterest" itself is seen as a value. In order to be able to approach any transpersonal situation at all in "moral" terms, one must, in short, cultivate the habit of the mature personality of reserving judgment for the sake of weighing the contrary sides of things in terms of their own integrity prior to any moral evaluation or ethical decision making. See Lippmann, *A Preface to Morals* (New York: Macmillan Company, 1929), especially pp. 204, 206, 209–10, 221, 225, 230–31. And see also the following note.

20. *The Sociology of Georg Simmel,* trans. and ed. by Kurt H. Wolf (New York: Free Press, 1950). This insight appears in Simmel's classic essay "The Stranger," pp. 402–8. Of the stranger who "moves on," Simmel writes, "he often receives the most surprising openness—confidences which sometimes have the character of a confessional and which would be carefully withheld from a more closely related person" (p. 404). This sharing of confidences, Simmel notes, is connected to the stranger's perceived objectivity. Again, however, this "disinterestedness" is not non-participation: "it is a positive and specific kind of participation" (p. 404) made more possible by the situation and role of the stranger. He is "freer practically and theoretically; he surveys conditions with less prejudice; his criteria for them are more general and more objective ideals; he is not tied down in his action by [local] habit, piety, and precedent" (p. 405). As with a kind of Lippmannian "distinterestedness," (see note 19) the picaro's realization of such Simmelian "objectivity" is a function and effect of his unbondedness, his exile, his unimplication.

21. Ninian Smart, *Worldviews: Crosscultural Explorations of Human Beliefs* (New York: Charles Scribner's Sons, 1983). As Smart puts it, the work of "structured empathy" is not simply or only the work of feeling—emotional participation in the sensible life of another—but is also rational in the sense that the effort has to be made "to comprehend the structure of another's world" (p. 16), that is, the background-views or belief-systems that are the sensical *context* of the other's feelings. See also the following two notes.

22. Richard Hill's picaro, Vic Messenger, perhaps because of his honed abilities as a jazz saxophonist, represents an illuminating example of this capacity to relinquish self-assertions temporarily in order to play the scene in its own terms. In several episodes of *Riding Solo with the Golden Horde,* his own "border music" (to borrow Waller's title) allows Vic to gain access just by way of his willingly entering the others' music, as for instance when he joins the band at the fraternity party (pp. 59–61), though he had agreed to go to the party only "as an observer and social critic" (p. 57). Even his own "riffs," solo improvisations, signal

his alertness to the music and the scene around him as much as his own originality: "Vic experienced a kind of surrender in which the important part of him had retreated behind the other part that was doing what the crowd demanded, giving just enough signals for the remote parts to keep working while he watched from there" (p. 61). For another kind of example, Least Heat Moon's afternoon of conversation with Barbara Pierre in *Blue Highways* (pp. 133–37) represents—in terms of its dialogical and reciprocating participation—another form of self-suspension, achieving what Ninian Smart calls the "epoche" (p. 24) for the sake of attuning to the other in acts of "structured empathy." Question follows upon question from the picaro, and his own, few observations are designed to elicit the woman's own fuller responses. Not only does this episode exemplify the work of involvement-detachment necessary to enter others' world views but also the shapes of that "interrogatory converse" discussed below. Of course, numerous, comparable scenes and episodes are repeated throughout the new American picaresque in various forms. From time to time, it also becomes clear that the picaro's ability in the empathetic arts has been aided by some once-stranger who has extended an empathetic hand, as when the black jazz singer Betty Boop puts a reassuring hand on Vic Messenger's back when he struggles with her band's music or when Least Heat Moon discovers early in his trip from J. M. Wheeler that "it's always those who live on little who are the ones to ask you to dinner" (p. 30).

23. Hortense Powdermaker, *Stranger and Friend: The Way of an Anthropologist* (New York: W.W. Norton & Company, 1966), pp. 291ff. As Powdermaker uses the phrase "psychological mobility," she means it to refer to the anthropologist's ability in the field to be able in a particular society to meet "hierarchical situations where[in] it is necessary to move easily between different levels in the power structure" (p. 291). But a broader sense of the term is required in characterizing this attribute in the new American picaro in order to discern it not only as a trait of personal stability that allows the figure to move with equilibrium between the "high" and the "low" social strata (like Vic Messenger's moving between the local artist "Tonto" and the world-famous "Satchmo" or Mort Rosenblum's moving between Carl Yannick and J. R. Simplot) but also a feature required to move, to move rapidly, and to move with sustained, empathetic balance across the borders of the numerous social and often conflicting "world views" in contemporary America. See also note 21.

24. George Steiner, *After Babel: Aspects of Language and Translation* (New York: Oxford University Press, 1975). For Steiner, all acts at the effort of understanding and communicating with another human being's "text" (written or spoken, from the past or in the moment, in one's own language or not) are at bottom acts of translation of the "speech-message" (p. 47): "no two historical epochs, no two social classes, no two localities use words and syntax to signify exactly the same things, to send identical signals of valuation and inference. Neither do two human beings" (p. 45). Larger or smaller degrees of "Time, distance, disparities in

outlook or assumed reference, make this act [of translation] more or less difficult. Where the difficulty is great enough, the process passes from reflex to conscious technique" (p. 47). For a socio- and ethno-linguistic approach to the very rudiments of "communicative interaction," see Nancy Bonvillain, *Language, Culture, and Communication: The Meaning of Messages* (Englewood Cliffs, N.J.: Prentice-Hall, 1993). Operating between or among varieties of "world views," of course, the picaro's or picara's translative efforts of understanding are pinned in a crucial way on his or her capacities for "structured empathy" (see note 21), not only to enter the others' worlds but to "deliver" or "translate" the other to the reader.

25. To move out of the status of complete stranger into the status of *engagement* with the other is also to move into the figurement of what Stonequist calls the "internationalist." Still marginal with respect to whatever social center he engages, this figure is a prime example of the occasion for "translation" just by dint of his or her being the "marginal" person. As Stonequist writes, "the individual who penetrates deeply enough into a foreign culture becomes a richer personality. He readily shifts from one language to another; from one set of habits, attitudes and values to another. Thus he is in a position to look at problems from more than one viewpoint, and to see the essential ethnocentrism of each" (pp. 178–79). But "engagement" is the key, without which the marginal person "can be confused with the *deracine* cosmopolitan . . . [who] is culturally adrift . . . lives on the surface of life, becomes blase and easily bored, and restlessly moves about looking for new thrills" (p. 179). In order to carry out the entire work of the new civility, in short, the picaro or picara must go well beyond *mere* cosmopolitanism (see note 26). Obviously, some picaros, like Bill Bryson in *The Lost Continent*, remain only the deracinated cosmopolitan, refusing to engage the world and, like Bryson, treating it only under the aegis of a smug, self-asserting dismissiveness. The point here surely is that if a concerted empathy is necessary for engagement with the other, this engagement bespeaks at least temporary, if somewhat "indifferent" or "disinterested," involvement or participation. Further discussion of the virtues of the bi- and multi-cultural figure Stonequist describes more precisely appears in chapter 7.

26. To accomplish these acts of civility, empathy, and translation, of course, does not require that the picaro or picara develop either solidarity with or even compassion for the others met en route. Even Least Heat Moon, who takes occasional recourse to Walt Whitman's expansive efforts at the inclusion into himself of all others, recognizes that the tour is too fast, that the others are too numerous, and that one cannot make room in one's feelings for everything and everyone. What is fundamentally required by the new civility, rather, is *respect* in the engagement for the other in all of his or her sheer and finally irreducible otherness. Like Lippmann, the works of Smart, Powdermaker, Steiner, and Clifford Geertz thus in their several ways extend the requirements of this form of "civility" and "translation" with respect to the strangers quite past Lofland's "new cosmopolitanism" and its skills and games to include a new chapter in what Geertz refers to as "the

social history of the moral imagination" (*Local Knowledge: Further Essays in Interpretive Anthropology* [New York: Basic Books, 1983], chapter 2). Each sees from her or his perspective that the encounter with the stranger is not only a social but a moral occasion, one that elicits a complex effort of respectful translation in attempting to determine, as Geertz puts it, "how the deeply different can be deeply known without becoming any less different" (p. 48) or, for the picaro in his own decidedly more rapid ethnographic work, how the stranger can be known at all without reducing him or her only to the picaro's terms.

27. David Rounds, *Celebrisi's Journey* (Los Angeles: J. P. Tarcher, 1982), p. 128. Hereafter, all page numbers in parentheses following quotations from this book refer to this edition.

28. Mort Rosenblum, *Back Home: A Foreign Correspondent Rediscovers America* (New York: William Morrow, 1989), pp. 237–39.

29. Richard Reeves, *American Journey: Traveling with Tocqueville in Search of Democracy in America* (New York: Simon and Schuster, 1982), pp. 257–60.

30. Although the idea cannot be developed here, there is some reason to think that the picaro's and picara's styles of successful communicative interactions with the strangers met along the sides of their various roads also have about them a "ritual" aspect or dimension, especially when there is a kind of "liminal" episode at the point of encounter and engagement and when there results some at least temporary affective bonding. See Victor W. Turner, *The Ritual Process: Structure and Anti-Structure* (1969; Ithaca: Cornell University Press, 1977), especially the chapter entitled "Liminality and Communitas." In another work, Turner discusses pilgrimage as "liminoid" or "quasi-liminal" experience associated with affliction rituals, but, while the picaro *and* pilgrim might well share a certain kind of road suffering, their ways of being on the road are quite different indeed. See Victor and Edith Turner, *Image and Pilgrimage in Christian Culture* (New York: Columbia University Press, 1978), especially the chapter entitled "Pilgrimage as a Liminoid Phenomenon."

CHAPTER 7: HOMO VIATOR, HOMO SPECTANS

1. In the final three chapters of this study, devoted to the cultural work of the new American picaresque, "culture" is used in the broadest anthropological sense to refer to the "human-made world," that is the numerous and disparate constructions people, consciously or not, have invented or devised to situate themselves in their natural and inherited environments, to understand and express themselves in both their material or functional and their more creative lives, to distinguish themselves in their forms of meaning and behavior from those with other identities and styles, and to interpret themselves in situ, in continuity and change, in relation to those forms of tradition giving them their past, bearing on their present circumstances, and conditioning their movement toward the future.

2. Giles Gunn, *Thinking across the American Grain: Ideology, Intellect, and the New*

Pragmatism (Chicago: University of Chicago Press, 1992), p. 1. Of course, Gunn is pointing generally to the cultural utility, indeed the cultural "health," of an intellectual situation in which a culture itself, first, supplies its critical thinkers or cultural critics with more than one set of terms for self-understanding, thus foiling any completely hegemonic outlook, and, second, even when one set of terms might seem decidedly dominant ideologically, reveals to view certain fissures or contradictions in those terms, thus exposing new or different interpretive possibilities. Although certainly not a species of cultural criticism in any intellectually systematic form, the new American picaresque might well be thought to provide "extra" or "other" sets of terms and, as the third section of this chapter proposes, sometimes to work on such slants as to illumine stress-cracks in some largely dominating conventions of American understanding.

3. E. Annie Proulx, *Postcards* (New York: Scribner, 1992), passim. Hereafter, all page numbers in parentheses following quotations from this book refer to this edition.

4. George Meegan, *The Longest Walk: An Odyssey of the Human Spirit* (New York: Dodd, Mead, and Company, 1988), pp. 282–83. Hereafter, all page numbers in parentheses following quotations from this book refer to this edition. Meegan is not American by birth, of course, and the travels recorded in this book are not confined to the United States, but, as a case in point in the present context, he is a concerted taker of inventory, large items and small, in the picaresque manner.

5. David Rounds, *Celebrisi's Journey* (Los Angeles: J. P. Tarcher, 1982), p. 129. Hereafter, all page numbers in parentheses following quotations from this book refer to this edition.

6. Geoffrey O'Gara, *A Long Road Home: Journeys through America's Present in Search of America's Past* (New York: W. W. Norton, 1989), 42. Hereafter, all page numbers in parentheses following quotations from this book refer to this edition.

7. Jonathan Yardley, *States of Mind: A Personal Journey through the Mid-Atlantic* (New York: Villard Books, 1993), p. 21. Hereafter, all page numbers in parentheses following quotations from this book refer to this edition.

8. James Crumley, *The Last Good Kiss* (New York: Pocket Books, 1978), p. 177. Hereafter, all page numbers in parentheses following quotations from this book refer to this edition.

9. Earl Thompson, *Caldo Largo* (New York: Signet Books, 1977), p. 30. Hereafter, all page numbers in parentheses following quotations from this book refer to this edition.

10. Jim Lehrer, *Kick the Can* (New York: G. P. Putnam's Sons, 1988), p. 171. Hereafter, all page numbers in parentheses following quotations from this book refer to this edition.

11. Pete Davies, *Storm Country: A Journey through the Heart of America* (New York: Random House, 1992), p. 14. Hereafter, all page numbers in parentheses following quotations from this book refer to this edition.

12. Some examples of the new American picaresque confine the picaro's or

picara's movement largely to a single large city, but, like their less restricted brothers and sisters on tour, they nevertheless locate those wide varieties of folk and forms making for abundant inventory. Among others, John Kennedy Toole's Ignatius J. Reilly in *A Confederacy of Dunces*, E. L. Doctorow's title picaro in *Billy Bathgate*, Richard Hill's Vic Messenger in *Riding Solo with the Golden Horde*, Jay McInerney's anonymous picaro in *Bright Lights, Big City*, Barbara Kingsolver's Taylor Greer in *The Bean Trees*, Ralph Ellison's nameless picaro in *Invisible Man*, Marilynne Robinson's Sylvie in *Housekeeping*, J. D. Salinger's Holden Caulfield in *The Catcher in the Rye*, and Walker Percy's Binx Bolling in *The Moviegoer*, preponderantly and respectively ramble about New Orleans, New York, St. Petersburg, New York, Tucson, New York, Fingerbone, New York, and New Orleans.

13. Thomas H. Rawls, *Small Places: In Search of a Vanishing America* (Boston: Little, Brown and Company, 1990), p. 12. Hereafter, all page numbers in parentheses following quotations from this book refer to this edition. With all of the nostalgia Rawls expresses for small-town, off the main highway, rustic America, he might find his counterpoint in Mark Winegardner. For the latter, the "real" American road zooms into a different kind of place, holds out a different kind of Americana. This is, Winegardner contends, "why I find so many American travel books pompous and sentimental: they focus on out-of-the-way hamlets and undertake microcosmic studies of 'our country,' thereby making us long for the past. That's valid, I suppose, but I'm more interested in the macrocosm. I don't doubt that Nameless, Tennessee [a reference to Least Heat Moon's *Blue Highways*], can be a splendid place to visit. But if everyone goes to Gatlinburg, Graceland and Disneyland, to Ruby Falls, the Sears Tower and the French Quarter, then it's irrational to dismiss out of hand what can be learned in such tourist meccas. And while I like traveling the back roads as well as the next person, the road we all share—our common road—is the turnpike, with its toll-booths and off-ramps, its service plazas and truckstops, its residents and its transients" (*Elvis Presley Boulevard: From Sea to Shining Sea, Almost* [New York: Atlantic Monthly Press, 1987]), p. 11. Hereafter, all page numbers in parentheses following quotations from this book refer to this edition.

14. Frances FitzGerald, *Cities on a Hill: A Journey through Contemporary American Cultures* (New York: Simon and Schuster, 1986). In The Castro in San Francisco, FitzGerald spots inventory within inventory in a gay parade, among the 138 contingents making it up, "the Gay Latino Alliance, or GALA . . . dancing down the street to mariachi music . . . [and] just behind them a group representing the gay Jewish synagogue . . . closely followed by a Marilyn Monroe look-alike on stilts batting six-inch-long eyelashes," and, among others, "the Order of Displaced Okies," "The Local Lesbian Association Kazoo Marching Band," "Dykes on Bikes," "the Gay Pagans, the Free Beach Activists, the Zimbabwe Medical Drive, and the Alice B. Toklas Democratic Club" (pp. 28–29). In Falwell's Lynchburg, Virginia, FitzGerald locates in the home of Gary Hunt, a ministerial student working with the Thomas Road Youth Ministries, a kitchen full of young-

sters, Hunt just having brought a number of boys "in from a basketball game outside [to where] . . . his wife, Angie, was showing the girls how to bake chocolate-chip cookies," all of this "in a confusion of twelve-year olds" (p. 139). "At the Sun City Inn on a Saturday night," FitzGerald observes, "the women lined up at the well-stocked buffet or dancing to organ music with their husbands wear flowered dresses in pink and green, pearls, and low-heeled sandals. On such occasions, the men—all close-cropped and clean-shaven—dress even more colorfully, in checkered trousers and white shoes, red or green linen slacks, pink shirts with blue blazers, madras ties, and the occasional madras jacket" (p. 217). And at the Rajneeshpuram in Oregon, FitzGerald catches a view of the *sannyasins,* those well-off devotees of the Bagwan Rajneesh, "all of them dressed in various shades of red," the men "bronzed and bearded, the women rosy-cheeked with their hair flying. . . . Handsome and healthy-looking, they appeared to work in a kind of good-humored chaos" (p. 255).

15. W. Hampton Sides, *Stomping Grounds: A Pilgrim's Progress through Eight American Subcultures* (New York: William Morrow & Company, 1992), p. 165. Hereafter, all page numbers in parentheses following quotations from this book refer to this edition.

16. David Lamb, *Stolen Season: A Journey through America and Baseball's Minor Leagues* (New York: Warner Books, 1991), p. 63. As the subtitle indicates, Lamb sees a connection between the small-town manifestation of the so-called national pastime and a "forgotten" America, remembered from his youth. Hereafter, all page numbers in parentheses following quotations from this book refer to this edition.

17. A fair number of examples of the new American picaresque narrative are, like those by Lamb (baseball), Winegardner (Elvisiana), Setterberg (literary sites), and Whaley (redneck culture), bent mainly on what might be called "thematic travel," travels that attempt to "grasp" America, no matter how concertedly the respective "theme" is followed. For some examples, John William's America tour (he is British) in *Into the Badlands: Travels through Urban America* (London: HarperCollins, 1993) takes him to the areas "storied" by crime- and detective-fiction to talk with the authors operating in this genre (Carl Hiassen, James Crumley, Sara Paretsky, and others); Alex Heard travels venues of American millennialist or "final days" outlooks in *Apocalypse Pretty Soon: Travels in End-Time America* (New York: W. W. Norton, 1999); Richard Reeves's *American Journey* (New York: Simon and Schuster, 1982) takes a picaresque course following the earlier travels in America of Alexis de Tocqueville; Karal Ann Marling tracks down "Colossi," those giant "figures" (ducks, cows, people, and so on) Americans have constructed at roadside in her quasi-picaresque tour in *The Colossus of Roads: Myth and Symbol along the American Highway* (Minneapolis: University of Minnesota Press, 1984). Or, for a final instance here, see Jim Lehrer's *A Bus of My Own* (New York: G. P. Putnam's Sons, 1992), in which the picaresque adventure follows from Lehrer's background in buses and bus memorabilia and into a narrative quest for such, elements of

which go to explain the bus "expertise" displayed by "The One-Eyed Mack," the young picaro in Lehrer's novel *Kick the Can.* Whether after crime, colossi, penal institutions, or buses, however, the picaros and picaras take not only that stock but broader inventory of America, often waylaid, as it were, by sights and sounds and places and people not on the thematic itinerary. All seem prepared to follow aspects of Lehrer's picaresque advice toward the end of his bus quest: "Don't travel by itinerary. Don't have to be somewhere at a certain time. It prevents you from following a 'Train Museum' sign down a road or taking an impromptu afternoon nap on a picnic table in a city park" (p. 226). For a critical account of one kind of "theme" in some American road narratives, namely the theme of landscape "ruminations," see Kris Lackey *RoadFrames: The American Highway Narrative* (Lincoln: University of Nebraska Press, 1997).

18. Michael Wallis, *Route 66: The Mother Road* (New York: St. Martin's Press, 1990), pp. 62–63. Hereafter, all page numbers in parentheses following quotations from this book refer to this edition.

19. Jim Lilliefors, *Highway 50: Ain't That America* (Golden, Colo.: Fulcrum Publishing, 1993), p. 17. Hereafter, all page numbers in parentheses following quotations from this book refer to this edition.

20. George Stewart, *U.S. 40: Cross Section of the United States of America* (1953; Westport, Conn.: Greenwood Press, 1973), p. 141. Hereafter, all page numbers in parentheses following quotations from this book refer to this edition.

21. Thomas R. Vale and Geraldine R. Vale, *U.S. 40 Today: Thirty Years of Landscape Change in America* (Madison: University of Wisconsin Press, 1983), p. 11. Hereafter, all page numbers in parentheses following quotations from this book refer to this edition. Although even less picaresque in tone and outlook than Stewart's or the Vales' narrative and constricted to the Indiana patch of the highway, Thomas J. Schlereth's *U.S. 40: A Roadscape of the American Experience* (Indianapolis: Indiana Historical Society, 1985) is likewise committed to the road, as his subtitle indicates, because of its disclosive character, when properly traveled, regarding American existence. If Stewart, the Vales, and Schlereth are prone to less narrative "vagabondage" than many another picaresque figure, they each nonetheless display forms of the picaro's and picara's attentiveness, curiosity, willingness to trespass, unwillingness respecting hard itinerary, and reluctance to sort the "high" from the "low." In all of this, each seems disposed to take inventory of America along the road as Stewart himself described the requirement: "we can forget neither the ancient trees that shadow it, nor the roadside weeds that grow upon its shoulders. We must not reject the wires that parallel it, or the billboards that flaunt themselves along its margins. We must accept the slums of 'Truck Route' as well as the skyscrapers of 'City Route,' and the fine churches and houses of 'Alternate Route.' We must not avert our eyes even from the effluvia of the highway itself—the broken tires, and rusting beer cans, and smashed jackrabbits. Only by considering it all . . . shall we come to know in cross section, the United States of America" (p. 5).

22. Perhaps the most consummately diffident, if more or less literal, stock-taker in the cumulative new American picaresque is Larry McMurtry's "Cadillac Jack" McGriff, whose life as a "scout," a procurer and trader of odds and ends, elegant and tacky, anything valuable to someone, takes him back and forth across the length of the land. For the most part, Jack has no personal or acquisitive interest in the "things" he scouts: they are simply the ostensible raison d'être for his being always on the road. And, on the road, taking enormous inventory just by way of his passion, he travels "in a pearl-colored Cadillac with peach velour interior, a comfortable vehicle in which to roam America" (*Cadillac Jack* [New York: Simon and Schuster, 1982], p. 3; hereafter, all page numbers in parentheses following quotations from this book refer to this edition). "Most scouts specialize," he reports, "but not me. I'm too curious, too restless, too much in love with the treasure hunt," and what he has bought and sold, quite beyond what he sees on the hunt, begins to suggest the size and scope of the narrative inventory: "continually crossing and recrossing the continent . . . I've sold Italian lace and Lalique glass, French snuff-boxes and pre–World War II Coke bottles, English silver and Chinese porcelain, Purdey shotguns and Colt revolvers, Apache basketry and Turkish ceramics, Greek cheese-boards, Coptic pottery, Depression glass, Peruvian mummy-wrappings, kilims, Aubussons, icons, Tibetan textiles, camel-pads, *netsuke*, scarabs, jewels, rare tools, early cameras and typewriters, barometers, Sevres, miniatures, lacquers, screens, tapestries, classic cars, railroadiana, Disneyana, Eskimo carvings, Belgian firearms, musical instruments, autographs, Swiss music boxes, Maori war clubs, and so on," all bought, sold, or traded in America from that "grid of dealers, collectors, accumulators, pack rats, antique shops, thrift shops, junk shops, estate sales, country auctions, bankruptcy sales, antique shows, flea markets, and garage sales that covers America like a screen" (p. 4).

23. John Steinbeck, *Travels with Charley: In Search of America* (New York: Bantam Books, 1963), p. 63. Hereafter, all page numbers in parentheses following quotations from this book refer to this edition. For his own part as picaro, Geoffrey O'Gara is comparably inclined to select a scene, a place, a thing, toward which to direct himself generally but to pursue it largely as an excuse simply to stay on the move: "travelers of my sort," he observes, "are always ready to aim ourselves at a weightless objective and take flight, because flight itself is the stimulant" (p. 195).

24. For another instance, among many possible examples, Mort Rosenblum attempts to work from the vantage-point of the "considerable remove" by taking advantage of the marginal status he has by virtue of long absence from his homeland and by seeing the place anew with as much as possible of his trained objectivity as a journalist: "as a foreign correspondent, an outsider, I would say what I saw. As an insider coming home, I would say what I felt" (*Back Home: A Foreign Correspondent Rediscovers America* [New York: William Morrow & Company, 1989], p. 15). Hereafter, all page numbers in parentheses following quotations from this book refer to this edition. In either case, like O'Gara, he wants to

remain unobliged to see and feel as the locals see and feel and, thus, to offer a different vantage on things.

25. Peter Jenkins, *A Walk across America* (New York: William Morrow & Company, 1979), p. 70. Hereafter, all page numbers in parentheses following quotations from this book refer to this edition.

26. James Leo Herlihy, *Midnight Cowboy* (New York: Simon and Schuster, 1965), pp. 174ff. Hereafter, all page numbers in parentheses following quotations from this book refer to this edition.

27. Bill Moyers, *Listening to America: A Traveler Rediscovers His Country* (New York: Harper's Magazine Press, 1971), pp. 241–42. Hereafter, all page numbers in parentheses following quotations from this book refer to this edition.

28. Peter DeVries, *The Blood of the Lamb* (1961; New York: Penguin Books, 1982), p. 70. Hereafter, all page numbers in parentheses following quotations from this book refer to this edition.

29. David Lamb, *A Sense of Place: Listening to Americans* (New York: Random House, 1993), p. 179. Hereafter, all page numbers in parentheses following quotations from this book refer to this edition.

30. After dealing with the obnoxious bartender, for instance, Mark Winegardner does not launch into critique. Once out of the bar and on the streets of Central City again, his friend Bob says about Rabbit "Of all the people I ever met" and then pauses, and Winegardner's response, closing the episode, is simply "He was one of them" (p. 140). For another, more serious kind of example, as O'Gara leaves New Orleans he drives through a scene on the streets in which an old disoriented, indigent man, is being tormented by a number of people. Cursing and swinging a knife about, the man seems to O'Gara "more dangerous to himself than anyone else," but the episode ends without further comment: "I saw a sign for the bridge, turned right, and was gone" (p. 139). Regarding such picaresque diffidence, the point is not that the picaros and picaras lack feeling—only, rather, that in their narrative lives the record of "what they see" generally has far greater priority than even momentary evaluation of what has been seen. Along with other items, bartender Rabbit and the old street man enter the picaresque inventory without judgments beyond those the reader might be disposed to add.

31. Bill Terry, *The Watermelon Kid* (Baton Rouge: Louisiana State University Press, 1984), p. 5. Hereafter, all page numbers in parentheses following quotations from this book refer to this edition.

32. Bo Whaley, *Rednecks and Other Bona Fide Americans* (Nashville, Tenn.: Rutledge Hill Press, 1986), p. 4. Hereafter, all page numbers in parentheses following quotations from this book refer to this edition.

33. B. C. Hall and C. T. Wood, *Big Muddy: Down the Mississippi through America's Heartland* (New York: Plume Books, 1993), pp. 202–3. As the forlorn woman is counted into the American inventory, Hall and Wood cannot maintain their usual picaresque disengagement from the scenes they witness (see note 30 above): "We have to watch ourselves down here sometimes or we start getting mad at things.

Mad at Vicksburg for letting its riverfront sink so wretchedly low. Mad at people back there for selling each other out. Mad mostly mad at Roy for running away and leaving that poor girl alone and hungry" (p. 203). Even as they state their anger, however, their very way of stating it—"we have to watch ourselves"— suggests their more usual picaresque propensity to remain unimplicated.

34. Andrei Codrescu, *Road Scholar: Coast to Coast Late in the Century* (New York: Hyperion, 1993), pp. 118–19. Hereafter, all page numbers in parentheses following quotations from this book refer to this edition.

35. All of the quotations of Rosenblum following immediately here are from this "Author's Note" preceding the table of contents.

36. This is not in the least to disparage the Salisburys, the Lambs, Steinbecks, or those others who travel America with perhaps higher degrees of social confidence than the nonwhite, nonmale, nonprivileged picaros and picaras. Even these more comfortable picaros venture the journey, indeed often elect to go rediscover what makes up America. But, clearly, the white, secure male on course, depending on his itinerary, is far less liable to feel extreme senses of picaresque contingency and far more likely to work with an "optics" of status and convention than more marginalized picaros. Mike McIntyre might very well record a trip across America in which every American encountered is more or less uniformly generous (*The Kindness of Strangers: Penniless across America* [New York: Berkley Books, 1996]), but this is certainly not the case for another white man, Lars Eighner, whose condition of homelessness gives him nothing of the social ease McIntyre can employ and much less is it the case for, say, Eddy L. Harris or Chet Fuller or John A. Williams, black men on route.

37. The matter of social advantage or disadvantage is, thus, also one of context. Vic Messenger and Walt Harrington, among others, are utterly marginalized in the particular worlds they travel: their "white," quite middle-class entries into black America simply forfeit the racial privilege they might have had on another picaresque itinerary, make them peripheral figures at best on their current courses in, respectively, Richard Hill's *Riding Solo with the Golden Horde* (Athens: University of Georgia Press, 1994) and Harrington's *Crossings: A White Man's Journey into Black America* (New York: HarperCollins, 1992).

38. The phrase "situationally disadvantaged" is borrowed from Carol Brooks Gardner, *Passing By: Gender and Public Harassment* (Berkeley: University of California Press, 1995). As Gardner uses the term, it refers clearly and immediately to those persons even temporarily made vulnerable in some public setting because their status, perhaps much more secure in some other social context, has been dislocated. Women, of course, suffer such disadvantage more or less continuously in the public sphere, but Gardner understands that "gender" in these terms is code for "race," "disability," "age," "appearance," and so on. By displaying a certain bravado and drinking a roadside beer, the young, white male "hippie," Peter Jenkins, might work through his situational disadvantage when cornered by the four rednecks in Shelby County, Alabama (pp. 221–25), but it is

decidedly more difficult to imagine such a "solution" to public harassment by a picaro like Eddy L. Harris or by picaras like Tom Robbins's Sissy Hankshaw or Laurel Lee in her *Godspeed: Hitchhiking Home* (San Francisco: Harper & Row, 1988). Even a "tough" picara like Barbara Kingsolver's Taylor Greer—consistently adept at meeting difficult situations—is perfectly aware that the gender "difference" ramifies as a category while she deals with a roadside mechanic who calls her "sassy," attempts to scare her with talk of tarantulas, hangs around "smoking and making me nervous," forces her to wonder "why men thought they could impress a woman by making the world out to be such a big dangerous deal," and leads her to decide "he was dumber than he was mean" (*The Bean Trees* [New York: Harper & Row, 1988], p. 38; hereafter, all page numbers in parentheses following quotations from this book refer to this edition). And the point is that when such "difference" is magnified by "situation," what is seen will be seen from an even further margin, with the slant or from the vantage point of such disadvantage.

39. S. E. Hinton, *The Outsiders* (New York: Viking Press, 1967), p. 149. Hereafter, all page numbers in parentheses following quotations from this book refer to this edition.

40. Marilynne Robinson, *Housekeeping* (New York: Farrar, Strauss & Giroux, 1980), p. 85. Hereafter, all page numbers in parentheses following quotations from this book refer to this edition. Once Sylvie appears on the scene in Fingerbone and begins to enact the peripatetic habits of a picara within the town's limitations, it grows increasingly clear that her gender "disadvantage" makes all the "difference": her late-night circumambulations, her intrepid pushing along the town's outer edges, are strange enough indeed in small-town America but are all the more strange or marginal forms of behavior for the townspeople when exhibited by a woman.

41. Anne K. Kaler's *The Picara: From Hera to Fantasy Heroine* (Bowling Green, Ohio: Bowling Green State University Popular Press, 1991) occasionally provides useful, if undeveloped hints on this matter of how the meanings and significance of the picara might play out as a narrative entry into the contemporary conversations about American cultural meaning. But Kaler's study, not centered on American narrative forms, is inclined to include under the rubric of "picara" virtually all female protagonists in myth and imaginative literature, and finally, seeing the figure in the broadest of archetypal terms and the picaresque everywhere from Greek myth to contemporary heroine-fantasy literature, veers away from many useful distinctions concerning the picaresque genre and thus turns away as well from interest in at least credibly presented women on at least recognizable roads. To include Scarlett O'Hara among the picaras, just for one instance, is automatically to attenuate the usefulness of Kaler's study.

42. As Ronald Primeau has pointed out, the narrations delivered by nonwhite male protagonists of American road literature over the past two decades suggest increased concerns to present American cultural diversity, especially as some of

these must alter many of the forms and conventions utilized by white, male authors. See his *Romance of the Road: The Literature of the American Highway* (Bowling Green, Ohio: Bowling Green State University Popular Press, 1996), pp. 107–25. Except for an occasional note, however, Primeau is not interested in the picaresque character of the road narratives he discusses. He wants to see them, as his title suggests, as a species of "romance" and tends therefore to approach them singly and cumulatively in terms of the mythic-symbolic and psychological dimensions they display as versions of quest literature. In a different set of terms, also bent on the romantic dimensions, Kris Lackey also approaches a number of American road narratives, past and present, with a concentration on nature, or, better, the Romantic pastoral. Again without any devoted attention to the picaresque elements, these books, for Lackey, yield a frequently bracing, if frequently poignant picture of the American landscape traveled anew in *RoadFrames: The American Highway Narrative* (Lincoln: University of Nebraska Press, 1997). Barbara Frey Waxman's *From the Hearth to the Open Road: A Feminist Study of Aging in Contemporary Literature* (New York: Greenwood Press, 1990) takes only a slightly different turn in her discussion of women's road novels, seeing them as unfolding a developmental pattern of aging, a form of *Reifungsroman*. As with Kaler, Lackey, and Primeau, the road for Frey is more "romanced" than real, more metaphorical than intractable, far more mythic than maculate. It should be repeated from earlier chapters that the picaresque narrative might well contain a romance impulse but, as well, that this impulse has to play out in a world that does not support "romance." Nevertheless, these several approaches suggest different facets of the road narrative phenomenon and serve as a reminder that each and every book here denominated as an example of the new American picaresque can also be fruitfully studied in a different framework.

43. Lars Eighner, *Travels with Lizbeth* (New York: St. Martin's Press, 1993), p. 170. Hereafter, all page numbers in parentheses following quotations from this book refer to this edition.

44. John A. Williams, *This Is My Country Too* (New York: New American Library, 1965), p. 22.

45. Eddy L. Harris, *South of Haunted Dreams: A Ride through Slavery's Old Back Yard* (New York: Simon & Schuster, 1993). In narrative recollection, Harris acknowledges how his road "optics" had been decisively angled by his expectation of racial hatreds and had put his approach to inventory on a bias: "Looking back now I see that not only was I eager to reach Charleston, my next significant destination, but I was impatient to reach my rendezvous with the evil in the haze. The evil spirit of the South. It was out there—somewhere—dressed in white, streaked with red, covered with blood, waiting for me" (p. 183). Already having admitted to "fear and trembling" about undertaking a comparable trip, Chet Fuller early on in his narrative about a black man's travels through the "new" South has car trouble near Salisbury, North Carolina, where his only alternative is a garage shop filled with "good ol' boys." It is clearly a scene Bo Whaley, he of

"redneck" travels, might approach with relish, and in fact it ends without harm, but the inventory Fuller takes is filtered not through a jovial perspective like Whaley's but one of "nightmarish horror and true evil." See *I Hear Them Calling My Name: A Journey through the New South* (Boston: Houghton Mifflin, 1981), pp. 25–35. If race puts a slant on the inventory for Williams, Harris, and Fuller, then gender colors the stock taken by Taylor Greer, the picara in Barbara Kingsolver's *The Bean Trees.* It is not simply that she will see clouds above the Arizona mesas as "pink and fat and hilarious-looking, like the hippo ballerinas in a Disney movie" (p. 35) in what is a decidedly non-male piece of metaphor-making that might freshen up a predictable American scene for the reader: that arrives in the course of picaresque defamiliarization. It is more significant that everything Taylor sees reaches the reader as angled through the marginality of the woman in male America. Stopped by her own car trouble, for instance, she anticipates the menace portended by the "dumb" automobile mechanic (see note 38). If race and gender create different "lenses," then sexual orientation surely does as well. How Michael Lane's "America" appears before the reader is decidedly refracted through his homosexuality. See *Pink Highways: Tales of Queer Madness on the Open Road* (New York: Birch Lane Press, 1995). In all such cases, how things are seen multiplies the inventory for the reader's perusal: the stuff recorded by a Lamb or a Salisbury must be re-entered in the accounting with at least slightly different tints when refracted through the eyes of Eddy Harris or Chet Fuller, Taylor Greer or Michael Lane.

46. Indeed, as minority views add their different angles on the "stuff" of America, those "acts" themselves might be thought at least an indirect participation not only in the revision of American culture but also as "actions" in "the politics of cultural difference," on which matter see Cornel West, *Keeping Faith: Philosophy and Race in America* (New York: Routledge, 1993), especially the chapter entitled "The New Cultural Politics of Difference," and Henry Louis Gates Jr., *Loose Canons: Notes on the Culture Wars* (New York: Oxford University Press, 1992), especially the chapter entitled "Writing, 'Race,' and the Difference It Makes." Such "actions" insure the culture's possession of *several* angles of self-understanding, as Gunn suggests is necessary for general cultural health (see note 2).

CHAPTER 8: ROAD WORK

1. John Steinbeck, *Travels with Charley: In Search of America* (New York: Bantam Books, 1963), p. 208. Hereafter, all page numbers in parentheses following quotations from this book refer to this edition. Andrei Codrescu, beginning his road work several decades later, knows from the outset what it takes Steinbeck most of a journey to calculate—namely, that the American identity in the contemporary moment is no exact and provable thing. With his typical penchant for overdetermination, Codrescu writes: "America in the last decade of the millennium is a complicated place. Our shoes come from Italy. Our cars come from Japan. Our patriots come

from Nazi Germany. Immigrants are buying Caddies. Romanians teach English to Americans. And the money is shit. You could buy a house twenty years ago for what it costs to buy a Caddie now" (*Road Scholar: Coast to Coast Late in the Century* [New York: Hyperion, 1993], p. 22).

2. In *States of Mind: A Personal Journey through the Mid-Atlantic* (New York: Villard Books, 1993), Jonathan Yardley, beginning to end, seeks to retrace his "home," that region that he feels the special locus of his well-being, his place to be. Even late in his narrative journey, he still seeks that defining "American" thing about it as he surveys the statue dedicated to movie actor Jimmy Stewart, the most famous son of Indiana, Pennsylvania: "The light of daybreak was still thin, but there he was, right in the middle of town, striking a pose that could have been from any of the dozens of movies in which he etched himself forever in the American imagination. How appropriate it was, I thought, that this quintessentially American figure should have been born in a small town in the Mid-Atlantic, a town named for a state in the Midwest. You couldn't get much more American than that" (p. 239). By journey's end, however, proud as he is of "home," Yardley is forced to conclude that people from the Mid-Atlantic "don't have a clearly definable human character, but then neither does any other [American] region. The crusty Yankee is as much a creature of myth as the hospitable Southerner or the quick-triggered Westerner; even the smallest of American regions is too large to permit facile generalizations" (p. 285). For others who travel the country in search of sustained American meaning, see, among *many* others, Richard Reeves, *American Journey: Traveling with Tocqueville in Search of Democracy in America* (New York: Simon and Schuster, 1982); Phillip L. Berman, *The Search for Meaning: Americans Talk about What They Believe and Why* (New York: Ballantine Books, 1990); and Michael Lee Cohen, *The Twenty-something American Dream: A Cross-Country Quest for a Generation* (New York: Dutton, 1993). Each of these forms itself largely in the "interview" mode, and some, obviously, possess more affinities with the picaresque narrative than others.

3. The phrase refers, of course, not only to meanings but to roads and to America itself. Codrescu, before embarking, wonders, "Was it too late to discover America, which seems to get discovered over and over and never definitely?" (p. 24)

4. For an interesting contention about the primacy of "space" in defining freedom—indeed in establishing the terms of other structures like the imported Christian formations—in the American mind as opposed to "Old World" ideas and definitions of freedom that emphasized "time," see the discussion in Sidney E. Mead, *The Lively Experiment: The Shaping of Christianity in America* (New York: Harper & Row, 1963), especially the first chapter, "The American People: Their Space, Time, and Religion," pp. 1–15.

5. On the literal matter of this mobility as a hallmark of the national character and how it "ramifies" in other facets of the country's existence, still instructive is George W. Pierson, *The Moving American* (New York: Alfred A. Knopf, 1973). This is perhaps the point also at which to call attention to the ways Phil Patton

has explored how the literal highways of America themselves "answered" to this native disposition to move and move and move. See his *Open Road: A Celebration of the American Highway* (New York: Simon and Schuster, 1986).

6. The quotation appears in the section called "Considerations by the Way" in Emerson's *The Conduct of Life*. See *Complete Works*, 12 vols. (Boston: Houghton, Mifflin and Company, 1903–4), VI, p. 266. It can also be found in Ralph Waldo Emerson, *Essays and Lectures* (New York: Library of America, 1983), p. 1090, and as the epigraph for Mona Simpson's novel, *Anywhere but Here*.

7. Along with Codrescu, on the metaphorical power attached to the automobile as an image, its triangulation of youth, freedom, and the car, see Anton Myrer's novel, *The Last Convertible* (New York: Putnam, 1978). For the excursus into the "psychology" of driving the car, explored "on the road" in new American picaresque fashion, see also both K. T. Berger, *Zen Driving* (New York: Ballantine Books, 1988) and K. T. Berger, *Where the Earth and the Sky Collide: America through the Eyes of Its Drivers* (New York: Henry Holt and Company, 1993). "K. T." is no single author but, rather, brothers Kevin and Todd, who write as one. When they/he set out to examine, in part, drivers' "thoughts about driving's impact on the environment," they/he report(s), "Only once did I make the mistake of referring to myself as a 'car biologist,'" to which reference an attendant at a Texaco station in Amarillo retorts, "'Whad'ya doin'? Studyin' how Buicks mate?'" (dust-jacket).

8. The sheer expanses of space in America are often, as with Codrescu, most immediately stunning to astonished foreigners who travel the continent, those for whom the "openness," the long horizons, have not been taken in from infancy like "mother's milk." See, for instance, the account rendered by a Scot, Gavin Young, as he surveys the *size* of everything in his *From Sea to Shining Sea: A Present-Day Journey through America's Past* (London: Hutchinson, 1995), especially the chapters in part 6, "Indian Territory." Then, of course, there is Jonathan Raban, so utterly taken by America in his travels that he sometimes feels himself, at least narratively, "going native." After an earlier observation that "No nation in the world had ever put such a high value on privacy and space as the United States, and nowhere in the country did people live so far apart . . . as here in the Midwest," he remarks, "Nothing does so much justice to the gargantuan scale of American life as its national weather maps. In Europe, one is allowed to see the weather only as scraps and fragments: a cake slice of a depression here; a banded triangle of a ridge of high pressure there. In the United States, every morning and evening, I was enthralled by the epic sweep of whole weather systems as they rolled across the country from the Pacific to the Atlantic, or coasted down from the Arctic Circle, or swirled up from Mexico and Cuba. The weathermen [without a flicker of wonder] . . . announced that people were being frozen to death in Butte, roasted in Flagstaff and blown off their feet in Tallahassee" (*Old Glory: An American Voyage* [New York: Simon and Schuster, 1981], pp. 30, 74). Hereafter, all page references following quotations from this book refer to this edition.

9. With respect to the ways "American space" answers not only to the restiveness of the American character but also the picaresque narrative form, see Frederick R. Karl's discussion of this "collusion" of ideas in some earlier "classic" American texts in "Picaresque and the American Experience," *Yale Review* 57:2 (December 1867): 196–212. Also see his chapter 2 ("American Space and Spatiality") in *American Fictions, 1940/1980: A Comprehensive History and Critical Evaluation* (New York: Harper & Row, 1985).

10. Saul Bellow, *The Adventures of Augie March* (New York: Viking Press, 1953), p. 607. Even as he gives up on the far-ranging adventures of the picaro, however, Augie does intend at least to fulfill the Emersonian prescription for fuller realizations "at home," so to speak. The quotation reveals also his sense that one can make discoveries "in this immediate *terra incognita* that spreads out in every gaze" (p. 607).

11. This holds for even the most incorrigible ramblers. Raban, for instance, identifying himself in *Old Glory* as an inveterate "runner away," one who cannot stand still in any status quo, with self-confessed "dubious talent as an escape artist" (p. 278), a picaro through and through, increasingly Americanized by the experiences he records here and in *Hunting Mister Heartbreak* (New York: Edward Burlingame Books, 1991), begins to prove just how American he is becoming when he observes that he was "really on much the same track, traveling hopefully, never arriving. I loved the audacity of that American principle which says, When life gets tainted or goes stale, junk it! Leave it behind! Go West. Go up. Move on" (*Old Glory*, p. 41) or, again, that he liked his "fellow vagrants . . . [whose] style of travel, at once feckless and compulsive, seemed much like my own" (p. 55). Even he, however, eventually reaches the point of seeking some repose and issues the signal that life on the picaresque route is coming to a close, as the Emersonian "want" for "anywhere but here" recedes into different desires: "I made my own list of wants. I wanted a long letter from home. I wanted calm weather. I wanted something else which I couldn't identify exactly. It was an ending" (p. 364). Still, Raban seems inveterately the picaro when he makes notes like his earlier observation: "*Travel*. It was an intransitive verb. It didn't involve any destinations. It was going for the going's sake, to be anywhere but where you were, with the motion itself its only object" (p. 293). For another instance, there is Larry McMurtry's Jack McGriff, vintage American picaro in his big Cadillac. After years and years "on the road," for trade—to be sure—but primarily for the life of the road, Jack finds himself proposing to settle down with Jean, one of several momentary "stalls" on course that the reader realizes would end the picaresque voyage. In this case, however, Jack becomes the picaro redux, remains throughout on the road, because Jean, like the reader, knows him, knows better, and sends him packing: "'Get out of here. . . . Hit the road. Find me something wonderful. You can't come back till you do.'" Slightly later, after this mandate, still dreading the road, Jack "didn't really want to start," but after a time, "as usual, once definitely on the

road, I felt a little better" (*Cadillac Jack* [New York: Simon and Schuster, 1982], pp. 327, 330, 332). Hereafter, all page references following quotations from this book refer to this edition.

12. In a telling instance, Steinbeck looks back in his mirror to the old black hitchhiker he had just frightened and troubled (p. 266), but the narrative transition out of the scene is quick and clean. As is most often the case when the picaro is operating at full picaresque hilt, the backward glances reveal no regrets about leaving—only, perhaps, regret about what has transpired in the episode. The narrators might be retrospective, but the picaro rarely is.

13. Barbara Kingsolver, *The Bean Trees* (New York: Harper & Row, 1988), p. 11. Hereafter, all page references following quotations from this book refer to this edition.

14. Elizabeth Berg, *The Pull of the Moon* (New York: Jove Books, 1997), p. 5. Hereafter, all page references following quotations from this book refer to this edition.

15. Jim Lehrer, *Kick the Can* (New York: G. P. Putnam's Sons, 1988), p. 4. Hereafter, all page references following quotations from this book refer to this edition.

16. The "license" of the picaresque form, of course, is to push the matter of physical mobility to a degree more possible in narrative than probable, ordinarily, in most peoples' actual lives. With such narrative "liberty," the form possesses the potential at least to heighten readers' senses of this American pattern by intensifying the presentation of it "in the extreme and with frequency." This is another way of noting, however, that the full-time, full-fledged picaros and picaras live only in books.

17. Mona Simpson, *Anywhere but Here* (New York: Vintage Contemporaries, 1992), p. 61. Hereafter, all page references following quotations from this book refer to this edition. For another picara who seems simply to have an innate need to stay in motion, there is the young Jean "Dutch" Gillis, who, from early childhood on, thinks that "when it's good in a car I want never to stop. Just keep going forever. The stopping makes me feel sick and tight like it's time to die. Just drive on, whoever was driving, not me. And I'd sit in the seat and we'd stop to piss and for gas and at drive-ins for hamburgers and get candy bars at gas stations and just go on fast down the road, not turning, just curving . . . and the car would never break down or run out of gas" (Katherine Dunn, *Truck* [New York: Harper & Row, 1971], p. 82). Hereafter, all page references following quotations from this book refer to this edition.

18. Exclamations and instances, trite and presaging, of the needs for cutting a broad swath and shaving close take a wide variety of forms in American life, but the examples, quite beyond those in major literary works, are legion. They range from corporate invocations to "just do it" (Nike) to the examples and injunctions of "Auntie Mame"—for everyone from nephew Patrick to Miss Gooch—to "Live! Live! Live!," from the pursued intensities of sky-diving and cliff-sailing to the extreme play of the triathletes, from Gretel Ehrlich's attempts to "encounter" the

landscape of Wyoming in *The Solace of Open Spaces* (New York: Penguin Books, 1986), to paint-fighting in simulated warfare, from the "athletics of the edge" practiced by Rob Schultheis and others (see his *Bone Games: One Man's Search for the Ultimate Athletic High* [New York: Random House, 1984]), to the adult "survival camps," with many more in between. In this context, the pedagogical value of hitting the road to gain deliberate experience was surely not lost on Douglas Brinkley, then American Studies Professor at Hofstra University, who took his students on the highways of the land to have them gain direct experience of significant sites and scenes of their country and who recounts the trip, as a kind of "group picaresque," in *The Majic Bus: An American Odyssey* (New York: Harcourt, Brace, 1993). See also the more personally motivated effort at experiential education mounted by Shainee Gabel and Kristin Hahn, abetted by consultation with Brinkley, as they describe it in *Anthem: An American Road Story* (New York: Avon Books, 1997).

19. Henry David Thoreau, *Walden and Civil Disobedience* (New York: New American Library, 1980), p. 66.

20. The remainder of this section, then, develops related but other facets of that drive for the possession of immediate or "unmediated" experience explored in the fourth chapter above in the section entitled "The Regimen of Road-Therapy in Self-Recovery." The emphases here are on this "experientialism" as one among other significant values in the American approach to life that comes in for reaffirmation in the new American picaresque narrative.

21. E. L. Doctorow, *Billy Bathgate* (New York: Random House, 1989), p 321. Hereafter, all page references following quotations from this book refer to this edition.

22. Elizabeth Berg, *The Pull of the Moon*, p. 174. That the discussion of the hunger for experience in the next several paragraphs takes its examples largely from narratives by and about females on the road is not at all accidental. Whereas the new American picaros most often simply assume and seldom speak of their liberty to pursue the next, intensified moments they hope await them, the picaras' drive often seems more urgent and more self-consciously acknowledged—surely because they have frequently felt, as they say, without "privilege" in the experiential domain or without the opportunity to enter experiences without the intermediations of the men around them. For a small instance, Nan literally bathes in the luxury of an extended time poking about by herself, people-watching, trying on clothes she would never buy, eating a ripe tomato by hand right at the farm stand, even later visiting a pet cemetery, and later still then writing to husband Martin "You would never have stood for it" (p. 36). Or there are Doris and Frannie in Pagan Kennedy's *Spinsters* (New York: High Risk Books, 1995), the former, one who cannot stand still, "despises idleness" (p. 10), the latter, a reluctant picara virtually to the last, as they follow out their 1968 tour across America, "spinning" now, not "spinsters." On course, Frannie discovers that the road obliterates her committed spinsterhood ("With each motel, each diner, I felt more

anonymous, wiped clean" [p. 58] and "I'd always thought of myself as some-how belonging with those objects that sat and gathered dust. But now I'd become another kind of thing entirely; I'd gotten used to the highway" [p. 106]), learns slowly to accept Doris's continuous detours along the way ("I had accepted this change of plans without arguing—without much thought, really" [p. 121]), and, indeed, finally, somewhere in New Mexico, her New Hampshire "life" now quite gone, realizes that "I was driving, alive to the road as never before" (p. 120).

23. Even late into her narrative, however, the runaway now brought back at least temporarily into captivity, "Dutch" fears that the intensely vibrant and difficult experience she has had is being stolen from her by her family: "They shouldn't have come here. I would have told them about it. Now I can never tell about it. It was mine and now it's not mine. It isn't theirs. They don't want it. It only isn't mine anymore" (p. 213).

24. From time to time, the intentional effort to experience life deeply and delib-erately appears in the new American picaresque as more decidedly "selective"—that is to say, the intention is aimed not at the realm of experience at large but at some particular slice of life that becomes the objective of experiential desire. For instances, Walt Harrington sets out quite consciously to enter, to probe, to get the feel of the nature of African-American experience in *Crossings: A White Man's Jour-ney into Black America* (New York: HarperCollins, 1992); Frances FitzGerald nar-rows the scope to alternative intentional communities in *Cities on a Hill: A Journey through Contemporary American Cultures* (New York: Simon and Schuster, 1986); and Hampton Sides enters into some other forms of communal association in *Stomp-ing Grounds: A Pilgrim's Progress through Eight American Subcultures* (New York: William Morrow & Company, 1992).

25. The quotations immediately above refer to *The Moviegoer* (New York: Alfred A. Knopf, 1979). Hereafter, all page references following quotations from this book refer to this edition. In terms that make quite clear the deliberate attentive-ness to experience required for him, as well as his picaro's hunch for the "detour," Binx immediately explains what he means by a "good rotation": "A good rota-tion. A rotation I define as the experiencing of the new beyond the expectation of the experiencing of the new. For example, taking one's first trip to Taxco would not be a rotation, or no more than a very ordinary rotation; but getting lost on the way and discovering a hidden valley would be" (p. 144).

26. Peter Jenkins, *A Walk across America* (New York: William Morrow & Com-pany, 1979), p. 128. Hereafter, all page references following quotations from this book refer to this edition.

27. Robert Penn Warren, *A Place to Come To* (New York: Random House, 1977), p. 26. Hereafter, all page references following quotations from this book refer to this edition.

28. Especially if one recalls Codrescu's assertion about television as "a death-trap for the American mind," that by the end of the century "no one will be able to distinguish between real people and TV people" (p. xv), the picaresque figure

David Bell in Don DeLillo's *Americana* (New York: Penguin Books, 1989) is a conspicuous example of one who takes to the road in America in order to avert "what is not life" and to take a new possession on reality through his direct or sensate experience of it. He leaves behind his successful life as a television executive wherein his dealings with the world occur mediated through the editing of electronic images, what he fears are ersatz simulacra at best, and, armed with his own camera, seeks America. As he tells Brand, "what I'm shooting now is just a small segment of what will eventually include more general matter— funerals, traffic jams, furniture, real events, women, doors, windows . . . people playing themselves" (p. 289). And so he plunges ahead into "matter" instead of devised images, often in highly "physical" terms (see the arm-wrestling episode following upon his comments to Brand) and most often into darker and more confusing experiences than he had anticipated. Hereafter, all page references following quotations from this book refer to this edition.

29. With a few notable exceptions like John Williams's *This Is My Country Too* (New York: New American Library, 1966) and some occasional episodes of horror or violence scattered about, the examples of the new American picaresque that propose themselves as nonfiction seem far less inclined to walk on the dark side than those that announce themselves as fictions, not surprising perhaps in view of the extra imaginative license the novelists might be thought reflexively to employ. For those writers who want their narratives to represent "true accounts" of what happened, regardless of the degrees to which they themselves "romance the facts," establishing credibility, cast in terms of likelihood or probability, impinges more than the novelists' charge to push into the realms of "possibility."

30. Albert Murray, *The Hero and the Blues* (Columbia: University of Missouri Press, 1973), p. 107. Hereafter, all page references following quotations from this book refer to this edition.

31. When Murray uses the term "hero" in this context, he means to refer neither to the traditional forms of the hero to be found in drama and epic (those outsized characters that make them different in imposing power) nor to the so-called anti-hero (those who stand in conspicuous rebellion against the crushing authority of their societies) but, rather, to those ordinary folks who struggle along, against hard times and numerous obstacles, to survive in the world while retaining their fundamental humanity. In most cases, this last form of heroism seems most appropriate in thinking of the focal figures of the new American picaresque, if one wants to think of them as "heroic" in any sense.

32. Stephen Wright, *Going Native* (New York: Farrar, Straus & Giroux, 1994), p. 3. Hereafter, all page references following quotations from this book refer to this edition.

33. Richard Hill, *Riding Solo with the Golden Horde* (Athens: University of Georgia Press, 1994), p. 61. Hereafter, all page references following quotations from this book refer to this edition. Several other examples of the new American pic-

aresque appear in which the jazz, blues, honky-tonk forms of extemporizing on musical grounds play prominently in the picaresque tour. See, for instance, Hugh Merrill's attempts to trace the old origins forward in *The Blues Route* (New York: William Morrow & Company, 1990). His conversation at Eddie Shaw's place on West Madison in Chicago with Bruce Iglauer of Alligator Records is telling in this consideration of blues, improvisation, and picaresque ingenuity. On why people listen to the blues, Iglauer remarks, "I feel like blues is music that allows people to express themselves with the music in a way they wouldn't do otherwise. It's as though these blues musicians are saying what you need to say to yourself. I keep telling people that if it weren't for the blues, I'd be a crazy person" (p. 86). For other examples, there are the erratic picaresque routes coursed by Bill Terry's A. J. Poole and cronies as they careen about from one honky-tonk road house to another in *The Watermelon Kid* (Baton Rouge: Louisiana State University Press, 1984) and Albert Murray's own eccentric novel formed around the jazz / blues scene, in which the musical variants of the road band and the unfolding motions of "Schoolboy" in space seem of a piece in *The Seven League Boots* (New York: Pantheon Books, 1995). Of course, many central figures in the new American picaresque, not themselves musicians, are accompanied on the road by their "musics." Among many others, there appears DeLillo's David Bell in *Americana*, for instance, who while riding with Clevenger, listens on his portable to "big beat, gospel, ghetto soul, jug bands and dirt bands, effete near-lisping college rock, electric obscenity and doom, wild fiddles of Nashville, ouds and tambourines and lusting drums . . . a scrap of catatonic Monk or Sun Ra . . . [with all of] the mad harmonics bringing most of what was sane to those who ran with death" (p. 350). Even if they themselves have nothing of Vic Messenger's or Schoolboy's artistic capacities, they often prove adept at that style of improvisational existence definitive for the picaro. See also, for a good case in point, the music that shoots through the road work of Robert James Waller's Texas Jack Carmine in *Border Music* (New York: Warner Books, 1995).

34. The remainder of this section indirectly follows out of and is indebted to an extended informal conversation in Indianapolis, on April 4, 1992, with Randall Balmer, Edward Linenthal, Steven Marini, James G. Moseley, and John K. Roth, in which the talk was about more or less uniquely or at least distinctively "American" contributions to the world, among which few "gifts" were numbered jazz / blues, basketball, African-American preaching styles, and democracy, all of which have sheets, scripts, texts, maps, rules, and boundaries, but all of which, also, permit—and indeed encourage—and, in some instances, ultimately require forms of the "riff," the arts and skills of improvisation, for those who would play them best. Each requires its shapes of tenacity, resilience, alacrity, dexterity, the capacities to negotiate the "givens," the reflexes for adventurous moves, the ingenuity to find a different path forward. All require a commitment to flow and process, an ability for rapid changes of course, an instinct for finding a way into the near future, and a certain amount of real acrobatic imagination. These "American

games," of course, both nourish and accommodate some of the defining traits of the picaro and picara, and many narratives of the new American picaresque suggest how these and other forms have helped "train" the picaresque figures for the road and how, in turn, their "riffs" on the road reassert the value of improvisation imbedded in such American forms.

35. Geoffrey O'Gara, *A Long Road Home: Journeys through America's Present in Search of America's Past* (New York: W. W. Norton & Company, 1989), pp. 272ff.

36. Late in the narrative, Wylie Jones, now Will Johnson after having gone through several other identity permutations, including one as Wylie Coyote, finds himself so completely absorbed into his own self-improvisations that he has not discovered any new, creative health through his riffing so much as he has lost himself altogether: "The loss of control, however temporary, frightened him, and incidents like this seemed to be accumulating. When you lost track of the names in your life, you relinquished contact with the reality of that life" (pp. 297–98). Completely unmoored, now unable even to locate the scripts so far have his improvisations gone, he can only return to the road of violence he has been traveling.

37. If Emerson, Thoreau, and other nineteenth-century thinkers were able in part to celebrate American space, American "experientialism," and American frontier virtues of ingenious improvisation, they and others also understood that the call of "open space" could lead to the disregard of possibilities nearer at hand, that the "actions" of saturating oneself in experience could overpower the necessity for "thought," and, with Francis Parkman, that frontier and wilderness improvisations could allow and even could lead to savage violence, each too arguably an American "trait."

38. James Leo Herlihy, *Midnight Cowboy* (New York: Simon and Schuster, 1965), pp. 169–70.

CHAPTER 9: POSTMODERN RELIGIOUS CONDITIONS AND PICARESQUE GIFTS

1. Pagan Kennedy, *Spinsters* (New York: High Risk Books, 1995), pp. 157–58. Hereafter, all page numbers in parentheses following quotations from this book refer to this edition.

2. In fact, a number of thinkers believe that it is in the American environment that the conditions of postmodernity appear most vividly and press most decisively because of the adventurous character of its corporate capitalism, commodities, and consumption, the arriving closures on industrialism, the sprawls of its urban centers, the pervasiveness of its bureaucracies, the looseness of the weave of its social fabrics, the rapidity of its technological advances, the omnipresence of advertising, and the like. Even when students of postmodern existence do not work on American culture per se, they often point up these characteristics that are, arguably, significant systems in American life. At least some of these most

prominent features—found here and now, of course, elsewhere—become "clear" cases in point for students of postmodernity, without much direct attention to American elements, in explorations, for instance, like those collected in *Postmodern Conditions,* Andrew Milner, Philip Thomson, and Chris Worth, eds. (New York: Berg Publishers, 1990).

3. Walker Percy, *The Message in the Bottle* (New York: Farrar, Straus & Giroux, 1975), p. 3. Hereafter all page numbers in parentheses following quotations from this book refer to this edition.

4. Peter Berger, Brigitte Berger, and Hansfried Kellner, *The Homeless Mind: Modernization and Consciousness* (New York: Vintage Books, 1974). This study sizes up how all of the bright promises of "modernity," founded on ideas of human capacity for social progress, dwindled into such fundamental dissatisfactions of contemporary consciousness. For other angles on this "story," see also, among others, Joshua Meyrowitz, *No Sense of Place: The Impact of Electronic Media on Social Behavior* (New York: Oxford University Press, 1985); Kenneth Gergen, *The Saturated Self: Dilemmas of Identity in Contemporary Life* (New York: Basic Books, 1991); and Christopher Lasch, *The Culture of Narcissism: American Life in an Age of Diminishing Expectations* (New York: W. W. Norton, 1978).

5. H. Paul Santmire, "Epilogue: The Birthing of Post-Modern Religion," in *Critical Issues in Modern Religion,* authored and edited by Roger A. Johnson and Ernest Wallwork et al. (Englewood Cliffs, N.J.: Prentice-Hall, 1973), p. 448. Hereafter, all page numbers in parentheses following quotations from this essay refer to this edition.

6. See Christopher Lasch, *The Minimal Self: Psychic Survival in Troubled Times* (New York: W. W. Norton, 1984). This book follows after his *The Culture of Narcissism* (see note 4) and seeks to explain why and how "minimalist life" virtually leads to and promotes narcissism as a response to such conditions.

7. See Paul Ricoeur's chapter entitled "The Symbol Gives Rise to Thought," in his *The Symbolism of Evil,* trans. Emerson Buchanan (New York: Harper & Row, 1967). Ricoeur's call for a "second naivete" occurs in the context of his argument about achieving a new immediacy with the world by way of a revision of consciousness, a revision altogether dependent upon what he refers to as an "empirics of the servile will." In brief, Ricoeur is suggesting, human consciousness must be forced into recognition that it occurs in the world and not, as with modern rationalism, that the world exists in human consciousness, "that the *Cogito* is within being, and not vice versa" (p. 356). Human outlook, thus chastened, subject again to the world and not simply to its own will, can then—newly-naive—make a re-entry into the world of being to regard it as potentially revelatory of meaning and not merely as a function of human interpretations. A recent, full critique of modernity's recourse to "overweening" rationalist approaches appears in Karlis Racevskis, *Modernity's Pretenses: Making Reality Fit Reason from Candide to the Gulag* (Albany: State University of New York Press, 1998).

8. For Cox's fullest discussion of this "People's Religion," and how it figures as a bulwark of community especially in times of trial, see the section with that title in his *The Seduction of the Spirit: The Use and Misuse of People's Religion* (New York: Simon and Schuster, 1973). For the power of carnival, festival, and concert for liminal moments of *communitas* and as alternatives to modern erosions of community, see his *The Feast of Fools: A Theological Essay on Festivity and Fantasy* (Cambridge: Harvard University Press, 1969).

9. The discussion in this paragraph draws broadly from the chapter entitled "Mazing Grace" in Taylor's *Erring: A Postmodern A/theology* (Chicago: University of Chicago Press, 1984), pp. 149–69.

10. Richard R. Niebuhr, *Experiential Religion* (New York: Harper & Row, 1972), p. 17. Hereafter, all page numbers in parentheses following quotations from this essay refer to this edition.

11. Robert Jay Lifton, *The Protean Self: Human Resilience in an Age of Fragmentation* (New York: Basic Books, 1993), p. 24. Hereafter, all page numbers in parentheses following quotations from this essay refer to this edition. A notable scholar of modern religious movements, Robert Ellwood, earlier referred to the necessary reprise of old Proteus. Under contemporary conditions, he observes, there is required "the formation of a Protean Man whose spiritual life is not tied to a monolithic cultural identity, but is changing based on individual experience" (quoted in T. A. English-Lueck, *Health in the New Age* [Albuquerque: University of New Mexico Press, 1990], p. 96).

12. At this point the reader should recall the views of Albert Murray on improvisational necessity for the sake of survival, shapeshifting as a form of "frontiering," as these views are discussed in chapter 8 in the section entitled "Contemporaneity and Improvisation: American 'Riffs.'" Like Murray, Lifton knows that the self-transformative capacity can have a dark result as well as admirable ones, that his frontier Proteanism in America "was tinged with blood" (p. 35), that it can lead to "deception and dissimulation" (p. 40) and "con-artistry" (p. 41). Nevertheless, he, like Murray, finds this standing trait a potentially useful one in times of fragmentation and trial for the "cornered" self.

13. Billy Bathgate, of course, closes by thanking God for his earlier, exclusively secular experiences on the picaresque way. Least Heat Moon's closing pages suggest that the picaresque trail has led him to the Lakota spiritual wisdom about the power of the circle, confirmation of the Hopi pattern he had earlier spotted, and ends thus in Native American religious insight, but the journey he has taken to this point is decidedly secular in cast. David Rounds's title picaro in *Celebrisi's Journey* (Los Angeles: J. P. Tarcher, 1982) finally comes to rest, quits as a picaro, in the calm of a Buddhist monastery in California, but his route to that point of closure is intractably secular and fully picaresque. Laurel Lee's *Godspeed: Hitchhiking Home* (San Francisco: Harper & Row, 1988) has her yet "on the road" on the book's last page, but the latter stages of her trip, although still on an inveterately secular track, tend her ever more deeply into her discovered Christian faith

and suggest, as the epilogue confirms, that she will soon leave the road for another life. As the subsequent discussion argues, however, the secular roads they all have followed do not disqualify them in the least as *resources* for postmodern religious sensibility even if they are not *examples* of discernibly religious lives: indeed, as should become clear, the secular journey enhances their possible assets for a burgeoning new form of spiritual existence.

14. In moving toward a conclusion, the remainder of this section draws together, under a different rubric for attention, many of the facets of the new American picaros and picaras and their picaresque narratives explored in the preceding chapters. Again, however, it should be noted that it is the *cumulative* nature of the form discussed here: not every picaro or picara or every picaresque narrative should be thought to possess every trait of the generic literary character, just as no single instance of the picaresque narrative fulfills every aspect of the form.

15. For a fuller rehearsal of the picaro's and picara's narrative "exile" cast in a different set of terms, the reader might want to return to chapter 4, especially the section there entitled "The Picaro as Symptom and Carrier" and to chapter 6 on the matter of "Curricula of Exile and Loneliness, Strategies of Approach."

16. William Least Heat Moon, *Blue Highways: A Journey into America* (Boston: Little, Brown and Company, 1982), p. 239.

17. For a more detailed account of picaresque ventures in "starting over," both at large and in terms of the cycles of experience from one episode to another, the reader can return to chapter 8 in the section entitled "Freedom in Space: The Renewal of an American Calisthenics."

18. On the matter of "experiential autonomy," the fuller discussion occurs in chapter 4 in the section entitled "The Regimen of Road-Therapy in Self-Recovery" and in the second section of chapter 8, entitled "Deliberate Life: Experience and Self-Possession."

19. These terms "creative resilience" and "shapeshifting" point especially to the rough and tumble arts of survival, of ingenuity in overcoming road-blocks, of probing for avenues of exit when the picaresque way seems to have hit trail's end. For a more nuanced account of this, readers should return to chapter 8, especially the section entitled "Contemporaneity and Improvisation: American 'Riffs.'"

20. A number of intermittent sections in the picaro's progress in the Proulx narrative are entitled "What He Sees" as Loyal Blood makes his complex journey across American grounds and into the cultural scenes and appearances he encounters. On the matter more generally of the size, scope, and various slants of the American "inventory" taken by the new American picaresque, the broader accounting appears in the three sections comprising chapter 7 on what, what else, and how the picaros and picaras see (and thus in the narratives "record") the stuff of American life.

21. Again, see note 17.

22. For a more ample discussion of this as a response to conditions faced by persons in late modernity, especially as it signals the kinds of self-predicaments in the face of experience persons suffer, see chapter 4, the section entitled "The Loss of the Creature and the Picaro's Dilemma."

23. Here, the reader can return for a broader discussion of the things that conspire against the "fresh view," the intermediations between the self and experience, to chapter 4, the section on "The Picaro as Symptom and Carrier."

24. Another, comparable way to accomplish the "innocent" or fresh vision of things is to travel America in the company of one who, like Turtle, has yet ever to see it, has yet not been predisposed to see it in customary ways, or has imagined it yet only in decidedly "alien" terms. New spiritual dimensions of the country appear all about, for instance, when Broughton Coburn "sees it anew" with the help of an old Nepalese woman, Aama, who digs out these facets of experience for his renewed scrutiny in different terms. See Broughton Coburn, *Aama in America: A Pilgrimage of the Heart* (New York: Anchor Books, 1996).

25. Geoffrey O'Gara, *A Long Road Home: Journeys through America's Present in Search of America's Past* (New York: W. W. Norton, 1989), p. xix.

26. On these possible advantages of a life in motion, on the margins, for certain kinds of social gains, the reader can return to the more extended discussion with a number of examples to be found in chapter 6, the section entitled "Cosmopolitanism, the New Picaro, and Tactics of Fuller Trespass." As the picaros and picaras surrender "community" for the sake of "motion," continuous motion itself creates certain social "virtues" in them if they are able to meet the road rising ahead with these assets.

27. Robert James Waller, *Border Music* (New York: Warner Books, 1995), p. 40.

28. Just as the Thorvalds' anniversary occasion enters the inventory as a possible kind of locus of "people's religion" in America, the new American picaresque contains numerous comparable examples, like, for instance, the spontaneous communities of commonality and celebration that David Lamb encounters over and again in his jaunting way through the baseball parks of small-town America. See *Stolen Season: A Journey through America and Baseball's Minor Leagues* (New York: Warner Books, 1991). For additional examples and discussion, see chapter 6, the section on "The New Civility: Arts of Inventory after Babel."

29. In this understanding of the "new vicar," Niebuhr again emphasizes just the secular character of this metaphorical figure: "This man does not so much care for sanctification as he longs for the justification of all his parts, as vicar and victim of a universe bursting into greater and greater variety. This is our new man. He is molded and informed by many powers, and he is more aware of his own variety than any generation before him. His vocation is to find a definition of his own humanity and so be a shaper of human nature, not disdaining any of the materials given him through and by his generation" (p. 24).

30. See chapter 8.

31. Charles Kuralt, *A Life on the Road* (New York: G. P. Putnam's Sons, 1990), p. 253.

32. For a more deliberate critique of what these emphatically and distinctively "American" traits, values, and styles can lead to in their most excessive forms, the reader should consult the closing pages of chapter 8.

33. Without making exaggerated claims for the literary "finesse" of most examples of the new American picaresque, the point here is that this narrative formation in many respects has the same kinds of "license" in its representational possibilities that always accompany literary expression. It can develop those imaginative renditions of experience that do not necessarily duplicate life as lived in some "documentary" insistence about presentational "realism" but, rather, that posit a narrative depiction of life as it might be lived out, felt, and understood under a certain set of hypothetical circumstances, no matter how much or little pushed to extremity. Readers will accredit this "depiction" as credible to the extent that the "world" proposed in the narrative possesses those structures of plausibility that make it a world to which those readers feel a compelling "tie" even while, perhaps, recognizing it as not *their* personal world precisely.

INDEX OF AUTHORS, TITLES,
AND PROTAGONISTS

Aama in America (Coburn), 310n9, 339n24

Abbey, Edward, 1, 21

Adams, Henry, 284n7

Adams, Percy G., 293n27

Adele (character in *Anywhere but Here*), 214, 220–21, 226

Adventures of Augie March, The (Bellow), 2, 55, 59–61, 212, 282n1, 329n10. *See also* March, Augie

Adventures of Huckleberry Finn, The (Twain), 17, 212, 282n1, 297n20. *See also* Finn, Huck

Aeneid, The (Virgil), 281n29

After Alienation (Klein), 286–87n20

After Babel (Steiner), 302n9, 314n24

Air-Conditioned Nightmare, The (H. Miller), 212, 288n5

Alcala, Jeronimo de, 12, 17

Aleman, Mateo, 3, 11, 13, 22, 25, 30, 37, 48. *See also Guzman de Alfarache*

Algren, Nelson, 2, 282n1

All the Pretty Horses (McCarthy), 183, 217

Alonso (Alcala), 12, 17

Alter, Robert, 277n5, 281n26

America in Change (Weber), 284n8

Americana (DeLillo), 240, 333n28, 334n33. *See also* Bell, David

American Adam, The (Lewis), 285n13

American Dream, An (Mailer), 2, 94, 215, 239. *See also* Rojack, Stephen Richards

American Fictions, 1940/1980 (Karl), 329n9

American Journey (Reeves), 60, 93, 182, 319n17, 327n2

American Mythologies (Blonsky), 284nn6, 8

American Sacred Space (Chidester and Linenthal), 296n12

American Scene, The (James), 212, 289n5

Ann (character in *Anywhere but Here*), 214, 220–21, 226

Anthem (Gabel and Hahn), 331n10

Anywhere but Here (Simpson), 2, 45, 214, 220, 226, 328n6, 330n17. *See also* Adele; Ann

Apocalypse Pretty Soon (Heard), 319n17

Artist's Journey into the Interior, The (E. Heller), 286n17

Autobiography (Franklin), 212

Babcock, Barbara, 278n9, 279n19, 280n21, 310n10

Back Home (Rosenblum), 67, 120–21, 128, 175, 182, 199, 321n24

Bad; or, The Dumbing of America (Fussell), 284n8

Banks, Russell, 2, 230. *See also Continental Drift*

Barth, John, 19, 287n21. *See also Giles Goat-Boy*

Bartram, William, 212

Bathgate, Billy (character in *Billy*

Bathgate): cultural values, 224–25, 227, 236; narrative inventory, 189; narrative issues, 70, 72; picaresque changes, 34, 44; picaresque continuities, 12, 22, 26, 28, 33, 281n26; picaresque social virtues, 146, 148, 155, 158, 161; postmodern facets, 253, 255–56, 337n13; selfhood dilemmas, 83; social dilemmas, 108, 117

Bean Trees, The (Kingsolver), 1, 214, 218, 229, 239, 259, 318n12, 324n38, 326n45. *See also* Greer, Taylor

Been Down So Long It Looks like Up to Me (Farina), 203, 257, 305–6n28, 310n11. *See also* Pappadopoulis, Gnossos

Bell, David (character in *Americana*), 230, 240, 333n28, 334n33

Bellow, Saul, 2, 212, 282n1, 287n20. See also *Adventures of Augie March, The; Seize the Day*

Bennett, William J., 302n8

Berg, Elizabeth, 2. See also *Pull of the Moon, The*

Berger, Brigette, 336n4

Berger, K. T., 60, 66. See also *Where the Earth and the Sky Collide; Zen Driving*

Berger, Peter, 246, 336n4

Berger, Thomas, 22. See also *Little Big Man*

Berman, Phillip L., 67. See also *Search for Meaning, The*

Berrigan, Philip, 111

Big Muddy (Hall and Wood), 67, 167, 183, 218, 297n20, 322–23n33

Billy Bathgate (Doctorow): cultural values, 213, 217, 224; narrative inventory, 196, 318n12; narrative issues, 59, 61, 289n7; picaresque changes, 34, 41; picaresque continuities, 11–12, 22; picaresque social virtues, 161; postmodern facets, 253; selfhood dilemmas, 83. *See also* Bathgate, Billy

Blas, Gil (character in *Gil Blas*), 13, 22, 35, 43, 73, 144, 189, 214, 219, 233, 281n26

Blonsky, Marshall, 284nn6, 8

Blood, Loyal (character in *Postcards*): narrative inventory, 178, 190, 257; picaresque social virtues, 147, 150, 153, 155, 157, 159, 168, 311n13; postmodern facets, 338n20

Blood of the Lamb, The (DeVries), 2, 74, 175, 215. *See also* Wanderhope, Don

Blue Highways (Trogdon), 1; cultural values, 215, 239; narrative inventory, 182, 184, 318n13; narrative issues, 57–61, 73, 80, 295n32; picaresque changes, 56; picaresque social virtues, 168, 314n22; postmodern facets, 253, 256, 259; selfhood dilemmas, 83, 98; social dilemmas, 305n26

Blues Route, The (Merrill), 334n33

Bohannan, Paul, 307n30

Bolling, Jack "Binx" (character in *The Moviegoer*), 75, 93–94, 106, 183, 215, 217, 228, 230, 233, 239, 258, 318n12, 332n25

Bone Games (Schultheis), 331n18

Bonvillain, Nancy, 303n9

Boorstin, Daniel, 87, 284n8

Booth, Wayne C., 292n25

Border Music (Waller): cultural values, 214, 334n33; narrative inventory, 182; narrative issues, 59, 74; picaresque changes, 37, 40–41, 52, 55; picaresque continuities, 21; picaresque social virtues, 309n5; postmodern facets, 255, 261; selfhood dilemmas, 84–85, 93, 106. *See also* Carmine, "Texas" Jack; Rhomer, Vaughn

Borges, Jorge Luis, 49, 54

Bound for Glory (Guthrie), 212

Brackenridge, Hugh Henry, 282n1

Breakfast of Champions (Vonnegut), 1

Bright Lights, Big City (McInerney), 21, 26, 217, 318n12

Brinkley, Douglas, 200, 304–5n26, 331n18

Brown, Joe David, 1. See also *Paper Moon*

Brown, Norman O., 248

Bryson, Bill: cultural values, 211; narrative inventory, 182, 184, 188, 200; narrative issues, 60, 66, 68, 71, 73–75; picaresque social virtues, 155, 315n25; selfhood dilemmas, 83, 92–94, 98, 298–99n24; social dilemmas, 123, 129. See also *Lost Continent, The*

Buck, Joe (character in *Midnight Cowboy*): cultural values, 208, 214, 227, 230, 239–41; narrative inventory, 192, 200–201; narrative issues, 59, 70, 72–73, 79, 289n7; picaresque changes, 39, 43–47; picaresque social virtues, 143–44, 158–61, 164, 167, 312n18; selfhood dilemmas, 91–92, 94–95, 97, 101, 299n26; social dilemmas, 108, 118, 138, 306n29

Bumppo, Natty (character in
Leatherstocking Tales), 44, 212
Bunyan, John, 18
Burroughs, William S., 49, 282n1
Bus of My Own, A (Lehrer), 295n32,
319n17

Cadillac Jack (McMurtry), 2, 37, 55, 61,
159, 175, 182, 217, 240, 321n22, 330n11.
See also McGriff, "Cadillac" Jack
Caesar, Terry, 290n15, 293n28, 298n24
Cage, John, 248
Caldo Largo (Thompson), 2, 183
Calvino, Italo, 287n21
Carmine, "Texas" Jack (character in *Bor-
der Music*): cultural values, 214, 240,
334n33; narrative inventory, 191, 205;
narrative issues, 59, 62, 73; picaresque
changes, 37, 40, 44–47, 52; picaresque
social virtues, 143, 148, 155, 309n5;
postmodern facets, 261–62; selfhood
dilemmas, 85
Catcher in the Rye, The (Salinger), 19,
318n12. *See also* Caulfield, Holden
Caulfield, Holden (character in *The
Catcher in the Rye*), 25–26, 44, 318n12
Cavell, Stanley, 283n2
Celebrisi, Joey (character in *Celebrisi's
Journey*), 1, 4, 168, 181, 190, 215, 217,
236, 253
Celebrisi's Journey (Rounds), 1, 59, 167,
215, 217, 236, 337n13. *See also* Celebrisi,
Joey
Celine, Louis-Ferdinand, 18, 279n14
Cervantes, Miguel de, 1. *See also* Don
Quixote
Chandler, Frank Wadleigh, 277n4, 278n8
Chidester, David, 296n12
Cities on a Hill (FitzGerald), 67, 318n14,
332n24
Coast, The (Thorndike), 67
Coburn, Broughton, 309n9, 339n24
Codrescu, Andrei, 2; cultural values, 216–
17, 220–21, 228–29, 233, 236, 240, 326n1,
327n3, 328nn7–8, 332n28; narrative in-
ventory, 197, 207; narrative issues, 64,
66; picaresque changes, 49, 286n18;
postmodern facets, 261. *See also* Road
Scholar
Cohen, Michael Lee, 327n2
Cole, John Grady (character in *All the
Pretty Horses*), 183, 217

Colossus of Roads, The (Marling), 319n17
Computing across America (Roberts), 67
Conduct of Life, The (Emerson), 328n6
Confederacy of Dunces, A (Toole): cultural
values, 215, 239; narrative inventory,
318n12; narrative issues, 59, 80, 294n32;
picaresque changes, 41, 55, 284n5; pica-
resque continuities, 19; picaresque so-
cial virtues, 312n18; selfhood dilemmas,
84, 298n23. *See also* Reilly, Ignatius J.
Confidence Man, The (Melville), 282n1
Conrad, Peter, 283n3
Continental Drift (Banks), 2, 55, 183, 214,
239. *See also* DuBois, Bob
Cooper, James Fenimore, 44
Country of Exiles (Leach), 276n3
Cox, Harvey, 248, 257, 260–61, 337n8
Crabb, Jack (character in *Little Big
Man*), 22, 72–73, 155, 159, 162, 193,
217, 234
Crevecoeur, J. Hector St. John de, 283n3
Critical Issues in Modern Religion (Johnson
and Wallwork et al.), 336n5
Crossings (W. Harrington), 60, 67, 175,
215, 239, 256, 323n37, 332n24
Crumley, James, 2, 21, 37. See also *Last
Good Kiss, The*
Crying of Lot 49, The (Pynchon), 2; cul-
tural values, 218, 229; narrative inven-
tory, 203; narrative issues, 64, 80; pica-
resque changes, 39, 41–43; postmodern
facets, 257; selfhood dilemmas, 91; so-
cial dilemmas, 129, 305n28. *See also*
Maas, Oedipa
Cultural Literacy (Hirsch), 302n8
Culture of Narcissism, The (Lasch), 296n14,
336nn4, 6
Culture Wars (Hunter), 302n6
Curtis, Ponyboy (character in *The Outsid-
ers*), 201–2, 310n11

Davies, Pete, 67, 183. See also *Storm
Country*
DeFoe, Daniel, 3, 17. See also *Moll
Flanders*
deHaan, Fonger, 284n10
Deliberate Speed (Lhamon), 284n7
DeLillo, Don, 230. See also *Americana*
Delta Time (Dunbar), 183, 217
DeVries, Peter, 2. See also *Blood of the
Lamb, The*
Dharma Bums, The (Kerouac), 275n1

Dilemmas of the American Self (Hewitt), 295n6

Dillard, Annie, 276n3

Disappearance of the Outside, The (Codrescu), 286n18

Doctorow, E. L., 11–12, 22, 34, 83. See also *Billy Bathgate*

Don Pablos, El Buscon (Quevedo), 12, 17, 30, 48. *See also* Pablos, Don

Don Quixote, 12, 276n2, 277n4, 278n11, 279n12, 281n28. *See also* Quixote, Don

Dramas, Fields, and Metaphors (V. Turner), 307n31

Dreiser, Theodore, 212

DuBois, Bob (character in *Continental Drift*), 183, 214, 230, 239

Dunbar, Anthony (Tony) P., 183, 217

Duncan, Dayton, 290n11

Dunn, Katherine, 182. See also *Truck*

Dunn, Peter N., 277n4, 281n31

Durant, Mary, 297n20

Dwight, Timothy, 212

Easy Rider (film), 276n2

Eco, Umberto, 49

Edel, Leon, 289n5

Education of Henry Adams, The (Adams), 284n7

Ehrlich, Gretel, 330n18

Eighner, Lars: cultural values, 208, 233; narrative inventory, 200–201, 205–6, 323n36; narrative issues, 61, 63–64, 69–72, 77, 80; picaresque social virtues, 145, 155, 157, 163; social dilemmas, 128. See also *Travels with Lizbeth*

Ellison, Ralph, 21, 26, 203, 251, 282n1, 287n20. See also *Invisible Man, The*

Ellwood, Robert, 337n11

Elvis Presley Boulevard (Winegardner), 67, 182, 185, 217, 290n11, 295n32, 318n13

Emerson, Ralph Waldo, 213–15, 221–23, 231, 283n2, 328n6, 335n37

Encounters (Goffman), 303n10

English-Lueck, T. A., 337n11

Erring (Taylor), 337n9

Espy, David, 60, 288n4

Esquire (magazine), 111–12, 138, 300n2

Estudio de la Novela Picaresca (Garriga), 278n7

Even Cowgirls Get the Blues (Robbins), 203. *See also* Hankshaw, Sissy

Everyman (anon.), 49

Exemplary History of the Novel, An (Reed), 281n28, 286n16

"Experience" (Emerson), 283n2

Experience of Place, The (Hiss), 290n11

Experiential Religion (Niebuhr), 250

Fanny, Being the True History of Fanny Hackabout-Jones (Jong), 12

Farina, Richard, 155. See also *Been Down So Long It Looks like Up to Me*

Faulkner, William, 49, 282n1, 297n20

Feast of Fools, The (Cox), 337n8

Feminine Mystique, The (Friedan), 301n3

Fielding, Henry, 3, 17. See also *Tom Jones*

Finn, Huck (character in *The Adventures of Huckleberry Finn*), 44

Fisher, Sylvie (character in *Housekeeping*), 204–6, 208, 215, 318n12, 324n40

FitzGerald, Frances, 67, 184, 196, 199, 318–19n14, 332n24

Flanders, Moll (character in *Moll Flanders*), 4–5, 35, 43, 49, 144, 219, 224, 233

Forgiving the Boundaries (Caesar), 293n28

For Love and Money (Raban), 293n28

Forrest Gump (Groom), 203, 312n18. *See also* Gump, Forrest

Fowler, Alastair, 53, 281n32, 288nn26–27

Franklin, Benjamin, 212

Frannie (character in *Spinsters*), 242, 255, 259, 331n22

Friedan, Betty, 301n3

From Ritual to Theatre (V. Turner), 307n31

From Sea to Shining Sea (Young), 328n8

From the Hearth to the Open Road (Waxman), 325n42

Fuller, Chet, 323n36, 326n45

Fussell, Paul, 284n8, 293n29

Future Shock (Toffler), 284n7

Gabel, Shainee, 331n18

García Márquez, Gabriel, 49, 287n21

Gardner, Carol Brooks, 323n38

Garriga, Francisco Javier, 278n7

Gates, Henry Louis, Jr., 326n46

Geertz, Clifford, 53–55, 58, 79, 88, 126, 137, 164, 288n28, 315–16n26

Gergen, Kenneth, 85–88, 90, 92, 100, 295–96n6, 336n4

Gil Blas (Le Sage), 3, 5; narrative issues, 61; picaresque changes, 35, 40, 48, 56; picaresque continuities, 12, 17–20,

277n4, 281n26; selfhood dilemmas, 84.
See also Blas, Gil

Giles Goat-Boy (Barth), 19, 310n11

Gillis, Jean "Dutch" (character in *Truck*),
4, 144, 226–27, 229–30, 239, 257, 330n17,
332n23

Ginsberg, Allen, 279n14

Gitlin, Todd, 301n3, 302n6

Godspeed (Lee), 60, 182, 214, 337n13

Goffman, Erving, 303n10, 306n29, 307n31

Going Away (Sigal), 212

Going Native (Wright), 234, 238. *See also*
Jones, Wylie

Goldberg, Natalie, 61, 66

Grass Roots (Duncan), 290n11

Greene, Bob, 111

Greer, Taylor (character in *The Bean Trees*),
4; cultural values, 214, 218–19, 229;
narrative inventory, 318n12, 324n38,
326n45; picaresque social virtues, 155,
161; postmodern facets, 239, 259; social
dilemmas, 109

Grimmelshausen, H. J. C. von, 17

Groom, Winston, 203. *See also Forrest
Gump*

Guillen, Claudio, 278n10, 279n15

Gump, Forrest (character in *Forrest
Gump*), 193, 203, 206

Gunn, Giles, 176, 316n2, 326n46

Guthrie, Woody, 212

Guzman de Alfarache (Aleman), 3; narrative issues, 294n32; picaresque
changes, 34, 48; picaresque continuities, 11, 13–16, 18, 24, 30, 277n4,
279n12, 281n31. *See also* Guzman de
Alfarache

Guzman de Alfarache (character in
Guzman de Alfarache), 22, 24–25, 30,
34, 44–45, 73, 159, 189, 279n12,
281n3

Habe, Hans, 61–62, 64, 66–67, 93–94, 98,
289n7. *See also Wounded Land, The*

Hahn, Kristin, 331n18

Halberstam, David, 111

Hall, B. C., 67, 123, 136, 167, 183, 218,
322n33. *See also Big Muddy*

Hand, Johnny (character in *Caldo Largo*),
183

Hankshaw, Sissy (character in *Even Cowgirls Get the Blues*), 197, 203, 207,
324n38

Harper's Magazine, 110–12, 120, 293n29,
300n2

Harrington, Michael, 110

Harrington, Walt: cultural values, 208,
215, 334n24; narrative inventory, 200–
201, 323n37; narrative issues, 60; picaresque social virtues, 143, 146, 155, 157,
161; social dilemmas, 118, 122, 135–36.
See also *Crossings*

Harris, Eddy L., 2; cultural values, 215;
narrative inventory, 205, 323n36,
324n38, 325–26n45; narrative issues, 60,
64, 66, 68–71, 73, 80; selfhood dilemmas, 93, 104, 106; picaresque social virtues, 155. See also *South of Haunted
Dreams*

Harwood, Michael, 297n20

Hassan, Ihab, 281n27

Hayduke, George (character in *The Monkey Wrench Gang*), 183

Health in the New Age (English-Lueck),
337n11

Heard, Alex, 319n17

Heller, Erich, 49, 286nn17, 19

Heller, Joseph, 282n1

Hemingway, Ernest, 222, 297n20

Henry James (Edel), 289n5

Herberg, Will, 301n5

Herlihy, James Leo, 21, 39, 64, 79. See also
Midnight Cowboy

Hero and the Blues, The (Murray), 333n30

Hewitt, John P., 295n6

Highway 50 (Lilliefors), 67, 186, 290n11

Hill, Richard, 143, 149. See also *Riding
Solo with the Golden Horde*

Hinton, S. E., 201. See also *Outsiders, The*

Hirsch, E. D., 302n8

Hiss, Tony, 290n11

Hoffer, Eric, 110

Homeless Mind, The (P. Berger et al.),
336n4

Hoosier Holiday, A (Dreiser), 212

Housekeeping (Robinson), 204, 208, 215,
318n12, 324n40. *See also* Fisher, Sylvie

Howells, William Dean, 282n1

Hughes, Langston, 288n5

Hunter, James Davison, 302n6

Hunting Mister Heartbreak (Raban), 283n2

Hurston, Zora Neale, 297n20

I Hear Them Calling My Name (Fuller),
326n45

Image, The (Boorstin), 284n8
Image and Pilgrimage in Christian Culture
    (V. Turner and E. Turner), 316n30
Imagining America (Conrad), 283n3
Into the Badlands (J. Williams), 283n3,
    297n20, 319n17
Invisible Man, The (Ellison), 21, 200, 215,
    289n7, 318n12
Ishmael (character in *Moby Dick*), 44, 212,
    222
I Wonder as I Wander (Hughes), 288n5

James, Henry, 212, 289n5
Jenkins, Peter, 1; cultural values, 215, 229,
    239–40; narrative inventory, 192, 200,
    207, 323n38; narrative issues, 70, 76, 79,
    295n32; picaresque social virtues, 145,
    155, 161; postmodern facets, 261;
    selfhood dilemmas, 84–85, 94, 103; so-
    cial dilemmas, 126, 133–36. See also
    Walk across America, A
Johnson, Roger A., 336n5
Jones, Tom (character in *Tom Jones*), 4, 22,
    43, 199, 233
Jones, Wylie (character in *Going Native*),
    234, 238, 240, 335n36
Jong, Erica, 12
Journey to the End of the Night (Celine), 18,
    279n14
Joyce, James, 49
Justina (character in *La Picara Justina*), 5,
    144

Kaler, Anne K., 324n41, 325n42
Karl, Frederick, 263, 285n14, 329n9
Kazin, Alfred, 290n11
Keen, Sam, 248
Keeping Faith (West), 326n46
Kelner, Hansfried, 336n4
Kennedy, Pagan, 242. See also *Spinsters*
Kerouac, Jack, 37–38, 212, 275n1. See also
    On the Road
Kesey, Ken, 111
Kick the Can (Lehrer), 1, 55, 73, 94, 183,
    217–18, 233, 259, 295n32, 312n18,
    320n17. *See also* One-Eyed Mack
Kindness of Strangers, The (McIntyre),
    323n36
Kinds of Literature (Fowler), 282n32,
    286n15, 288n26
Kingsolver, Barbara, 1. See also *Bean
    Trees, The*

Klein, Marcus, 50, 286n20
Knaves and Swindlers (Whitbourn), 280n21
Kowalewski, Michael, 288n4
Kuralt, Charles, 1, 265, 295n32

Lackey, Kris, 320n17, 325n42
Lamb, David, 2; cultural values, 209, 218;
    narrative inventory, 184–85, 188, 193,
    199–200, 205–6, 319nn16–17, 323n36,
    326n45; narrative issues, 62–66, 68, 71–
    72, 76–78, 289nn10–11; picaresque so-
    cial virtues, 155, 161–62, 164, 167;
    postmodern facets, 255, 257, 339n28;
    selfhood dilemmas, 83, 85, 88, 91–92,
    101, 104; social dilemmas, 108–9, 125,
    127, 131. See also *Sense of Place, A; Sto-
    len Season*
Lane, Michael, 295n32, 326n45
Language, Culture, and Communication
    (Bonvillain), 303n9, 315n24
Lasch, Christopher, 89–90, 248, 296nn6,
    14, 298n23, 303n10, 336n14
Last Convertible, The (Myrer), 328n7
Last Good Kiss, The (Crumley), 2, 21, 37,
    145, 182, 217. *See also* Sughrue, C. W.
Lazarillo (character in *La Vida de Lazarillo
    de Tormes*), 4; cultural values, 214, 219,
    224, 233; narrative inventory, 189; nar-
    rative issues, 73, 76; picaresque
    changes, 34, 43, 49; picaresque continu-
    ities, 11–12, 14, 22–25, 29, 279n12,
    281n31; picaresque social virtues, 144;
    selfhood dilemmas, 97
Lazaro (character in *La Vida de Lazarillo de
    Tormes*), 14, 24, 278n10
Leach, William R., 276n3
Least Heat Moon, William. *See* Trogdon,
    William (Least Heat Moon)
Lee, Laurel, 60, 126, 208, 214, 217, 253.
    See also *Godspeed*
Leed, Eric, 291n19
Lehrer, Jim, 1, 73, 94, 319–20n17. See also
    Bus of My Own, A; Kick the Can
Le Sage, Alaine-Rene, 3, 12, 17, 25, 37, 48.
    See also *Gil Blas*
Lévi-Strauss, Claude, 54–55
Lewis, R. W. B., 277n5, 285n13
Lhamon, W. T., Jr., 284n7
Life and Death of Mr. Badman, The
    (Bunyan), 18
Life on the Mississippi (Twain), 297n20
Life on the Road, A (Kuralt), 1

Lifton, Robert Jay, 251–52, 263, 337nn11–12

Lilliefors, Jim, 67, 186, 188–89, 200, 290n11

Linenthal, Edward T., 296n12, 334n34

Lippman, Walter, 312–13n19, 315n26

Listening to America (Moyers), 60, 74, 83, 121, 182, 292n23, 310n13

Literature and the Delinquent (Parker), 277n5

Literature as System (Guillen), 278n10, 279n15

Literature of Roguery, The (Chandler), 277n4

Little Big Man (T. Berger), 22, 162, 182, 193, 217, 234, 256. *See also* Crabb, Jack

Lively Experiment, The (Mead), 327n4

Living by Fiction (Dillard), 276n3

Lizardi, Jose Joaquin Fernandez de, 17

Local Knowledge (Geertz), 288n28, 304n24, 316n26

Lofland, Lyn, 151–60, 311–12nn16–18, 315n26

Lonely Crowd, The (Reisman), 296n6

Longest Walk, The (Meegan), 180, 317n4

Long Quiet Highway (Goldberg), 61

Long Road Home, A (O'Gara), 67, 194, 237, 256, 310n9

Loose Canons (Gates), 326n46

Lost Continent, The (Bryson): narrative inventory, 182, 184; narrative issues, 60, 73–75, 78; picaresque social virtues, 315n25; postmodern facets, 257; selfhood dilemmas, 83, 98; social dilemmas, 129, 305n28

Love and Will (May), 296n13

Maas, Oedipa (character in *The Crying of Lot 49*): cultural values, 208, 211, 218, 229, 233; narrative inventory, 203, 206; narrative issues, 64, 72–73; picaresque changes, 40, 42–47, 51, 288n24; picaresque social virtues, 161; selfhood dilemmas, 88, 91, 95, 97, 101, 104, 296n15; social dilemmas, 129, 136, 306n28

Mailer, Norman, 2, 54, 203. *See also American Dream, An*

Majic Bus, The (Brinkley), 304n26, 331n18

March, Augie (character in *The Adventures of Augie March*), 51, 74, 217, 329n10

Marginal Man, The (Stonequist), 308n1

Marling, Karal Ann, 319n17

Marty, Martin, 301n5

May, Rollo, 89, 296n13

McCarthy, Cormac, 183. *See also All the Pretty Horses*

McGriff, "Cadillac" Jack (character in *Cadillac Jack*), 4; cultural values, 208, 237–38, 240, 329n11; narrative inventory, 196, 200, 206, 321n22; narrative issues, 74; picaresque social virtues, 155, 159

McInerney, Jay, 21, 26. *See also Bright Lights, Big City*

McIntyre, Mike, 323n36

McMurtry, Larry, 2, 37. *See also Cadillac Jack*

McPhee, John, 60, 288n4

Mead, Sidney E., 327n4

Meegan, George, 180, 182, 317n4

Melville, Herman, 44, 212, 222. *See also Confidence Man, The*

Merrill, Hugh, 334n33

Merton, Thomas, 248

Message in the Bottle, The (Percy), 86, 296n7

Messenger, Vic (character in *Riding Solo with the Golden Horde*): cultural values, 217, 230, 234–35, 240, 334n33; narrative inventory, 200, 318n12, 323n37; picaresque social virtues, 144, 149, 155, 157–59, 161–62, 168, 310n11, 311n15, 313–14nn22–23

Meyrowitz, Joshua, 87–88, 90, 284n9, 336n4

Midnight Cowboy (Herlihy): cultural values, 214, 227, 239; narrative inventory, 182; narrative issues, 59, 61, 79, 289n7, 292n23, 294n30; picaresque changes, 39, 43, 55; picaresque continuities, 21; picaresque social virtues, 158, 167, 312n18; selfhood dilemmas, 94, 97; social dilemmas, 118, 305n28. *See also* Buck, Joe

Miller, Henry, 212, 288n5

Miller, J. Hillis, 286n19

Miller, Stuart, 277n4

Milner, Andrew, 336n2

Mind of the Traveler, The (Leed), 291n19

Minimal Self, The (Lasch), 296n14, 303n10, 336n6

Moby Dick (Melville), 212, 222

Modern Chivalry (Brackenridge), 282n1

Modernity's Pretenses (Racevski), 336n7

Moll Flanders (DeFoe), 3, 17, 40. *See also* Flanders, Moll

Monkey Wrench Gang, The (Abbey), 1, 21. *See also* Hayduke, George

Moriarity, Dean (character in *On the Road*), 94

Morris, Wright, 287n20

Moviegoer, The (Percy), 75, 93, 183, 215, 217, 228, 233, 239, 258, 318n12, 332n25. *See also* Bolling, Jack "Binx"

Moving American, The (Pierson), 327n5

Moyers, Bill: cultural values, 230, 233; narrative inventory, 189, 193, 199–200, 205–7; narrative issues, 60–64, 66–68, 71–74, 292n23; picaresque social virtues, 147, 155, 161, 310n13; selfhood dilemmas, 83, 93; social dilemmas, 109, 118–19, 123, 126, 131–32, 304n16. *See also Listening to America*

Muir, John, 212. *See also Thousand Mile Walk to the Gulf, A*

Murray, Albert, 231–33, 235, 238, 263, 333n31, 334n33, 337n12

My Literary Passions (Howells), 282n1

Myrer, Anton, 328n7

Nan (character in *The Pull of the Moon*): cultural values, 217–19, 225, 229, 238–39, 331n22; picaresque social virtues, 155, 157; postmodern facets, 257, 261; selfhood dilemmas, 94, 102, 106

Nashe, Thomas, 3, 12, 17, 25. *See also Unfortunate Traveller, The*

"Nature" (Emerson), 222

Niebuhr, Rheinhold, 250, 254, 257–58, 262, 339n29

No Sense of Place (Meyrowitz), 284n9, 303n11, 336n4

Novak, Michael, 301n4

O'Gara, Geoffrey: cultural values, 236–37, 259; narrative inventory, 181–82, 190, 194–95, 200, 202, 207, 321nn23–24, 322n30; narrative issues, 67; picaresque social virtues, 310n9. *See also Long Road Home, A*

Old Glory (Raban), 218, 283n3, 297n20, 328nn8, 11

Old Man and the Sea, The (Hemingway), 222

One-Eyed Mack (character in *Kick the Can*), 94, 155, 183, 217–19, 230, 233, 259, 312n18

On the Road (Kerouac), 37, 43, 59–60, 94, 275n1. *See also* Paradise, Sal

On the Road with Charles Kuralt (Kuralt), 1

On the Road with John James Audubon (Durant and Harwood), 297n20

Open Road (Patton), 328n5

Orvell, Miles, 284n8

Outline of the History of the Novela Picaresca in Spain, An (deHaan), 285n10

Outsiders, The (Hinton), 201, 310n11. *See also* Curtis, Ponyboy

Pablos, Don (character in *Don Pablos, El Buscon*), 12, 22, 24, 30, 35, 224

Paper Moon (J. Brown), 1, 214

Pappadopoulis, Gnossos (character in *Been Down So Long It Looks like Up to Me*), 155, 197, 203, 206, 240, 306n28, 310n11

Paradise, Sal (character in *On the Road*), 43–44, 73, 94, 205

Parker, A. A., 277nn4–5, 278n11

Parkman, Francis, 335n37

Passing By (Gardner), 323n38

Patton, Phil, 327n5

Pellon, Gustavo, 279n17

Percy, Walker: picaresque continuities, 21; postmodern facets, 244–46, 248, 250, 257–58; selfhood dilemmas, 86–90, 92–93, 100, 102, 105, 297n20, 298n23. *See also Message in the Bottle, The; Moviegoer, The*

Periquillo Sarniento, El (Lizardi), 17

Phaedrus (character in *Zen and the Art of Motorcycle Maintenance*), 205, 215, 309n9

Picara, The (Kaler), 324n41

Picara Justina, La (Ubeda), 5, 17, 19, 279n12, 294n32. *See also* Justina

Picaresque, The (Sieber), 278n6

Picaresque Narrative, Picaresque Fictions (Wicks), 279nn12, 19, 281n30, 283n1, 289n7

Picaresque Novel, The (S. Miller), 277n4, 282n1

Picaresque Saint, The (Lewis), 277n5, 282n1, 285n13

Picaros, Madmen, Naifs, and Clowns (Riggan), 278n10, 282n1, 293n25

Picture Palace (Theroux), 60

Pierson, George W., 327n5

Pilgrim, Billy (character in *Slaughter-House Five*), 83

Pink Highways (Lane), 295n32, 326n45

Pirsig, Robert, 1. See also *Zen and the Art of Motorcycle Maintenance*

Place to Come To, A (Warren), 2, 59, 215, 236. See also Tewksberry, Jed

Plimpton, George, 111

Poets of Reality (J. Miller), 286n19

Poole, A. J. (character in *The Watermelon Kid*), 21–22, 44, 59, 155, 195, 294n32, 334n33

Postcards (Proulx), 147, 168, 178–79, 257. See also Blood, Loyal

Postmodern Conditions (Milner et al.), 336n2

Powdermaker, Hortense, 138, 165, 315n26

Preface to Morals, A (Lippman), 313n19

Presentation of the Self in Everyday Life, The (Goffman), 303n10

Primeau, Ronald, 324n42

Protean Self, The (Lifton), 337n11

Protestant, Catholic, Jew (Herberg), 301n5

Proulx, E. Annie, 147, 168, 182, 338n20. See also *Postcards*

Pull of the Moon, The (Berg), 2, 45, 106, 157, 218–19, 225, 229, 238–39, 257, 261, 331n22. See also Nan

Pynchon, Thomas, 2, 39, 282n1. See also *Crying of Lot 49, The*

Quevedo, Francisco de, 12, 17, 30. See also *Don Pablos, El Buscon*

Quinn, Sally, 111

Quixote, Don (character in *Don Quixote*), 295n32

Raban, Jonathan, 218, 241, 283n3, 293n28, 328nn8, 11. See also *Old Glory*

Racevski, Karlis, 336n7

Radical Innocence (Hassan), 281n27

Rainman (film), 276n2

Rawls, Thomas, 67, 184, 200, 318n13

Real Thing, The (Orvell), 284n8

Rednecks and Other Bonafide Americans (Whaley), 67, 185

Reed, Walter L., 281n28, 286n16

Reeves, Richard: cultural values, 208–9, 327n2; narrative inventory, 199; narrative issues, 60, 62–68, 70, 72, 76, 78, 290n11, 295n32, 297n20; picaresque so-cial virtues, 155, 168; selfhood dilem-mas, 93, 101–2, 297n20; social dilem-mas, 108. See also *American Journey*

Reilly, Ignatius J. (character in *A Confed-eracy of Dunces*): cultural values, 215, 217, 239; narrative inventory, 189; nar-rative issues, 59, 70, 72, 294n32; pica-resque changes, 44, 284n5; picaresque continuities, 20–22, 27–28, 31; pica-resque social virtues, 312n18, 318n12; postmodern facets, 255; selfhood di-lemmas, 88, 298n23; social dilemmas, 108

Reisman, David, 296n6

Religion and the Life of the Nation (Sherrill), 300n2

Reversible World, The (Babcock), 278n9, 310n10

Rhetoric of Fiction, The (Booth), 292n25

Rhomer, Vaughn (character in *Border Mu-sic*), 37–38, 74, 85, 93, 106, 157, 191, 214

Ricoeur, Paul, 248, 259, 287n23, 336n7

Riding Solo with the Golden Horde (Hill), 143, 217, 234, 256, 295n32, 313n22, 318n12, 323n37, 333n33. See also Mes-senger, Vic

Riggan, William, 278n10, 293n25

Rise of the Novel, The (Watt), 281n28

Rise of the Unmeltable Ethnics, The (Novak), 301n4

Ritual Process, The (V. Turner), 316n30

RoadFrames (Lackey), 320n17, 325n42

Road Scholar (Codrescu), 2, 61, 182, 217, 261, 327n1

Roads Taken, The (Setterberg), 185, 290n11, 297n20

Robbins, Tom, 197. See also *Even Cowgirls Get the Blues*

Roberts, Stephen K., 67

Robinson, Marilynne, 204. See also *Housekeeping*

Roderick Random (Smollett), 17, 19, 56

Rodriguez, Richard, 110

Rogue's Progress (Alter), 277n5, 281n26, 282n1

Rojack, Stephen Richards (character in *An American Dream*), 94, 215, 230, 239

Romance of the Road (Primeau), 325n42

Rosenblum, Mort: cultural values, 208; narrative inventory, 321n24, 323n35; narrative issues, 67; picaresque social virtues, 155, 168, 199–202, 206; social dilemmas, 120–21, 123, 126, 128–29. See also *Back Home*

Rounds, David, 1, 67, 181–82. See also *Celebrisi's Journey*

Route 66 (Wallis), 320n18

Salinger, J. D., 19, 25. See also *Catcher in the Rye, The*

Salisbury, Harrison, 2; cultural values, 208–9, 215, 230, 240; narrative inventory, 200, 205, 323n36, 326n45; narrative issues, 60, 63–64, 66–68, 71–72, 294n29, 295n32; picaresque social virtues, 161; postmodern facets, 255; selfhood dilemmas, 84, 91–93, 97, 101; social dilemmas, 124. See also *Travels around America*

Santmire, H. Paul, 247, 258, 336n5

Saturated Self, The (Gergen), 295n4, 336n4

Schlereth, Thomas J., 320n21

Schultheis, Rob, 331n18

Search for Meaning, The (Berman), 67, 290n11, 327n2

Secular City, The (Cox), 249

Seduction of the Spirit, The (Cox), 337n8

Seize the Day (Bellow), 215

Sense of Place, A (Lamb), 61, 91, 167, 184, 217, 257

Setterberg, Fred, 185, 319n17. See also *Roads Taken, The*

Seven League Boots, The (Murray), 334n33

Shaw, Patrick W., 285n12

Sherrill, Rowland A., 296n12, 300n2

Sides, W. Hampton: cultural values, 332n24; narrative inventory, 184, 196, 199, 207; narrative issues, 61, 63, 66, 79; picaresque social virtues, 155, 159; social dilemmas, 123. See also *Stomping Grounds*

Sieber, Harry, 278n6

Sigal, Clancy, 212

Simmel, Georg, 163, 306n29, 313n20

Simplicius Simplissimus (Grimmelshausen), 17

Simpson, Mona, 2. See also *Anywhere but Here*

Sir Gawain and the Green Knight (anon.), 15, 48

Sixties, The (Gitlin), 301n3

Slaughter-House Five (Vonnegut), 83

Small Places (Rawls), 67, 184, 318n13

Smart, Ninian, 164, 313n21, 314n22, 315n26

Smollett, Tobias, 17, 281n26. See also *Roderick Random*

Sociology of Georg Simmel, The (Wolf), 313n20

Solace of Open Spaces, The (Ehrlich), 331n18

South of Haunted Dreams (Harris), 2, 56, 60, 63, 73, 93, 200–201, 206, 215, 239, 325n45

Spanish Picaresque Fiction (P. Dunn), 277n4, 281n31

Spanish Picaresque Novel, The (P. Dunn), 277n4, 281n30

Spender, Stephen, 283n3

Spinsters (Kennedy), 242, 259, 331n22

Spirit of Place (F. Turner), 290n11

States of Mind (Yardley), 67, 83, 182, 217, 257, 327n2

Steinbeck, John, 1; cultural values, 209–11, 217, 230, 234, 236, 239–40, 326n1, 330n12; narrative inventory, 179, 185, 189, 200, 205, 323n36; narrative issues, 59–60, 63, 67, 76, 80, 295n32; picaresque changes, 282n1; picaresque social virtues, 143, 145, 148, 150, 158–59, 309n9, 311nn13–14, 312n18; postmodern facets, 259, 263, 267–68; selfhood dilemmas, 88, 95–98, 290n22, 300n29; social dilemmas, 119, 121–23, 125–26, 128–33, 135–38, 305n27. See also *Travels with Charley*

Steiner, George, 165–66, 279n14, 314n24, 315n26

Stewart, George, 186–89, 320n21

Stolen Season (Lamb), 2, 67, 188, 218, 319n16, 339n28

Stomping Grounds (Sides), 61, 80, 294n31, 332n24

Stone, Ruthie (character in *Housekeeping*), 204

Stonequist, Everett V., 308n1, 311n15, 315n25

Storm Country (Davies), 67, 290n11

Stranger and Friend (Powdermaker), 307n30, 314n23

Stritch, Thomas, 284n8

Sughrue, C. W. (character in *The Last Good Kiss*), 37, 145, 155, 182–83, 217, 230

Symbolism of Evil, The (Ricoeur), 287n23, 336n7

Taylor, Mark C., 249–50, 255–56, 337n9

Temperamental Journeys (Kowalewski), 288n4

Terry, Bill, 1, 21, 195. See also *Watermelon Kid, The*

Tewksberry, Jed (character in *A Place to Come To*), 59, 72, 215, 229, 236–37, 255

Thelma and Louise (film), 276n2

Theroux, Paul, 60, 67, 73, 293n29

Thinking across the American Grain (Gunn), 316n2

This Is My Country Too (J. A. Williams), 206, 239, 333n29

This New Yet Unapproachable America (Cavell), 283n2

Thompson, Earl, 2. See also *Caldo Largo*

Thomson, Phil, 336n2

Thoreau, Henry David, 44, 212, 222–23, 225, 227, 230–31, 297n20, 335n37

Thorndike, Joseph J., 67

Thousand Mile Walk to the Gulf, A (Muir), 212, 295n32

Toffler, Alvin, 284n7

Tom Jones (Fielding), 3, 17, 19, 38. See also Jones, Tom

Toole, John Kennedy, 19, 64. See also *Confederacy of Dunces, A*

To Reclaim a Legacy (Bennett), 302n8

Travelers and Travel Liars, 1660–1800 (P. Adams), 293n27

Travels (Bartram), 212

Travels around America (Salisbury), 2, 60, 63–64, 83, 182, 215, 240, 294n29, 295n32

Travels in New England and New York (Dwight), 212

Travels with Charley (Steinbeck), 1; cultural values, 209, 217, 326n1; narrative inventory, 182, 321n23; narrative issues, 59–60, 76; picaresque changes, 56; picaresque social virtues, 167, 309n9, 312n18; postmodern facets, 255; selfhood dilemmas, 84, 95–96, 167, 298n22; social dilemmas, 121

Travels with Lizbeth (Eighner), 61, 163, 205, 214, 233, 255

Trogdon, William (Least Heat Moon), 1; cultural values, 215, 230, 236, 239–40; narrative inventory, 184, 188–89, 202, 318n13; narrative issues, 57–60, 63–64, 67, 71–73, 80, 295n32; picaresque social virtues, 143, 145–49, 155, 157, 159, 161–62, 167–68, 311n14, 314n22, 315n26;

postmodern facets, 256, 257, 259, 337n13; selfhood dilemmas, 83, 98–99, 102, 104–6, 299–300n29; social dilemmas, 127, 131, 305n26. See also *Blue Highways*

Truck (K. Dunn), 182, 226, 229, 239, 257, 330n17. See also Gillis, Jean "Dutch"

Turner, Edith, 316n30

Turner, Frederick, 290n11

Turner, Victor W., 307n31, 316n30

Twain, Mark, 17, 212, 297n20

Twenty-something American Dream, The (Cohen), 327n2

Twilight of Common Dreams, The (Gitlin), 302n6

Ubeda, Lopez de, 17. See also *Picara Justina, La*

Unfortunate Traveller, The (Nashe), 3, 5, 12, 19, 36, 49, 61. See also Wilton, Jack

Upstarts, Wanderers, or Swindlers (Pellon and Rodriguez-Luis), 279n17

U.S. 40 (Schlereth), 320n21

U.S. 40 (Stewart), 320n20

U.S. 40 Today (T. Vale and G. Vale), 320n21

Vale, Geraldine, 186–87, 320n21

Vale, Thomas, 186–87, 320n21

Van Gennep, Arnold, 306n29

Vanity of Duluoz, The (Kerouac), 275n1

Vida de Lazarillo de Tormes, La, 3; narrative issues, 61, 76, 289n7, 294n32; picaresque changes, 35–36, 38, 39–40, 48, 56; picaresque continuities, 11–16, 18, 22, 29–30, 277n4, 279n12, 281n31; selfhood dilemmas, 84. See also Lazarillo; Lazaro

Virgil, 281n29

Vonnegut, Kurt, 1, 83

Walden (Thoreau), 222–23

Walk across America, A (Jenkins), 1, 67, 70, 94, 182, 192, 215, 261

Walk on the Wild Side, A (Algren), 2

Waller, Robert James, 21, 37, 313n22. See also *Border Music*

Wallis, Michael, 185, 188. See also *Route 66*

Wallwork, Ernest, 336n5

Wanderhope, Don (character in *The Blood of the Lamb*), 4, 74, 155, 193, 200, 215

Warren, Robert Penn, 2. See also *Place to Come To, A*
Watermelon Kid, The (Terry), 1, 21, 61, 294n32, 334n33. *See also* Poole, A. J.
Watt, Ian, 281n28
Waxman, Barbara Frey, 325n42
Weber, Ronald, 284n8
West, Cornel, 326n46
We, the Aliens (Bohannan), 307n30
Whaley, Bo, 67, 185, 195–96, 200, 207, 319n17, 325n45
Where the Earth and the Sky Collide (K. Berger), 60, 328n7
Whitbourn, Christine, 280n21
Whitman, Walt, 222, 295n32, 315n26
Wicks, Ulrich, 276–77nn2–4, 278n7, 279nn16, 19, 282n1, 285n11
Wilhelm, Tommy (character in *Seize the Day*), 215
Williams, John, 283n3, 319n17. See also *Into the Badlands*
Williams, John A., 205–6, 239, 323n36. See also *This Is My Country Too*
Wilton, Jack (character in *The Unfortunate Traveller*), 4, 12–13, 17, 22, 24, 144, 189, 214
Winegardner, Mark, 67, 185, 187, 189–90, 199, 318n13, 319n17, 322n30. See also *Elvis Presley Boulevard*
Wolf, Kurt, 313n20
Wood, C. T., 67, 123, 136, 167, 183, 218, 322n33. See also *Big Muddy*
World of Strangers, A (Lofland), 151, 306n29, 311–12nn16–17
Worldviews (Smart), 313n21
Worth, Chris, 336n2
Wounded Land, The (Habe), 61, 73, 93, 98
Wright, Stephen, 234, 240. See also *Going Native*
Writer's America, A (Kazin), 299n11

Yardley, Jonathan, 67, 200, 257, 294n29, 327n2. See also *States of Mind*
Young, Gavin, 328n8

Zen and the Art of Motorcycle Maintenance (Pirsig), 1, 59, 205, 215, 309n9
Zen Driving (K. Berger), 182, 328n7

ROWLAND A. SHERRILL is professor and chair of religious studies and director of the Center for American Studies at Indiana University / Purdue University Indianapolis. The author of *The Prophetic Melville* (1979), editor of *Religion and the Life of the Nation* (1990), and coeditor of *Religion, the Independent Sector, and American Culture* (1992), he also serves as a coeditor of *Religion and American Culture: A Journal of Interpretation.*

Typeset in 10/13 Palatino
with Copperplate display
Designed by Paula Newcomb
Composed by Celia Shapland
for the University of Illinois Press
Manufactured by Thomson-Shore, Inc.

University of Illinois Press
1325 South Oak Street
Champaign, IL 61820-6903
www.press.uillinois.edu